# Robert Lowell

## THE POET AND HIS CRITICS

# Robert Lowell

## THE POET AND HIS CRITICS

NORMA PROCOPIOW

AMERICAN
LIBRARY
ASSOCIATION
CHICAGO
1984

THE POET AND HIS CRITICS

A series of volumes on the meaning of the
critical writings on selected modern British
and American poets.

Edited by CHARLES SANDERS, University of Illinois, Urbana

*Robert Frost* by Donald J. Greiner
*William Carlos Williams* by Paul L. Mariani
*Dylan Thomas* by R. B. Kershner, Jr.
*Langston Hughes* by Richard K. Barksdale
*Wallace Stevens* by Abbie F. Willard
*T. S. Eliot* by Robert H. Canary

Designed by Vladimir Reichl

Title lettered by Jack Sugioka

Composed in Linotype Janson by FM
  Typesetting Co.

Printed on 50-pound Glatfelter, a
  pH-neutral stock, and bound in
  C-grade Holliston cloth and
  printed cover stock
  by Braun-Brumfield, Inc.

LIBRARY OF CONGRESS CATALOGING IN PUBLICATION DATA
Procopiow, Norma.
    Robert Lowell, the poet and his critics.
    (The Poet and his critics)
    Includes index.
    1. Lowell, Robert, 1917–1977—Criticism and
interpretation.  I. Title.  II. Series.
PS3523.O89Z835   1984        811'.52        84-467
ISBN 0-8389-0411-4

*For Bill*

# Contents

# Acknowledgments

I wish to thank Professor Charles Sanders of the University of Illinois for his support in this project. His editorial suggestions proved invaluable; more importantly, his belief in the creative potential inherent in reception scholarship helped to make this labor one of love. Thanks are also extended to Beth Alvarez for her expert bibliographical assistance.

# Introduction

Lowell's poetry has never been without good critics. Today, when we read the Introduction to Lowell's first volume, written by his advisor and friend Allen Tate in 1944, we are struck by its lasting freshness and force. Tate considered *Land of Unlikeness* a brilliant poetic debut, but he tempered his enthusiasm with a high form of aesthetic objectivity. He brought home to us the central themes in Lowell's verse, themes which would form an imprint on all of Lowell's writing. What Tate liked, other critics disliked, and the debate was under way. For nearly four decades the strain of critical opposition continued, sometimes matching in its collective excitement the excitement of the poetry itself. Taken as a whole, the criticism is more than an attempt at clarification or judgment of often unwieldy texts; it is also the signature of an evolution in taste, both restricted by and liberated from a tradition. The wide sampling of Lowell commentary instructs us that while the words of a poem remain constant, interpretations of these words change, and that in modern critical practice the change is a function of expectations—which will, in turn, affect the commentary still to come.

Contemporary literary theory has viewed the work of art less in the fixed and objective mold envisioned by earlier theorists and more as the protean matter from which the contributing reader "constructs" a poem. A horizon of expectations, affecting the author and his or her contemporary readers, as well as the changing expectations for the literary work itself, is shaped through time by critical commentary. Lowell responded almost dutifully to what might be considered the horizon of expectations he sensed. First he took up the imagistic mode of his mentors (particularly Tate) in the New Critical school. It was customary for this group to emphasize cultural identity in one's verse by keeping tradition and orthodoxy as pervasive as possible. Tate's obsessive ruminations about cultural identity proved a catastrophe to Lowell, however. By attempting to satisfy Tate's expectations, Lowell brought a verbalism and unreality to his early poems; his powerfully sensual mind was nearly lost in ahistorical abstractions.

Integral to Tate's formal view of poetry was the tough ironic stance of the poet as New England Puritan. No American writer of Lowell's generation was more insistent on expressing this stance, heavy with complaints of alienation, loneliness, and the search for a usable past. Then, too, war in the world and war in the self added tensions which, with conversion to Catholicism, brought strains in Lowell's poetry which echoed modes dating as far back as the seventeenth century. As Lowell's works entered the public world, the critics "constructed" them through their own expectations. The first formalist critics, expecting a tough, dense poetry, announced that they had found it. Thus began a dialectic in which the critics took in the poems and, where those critics were most successful and persuasive, formed a new expectation for them which was shaped by their own experience with the poems. Lowell, too, entered into this dialectic, both with the creation of new poems (or, as was one of his idiosyncrasies, the reworking of older poems) and with his own comments on the craft of poetry. The attitudes—the expectations of the Viet Nam War period, for example—revised readings of Lowell's earlier poems. When critics who had read *Day by Day* and the *Notebooks* reread *Mills of the Kavanaughs, Life Studies,* and *For the Union Dead,* the poems of the forties and fifties became, as they never could have in their own day, documents of "Modernism" in a time of "Postmodernism." Lowell himself never spoke of his poetry as moving from Modern to Postmodern. Rather, he spoke of relationships with poets whom he admired and learned from as though wishing to protect them and—indirectly—himself. Mainly, he had a horror of being commonplace, and his way of meeting expectations was to be distinguished among the best, whatever the "best" meant at the moment.

In this interaction of expectation, poem, reception, and new expectation, Lowell constructed and developed his themes. The Puritanism, sense of history, family geography, echoed and re-echoed, but they always brought new critical readings. Chronology, then, is a factor (though secondary) in my analysis. I present a chronological review of the criticism when it reveals decisive trends or junctures in the record of Lowell's reputation.

By and large, Lowell was not in conflict with the expectations in the critical community. He moved from one phase to another, bringing his self-questioning personal style, and sometimes, himself, becoming the force which altered the horizon of expectations.

The chapters in this study are arranged according to the subjects most frequently discussed in Lowell criticism. In chapter 1 we learn how the critics apprehended Lowell's public and private life and how they evolved an image of Lowell the man. Lowell did not live at the best address on Boston's Beacon Hill (Louisburg Square), but "less than fifty yards" from it (91 Revere Street). He attended the—private—Brimmer School and played in the Boston Public Garden. He entered Harvard but transferred to Kenyon, to finish college in 1940. At Kenyon, he worked with one of the important "new" critics of midcentury, John Crowe Ransom. And in 1944 he published, in a limited edition, his first volume of verse. His next book, *Lord Weary's Castle* (1946), won the Pulitzer Prize in 1947. Lowell was thirty. An auspicious beginning, by any standard. But this impressive compilation of facts conceals the dark experiences attendant upon them.

Lowell's ancestral background was fascinating and complex. From the paternal Lowell blood, mixed a few generations back with the Jewish blood of Major Mordecai Myers and more recently with the iconoclastic habits of Amy Lowell, together with the maternal Winslows and slightly more Northern (New Hampshire) Starks, Lowell inherited the "Puritan Burden." Never quite comfortable with the Irish and Italians who had invaded "the Hill" or even with their ultimate product, the Kennedy clan, Lowell nonetheless converted to Catholicism and—but not necessarily as a consequence—joined the various and sometimes abortive protests against the injustices he felt his ancestry had inflicted. Yet Lowell's life was the life of a poet and his public modes were always shaped by his true profession. When he marched on the Pentagon to protest the Viet Nam War, his motive was less patriotic than artistic: to gather material for his poetic imagination. At the same time, Lowell's stands—against the Pentagon, against World War II, against Lyndon Johnson, even against his ancestors—were a necessary public component of the Arnoldian figure whose life struggles brewed a poetry for his age. The obscure early poems which mix New England geography with Marian symbolism and Puritan preachers caught many themes which later ran through the easier lines of, say, *For the Union Dead* or the sonnets of the penultimate books. In chapters 2, 3, and 4 we evaluate these themes as the critics found them, developed them, and reexamined them. The Lowell these critics left us is sometimes a strangely dismembered man. Some critics held that Lowell had a great, perhaps a unique sense of the history which culminated in the midcentury in the battle of faith against fascism and despair. Some held that Lowell's poetic concern with the nuclear threat, "Johnson's war"—even with figures out of the past, like Caesar or Jonathan Edwards—was always painfully personal. Yet it is surely out of a personal life that a poet creates that history which Aristotle and Sidney would hold "truer" than that of the historians. And in these chapters we see how the critics received and revised interpretations of the century's moments. The century comes to life in Lowell's poems—in the immediate world of his grandfather, mother, wife, daughter.

*Life Studies* became a fulcrum in Lowell's reception, inevitably coloring, in the minds of those who read it, the earlier—now seemingly more contrived—poems. The expectations with which *Life Studies* was met, became, after its arrival and after the various fixings which critics made upon the volume, an expectation for the succeeding volumes. Confessional portraits of the family became a diary in the sonnets, and though wives changed, the personal agony did not. In the meantime, in the soul-searching years of the Viet Nam War, Lowell offered three plays (collected under the title *The Old Glory*). A New York production of two of these plays achieved some success and focused attention on Lowell in a different way. Themes of both the "Puritan Burden" and of disorder in our culture were reflected in these dramatizations of stories by Hawthorne and Melville. By the end of the sixties, critics began to wonder if the nation's greatest "confessional" poet would become one of its most distinguished playwrights.

Throughout his career Lowell had a fondness for what the Renaissance, with a much more positive view of the word than now, would call *imitation*, even using this as a teaching device. Largely, Lowell's work in this mode consists of the translations of poems published in *Imitations* and in parts of *Near the Ocean*. Lowell's range was great, from the ancients to Baudelaire and Pasternak. This was an important part of his creativity, one that he obviously took quite seriously, but the critics were mixed on its success. Chapter 2, specifically, considers *imitation* as a basis for Lowell's poetics and the critics' dispute

about its purposes. Again, the question seems to turn on whether
or not Lowell ever transcended the personal.

Lowell's themes have received much more attention than the
techniques of the poems which embody them. In chapter 5 we
sort out the major statements on this poet's *style*, a term which
covers a sometimes puzzling group of traits. Clearly, Lowell's
style changed in the obvious aspects of prosody when he moved
from relative regularity to looser structures, then back to
rhyme, and finally to a mode freer than anything he had ever
written. The critics have paid most attention here to the stylistics of confessionalism, in effect focusing a Lowellian poetics on
part four of *Life Studies*. In this, as well as in comments on the
earlier and later poems, critics show great interest in the poet's
"voice," but their comments provide more confusion than information. They have not gone far toward defining either the
sense of distanced nostalgia in the "voice" or the techniques of its
considerable music. The problems with Lowell's lifetime habit
of revision—most markedly practiced in *History*, a reworking of
sonnets from the previous books *Notebook 1967–68* and *Notebook*—are also noted in this chapter. The last poems have suffered somewhat in reception, receiving neither as much attention nor favor as the earlier volumes. We do, however, find
some champions of *Day by Day*, and suggest that Lowell may
have been working out a new poetics, based upon his views of
realism in the visual arts. In chapter 6, we turn to Lowell as he
assumes the role of critic, and learn that all the characteristics
observed in him as a poet are present in this role as well. He is
personal, puritanical, self-questioning. He instructs us, in his
ever penetrating judgments of other writers, in what to demand
from his oeuvre. Lastly, in chapter 7, we address the newly
offered theories of Modernism and discuss the ways it challenged the English poetic tradition, and how Lowell contributed to that challenge.

# CHAPTER 1

# The Man: Public and Private Life

Poet, playwright, translator, critic, teacher, public figure, father, husband, friend. There are many ways to see Robert Lowell, whose stature derives from his courage to accept—always with a fierce sense of mission—the simultaneous challenges these diverse roles thrust at him. Yet, despite his distinction in several of these categories, there is no question that the poet predominates. It was Lowell the poet who determined his performance in the other roles; it was Lowell the poet who was lionized, judged, eulogized. In bulk and excellence, Lowell's poetry supersedes engagement with drama, translation, criticism, academia, politics. There are commentators who champion the "imitations" or the plays, but they remain in the minority; and it is doubtful that future scholarship will reverse the proportion.

When Randall Jarrell was asked to deliver a lecture, "Fifty Years of American Poetry," at the National Poetry Festival in Washington, D.C., he concluded with a tribute to Lowell, predicting that one would always come to Lowell's new work with the renewed expectation of "encountering a masterpiece" (this speech was published in *Prairie Schooner*, Spring 1963). There was a toughness to this "poet of shock," said Jarrell, and added, in a striking phrase, a "senseless originality" that would continue to stun his readers. Jarrell died shortly after (1965), and never learned the outcome of his prediction. In truth, the reception of Lowell's late work was mixed, but his reputation never reached low ebb; and whenever he delivered a new volume, the critics were invariably challenged.

Because of Lowell's untimely death in 1977 at age sixty, his "story" as a poet seems unfinished. Not only was his voice stilled relatively early in the life of a man, but his last volume, *Day by Day*, signaled a departure which left critics speculating about new directions. In *Day by Day* Lowell had shed his recently adapted sonnet form, which, according to observers, had limited his lyric range and dulled his products of the seventies: *The Dolphin, For Lizzie and Harriet, History.* *Day by Day* was a fresh start; at the same time, it was said to bear a striking resemblance to *Life Studies.* Could Lowell reconcile the turning back with moving forward? And could he avoid the pitfalls of repetition or self-parody? Death obviated these questions and the critics began the testy business of measuring his influence—not, this time, as it was felt during his stages of creativity, but as a means of locating his position in literary history. The search for a position will not be so much limited to evaluation of Lowell's canon as subject to appraisals of modern symbolist and confessional modes in twentieth-century American poetry. That Lowell should figure in this peerage, which includes poets like Eliot and Pound, is sufficient authentication of his stature.

In many ways the making of Lowell's reputation has been unfortunately impressionistic. Too often critics allowed causes and theoretical fixations to color their judgments. Too often political and cultural prejudices became the basis for interpreting the work. The criticism of the sixties, for example, tended to grade Lowell in political terms, global as well as national. In 1966 Thomas Parkinson argued that the period from the midforties to the mid-sixties was not "The Age of Lowell" (*Salmagundi,* 1966–67). Instead, Lowell was "something we reacted to and against." The intellectual shapes and dictates of a generation were being redefined, and Lowell no longer qualified as spokesman.

Fame came early to Lowell. Unlike those poets who suffer neglect and bitter struggle, Lowell had little difficulty drawing attention to himself. His family name, enhanced by notable ancestry in statesmanship and letters, swept him into the limelight. With characteristic angst and peevishness, Lowell claimed, in interviews, that he regarded this automatic publicity a handicap. Observers have remained skeptical of this claim and argued that Lowell not only enjoyed adulation but depended on it as a stimulus to writing. The image of conflict within this sometimes tortured man who was both exhibitionistic and retiring may confuse any simplistic biography, but surely was a factor in his creativity. At the least, we must remember that Lowell's familial heritage has been an interpretive handle for critics, who prefaced their analyses of the poetry with biographical references to the poet's New England background. In *The Armies of the Night* (1968), Norman Mailer even traced the poet's posture to that elite ancestry:

> One did not achieve the languid grandeurs of that slouch in one generation—the grandsons of the first sons had best go through the best troughs in the best eating clubs at Harvard before anyone in the family could try for such elegant note.

In the seventies, critics better understood that Lowell's image of the suffering self was a conscious cultivation, serving his need for a mythic persona. Lowell, as poet and public figure, was a poseur.

In addition to their notes on Lowell's family heritage, most critics (even in their detraction) paid homage to his erudition. Exegetes of the Christian and classical symbolism of the early work were sometimes forced to retreat from enigmatic passages (as in "Mills of the Kavanaughs"), a reluctant tribute to the learning there embedded. Exegetical studies of Lowell's early volumes have fallen off, and now expressions like "clotted" and "obscure" are used to pass dismissively over works like "Mills" as critics show growing interest in the later work. What has also flagged is the tendency to identify Lowell's poetry with that of Ransom and Tate, with the Metaphysical poets, or to ascribe his technical development to the platform of the New Criticism. The terms "irony" and "tension" have all but vanished from the critical commentary.

When we scan the corpus of scholarship, we discover that the perception of Lowell as poet was formed in no little degree by his statements in interviews. The interviews, which number about a dozen (plus a handful of symposia remarks), became "digs" from which the critics pieced together opinions as they would precious shards. Who were his favorite poets, what were his writing habits, and so on. With the exception of a brief account by John McCormick (*Poetry*, January 1953) of his conversations with Lowell in Germany, the publication of interviews did not commence until the early sixties. At that time, the favorite interview topic was the stylistic novelty of *Life Studies*. Lowell, when asked why he had departed from his early style, expressed concern that the proficient poets of the fifties had, in their obsession with stylistics, divorced themselves from their culture, and said that he attempted to make a breakthrough back into life by imitating the European prose realists. Critical acknowledgments of this turn from poetic "high seriousness" were frequently accompanied by the sweeping pronouncement that the modern Symbolist mode had finally gone out of style. Unlike the conventional accounts of other poets' critical receptions, in which their stature was either confirmed or altered by a critical work (J. Hillis Miller's essay in *Poets of Reality* on Williams' "poetry of immanence" is an example), Lowell himself defined his contribution. Yet, despite the transition in Lowell criticism during the sixties, a basic approach to his poetics, which had been delineated by Blackmur, Tate, and Jarrell, was never fully erased. Nor did it supersede the acceptance of Lowell's definition of his poetry. This approach fostered an ethical slant—as opposed to a Freudian or mythopoeic one, for example—to analyses of Lowell's work. Lowell's endorsement of Jarrell in his *Paris Review* interview (1961) gave Jarrell (and, by implication, critics of Jarrell's leaning) a certain authority: "Jarrell's a great man of letters, a very informed man, and the best critic of my generation." In essence, Jarrell had registered the notion that Lowell's imaginative energy derived from religious tension, which, when organically fused in form and theme, resulted in major poetry.

## Lowell's Reputation as a Poet

We must draw a distinction between the sources of authority for Lowell's reputation as a poet. How uniform was agreement between the academic critics and those critics who were poets themselves? And which of the two will have more sway in the deliberation over Lowell's stature? It is too early to answer the second question, but we can confidently cite the very different landmarks of recognition he received from academia and from his fellow poets. Among publications rooted largely in academia, special journal issues have been devoted to Lowell: *Harvard Advocate* (November 1961); *Salmagundi* (1, no. 4, 1966–67); *The Hollins Critic* (February 1967); *Salmagundi* (Spring 1977); *American Poetry Review* (September/October 1978); *Agenda* (Autumn 1980). Primary and critical bibliographies have been compiled, the former by Jerome Mazzaro (*The Achievement of Robert Lowell*, 1960); the latter, also by Mazzaro, has been appended to an anthology of criticism: *Robert Lowell: A Portrait of the Artist in His Time* (1970). By 1970 the Twayne Authors Series had added a Lowell volume to its collection (Richard Fein, *Robert Lowell*), and in 1979

Fein completed a revised and expanded second edition. The University of Minnesota pamphlet series on American writers also furnished a study on Lowell in 1970 (Jay Martin, *Robert Lowell*). In addition to the critical anthology mentioned above, we have Thomas Parkinson's *Robert Lowell: A Collection of Critical Essays* (1968) and Jonathan Price's *Critics on Robert Lowell* (1972). Last but not least, there is Mazzaro's *Profile of Robert Lowell* (1971), a gathering of essays and interviews. A quick check of these volumes' publication dates indicates that Lowell was scoring well in academia during the sixties and continued to do so in the seventies, when seven book-length studies complemented the listings.

When we turn to publications written or edited by other poets, Lowell's election to the pantheon seems much less sure. Nor do we have a sense that editors who were on the fringe of academia considered Lowell an innovator. Lowell did not qualify for inclusion in *The Poetics of the New American Poetry* (ed. Donald Allen and Warren Tallman, 1973), an anthology of statements on poetics by twenty-five poets who "achieve spectacular fulfillment in our century of what Whitman was calling for in his." Some of the poets represented in this volume are Pound, Hart Crane, Gertrude Stein, William Carlos Williams, and Charles Olson. Given this roster, one might ask about *Life Studies*: Just how radical or innovative was it? When we turn to that group of poets who write a kind of "surrealist" poetry, which is heightened by fantasy and dreamlike imagery, we discover that they have neither championed nor attributed inspiration or tutelage to Lowell (e.g., W. S. Merwin, Charles Simic, Galway Kinnell). This despite Robert Hass's linkage of Lowell's poetry with "the strategies of the French surrealists" (*Salmagundi*, Spring 1977). The New York school of poets (e.g., Frank O'Hara, Kenneth Koch, John Ashbery) were either contemptuous toward Lowell or remained indifferent to him. The much touted "Skunk Hour" (*Life Studies*) failed to charm O'Hara: "I don't think that anyone has to get themselves to go and watch lovers in a parking lot necking in order to write a poem, and I don't see why it's admirable if they feel guilty about it." The confessional manner, said O'Hara, let Lowell get away with things that are "just plain bad but you're supposed to be interested because he's supposed to be so upset" (*Studio International*, September 1966). The poets of the Black Mountain school—Olson especially—felt that Lowell's poems were written as though they should hang in a museum. The Beat poets, Allen Ginsberg in particular, enjoyed political fraternity with Lowell but said little about his technical virtuosity. And the performance or "talking" poets, like Jerome Rothenberg and David Antin, either remained silent or debunked his "pseudo-narrative and pseudo-history of America" (*Boundary 2*, Fall 1972).

Taken collectively, poets have admired Lowell less than has the scholarly community. And the more recent the tally the greater the difference between the two camps. Even that coterie of political poets (e.g., Bly, LeRoi Jones, Ginsberg) who aligned themselves with Lowell during the sixties, often sharing platforms with him at poetry readings, considered him an alienated intellectual who had never really left the establishment. In fact, the only bloc of poets who consistently supported Lowell were the "confessionals": Stanley Kunitz, W. D. Snodgrass, and Anne Sexton (Sylvia Plath died in 1963). Although each of these poets had a distinctive style, their poetry had several features in common with Lowell's: clinical atomizing of psychic disturbance; diction and imagery which suggested states of incoherence; exposure of private thoughts and actions which are ordinarily reserved for the psychiatrist. The "confessionals" learned from Lowell how to bring their unelevating dailiness into their poems, at no cost to technical rigor. Kunitz, whose verse volume *The Testing Tree* (1971) closely resembles *Life Studies*, said of Lowell: "He wanted to see how much of his personal story, memories, family history he could pack into his verse. In the best of these constructions there is so much art that it is misleading to refer to them as 'confessions' " (*Salmagundi*, 1966–67).

During the early forties, Lowell's publications were few in number: isolated poems which made their way into select journals. His first volume, *Land of Unlikeness* (1944), was printed in a limited edition by an "unknown" press (Cummington). Consequently, little was written about Lowell the poet until the appearance of *Lord Weary* (1946). His selection for the Pulitzer Prize in 1947 brought him status in the academic community, and he quickly became the recipient of a Guggenheim Fellowship (1947). That same year, he was invited by the Library of Congress to serve as Consultant in Poetry. During the late forties, Lowell was better known as the ivory-tower poet—the dignified man of letters—than as the tortured artist. Only a few friends were aware of his bouts with nervous disorder, which exacerbated his already tormented creative process.

When Lowell gave poetry readings, his demeanor was far from imposing. John Ciardi's account of one of these readings suggests that Lowell lacked confidence in his work:

> I was especially struck by a trick Lowell has of throwing away the last line of a poem and shying away from it as if making good an escape. But whether or not a man puts forth a good platform is fairly irrelevant [*Poetry*, August 1948].

Ciardi recalled that Lowell's voice didn't "carry too well" but that this did not lessen his audience appeal. He seemed automatically to command respect.

During these years he was numbered in that company of writers who were the darlings of academe. As a Pulitzer Prize winner he joined the company of Auden and Karl Shapiro, who had recently been granted that honor as well. Lowell's popularity was simple to explain: he was writing in a mode that met with current approval. The New Critics' formalist stronghold was not yet shaken, and Lowell qualified in the ranks of "American Formalists," the title of an essay in *South Atlantic Quarterly* (October 1950). In this essay Lowell was placed side by side with Peter Viereck, Richard Wilbur, and James Merrill. Today it is obvious that Lowell had little in common with these three poets, whose urbane verse never lost its smooth veneer, as Lowell's did when his fierce intensity took control; but Lowell *did* share with these poets a penchant for erudite allusions, and this delighted the scholars.

The June 1951 issue of *Explicator* was almost entirely devoted to source studies and symbol explication of Lowell's poetry. His abstruse mixture of mythical, biblical, and historical references impressed English-department heads, who competed vigorously to lure Lowell to their respective campuses. The years 1953 to 1960 found Lowell at the University of Iowa (1953), University of Indiana (summer workshop, 1953), University of Cincinnati (1954), and Boston University (1955–60). Foundation awards began to pour in: National Institute of Arts and Letters (1954), Ford Foundation Fellowship (1960), Boston Arts Festival Prize (1960). National publicity began to run high: *Life* magazine featured "The Lowells at Massachusetts" (March 18, 1957), replete with photographs and anecdotes. It was as though America had found a new poet laureate, and in Robert Fitzgerald's view, Lowell was the fitting choice (*American Review*, Autumn 1960).

The appearance of *Life Studies* (1959) caused a fluctuation in

Lowell's reputation which did not so much damage his artistic record as stir up controversy about it—further increasing his visibility. There had been an interlude of quiet in the American political scene during the late fifties, and when the maelstrom began in the early sixties, *Life Studies* was a perfect target for those literary critics who had become infected with the nation's polemical mood. This volume confirmed their conviction that literature, like the nation, would never again be the same. A few years earlier, George Steiner had predicted that Lowell would march in the vanguard of literary revolution (*Time and Tide*, August 29, 1959), and Hugh Staples had noted that Lowell took more risks than most poets of his time (*Tri-Quarterly*, Winter 1959). But when we look closely at the tributes paid *Life Studies* at the time it was chosen for the 1960 National Book Award, we discover that the volume was little understood (*Saturday Review of Literature*, April 9, 1960; *New York Times Book Review*, March 20, 1960). Critics talked about it as a "breakthrough," and some of the rhapsodic reviewers were reminded of "Song of Myself," perhaps mindful that Whitman's poem, in its day, also stunned readers.

Nonetheless, when the *Harvard Advocate* brought out a special Lowell issue in November 1961, encomia and personal anecdotes took the place of close analysis of *Life Studies*. Ransom recalled the Kenyon days and Lowell's distinction as a classics student; Anne Sexton described the course Lowell taught at Boston University. The only essay containing technical commentary was by William Carlos Williams, and he focused on *Imitations*. When we look back at the controversy surrounding *Life Studies*, and consider the radical experiments of other poets, the teapot does seem tempestuous. It was a time to relish: had *Life Studies* made its debut in the seventies, the criticism might have been less volatile.

When we glance at Lowell's reputation in England during these years, we find that, with a few exceptions (Staples, who wrote the first book on Lowell; Spender, who called Lowell a pioneer), the critics invariably compared his experiments with England's time-honored works. Thus when Lowell wrote dramatic monologues he was, in their view, a poor copyist of Browning. (Ironically, Lowell had remarked in his *Paris Review* interview that he rejected Browning's monologues as models because "You feel that the people are made up.") When he wrote "public" or history poems, such as "For the Union Dead," he was no match for the eighteenth-century poets. In

John Holloway's words, Lowell lacked the "public dimension" and was inclined to "take history where it is at its most personal, and private resonances can compensate when public resonances fail" (*Encounter*, April 1968). Finally, when he wrote elegies, critics were reminded of how magnificent "Lycidas" is. Nonetheless, Lowell's reputation was substantial enough to win him a nomination in 1966 for the Oxford poetry chair. Edmund Blunden, his opponent, was the victor. Little time elapsed before observers castigated the inadvertence of the judges' choice.

On native shores, in this interim Lowell continued to entice the scholars. *Imitations* (1961), Lowell's adaptation of classic poetry to modern setting and diction, opened new channels for exploration. Although Lowell, along with Richmond Lattimore, would capture the Bollingen Translation Prize for 1962, *Imitations* was not greeted with enthusiasm. Critics were more impressed with his prolixity than with his talent as a translator. At the same time they knew that Lowell's new undertaking required them to reevaluate him as a poet. Edmund Wilson now believed that Lowell was the only contemporary poet worth reading (*New Yorker*, June 2, 1962) and Robert Bly decided that Lowell's poetry was of no value (*Choice*, 1962). Wilson's and Bly's verdicts came in a year when the literary establishment was busily engaged in summation, and the impetus for this activity was indirectly related to the national political mood. The Kennedy administration had launched its New Frontier and there was sudden interest in the national cultural status. Arts and artists were at a juncture, said Malcolm Cowley, who sealed off one phase of American literature with dates and names and then prepared for the next with a new list of names (*New York Times Book Review*, October 7, 1962). Cowley numbered Lowell among the replacements for former masters. *Saturday Review* (February 17, 1962) and *Time* (November 9, 1962) also made inventories, selecting their leading candidates for the poets of the New Frontier, and Lowell was again named. Not surprisingly, these omnibus articles said virtually nothing about Lowell's poetry. What *is* surprising is that the less specialized the publication the more Lowell's technical skill was praised. It was really praise by negation: Lowell was less obscene than the Beats, less graphically descriptive than some other "confessionals." Critics were really deferring to Lowell's image as the eminent and dignified poet, an image that was never really jeopardized.

As we know, the New Frontier was soon pushed back by assassinations and other national tragedies, and the establishment turned to more pressing matters than the status of the arts. With this turn in the national interest there was less adulatory coverage of Lowell in wide-readership publications. Another change was taking place in the academic community at this time: critics were beginning to lose interest in whipping the New Critics and to concede that formalist standards and the confessional mode could be successfully united. Even Leslie Fiedler, that habitual provocateur of academia, was willing to grant Lowell's ability to fuse the intimate confession with the high style (*Kenyon Review*, Winter 1964). Ralph Mills made the same point about Lowell, to whom he devoted a chapter in his *Contemporary American Poetry* (1966). And Stephen Stepanchev attributed Lowell's success to the release from those restrictions that the new critics had forced on him, but insisted that Lowell had learned to handle, rather than abandon, symbolism in *Life Studies*:

> what symbolism remains in the poems—poetry, after all, cannot exist without symbols—is intrinsic and so subtle that the reader is not offended by the need to make continual equations [*American Poetry Since 1945*, 1965].

Appraisals, then, were contingent upon the whims of the critical community and, to some extent, upon Lowell's whims, for in 1964 he published his verse drama *The Old Glory*, which forced the critics to reevaluate Lowell as a poet. Indeed, *Union Dead*, which appeared the same year, did not represent any dramatic break, as Christopher Ricks correctly observed (*New Statesman*, March 25, 1965), but *Old Glory* led critics to believe that the poet would now turn playwright and universalize his earlier, more personal vision. They were proved wrong; Lowell ventured no further with drama than to translate two Greek tragedies, *Prometheus Bound* and *The Oresteia* (he never completed the latter). But the critics scurried back to Lowell's earlier dramatic monologues and redefined their function: they were preludes to Lowell's greater artistic genre, the drama. The virture of this notion was that it generated a spate of revisionary assessments of neglected work, primarily "The Mills of the Kavanaughs." The volume which contained this title poem now had special value: "The Mills" and *Life Studies*, despite their stylistic differences, had identical confessional qualities which were brought together in Lowell's new idiom, history (the dramatized history which constituted the three plays in *Old Glory*). This was how Josephine Jacobsen explained Lowell's poetic evolution (*Commonweal*, December 4, 1964), and at the time her argument made sense. Moreover, it gave critics further cause to plump Lowell's poetic reputation. How versatile of this poet to number such dissimilar works in his canon! Stephen Spender had, after all, warned of the danger of limiting oneself to confessionalism, which leaves poets at a spirtual dead end (*New Republic* June 8, 1959). And while "Mills" had different personae than the obviously first-person speaker in *Life Studies*, the Kavanaughs were little more than projections of Lowell's own family, and the fall of the Winslow and Lowell ancestral houses was the true subject of the poem. Thus Lowell's movement beyond the dramatic monologue to *Old Glory* was instrumental to his changing image as a poet. The play's the thing, said Roger Bowen:

> In the first few months of 1967, Lowell's newest book of poetry, *Near the Ocean*, was published in the United States, and *Benito Cereno* had its London premiere. . . . Of the two events, the new production of his now four-year-old play remains the more significant [*Criticism*, Winter 1969].

Lowell's remarks in interviews helped to reinforce such claims, for he said that he planned to write plays on Trotsky and Malcolm X in the near future (*The Observer*, March 12, 1967). What happened, of course, was that Lowell put his views about revolutionary leaders into his sonnet cycles of the seventies. But, again, it had been Lowell's interview remarks that sent critics to corners they would have ordinarily overlooked.

When Twentieth Century Views presented its collection of critical essays on Lowell in 1968, the Introduction, by Parkinson, which emphasized Lowell's "relevance," fit the sixties framework:

> Lowell as much as any current poet deserves systematic study in universities. He is entwined in the great moral issues of our age with compelling fullness, reacting against the savagery and barbarism of great and small wars.

But despite the tone of the Introduction, the essays in the collection (with a few exceptions) were reprints of the standard ones up to that period; here again were Tate, Blackmur, Jarrell,

Staples, Ehrenpreis, Berryman. Thus the essays focused on "war horses" like "Quaker Graveyard in Nantucket" while the Introduction depicted Lowell as our latest scoop. In effect, academia was looking for a spokesman for the period and Lowell was a problematic choice.

Since Parkinson's edition of essays was a watershed of sorts, we must ask if it signaled any progress in the scholarship on Lowell's literary heritage: In the Parkinson collection or elsewhere, had any systematic study of the influences on Lowell's style been undertaken? The answer is no—then and now. Commentary has gone no further than the customary references to Ransom and Tate. A few critics sensed a Crane or Eliot connection, but merely suggested it. A. Alvarez' piece in *Times Literary Supplement* (March 23, 1967) demonstrated the extent of the analysis: "Lowell is not only the most brilliant and assured technician now writing, but he is also—in background, preoccupations and intellectual tone—most naturally heir to T. S. Eliot." Gabriel Pearson also made some show of interest in influences, but only to acknowledge that Winters and Tate were the two dominant figures (*Review*, March 1969). Pearson believed that Lowell had surpassed them: "In the end his despair is more bracing and more buoyant, his exposure more eager, his insistence on order and virtue more unremitting." Precisely. And that is why the evocation of Winters' and Tate's names is misleading; apart from sharing their intellectual metier, Lowell had little in common with them as a poet. Alvarez was closer to the mark in his mention of Eliot. Eliot's cosmopolitanism, traditionalism, and impersonality, balanced by his colloquialism and modernity, taught Lowell more than did any other poet of the twentieth century. Lowell himself commented on Eliot's monolithic genius in the *Paris Review* interview: "All his poems are one poem, a form of continuity that has grown and snowballed."

Turning back from this look at Lowell's sources to the more conventional treatments of his reputation, we note that the predictions about Lowell becoming a playwright, the debate over Lowell's true role as our national poet, began to lose momentum when the new decade arrived. Lowell won the Pulitzer Prize for *The Dolphin* in 1973 and the Copernicus Award for *Robert Lowell's Poems: A Selection* in 1974, but he maintained a low profile in the seventies, shunning publicity entirely. Perhaps because of declining physical health, he had intimations of death, and the poems evince exhaustion and a tendency to sum up or tie together the stray strands of his life and art. Again, the critics took the cue from him, indulging in summations. *Salmagundi* celebrated his sixtieth birthday by devoting a special issue to him (Spring 1977). Robert Boyers wrote a preface which clearly indicated that the poet to whom these essays were dedicated had become the nation's laureate.

The issue, I might add, contains some of the best scholarship in the late Lowell criticism: Helen Vendler, Robert Fitzgerald, G. S. Fraser, among others. Vendler and Fitzgerald confront the difficult "Ulysses and Circe," which found its way into *Day by Day*. While Fitzgerald gave a close reading of the mythical echoes in the poem (see chapter on stylistics), Vendler, uncannily sensing that this poem was "the finale of the long effort," used the work to verify Lowell's indisputable reputation. Lowell's version of the Odyssey now belonged in the pantheon with Pound's, Joyce's, Tennyson's, Dante's, DuBellay's. To Vendler, the poem embodied the archetypal return from the exploration of the world, and at the end "what emotion is left to age but fury?" Fury, violence, rage—these emotions were not just symptomatic of old age, said Christopher Ricks in his radio tribute to Lowell (March 1, 1977, Radio 3, BBC), adding that violence is Lowell's "essential subject." Ricks wondered whether Lowell would react to his sixtieth birthday in this characteristic way: "Robert Lowell is 60 today; it will be a while before there is a poem which knows and shows the conflicting emotions that this must mean for him." Lowell did not live to write about it, but what is germane to our present discussion is that Lowell, abroad, had the honor of a nationally broadcast tribute.

England, for some reason, grew fonder of Lowell after his death. He was the "Last Parnassian," said John Haffenden (*Agenda*, Summer 1978), and at the end he was not violent but "tender-hearted, enduring without demanding." At the risk of presuming to read Haffenden's mind, I believe that he—and other British critics—were pleased that Lowell had reverted to traditional forms at the end of his career, having largely abandoned his confessional voice. Indeed, Haffenden, although deferent to *Day by Day*, called it a "wilful regression" to the earlier expression of *Life Studies*. John Bayley, too, expressed appreciation of the late Lowell, who in his commitment to the artist's role resembled Horace (*Times Literary Supplement*,

August 22, 1980). Lowell's Horatian tone "depends on a curious kind of sophisticated intercourse—rather un-American—between poet and reader, a relation borrowed as it were from the intimacy of aristocrats, even though it is not confined to that social tone." Horace's extreme compactness and ability to be at once intimate, easy, and allusive was repeated in Lowell. Bayley's précis was a paradigm of British literary principles: through classic, urbane restraint the full emotive and quotidian force of life is best conveyed.

No account of Lowell's reputation as a poet is complete without a glimpse of his performance as a teacher. To date, there is little on record about this important aspect of Lowell's career, which he came to "voluntarily," having no need to worry about finances. In a "Talk with Robert Lowell" (*New York Times Book Review*, October 4, 1964), Lowell registered his pleasure at preparing his courses, which helped him to place his own writing in perspective. Helen Vendler's recollection of Lowell as a teacher—at Boston University, where she was a student; at Harvard, where she audited his Nineteenth-Century Poetry course—attests to the fact that Lowell turned his lectures into the anecdotal and the personal (*New York Times Book Review*, February 3, 1980). His approach was neither conventional nor categorical. He proceeded through literary history with a barrage of aperçus which ranged from the "wittily malicious" to the "piercing," says Vendler. He always talked about poets with an eye toward his own work. Thus he skipped over middle Hopkins and "dwelt instead on the sonnets, perhaps because he had been so recently engaged in sonnets himself, talking about how well Hopkins 'did' ecstasy and despair." Or when he spoke of Whitman's "Song of Myself," Lowell seemed to identify with this poet who habitually rewrote, for he concluded that the revisions didn't improve Whitman's poem. His lectures on Coleridge showed a bit of envy, Vendler felt, for that Romantic's ability to "render the domestic, in all its tangles and dailiness and anguish." And when it came to pedagogy, Lowell was somewhat impersonal, occasionally soliciting opinion but more often murmuring a "monologue." On the whole, "he did not know his students' names; there was no 'discussion.' " Vendler is quick to add that, outside the classroom, Lowell eagerly engaged in "give-and-take" with students, which suggests that he never lost sight of his public image; playing professor necessitated a certain formality.

In 1968 Lowell taught a creative writing course at Harvard,

whose description read: "The emphasis will be primarily on poetry. Not more than ten students will be enrolled." James Atlas was admitted to this course (which was so inundated with visitors that there were seldom fewer than forty people in the hall) and wrote a fascinating account of his experience as Lowell's student (*Atlantic*, July 1982). Lowell delivered mono-logues about dead poets, said Atlas, often forgetting to com-ment on the students' poems, although they were dutifully mimeographed and distributed. Then, when he *did* turn to a student composition, he would "rewrite" it as if it had been written by Wallace Stevens or Eliot. The students were struck by Lowell's knowledge of metrics and his ability to isolate the weak points of major poets:

> "You feel that Arnold's trying too hard here," he remarked once, poring over "The Buried Life." "You'd almost say he [Arnold] wants to feel more than he does; the terse lines are there to goad on his emotion."

Atlas does not extrapolate from this little anecdote, but it would not be presumptuous to claim that Lowell was recalling his own "willed" lines (as Jarrell once described them) and his effort, in certain periods of creative drought, to feel more than he did. Atlas said that students watched eagerly for "manic soliloquies, references to Hitler, or outbursts of unnatural gaiety," which, according to hearsay, were the former signs of Lowell's break-downs. None occurred that semester, said Atlas; but the details about Lowell's behavior during one of these breakdowns were familiar to the student body:

> Lowell showing up at William Alfred's house and declaring that he was the Virgin Mary; Lowell talking for two hours straight in class, revising a student's poem in the style of Milton, Tennyson, or Frost; Lowell wandering around Harvard Square without a coat in the middle of January, shivering, wild-eyed, incoherent.

Atlas renders his essay as though he has total recall of that fall semester at Harvard, even to the point of placing quota-tion marks around Lowell's words. This is disconcerting and detracts from the credibility of the profile. Nonetheless, much of Atlas' profile corroborates Helen Vendler's account of Low-ell, and the dialogue format gives a convincing evocation of Lowell at Harvard in 1968.

## Lowell the Public Figure

Lowell's public activities, especially when they resulted in confrontations with the White House and other organs of political authority, were of interest to critics and journalists at intermittent periods in his career. Stories reported in the press, anecdotes related by friends and colleagues, have yet to be sifted to gain a reasonably accurate account of his behavior in the public arena and the motivations behind this. The political image of Lowell, as it now stands, is built on a myth which had its inception in the early forties: the man of principle who, as a descendant of a line of patriotic ancestors, considered it his proper burden to participate in the forum in times of national crisis. In October 1943 Lowell sent a letter to President Roosevelt, stating his reasons for refusing to report for induction into armed service. The *New York Times* (October 12) covered the story with a fierce caption: "A "BOSTON" LOWELL IS A DRAFT DODGER." Two days later, again in the *Times*, Lowell was placed in less than august company when his sentence was briefly mentioned as part of a story on another defendant: "NAZI DRAFT DODGER GETS 3–YEAR TERM." Flares of patriotism brought censure to Lowell at the time, but later judgments were milder. As the memory of World War II receded, so did Lowell's notoriety. Poets in modern society were "different drummers," after all, and Lowell, having been denied privileged treatment, had dutifully served five months in federal prison.

The publicity about Lowell's incarceration as a conscientious objector had no sooner abated than Lowell was embroiled in another issue which would put his name in headlines again. Between 1948 and 1950 he was a participant in the Bollingen Prize controversy over Ezra Pound. As one of the twelve judges who figured in the debate about honoring a "turncoat" who, according to the *New York Times* (February 20, 1949), had composed *Cantos* in a "treason cell," Lowell defended Pound on purely artistic grounds. The broadcast media and magazines which catered to a nonspecialized readership exhibited a strong postwar disaffection toward Pound. For example, Norman Cousins and Harrison Smith wrote editorials for the *Saturday Review of Literature* (July 30, 1949) in which they chastised the Bollingen jury for separating art from life. But a different response came from poets and academicians, who feared precedents of censorship and the stifling of expression that might result if Pound were denied the prize. Dwight Macdonald's was one of the more articulate editorials of this persuasion (*Politics*, Winter 1949). Macdonald praised the committee in general: "By some miracle the Bollingen judges were able to consider Mr. Pound the poet and not the fascist." Then he defended Lowell for championing Pound and visiting him during his internment at St. Elizabeth's Hospital.

In the wake of the Bollingen Prize dispute, Lowell temporarily withdrew from the political scene. During the fifties, he seemed to have little interest in affairs of state. He made no show of objection to President Eisenhower's foreign or domestic policies, outside such despairing lines as these from "Inauguration Day: January 1953" (*Life Studies*):

> The Republic summons Ike,
> the mausoleum in her heart.

In contrast to the great concern he voiced about "American aggression" in World War II and Viet Nam, Lowell remained quiet about our bid for sovereignty in Korea. At a *Partisan Review* symposium on "The Cold War and the West," he registered his disapproval of the use of nuclear weaponry—for any reason—but his statement lacked fervor (Winter 1962). The record of his political activism, then, is marked by inconsistency. In his 1965 interview with Alvarez (*Encounter*, February), Lowell, recalling a Kennedy White House dinner he had attended, made it clear that he believed artists are not taken seriously in the political sphere:

> We all drank a great deal at the White House, and had to sort of be told not to take our champagne into the concert, and to put our cigarettes out like children—though nicely, it wasn't peremptory. Then the next morning you read that the Seventh Fleet had been sent somewhere in Asia and you had a funny feeling of how unimportant the artist really was; that this was sort of window dressing and that the real government was somewhere else.

This feeling of powerlessness may explain his ambivalent feelings about public duty. However, special-interest groups persisted in soliciting his support or participation in different ways, and in 1965 he was once again thrown into the political whirlwind. Lyndon Johnson had been inaugurated for a full term as president and one of his first actions was the initiation of American bombing raids on Communist targets in Viet Nam. Teach-ins and demonstrations were staged, and Lowell num-

bered himself among the antiwar minority. *Life* magazine
featured another article on Lowell, launching a new phase of
publicity for him (February 19, 1965). In May of that year,
when President Johnson invited him to recite his poetry at the
White House Festival of the Arts, Lowell replied by sending a
telegram of refusal, after having tentatively accepted the invi-
tation by telephone. His decision made the front page of the
*New York Times* (June 6) and inspired magazine articles with
captions like "REJECTION SLIP" (*Newsweek*, June 14) and snide
summaries of his exchange with the White House (*Time*, June
11). An editorial in *Nation* (June 21) commended his action,
but journals of less liberal persuasion printed letters of censure
from their readership.

National disaffection with the war was still several years
away, and Lowell's position was by and large unpopular. The
entire matter generated comparisons between Johnson and
Kennedy: Johnson's annoyance at Lowell demonstrated the
president's contempt for the intelligentsia, which made that
segment of the population nostalgic for the Kennedy style.
Eric Goldman, who had served as special consultant to Johnson at the time of the arts festival, described the White House
reactions to the telegram in *The Tragedy of Lyndon Johnson*
(1969). The president was in a rage, said Goldman, and "The
roar in the Oval Office could be heard all the way into the
East Wing." Goldman initially agreed with the president:

> This, I told myself, was arrant troublemaking and publicity seek-
> ing—the acceptance of a White House invitation, then turning it
> down, the injection of irrelevant grand issues in high-sounding
> language, the play to the newspapers. Then, studying the actual
> contents of the letter and reflecting on what I knew of Lowell . . .
> I decided that my initial reaction was off base and that the letter
> had been written by a sincere and troubled man.

Goldman came to respect Lowell for his judgment and the
"gracious" manner with which he carried it out. Even Johnson
volunteered a show of regard for Lowell when, several months
after the Festival episode, he recited several lines from "Dover
Beach" during a speech and mistakenly attributed them to
Lowell. (As we shall see, the association of Lowell with Arnold
has a certain logic, though Johnson presumably would not have
known this.) Johnson's placation of Lowell brought derision
from the *New York Times* (August 5, 1965), which reported
the error with a certain relish.

The reactions to Lowell's confrontation with the White House were registered in academia. British critic John Bayley believed that Lowell had shirked his responsibility and that his disillusionment with national policy exhibited a destructive "style of cancellation" (*London Magazine*, June 1966). Lowell showed a capacity for self-extinction, said Bayley, who called the withdrawal a syndrome of Lowell's "death-wish"—a syndrome present in Lowell's poetry as well. Hayden Carruth took the opposite view and insisted that Lowell had earned renown as a leader: "One thinks of his conscientious objections during the war [World War II] and all that it entailed, his refusal to attend White House sociables, and many other such actions—to substantiate his moral fitness for the role" (*Hudson Review*, Autumn 1967). Carruth's response to Lowell's "firmness and integrity" was more representative of poets and other artists of the period, even those affiliated with academia, than Bayley's was. Another group that deified Lowell in the mid-sixties was American college youth. They inundated him with letters of congratulations and initiated a rush of demands for his support in public activities, especially draft protests. Lowell's new prominence won him a story in *Time* (June 2, 1967), which featured a cover portrait by Sidney Nolan depicting the poet as a sorrowful figure, crowned with a wreath of laurels. The seven-page story characterized Lowell as "an intensely private man" who was pleased by the younger generation's approval, yet reluctant to throw himself in their midst. *Time* also depicted him as something of a "grandee," who was inclined to make outlandish—or, at best, curious—remarks about America's enemies. For example, when he introduced Soviet poet Andrei Voznesensky at a reading at Manhattan's Town Hall, he said: "Both our countries, I think, have really terrible governments. But we do the best we can with them, and they better do the best they can with each other or the world will cease to be here." Voznesensky, when asked later what he thought of the comment, looked away without answering.

The climate of the middle sixties brought a new selfhood to Lowell. The antiwar movement, while small, was more idealistic and more consolidated than at the end of the decade, and Lowell found it easier to identify with the philosophical leanings of this new Left than with the protest movements in the Cold War years of the fifties. The force for evil, which the Left saw embodied in Johnson and his administration, was a concrete target for Lowell, who needed to unleash his own proclivity toward struggle. As much as he deplored causes (in the Naipaul interview he had complained that the country was "cause-mad"; *Listener*, September 4, 1969), he was reluctant to recognize his own pleasure at playing the protestor, though even this role was undertaken in an ambivalent way, as the October 1967 Pentagon March amusingly demonstrates. Lowell was a participant at this antiwar demonstration, along with a crowd of marchers who were numbered at from 50,000 to 200,000, the figure depending on which side's estimates we accept: those of the government representatives or of the left-wing pacifists. Lowell marched in the vanguard with such notables as Noam Chomsky, Allen Ginsberg, Norman Mailer, Dr. Benjamin Spock. Mailer's book on this event, *The Armies of the Night*, reports on Lowell's behavior prior to and during the march. While the two men were having dinner the night before the march, Lowell told Mailer that he hoped the event would end quickly because he wanted to get back to New York in time for a dinner party he was hosting. They talked about the possibility of getting arrested:

Mailer:   "No Cal, if you get arrested, you had better plan on not making dinner before nine."
Lowell:   "Well, should we get arrested? What do you think of the merits?"

Mailer felt that it was the best way they could serve the occasion: "The papers can't claim that hippies and hoodlums were the only ones guilty." At the march, by pure coincidence, Mailer was arrested but Lowell was turned back by MPs and forced to remain at a rear parking lot during the speeches. Mailer said that Lowell was one of the first to leave, presumably to meet his plane for New York. Mailer's vignette suggests, perhaps more than any other accounts of Lowell's political activities, that he was never fully committed to political causes.

No sooner had Lowell sprung to the center of attention through the antiwar movement than he began to campaign for Eugene McCarthy, a presidential candidate in 1967. This new cause seemed to please him more than his antiwar activities, for his participation in the October march on the Pentagon had left him fearful and self-questioning—indeed, overwhelmed by the seemingly endless symbols of power surrounding him:

Under the too white marmoreal Lincoln Memorial,
the too tall marmoreal Washington Obelisk,
gazing into the too long reflecting pool,
the reddish trees, the withering autumn sky.

["The March," *Notebook*]

He was too reticent and psychically delicate to move with masses of people, but he had a temperamental affinity with McCarthy, a poet himself. The two men covered the campaign trail with an aristocratic flair, comparing views on Shakespeare, assessing issues with cavalier wit. Lowell's enthusiasm for McCarthy was spurred by his objections to Robert Kennedy, the other Democratic candidate. To Lowell, the Kennedy clan represented the kind of pride and ambition which fostered tyrants. In effect, Lowell could—by supporting McCarthy— put into action the beliefs he had expressed in his poetry about such leaders as Jonathan Edwards and Colonel Shaw. Kennedy, like these American heroes, was doomed by his irrational ideals, Lowell felt. Toward the end of the campaign, just prior to Kennedy's death, Lowell became more drawn to Kennedy's charisma and toned down his support for McCarthy. Nonetheless, Lowell composed an official statement for the *New Republic* (April 13, 1968) in which he explained why McCarthy had his endorsement: "McCarthy is preferable, first for his negative qualities: lack of excessive charisma, driving ambition, machine-like drive, and the too great wish to be President."

The circle of advisors and friends in the McCarthy camp were somewhat resentful of Lowell's behavior during the campaign. In *McCarthy for President* (1969), Arthur Herzog recalls how Lowell would draw McCarthy away from the business at hand "while speech writers, press aides, and others waited in the hall." And in *People* (1970), Andreas Teuber, a campaign worker, attributes McCarthy's poor showing in his televised debate with Kennedy to Lowell's way of taking "the edge off things" and making McCarthy feel detached or olympian. The most critical account of Lowell's conduct is in *American Journey: The Times of Robert Kennedy* (1970), which describes the limousine ride that Lowell and McCarthy took to the television studio for the debate: the two men composed "a twentieth-century version of 'Ode to St. Cecilia's Day' in the back seat. So by the time McCarthy got to the studio, yes, he was then like Henry the Fifth at Agincourt."

There was, then, an air of unreality about Lowell's engagement in politics. He had a habit of separating himself from his consciousness and behaving as though another self was immersed in the scene. This was not immediately obvious to his critics, and even as late as 1972 Harry Cargas, in his essay "Robert Lowell: Protestor as Link Between Past and Present," gave a party-line profile of Lowell as one who could not resist political involvement (*Daniel Berrigan and Contemporary Protest Poetry*). Lowell was the standard liberal, in line with other political poets like Ginsberg, LeRoi Jones, and Daniel Berrigan. That image was later obliterated, both with venom (Louis Simpson) and with sympathy (Robert Boyers). Simpson implied that he was not duped by Lowell, who made a show of interest in social issues but really understood very little about history, the common man, and liberalism (*Saturday Review of Literature*, October 1, 1977). Describing Lowell's participation at marches and campaign meetings, Simpson reminded us that Lowell was never capable of relating to the masses, even though he tried to make imaginative connections between his own suffering and the suffering of the masses. This was not Boyers' perception; there was an unflinching honesty in Lowell which endeared him to people, who shared with him the role of the "victim" (*Salmagundi*, Summer 1979). Boyers suggested that Lowell's capacity to "assuage, never goad" was what drew us to him, whether on a stage, speaking out for a candidate, or in the poetic mask of a persona. His suffering is our suffering and we share with him the belief that sometimes the "will to keep going may be all we have." This kind of rhetoric sounds hyperbolic now, but there is no question that in the sixties Lowell's gaunt, slightly removed presence had a certain appeal. The photographs of him in the *Time* story (mentioned above) substantiate Boyers' view. Lowell exploited his image of frail saintliness.

In assessing the place of Lowell as "public figure," one must admit that, unlike the opinions of most poets, his views were clearly noted by several of America's presidents. (How many letters and telegrams to the Chief Executive have had the effect that Lowell's missives to Roosevelt and Johnson had?) Yet this whole performance, including the role he played in trying to elect a friend and fellow poet to the highest office, is questionable. Can Lowell's firmly established professionalism as poet excuse what seems to be forming more and more as a charge of dilettantism in politics? This is hardly the place to debate the roles of the poet—Lowell would hardly have qualified as a philosopher-king—but in any study of the Lowell phenomenon it must be noted that this man of literature had a public presence, that he was taken seriously by men of action in the highest reaches of our government.

After the McCarthy campaign, Lowell, like McCarthy, withdrew from the public scene. The seventies aftermath was a decade of relative apathy for the political liberals, but this national climate was not so much the cause of Lowell's withdrawal as was his domestic situation, which permanently removed him from politics.

## Lowell in Private Life

Prior to the first full-scale biography of Lowell, Ian Hamilton's *Robert Lowell* (1982), we had to content ourselves with fragmentary segments of scholarship which provided glimpses of the man in disconnected anecdotes, memoirs, and reports of conversations. The composite portrait was a complex one; yet, because most of the accounts of Lowell are by admirers, they are perhaps more flattering than authentic. What emerges from the descriptions, nonetheless, is a troubled, often tortured, personality. We might begin with that version of Lowell which is included in a three-part biography of the Lowells who distinguished themselves as writers: David Heymann's *American Aristocracy: The Lives and Times of James Russell, Amy and Robert Lowell* (1980). Heymann does not pretend to offer a fully documented history of the lives of these figures; his purpose is to depict the Lowells as offspring of a dynasty which determined their roles as artists. Thus their "regal legacy" included the "virtues of piety, sobriety, frugality, productivity, and diligence." In Robert's case, the inability—or unwillingness —to accept this inheritance was compounded by the fierce pride he felt in his patrician ancestry. Heymann reprints several statements by Lowell about his "writing relatives," which indicate that Lowell did not enjoy being identified with Amy or James Russell:

> I think James Russell in his *Biglow Papers* about the Mexican War and the Civil War was a minor great poet, really, and a really . . . not very interesting poet the rest of the time. And Amy I can't get at all but I admire her character and admire her poetry in a way.

Heymann argues the obvious, namely, that Robert climbed higher than either of his kinsmen because of his greater talent. James Russell was at best a period poet, and Amy was a "shooting star that blazed and faded." Robert, despite his irreverence, suffered his heritage more profoundly than the other two, says Heymann. Amy Lowell, pierced by the self-consciousness of her heritage, had protested earlier: "I'm the only member of my family who is worth a damn." Heymann never delves into the extent of the influence James Russell and Amy may have exerted on Robert, either in lifestyle or literary matters. A very brief section of "91 Revere Street" describes the grudging admiration that Lowell's parents accorded their relative, Amy, who was "never a welcome subject in our household." She was respected more for her pluck and hard work than for her "loud, bossy un-ladylike *chinoiserie*—her free verse!"

Lowell's mental illness is a subject which has been largely skirted in the scholarship. When working with thematic—and on occasion stylistic—analyses of Lowell's poetry, critics intermittently referred to Lowell's breakdowns. But the personal accounts of Lowell pointedly avoided the subject. Philip Booth's "Summers in Castine," which presents in diary-like form a chronological portrait of Lowell between 1955 and 1965, gives the impression that Lowell was a genial, untroubled man (*Salmagundi*, Spring 1977). Castine, Maine was Lowell's summer haven and Booth, his neighbor, was his sailing companion and frequent guest. Booth depicts Lowell (referred to as "Cal") as immersed in a happy domestic world where he was the devoted husband and doting father: "Cal tends to her [Harriet]. All this is but wordless, as basic as pats and murmurs." Lowell is given to frequent entertaining and plays the witty host. When a member of the Kennedy family spends an evening with Cal, the atmosphere is at once stimulating and friendly. Booth says of Ted Kennedy: "His respect for Cal is obviously considerable; his courtesy is total. It occurs to me that Kennedy Boston is astounded to find patrician Boston so passionately informed."

It is hard to square Booth's description of the tenderness shown by Lowell with some of the domestic poems in *Life Studies* and *Union Dead*. In "Man and Wife," for example, the wife is distant and unaffectionate:

> Now twelve years later, you turn your back.
> Sleepless, you hold
> your pillow to your hollows like a child—

Granting the element of fiction in Lowell's poetry, and granting that we must not presume to read his verse as autobiography, Booth is still a bit too adulatory to be convincing.

Booth is better when he turns to Lowell's conversations on poetry. Lowell evidently had a need to dominate: "Given an audience of more than one, Cal turns conversation into his best competitive sport." Playing the acolyte, though only eight years younger, Booth brings his own manuscripts to Lowell and carefully records Lowell's advice: "I should read say three poets for a month, maybe copying-out poems to see what I can learn to use, to extend my range." Lowell had certain models for extending his creative range: Empson showed him how to use his intellect; Marianne Moore showed him how to study an object; Frost showed him how to organize a poem. Booth also noted that Lowell often used prose as his stylistic model or touchstone, offering such observations as that description in a poem should be as solid as the river-crossing section of *As I Lay Dying* and that all of Hardy's novels had the knack of implying narrative without sacrificing the sense of documentary realism. Little gems of insight such as these are valuable contributions toward a survey of Lowell's reading tastes and the resultant chronology of literary influence on his verse. Finally, Booth stresses that although Lowell was obsessed with realism in literature (he loved the "thereness" of "Tintern Abbey"), he was strikingly unaware of actualities in the real world. For example, on a family excursion to the Town Wharf to visit a submarine on exhibit to the public, Lowell said to Booth, "Tell me, are the men who sail that thing *Marines?*" This, naturally, charmed Booth, who felt that associative leaps of this sort were what made Lowell a great poet.

Lowell was evidently loved by his colleagues and peers. The tales about poets vying for prizes, jockeying for first place among the nation's poets (Frost immediately comes to mind), have not—at least, as yet—surfaced about Lowell. By all reports, he was so absorbed in his work that he was oblivious to such pettiness. John McCormick's piece on his meeting with Lowell in Germany (*Poetry*; see above) reinforces the notion that Lowell grasped reality largely by identification. For example, Lowell, not inclined to suicide, felt that when Hart Crane leapt off a ship into the Mexican Gulf, he had "only an intense desire to cool and wet his exhausted body." On another subject, McCormick was interested in sounding Lowell about the American writer who has a long residence abroad. Lowell replied

that he had always wanted to live abroad and that, now he had
done so, he discovered how attached he was to America. England was the only possibility, he felt, but it contained its risks
as well as its rewards. Then he cited Pound, who had wasted
twenty years at Rapallo, or so it seemed, until he produced
the reveries of recollection in *Pisan Cantos*. There were, perhaps, advantages to be gained by leading the expatriate life.
McCormick concluded his essay by remarking that Lowell
worked with such intensity that he was constantly weary. Part
of his exhaustion derived from his intolerance of the dissension
and stupidity he encountered in the literary world. Essentially
polite, he internalized his intolerance, which further sapped his
strength. He was not a vigorous man, and confessed to McCormick that the "best thing about writing verse is that you can
work lying down."

As we rummage through the scholarship, looking for privileged peeks at the person known as Lowell, we discover a certain protectiveness on the part of the writers. Perhaps the most
disappointing text—disappointing because it is the only extended
personal account of Lowell in the years of his first marriage—
is Eileen Simpson's *Poets in Their Youth: A Memoir* (1982).
Simpson, who married John Berryman in 1942 and divorced
him fourteen years later, purports to present a firsthand memoir
of her husband and his gifted circle of friends. She and Berryman spent a brief period during the summer of 1946 visiting
Lowell and Jean Stafford at their vacation home in Damaris-
cotta Mills, Maine. (The Lowells were divorced two years later.)
Simpson describes the visit in great detail, but she emphasizes
that the atmosphere of tension between the Lowells bespoke
their crumbling marriage. And yet, treated to so much information, we cannot feel that we have become acquainted with
Lowell. Lowell seems concerned that Jean drinks too much,
says Simpson:

> Jean worried that we might run out of "hootch." The bottle of
> rum opened when we arrived was almost empty. Cal said we
> could do without liquor; John and I drank little and he [Lowell]
> wasn't drinking at all. "Maybe *you* can do without it," Jean said,
> "but it gives me the wimwams to be in a house that's bone-dry."

And Jean talks about how difficult it is to live with Cal, now
that he isn't drinking: "I fell in love with Caligula and am
living with Calvin." Simpson, a Catholic, accompanied the

Lowells to Sunday Mass and during the walk to church Jean
whispered that Cal is a "puritan at heart," that he was rigidly
devout, and focused on the least attractive aspects of Catholicism: "spiritual exercises, retreats, good works." The two
weeks spent with the Lowells are taken up with lovely excur-
sions to the mill (setting of "Mills of the Kavanaughs") and to
the lake, but we never get a convincing picture of what it was
like to be in this idyllic setting with the sparring Lowells.

It may be that the air of unreality which permeates the account of this visit is attributable to the passage of time and that
Simpson cannot re-create an experience so long past. Further
along in the book, Simpson reintroduces Lowell into the narrative, this time to recount his experience at the Yaddo Writers'
Colony (1948–49). Here the evocation of Lowell is much more
vivid, and the factual information, which is new to the scholarship, is of value. Lowell was presumably in a manic stage at
Yaddo, for he was writing continuously and, at the same time,
becoming involved in the management of the colony. He convinced himself that Elizabeth Ames, the director, was an active
Communist and requested that she be dismissed. Other past and
present residents, who knew Ms. Ames, rallied to her defense.
A decision was made in her favor, and Lowell, deeply per-
turbed, left the colony (Saratoga Springs) for New York City.
Lowell attended a party at Dwight Macdonald's Manhattan
apartment soon after the episode, and his bizarre behavior
alarmed everyone. When, finally, he was committed to a mental
hospital, Elizabeth Hardwick, his soon-to-be second wife, revealed the events which led to his hospitalization. In addition to
telephoning everyone he knew and sending telegrams all over
the country, in each instance to declare that he felt "marvelous"
and loved everyone, he called Allen Tate's wife (the novelist
Caroline Gordon) to inform her of Allen's infidelity. Moreover, Lowell told Tate that he must repent of his sins and he
summoned him to New York. There was a fracas at the meeting
between Lowell and Tate and the police were called. Lowell
was given shock therapy when he was hospitalized. When
Simpson spent an evening with him several months after his
release from Baldpate Hospital (outside Boston), Lowell revealed
that he lived in terror of another breakdown:

> What haunted him was not simply the idea of another period of
> mania, during which he would do God knew what, nor even the
> incarceration in an institution and the horrors of electroshock

therapy. It was the fear that the next time, or the time after, he
would not recover. Or, if he did, that he would be released with
the part of his brain he used for writing poetry burned out by the
high voltages of the shock machine.

In 1954 Simpson met Lowell again, this time in a Cincinnati
hospital where he was recovering from his third breakdown.
He told her that his illness had been triggered by the death of
his mother, and that during his manic period he had left Elizabeth, who was his current wife. He was later reunited with
Elizabeth, only to separate from her again in 1970. In the years
between 1955 and 1960, Simpson continued to see Lowell intermittently and her impression was that Elizabeth had been a
buoy for him, keeping him afloat. He was well, but it should
be noted that he was doing more teaching than writing, which
may account for his calmer psychic state. There (with the exception of a few insignificant references) Simpson concludes
her memoir of Lowell. It will surely be replaced by a more
thorough treatment at a future date, but for the present it provides us with necessary information, the most important of
which is his constant terror of irreversible madness.

Helen Vendler, who knew Lowell during the last years of
his life, wrote a brief piece on him for *Robert Lowell: A Tribute*, which was published in Italy in 1979. He was in those last
years a sad, broken man. In conversation with Vendler about
critics' perceptions of him, Lowell indicated that Christopher
Ricks had called him "violent" and that he was wrong. "Why
don't they ever say what I'd like them to say. . . . That I'm
heartbreaking." Vendler believes that what dismays readers
most about Lowell is the unhappiness he projects; his truths
are "deadly truths, unrelieved by any prospect of afterlife or
immortality." His last volume, *Day by Day*, flickers with desire but is saturated with despair. Nothing remains for Lowell
at the end of his life, she says, after he has "jettisoned formal
religious belief, social protest, a twenty-year marriage, even residence in America." Vendler emphasizes that Lowell's chaotic
domestic life was instrumental in changing him from a New
England poet, with all the qualifications that rubric implies, to
a poet of New York, Washington, Kent (England), Ireland. He
had become an expatriate not only in terms of residence but in
terms of the values his New England upbringing had imposed
on him. Vendler does not elaborate on this insight, but the
notion of Lowell as an expatriate deserves further study. How

did changing locale alter the thematic elements of his writing, if it did? *Day by Day*, for example, his loosest prosodic mode, was composed while he was living in England, where metrical conventions are more conservative than they are in America. Was this another form of Lowell's rebellion?

Apart from Booth's portrait of Lowell tramping outdoors with his little daughter (*Salmagundi*; see above) and some passing references in Hamilton's biography, there is little material on Lowell as a parent. When we look at the poems on his children, the passages on his daughter Harriet seem much more tender than those on his son Sheridan. Is this poetic phenomenon the basis of another topic for the critics? At Lowell's funeral, his second and third wives, his daughter and his son, and his three stepdaughters sat together in what appeared to be a common state of grief. Because Lowell was so characteristically a poet of autobiography, the knowledge of his relationships with family members is essential to understanding the tonal complexity of the verse.

We have a clearer picture of Lowell as a friend, and (apart from his unfortunate behavior toward the Tates) his reputation in this area of relationships is high indeed. As we might expect, most of his friends were writers or members of academia. He had no need to exploit individuals for his advancement and, consequently, associated only with people he liked and respected. One of Lowell's closest friends, Randall Jarrell, helped him ride out his religious crises by constantly making light of them. Simpson remembers that Jarrell invented witty parodies of Cal's poems, full of sermons, Mariology, graveyards, and ancestors, which invariably cheered the morose Lowell. Lowell was also deeply fond of John Berryman, but felt that he became more a "happening" poet and poorer company after *Dream Songs* had brought him fame. Nonetheless, he wrote a dedicatory poem for Berryman after his death in 1972, the closing lines of which are:

> To my surprise, John
> I pray *to* not for you,
> think of you not myself,
> smile and fall asleep.
> ["For John Berryman," *Day by Day*]

The poet Frank Bidart wrote a very short piece on Lowell which is interesting for its "between the lines" defense of his friend (*Salmagundi*, Spring 1977). This issue of *Salmagundi*, celebrating the sixtieth birthday of a man it styled as one of the nation's foremost poets, appeared at a time when the author's personal life was causing him no little notoriety. Lowell had not only married for the third time, but by 1976 the news had circulated that this marriage, too, had failed and that he was again in contact with his former wife Elizabeth. Bidart, presumably, tried to fend off the critics' intolerance and stressed Lowell's courage: "Many of us would be terrified to face or write the record of our lives." In his long affair with poetry, Bidart added, Lowell was not afraid to judge himself and then begin again. The implication is palpable that this zest for renewal is also a factor in his personal relationships. To conclude his tribute, Bidart recalled that the U.S. First Circuit Court of Appeals, in upholding Boston's school desegregation, had quoted this line from "For the Union Dead" on the Beacon Hill statue commemorating the young, white Colonel Shaw and his black regiment: "Their monument sticks like a fishbone in the city's throat." Bidart was evidently trying to divert attention from Lowell's personal life by demonstrating his political liberalism. The essay is, consequently, a curious one but, at the same time, a lovely proof of friendship.

Perhaps the most eloquent proof of friendship is novelist Peter Taylor's "Robert Trail Spence Lowell: 1917–1977" (*Ploughshares*, 5, 1979). Taylor, a famous author in his own right, retained a longstanding friendship with Lowell from their years together at Kenyon and supplies the kind of information on the heart of a man which only such an old friend could offer. He praised Lowell for precisely those irregularities which brought him censure:

> He never even wanted to give up a marriage entirely. He wanted his wife and children around him in an old fashioned household, and yet he wanted to be free and on the town. Who wouldn't wish for all that, of course? But he *would* have both. He wanted it so intensely that he became very sick at times.

Lowell simply needed to have every kind of experience, says Taylor, who recalled attending Palm Sunday services with Lowell and watching the poet go from an elated, transported moment of prayer to a playful tickling of his friend's ear with a palm frond. This combination of prankish boy and dignified adult indicated the kind of split that Lowell was continually trying to mend, the split that attracted him, at the same time, to Marxism and to the elegant haberdasheries of London. He was known for taking the most conservative position in arguments with his (mostly) liberal friends. He even wanted to be allowed to take both sides of the arguments, Taylor recalls, and this was especially the case when he was in the company of doctrinaire liberals. But none of this quirky intransigence seemed to lessen the affection his friends and even casual acquaintances felt for him. Lowell, somehow, never made enemies. Taylor also mentioned Lowell's fidelity as a friend: "I believe Lowell was about as good a correspondent as you will find in our generation—especially during the last years. He sometimes wrote me two or three times a week." (What a boon to the scholarship if these letters would be prepared for publication.)

Finally, Taylor made a deliberate effort to stress the importance of Boston to Lowell. Lowell would often take walking tours of the streets which figured so largely in his youth: Revere, Brimmer, Pinckney, Marlborough. During his marriage to Elizabeth he had tried to be a Bostonian again, setting up house on Marlborough Street, but he could not restore the past. We wonder, of course, in light of Lowell's often deprecating comments on Boston, why he would *want* to reactivate such memories, yet the ambivalent love and hate of such a place and such a tradition obviously was lodged in this poet's soul.

On another tangent, Taylor's remarks about Boston remind us that there is a paucity of scholarship on Lowell as a poet of place. Just a glance at the index of titles of his poems tells us how crucial locale must be to Lowell's poetics; and in such an index, Boston and its environs figure prominently. In 1978 Richard Fein suggested this vein of research in "Looking for Robert Lowell in Boston," a literary guide to the landmarks which act as settings for the poems (*Literary Review*, Spring). In his stroll through the city, Fein looks for versions of Boston as they were informed by Lowell's imagination. He claims that Lowell transformed many of the sights and often created details that simply did not exist. There were no swanboats at the Public Garden; 91 Revere Street looked "seedier" than Lowell's depiction of it in his prose memoir; and Lowell's "studied decor" for the iron fence in the King's Chapel graveyard poem ("At the Indian Killer's Grave") is missing. While it is true that swanboats have not paddled the little lake in Boston Public Garden for many years, they were, in Lowell's younger years, as prominent a feature of that area as the Ritz Carlton across the way. It must be remembered, too, that a number of Boston's most elite institutions have always seemed depressingly plain to the outlander who might catch a glimpse of them.

Perhaps this native conservatism stems from the "Puritan Burden" we discuss in chapter 3, but Boston society has long regarded any untoward show of elegance as more appropriate to that sinful city 200 miles to the south. Yet the names and places of Boston; the streets, Arlington, Berkeley, Clarendon, that stretch alphabetically from the foot of Beacon Hill into the Back Bay; and the names of the old families who speak only to each other or God form a kind of American mythology of which Lowell, no matter how he moved around, was a native speaker. Surely the Yeatsian ancestral home, or the "great house" tradition itself, appropriately modified from the Cavalier to the Puritan tradition, must have been in the recesses of Lowell's mind when he wrote "Father's Bedroom" or "Home after Three Months Away" (*Life Studies*). Indeed, I would argue that Lowell's reconstruction of Boston—in a volume even as "realistic" as *Life Studies*—reveals how strongly Lowell leaned to the Symbolist imagination in life as well as in art.

Lowell confided in one of his letters to Peter Taylor (snatches of which were first printed in the *Ploughshares* essay), "We're having a good fall, and feel very lordly and pretentious in our new Boston house. It's just exactly a block from the one I grew up in." It was as though he had achieved a oneness between his real self's memory and the memory of his fictional persona of *Life Studies*. This importance of place, in real life and in fictional life, is investigated a little more specifically by Michael North (*Contemporary Literature*, Spring 1980), who argued that "monuments" were the most important part of Lowell's relationship to place. Whether he is in Buenos Aires, Washington, D.C., or Boston, statues, chapels, municipal edifices seem to take on a significance which is transcendent. Lowell does not necessarily feel that they represent a golden past or a tradition which cannot be restored, says North. The monuments are often unreal and useless, or recall a shameful moment in history. Moreover, the rigidity of monuments, as opposed to natural landmarks like lakes or gardens, emphasizes their "deadness." This is a fascinating premise, which will likely be strengthened by that biographical information which charts Lowell's manic, as opposed to depressive, phases.

For example, what was happening in Lowell's personal life

when he wrote that Colonel Shaw had the "peculiar power to choose life and die"? Answers to such questions must replace the sort of analysis made by Ronald Hayman, who assessed Lowell's personality in too general terms: "Lowell is the great survivor, but he had been living close to the brink . . . the drive towards sanity has been stronger, the awareness of the external world keener" (*London Magazine*, November 1970). But to return to the topic of locale: a study that is sensitive to what names and places truly meant to a Bostonian of Lowell's day (when an address of over 100 on Beacon Street was outside the pale of fashion) would be helpful in discovering the artistic manipulations by which these cultural realities were transformed to poetic symbols.

We might supplement our commentary on Lowell the man by asking if the personal memoirs contain uniform reflections or whether differences are explained by the periods in which these associations with Lowell took place. While each memoir presents Lowell in a different context, certain constants are observed in his behavior: marked absence of arrogance; greater interest in ideas and literature than in people; intensity of presence that conflicted with his frail demeanor and gentle speech. This curious combination of qualities was disarming to those who met him for the first time. When J. D. McClatchy described his first meeting with Lowell, he said he was reminded of Colonel Higginson's report of his introduction to Emily Dickinson: "I never was with anyone who drained my nerve power so much" (*American Poetry Review*, September/October 1978).

Other sides to Lowell the man have recently become known to us through Hamilton's biography, an absorbing and sympathetic account that should be acknowledged in this chapter. Hamilton's dominant focus is clinical: Lowell's mental illness, and how it affected his creativity as well as his familial and social behavior, is highlighted. Now that we have Hamilton's heavily documented book we may well ask: Who but the closest of Lowell's friends and relatives would have known that this prolific poet, playwright, translator, and critic had spent so many years of his adult life in "the kingdom of the mad"? Though readers and critics alike had always acknowledged his obscure, anguished verse and dark vision, the entire canon nonetheless bespoke a brilliant, lucid mind that was well acquainted with the meaning of history and the cultural sway of literature.

Now, in the first and in many ways invaluable biography of Lowell, Hamilton reveals the tormented figure from close range, and it is difficult to match this figure with the man who became a major post–World War II American writer.

Hamilton's account is one we cannot bear to put aside, yet cannot bear to read. As a narrative strongly supported by letters and frank interviews, it has the impact of authenticity—perhaps at the expense of a more integrative analysis which would mesh the work with the man. But then, one is reminded of the various options for writing literary biography. Does Hamilton want to tell us the life story or what the story means? Does he find in his subject a configuration, myth, or psychic pattern? Does he feel obliged to explain Lowell's role in American letters and the reasons (warranted or not) for Lowell's inflated reputation at a particular juncture in literary history?

Hamilton's is a popular, narrative, trade-published life of Lowell, rather than a scholarly, analytical life written for a select audience of specialists. At the same time, Hamilton, a poet himself, suffuses his commentary with literary expertise; he also chronicles with acuity both the cogent and the sensational reviews of Lowell's volumes as they appeared on the literary scene. Rather than make a theoretical assessment of the works, Hamilton relates the gestation of a volume to a stage in Lowell's life, supplying geographic, marital, and social details as context for the imaginative world of the verse. This is perhaps the least satisfying aspect of the book. Lowell's creativity is discussed in time slots, with little or no retrospection or foreshadowing. Chronology may suggest causality, but real genesis, in the realm of poetics, is never truly broached. One is inclined to skim through the sections which record Lowell's writing projects, especially those which culminated in the "confessional" volumes: *Life Studies* (1959), *For the Union Dead* (1964), *Near the Ocean* (1967). Lowell's transition from a mannered symbolist poet, working under the aegis of New Critics, to a confessional poet, in pursuit of loosely structured modes, has been too often recited. It is the new material—anecdotes garnered from friends, wives, lovers—that makes the indelible impression.

The irony about Lowell's reputation as a confessional poet is that an ornate screen stands between his "nakedly honest" verses and his actual life. Real people and real events fill *Life Studies*, but they are not actually recoverable. For example, meter and manner obscure the credibility of these lines on Lowell's confinement in a mental hospital:

After a hearty New England breakfast,
I weigh two hundred pounds
this morning. Cock of the walk,
I strut in my turtle-necked French sailor's jersey
before the metal shaving mirrors,
and see the shaky future grow familiar
                              ["Waking in the Blue"]

The intended informality of such lines gives way to inescapable artifice. Hamilton's description of parties in the period of Lowell's madness (from an account by W. S. Merwin's wife) rings far truer. He gives us the unfiltered view of Lowell's illness: the violent quarrels; the impromptu parties to which Lowell invited *everyone* he knew and during which pandemonium prevailed ("Edmund Wilson fell down, or someone knocked him down. . . . He [Lowell] sat down in a chair and dashed the glasses off the table with his feet and sat there, with his feet on the drinks table, surrounded by broken glass"). Thus Hamilton's first (and giant) step of research deserves a second step: analysis. If anything and everything was fit material for poetry, by what procedure did Lowell judge and transform his experience?

Lowell's recuperative periods, following his frequent hospitalizations, were stabilized by intensive drug therapy. With Hamilton's calendar reading of Lowell's medical treatments, the creative lulls and peaks, as well as the genre experiments, are better understood. Formerly, they were perfunctorily attributed to more external causes: a schism with the New Critics, a discovery of William Carlos Williams' "natural speech," an attendance at a Beat poetry reading on the West Coast. Now, the creative stages may be classified differently. For example, when Lowell was on tranquilizer therapy he tended to avoid the emotional excitement of writing poetry. In the sixties, fired by the national obsession with politics, he entered the forum and wrote plays about American history, marched in peace demonstrations, campaigned in a presidential primary for his poet-friend Eugene McCarthy. Lithium, the new wonder drug of the sixties, helped Lowell avoid the extremes of his manic-depressive illness; but it made him creative in a different way. When he reverted to full scale poetry in the seventies, a tame, almost dreamlike style characterized his *Notebook*. A new perception of Lowell's poetics could be grasped from this sort of information. Thanks to Hamilton's biography, certain critical and exegetical problems may eventually be solved. For example, the cryptic poems about Lowell's mother in *Notebook* contain fragments of previously unreleased letters from Mrs. Lowell to the poet-psychiatrist Merrill Moore. There is a suggestion that Lowell knew about a clandestine affair between Moore and his mother, but that Lowell suppressed the information. As a result, he produced incoherent sonnets about his mother and his tone of rage seemed both inexplicable and excessive.

Hamilton offers no definitive verdicts on Lowell's character. It is fairly safe to predict that despite (or perhaps because of) his biography, oppositional readings of Lowell as a misogynist (who tried to strangle his first wife, Jean Stafford) or committed humanist (dedicated teacher, peace marcher), as artistic innovator or mere purveyor of literary fads, as private poet or public poet, will continue for some time. In the interim, we have a compelling portrait of this man who, among other caprices, constantly added new lovers to his life and expected his wives to sympathize with and encourage his irregularities. Hamilton provides his information without the sensationalism so often found in celebrity biographies. Alas, he falls short of relating Lowell's profligacy to Oedipal conflicts which reach back to childhood, to the domineering mother (who later termed his poetry "nice but valueless"), to the passive father. We have, then, neither a psychobiography (such as Leon Edel's *Henry James*) nor a patent canonization (such as Paul Mariani's *William Carlos Williams*). We have, as I noted, an absorbing and sympathetic story of Lowell.

Finally, a word about Hamilton's treatment of Lowell's cultural heritage. While he systematically reports Lowell's fanatical behavior as a Catholic convert, he does not delve into the impact of New England Puritanism on this poet's vision. When this is done, we will learn what the story means.

From his student days at Kenyon, Lowell saw his practice at poetry as repetition, revision, imitation—of himself and other artists. Beyond his need to contemporarize or desymbolize either his earlier poetry or the poetry of others, Lowell rewrote to create an ironic locus from which to reevaluate the past. Since this was the dominant impulse in his writing, we must consider Lowell's theory of "imitation" and the critics' assessments of it.

# References

Allen, Donald, and Warren Tallman
  1973. (editors) *The Poetics of the New American Poetry.* New York: Grove Pr.
Alvarez, A.
  1965. "A Talk with Robert Lowell." *Encounter* Feb., pp. 39–43.
  1967. "Something New in Verse." *Times Literary Supplement* Mar. 23, pp. 229–32; reprinted in his *Beyond All This Fiddle.* New York: Random House, 1968.
Anonymous
  1943. "A 'Boston' Lowell Is a Draft Dodger." *New York Times* Oct. 12, p. 29.
Anonymous
  1943. "Nazi Draft Dodger Gets 3-Year Term." *New York Times* Oct. 14, p. 13.
Anonymous
  1949. "Pound, in Mental Clinic, Wins Prize for Poetry Penned in Treason Cell." *New York Times* Feb. 20, pp. 1, 14.
Anonymous
  1965. "Applause for a Prize Poet." *Life* Feb. 19, pp. 49–58.
Anonymous
  1965. "President and Poet." *New York Times* June 6, sec. 4, p. 4.
Anonymous
  1965. "Rejection Slip." *Newsweek* June 14, p. 68.
Anonymous
  1965. "The Presidency." *Time* June 11, p. 29.
Anonymous
  1965. "The Occasion to Protest." *Nation* June 21, pp. 658–59.
Anonymous
  1965. "Johnson Hails College Students as His 'Fellow Revolutionaries.'" *New York Times* Aug. 5, p. 13.
Anonymous
  1967. "The Second Chance." *Time* June 2, pp. 67–74.
Antin, David
  1972. "Modernism and Post Modernism: Approaching the Present in American Poetry." *Boundary 2* Fall, pp. 98–133.
Atlas, James
  1982. "Robert Lowell in Cambridge: Lord Weary." *Atlantic* July, pp. 56–64.
Bayley, John
  1966. "Robert Lowell: The Poetry of Cancellation." *London Magazine* June, pp. 76–85.
  1980. "Robert Lowell." *Times Literary Supplement* Aug. 22, p. 432.
Bidart, Frank
  1977. "On Robert Lowell." *Salmagundi* Spring, pp. 54–55.

Booth, Philip
1977. "Summer in Castine: Contact Prints, 1955–1965." *Salmagundi* Spring, pp. 37–53.

Bowen, Roger
1969. "Confession and Equilibrium: Robert Lowell's Poetic Development." *Criticism* Winter, pp. 78–93.

Boyers, Robert
1970. "On Robert Lowell." *Salmagundi* Summer, pp. 36–44.

Cargas, Harry
1972. "Robert Lowell: Protestor as Link Between Past and Present." In his *Daniel Berrigan and Contemporary Protest Poetry.* New Haven, Conn.: College and University Pr., pp. 47–61.

Carruth, Hayden
1967. "A Meaning of Robert Lowell." *Hudson Review* Autumn, pp. 429–47.

Ciardi, John
1948. "Letter." *Poetry* Aug., pp. 261–63.

Cousins, Norman, and Harrison Smith
1949. "More on Pound." *Saturday Review of Literature* July 30, p. 22.

Cowley, Malcolm
1962. "Who's to Take the Place of Hemingway and Faulkner." *New York Times Book Review* Oct. 7, p. 4.

Fein, Richard J.
1970. *Robert Lowell.* New York: Twayne. 2d ed., 1979.
1978. "Looking for Robert Lowell in Boston." *Literary Review* Spring, pp. 285–300.

Fiedler, Leslie A.
1964. "A Kind of Solution: The Situation of Poetry Now." *Kenyon Review* Winter, pp. 54–79.

Fuller, John G.
1960. "Trade Winds." *Saturday Review of Literature* Apr. 9, p. 16.

Goldman, Eric F.
1969. *The Tragedy of Lyndon Johnson.* New York: Knopf.

Haffenden, John
1978. "The Last Parnassian: Robert Lowell." *Agenda* Summer, pp. 40–47.

Hamilton, Ian
1982. *Robert Lowell: A Biography.* New York: Random House.

Harrigan, Anthony
1950. "American Formalists." *South Atlantic Quarterly* Oct., pp. 483–89.

Hass, Robert
1977. "Lowell's Graveyard." *Salmagundi* Spring, pp. 56–72.

Hayman, Ronald
  1970. "The Imaginative Risk: Aspects of Robert Lowell." *London Magazine* Nov., pp. 8–30.
Herzog, Arthur
  1969. *McCarthy for President*. New York: Viking.
Heymann, David
  1980. *American Aristocracy: The Lives and Times of James Russell, Amy and Robert Lowell*. New York: Dodd, Mead.
Holloway, John
  1968. "Robert Lowell and the Public Dimension." *Encounter* Apr., pp. 73–79.
Jacobsen, Josephine
  1964. "Poet of the Particular." *Commonweal* Dec. 4, pp. 349–52.
Jarrell, Randall
  1962. "View from Parnassus." *Time* Nov. 9, p. 100, 102.
  1963. "Fifty Years of American Poetry." *Prairie Schooner* Spring, pp. 1–27.
Kunitz, Stanley
  1964. "A Talk with Robert Lowell." *New York Times Book Review* Oct. 4, pp. 34–39.
  1966–67. "Telling the Time." *Salmagundi* no. 1, pp. 22–25.
Lowell, Robert
  1962. "The Cold War and the West." *Partisan Review* Winter, p. 47.
  1968. "Why I Am for McCarthy." *New Republic* Apr. 13, p. 12.
Macdonald, Dwight
  1949. "Homage to Twelve Judges." *Politics* Winter, pp. 1–2.
Mailer, Norman
  1968. *The Armies of the Night*. New York: New American Library.
Martin, Jay
  1970. *Robert Lowell*. Minneapolis: Minnesota Univ. Pr.
Mazzaro, Jerome
  1960. *The Achievement of Robert Lowell: 1939–1959*. Detroit: Detroit Univ. Pr.
  1970. "Checklist: 1939–1968," in *Robert Lowell: A Portrait of the Artist in His Time*, ed. Michael London and Robert Boyers. New York: David Lewis.
  1971. (editor) *Profile of Robert Lowell*. Columbus: Merrill.
McClatchy, J. D.
  1978. "Some Photographs of Robert Lowell." *American Poetry Review* Sept./Oct., pp. 28–29.
McCormick, John
  1953. "Falling Asleep over Grillparzer." *Poetry* January, pp. 269–79.

Mills, Ralph, Jr.

  1966. *Contemporary American Poetry*. New York: Random House.

Naipaul, V. S.

  1969. "Et in America Ego." *Listener* Sept. 4, pp. 302–4; reprinted in *Profile of Robert Lowell*, ed. J. Mazzaro. Columbus: Merrill, 1971.

Nicols, Lewis

  1960. "In and Out of Books." *New York Times Book Review* Mar. 20, p. 8.

North, Michael

  1980. "The Public Monument and Public Poetry: Stevens, Berryman, and Lowell." *Contemporary Literature* Spring, pp. 267–86.

Parkinson, Thomas

  1966–67. "For the Union Dead." *Salmagundi* 1: 87–95.

  1968. (editor) *Robert Lowell: A Collection of Critical Essays*. Englewood Cliffs, N.J.: Prentice-Hall.

Pearson, Gabriel

  1969. "Robert Lowell." *Review* Mar., pp. 3–36.

Piper, Henry Dan

  1962. "Modern American Classics." *Saturday Review of Literature* Feb. 17, p. 20.

Price, Jonathan

  1972. (editor) *Critics on Robert Lowell*. Coral Gables: Miami Univ. Pr.

Ricks, Christopher

  1965. "The Three Lives of Robert Lowell." *New Statesman* Mar. 25, pp. 496–97.

Seidel, Frederick

  1961. "Interview with Robert Lowell." *Paris Review* Winter–Spring, pp. 56–95; reprinted in *Robert Lowell: A Portrait of the Artist in His Time*, ed. Michael London and Robert Boyers. New York: David Lewis, 1970; in *Robert Lowell: A Collection of Critical Essays*, ed. Thomas Parkinson. Englewood Cliffs, N.J.: Prentice-Hall, 1968; in *Writers at Work, Second Series*, ed. Malcolm Cowley. New York: Viking, 1963; in *Modern Poets on Modern Poetry*, ed. James Scully. London: Collins, 1966.

Spender, Stephen

  1959. "Robert Lowell's Family Album." *New Republic* June 8, p. 17.

Staples, Hugh

  1959. "A Graph of Revelations." *Tri-Quarterly* Winter, pp. 7–12.

Stein, Jean, and George Plimpton

  1970. *American Journey: The Times of Robert Kennedy*. New York: Harcourt Brace Jovanovich.

Steiner, George
    1959. "A Literature Enters the Sixties." *Time and Tide* Aug. 29, pp. 927–28.
Stepanchev, Stephen
    1965. *American Poetry Since 1945: A Critical Survey*. New York: Harper & Row.
Taylor, Peter
    1979. "Robert Trail Spence Lowell: 1917–1977." *Ploughshares* 5, no. 2: 74–81.
Teuber, Andreas
    1970. *People*. New York: Harper & Row.
Vendler, Helen
    1979. "Robert Lowell's Last Days and Last Poems." *Robert Lowell: A Tribute*, ed. Rolando Anzilotti. Pisa: Nistri-Lischi Editori.
    1980. "Listening to Lowell." *New York Times Book Review* Feb. 3, pp. 9, 28–29.

# CHAPTER 2

# The Poetics of Imitation

As the term "imitation" suggests, a body of Lowell's work builds directly on literary sources. Lowell believed that literature in the Western tradition was reusable. Imitation was not, in his view, a form of stealing or proof of creative impoverishment. Possessed of a classical temper, he respected past literary masters and apprenticed himself to them. He also believed that classics were, by definition, convertible to modern context and significance. In addition to his original volumes of verse, he completed dramatic adaptations of tales by Hawthorne and Melville (*The Old Glory*, 1964), translations of eighteen European poets (*Imitations*, 1961), versions of Racine's *Phèdre* (*Phaedra*, 1961) and Aeschylus' *Prometheus Bound* (1967), and at the time of his death he was working on an adaptation of Aeschylus' *Oresteia*. In each of these works he merged the original material with his own ideas and sensibility. According to the corpus of commentary, he did so with varying degrees of success; but the diversity of critical opinion generated from an argument which was only tangential to Lowell: the nature and extent of license any author is permitted when tinkering with established texts. Apart from this consideration, the critical consensus is that Lowell's imitations embody a message similar to that in his own poetry. The imagination which commands the personal poetic and the borrowed poetic is all of a piece.

Lowell's imitations were discussed in categories pertinent to their three distinct genres: the transformation of early American narratives to a verse drama on the American character (*Old Glory*); the imitation of European poets and the ongoing debate on translation (*Imitations*); the intrusion of autobiographical and political elements into classical drama (*Phaedra*, *Prometheus Bound*, *Oresteia*). In the first and third categories, "theatre" criticism entered the canon.

## *Verse Drama*

It would be useful to summarize the status of American verse drama prior to the period Lowell experimented with the mode. His contribution was small, but its merit and reception were related to and contingent upon the destiny of this form in modern theatre.

"One of the surest of tests is the way in which a poet borrows. . . . The good poet welds his theft into a whole of feeling which is unique, utterly different from that which it was torn." These are the words of T. S. Eliot (*Selected Essays*, 1960), but they are a suitable paraphrase of Lowell's objectives. Growing up in the heyday of New Criticism, Lowell was bound to internalize Eliot's attitudes. But apart from Eliot's pronouncements in his essays, Lowell had Eliot's verse plays—several of which derived from classical sources—as palpable models for his own dramatic compositions. Indeed, the success of *Murder in the Cathedral* (1935) and *The Cocktail Party* (1949) attracted Lowell, as well as other poets, to the theatre. Eliot had proved that a modern poet could effectively turn his talents to drama; in many ways he was the force behind the American verse-drama movement in the twentieth century.

The intelligentsia of Lowell's generation were tantalized by the idea of a contemporary verse drama. Eliot had told them that there is a "peculiar range of sensibility" necessary to drama which cannot be adequately supplied by prose. Time had verified Eliot's pronouncement—the passing of 2,000 years could not dim the brilliance of Euripides or Aeschylus. The inescapable spectacle of the Elizabethan drama, which has never lost its popularity, convinced poets that where there is vital poetry there should also be vital drama, written in their own medium. *Murder in the Cathedral* and *The Family Reunion* (1939) seemed adequate proof of this assumption; they were admired by critics and audiences alike. Eliot's later plays, *The Cocktail Party* (1949) and *The Confidential Clerk* (1954), had impressive Broadway productions, but it took the passage of time and numerous experiments before poets realized that Eliot's successes were seldom matched by other playwrights. Even Eliot's immediate predecessor, Maxwell Anderson, who was initially hailed as a major dramatist, declined in favor as Eliot rose. Anderson had tried his hand at verse drama which dealt with historical themes (*Elizabeth the Queen*, 1930; *Mary of Scotland*, 1933) and contemporary themes (*Winterset*, 1935), but the poetic medium

did not truly suit either. In the historical plays, the loose Shake-
spearean style seemed imposed on the material by its subject
matter. In *Winterset*, a play based on the Sacco-Vanzetti case
and set in Depression-era Brooklyn, the blank verse seemed
strained in the mouths of the characters. In fact, *Winterset*
never won the box-office appeal Anderson hoped for (it made
a greater impression when converted to a gangster film). Anderson was a popular poet-playwright despite these drawbacks,
and apart from Eliot, he suffered little formidable competition;
but his reputation did not endure. Although his plays are considered unique and valid works, they did little to change the
course of American drama.

Enthusiasts of verse on stage were again heartened when *The
Lady's Not for Burning* (1949) scored at the box office. It
seemed as though Christopher Fry would bring impetus to the
cause. *Not for Burning* had lengthy runs both on and off
Broadway, but critics were aware of the play's British author-
ship and the more natural disposition of British writers to verse
drama. Did American playwrights really have a knack for this
mode? Subsequent plays by Fry tended to blur this question,
however; *Not for Burning* was Fry's only triumph. Although
he continued to offer new poetic scripts for production during
the fifties, none came up to his earlier success. Then, too, *Not
for Burning* poorly withstood the test of time, largely *because*
of its poetic diction. Critics decided that it had a supple ver-
bosity but that its language decorated themes without deepen-
ing our perceptions of them. Nonetheless, Fry rekindled an
interest in verbal eloquence on stage; and the sort of audience
that welcomed Fry also welcomed the translations of Giraudoux which found their way to Broadway in the fifties. While
Giraudoux's plays, technically, were not in verse, they seemed
to possess a "poetic" quality. This was achieved through the
heightened language of the speeches and the archetypal nature
of the characters (contemporary, as in *Madwoman of Chaillot*,
or biblical, as in *Judith*). Giraudoux brought fantasy to characterization, a refreshing change from the naked realism of
prose drama.

The fifties saw a burst of interest in verse drama which contained religious themes. Union Theological Seminary in New
York City encouraged playwrights to compose religious drama,
sponsored prize contests for new works, and produced winning
submissions. With the influence of Eliot still much in the air,
it seemed that a great verse drama might well be a religious one,

but the campaign yielded few memorable texts. The best one to emerge was *J.B.* (1958), Archibald MacLeish's contemporary retelling of the Job story. It was MacLeish's only significant contribution; after *J.B.* he wrote more plays, but devoted his better talents to the composition of political and literary criticism.

If the search for religious verse drama uncovered few American successes, it helped Americans to rediscover European equivalents in the experiments of Claudel and deGelderhode. But it also meant that the mode might be more congenial to foreign writers.

The notion of religious drama inevitably brought to mind Greek tragedy. The academic minds of the period were occupied with the new, presumably "more Greek" translations of the classics which issued from university presses. Of these, Richmond Lattimore's Aeschylus renditions captured much attention. (Lowell remarked, in an interview in *Delos* [1968], that he admired Lattimore and had used Lattimore's texts when he taught at the University of Iowa.) The *Oresteia* (which was a source for Eliot's *Family Reunion*, a favorite of Lowell's) was one of the most popular "revived" classics. Lowell himself worked on his version of it for two decades. Interest in Greek drama and its potential for modern adaptation was sustained on the theoretical level by scholars, the most influential of whom was Francis Fergusson. Fergusson's *The Idea of a Theatre* (1949) traced the development of classical themes in various periods of dramatic literature. He concluded his study with a discussion of Eliot's plays, which were to his mind the best modern offerings of classical themes.

Lowell could not escape involvement in the verse-drama vogue. He was affiliated with the academies of New York and New England which produced and discussed the plays. He numbered among his friends and colleagues such scholars as Robert Fitzgerald and Eric Bentley. Bentley, whose *Playwright as Thinker* (1946) dealt with poetic re-creations of classical themes, was one of the most ambitious anthologizers of, and apologists for, new verse drama. He was not consistently flattering or encouraging about the experiments, but he kept the arena of controversy alive. So did Moody Prior, whose *Language of Tragedy* (1947) voiced strong reservations about contemporary verse drama.

Lowell's participation in the movement came to fruition through a commission: he was invited by Bentley to prepare a translation of *Phèdre* for the "French" volume of Bentley's collection *The Classic Theatre* (1961). This sparked his interest even further, since translation was a way to use and sharpen his poetic tools. But it was not the translation of Racine which made him such an interesting poet-turned-playwright; it was *Old Glory*, which had a certain kinship with Eliot's work, but possessed remarkable individuality.

## *The Old Glory*

In *Old Glory*, Lowell observed the authority and posture of three centuries of American experience, but he did so second-hand and through the eyes of Hawthorne and Melville. Although he ultimately converted the facts of American history to an observation about his own period, Lowell literally "lifted" Melville's and Hawthorne's plots, their concern with rebellion, and their theory that a nation pays a price for rebellion. He also wanted American audiences to understand their hidden loyalties and (sometimes) tyrannical tendencies. By using older American material, he was simultaneously imitating and modulating a central theme of drama: the collision of social forces and the subsequent effort to restore social order. The three plays in *Old Glory* are not only vehicles for ideas that might be considered commonplace, especially since the French and Russian revolutions; they are also an imitation of the Jamesian notion that Americans abroad and at home can suffer disastrous consequences because of their ideals.

Lowell also indirectly suggests that the notion of the Whitmanian expansive ego is partly ironic. He warns about our aggressive, unleashed selves in a kind of inverse imitation of Whitman's vision. Thus, while he borrows directly from Hawthorne and Melville, he indirectly imitates the standard illusions (and delusions) of the American ideology. Critics were not surprised that Lowell should imitate the works of other writers; *Imitations*, which had appeared four years earlier, actually paved the way for *Old Glory*. However, while they were not surprised, neither were they especially apt at recognizing that the same creative process was inherent in both volumes.

The composition of *Old Glory* resulted from an amalgamation of aesthetic and cultural imperatives. If Lowell was to be a dramatist at all, he wanted to be a verse dramatist. Even

*Prometheus Bound*, his only prose play, evinced poetic cadence and diction; but his decision to write a historically based work like *Old Glory* came from another impulse. He was caught up in the activist fever which permeated American life in the sixties, and his need to participate in the national mood could not be fully satisfied by poetry. Interaction with the public required a more immediate medium. But Lowell was torn; drama was not his first love. At the same time that he was writing plays, he would insist (during interviews) that drama would never be his forte, and what is more, other playwrights bored him. He quipped in the *Review* (1971) interview with Ian Hamilton that it was "a backache to sit through a whole play." The form was not compressed enough for him. When Hamilton asked if he planned to continue writing plays in the future, he replied: "I am gunshy of the theatre. . . . I can't love the game." His remarks could be taken as disingenuous or, possibly, slightly defensive. But what he said and what he did about drama made two different topics. The fact is that he was not deterred from accepting commissions or residencies from institutions which were considered "establishment." He even accepted the writer-in-residence offer at Yale School of Drama in 1967.

Whatever forces signified in the composition of *Old Glory*, its poetic style had a familiar ring to Lowell followers. The switch in genre did not prevent Lowell from pulling out all his rhetorical stops. The intense imagery and strong meters of his early verse were here restored in abundance. In the Hamilton interview, Lowell said that he had chosen the verse medium for *Old Glory* because he was a "word-man." The text was proof of this. While this gave the trilogy a traditional flavor, the eccentric characters and their even more eccentric dialogues gave it an almost radical flavor. This mixture came from Lowell's ambivalence about what a play should be. Although he admired the "new theatre," as he called it, by which he meant the prose plays of Albee, Kopit, and several off-off Broadway writers, he felt it restricted language too heavily. In effect, he was separating theatrical devices—such as Albee's Absurdist staging of *The Sandbox*—from the language medium of a text.

He liked what was done on stage in "new theatre," but not what was said—but he was also ambivalent about the established verse dramas. He told Hamilton that, except for Yeats's last plays and Eliot's *Sweeney Agonistes*, there was little else in twentieth-century theatre he admired. In another interview he was less deferential to Eliot (*London Times*, March 8, 1967);

this time he said that although he learned about drama through
Eliot's essays on the Elizabethans, Eliot's *own* plays needed "a
more gaudy style, something like the Elizabethans themselves."
Actually, he made no definitive statements about the use of
prose or verse—at least in print. He jumped boundaries and
judged genres by impulse. For example, in the Hamilton interview he said that Brecht was the "strongest modern dramatist,"
a "poet even though he writes in prose." And about his own
work, he said of "Benito Cereno," which is in free verse: "I think
of 'Benito' as prose, my best."

Within the large framework of verse drama, *Old Glory*
eludes subclassification. Based on stories by Hawthorne and a
novella by Melville, it has been variously labeled historical
drama, adaptation, imitation—indeed, even translation. It is all
of these, depending on the critical approach. As historical
drama, it incorporates documented episodes that were used as
source material for Hawthorne's and Melville's fictions. As imitation, it is what Lowell intended imitation to be: the rewriting
of a classic text with full interpretive latitude. And in the loosest
use of terminology it has been called a translation, meaning the
conversion of a text from its original narrative form to dramatic form (*Hollins Critic*, February 1967). But since scholars
generally appropriate the term "translation" to language conversion, it is improbable that *Old Glory* will be ultimately
classified as such. As yet, there has been no uniformly established term. This is more an indication of the text's singularity
than of critical dispute. In theory, *Old Glory* best satisfies the
notion of imitation.

What Lowell himself felt about *Old Glory* can be glimpsed
from passing statements in interviews or from comments repeated in reviews or theatre announcements. For example, in
the *London Times* article (above), Michael Billington gives
snatches of his conversation with Lowell at the opening of
*Cereno* at the Mermaid Theatre in London. Lowell said the
play simply "came" to him; he had no preconceived design in
mind. And his cavalier remarks in Richard Gilman's column
(*New York Times*, May 5, 1968), which announced the opening
of *Endecott and the Red Cross*, were similarly offhand: since
he found plots too "boring" to create, "using Hawthorne and
Melville spared me a lot of work and gave me the confidence
that something was there." After all, Lowell argued, Shakespeare borrowed plots all the time! He added that when he
read *Macbeth* he would skip all the passages in which Macbeth

and Lady Macbeth did not speak: "What I found was that it would have made a great poem, one of the greatest, with all those plot elements removed." Perhaps this was Lowell's rationalization for his weakness at writing plot. "The Mills of the Kavanaughs," his one sustained narrative poem, had been considered faulty storytelling. Whatever his motive for debunking plot, he was sufficiently objective to concede that there was a nonverbal dimension in drama—what he called "a reality *beneath* the words"—which made theatre more satisfying than "any reading." He was obviously referring to the importance of action and acknowledging that drama needs more than speeches or dialogues. His aversion to plot is not evident in *Old Glory*, however; the trilogy is conventionally sequential. Moreover, the order of episodes in the plays is chronological.

Thus Lowell was impressionistic when he vouchsafed remarks on the theatre. When *Old Glory* appeared, he called it an alternative to "naturalistic" drama, a mode which presented a limited view of life. When Lowell used the term "naturalistic," he meant a kind of well-plotted play in prose about ordinary people, rather than a kind of drama which followed the principles of literary Naturalism. He was referring to playwrights like Arthur Miller, who resolved their work too simplistically: "This business of naturalistic plays, life doesn't offer such neat conclusions" (*New York Times*, May 5, 1968). He also wanted his plays to extend beyond a fixed temporal setting. Despite the impression that the events in *Old Glory* were authentic, their "dramatic world" was intended to be broadly archetypal. Lowell grew impatient with inquiries about specific historical references. His flags, for example, were not intended to symbolize particular nations or periods—this narrowed their meaning. He said that the flags served as "harmonic repetition" (ibid.). His reply suggests that he and the critics were using a different level of discourse. To Lowell, the flag in its various representations (British rule, piracy, colonial revolution) embodied the "tensions and antinomies" which have characterized the American experience for the past three centuries. To critics, this amounted to a symbol—by any other name. They thought the title itself gave the work its meaning, but Lowell refused to be pigeon-holed into admitting that *Old Glory* was an elaborate poem which, with the trappings of character and action, happened to be a drama. Discussions of symbols smacked too much of the poetic.

Apart from the classification quibble about the flag, *Old*

*Glory* gave little interpretive difficulty to the critics. Some (correctly) found passages or scenes in all of the plays confusing or obscure, but the dominant thematic elements were easily recognized. Divergence of interpretation surfaced mainly in analyses of the characters—especially, how they departed from the functions that Hawthorne and Melville had assigned to them. The bulk of the commentary was comparative: How had Lowell changed Hawthorne and Melville? In effect, was he a successful imitator? A secondary critical consideration was the theatrical viability of this "poetic" work. *Old Glory* reinvoked the debate about the value of modern verse drama. Critics made comparisons between Lowell and Eliot, but they were superficial. They were more interested in whether Lowell's contribution could strengthen a genre whose future was doubtful. Did the trilogy's political overtones interfere with its poetic texture? Eliot's plays, after all, were uncorrupted by political topicality.

*Old Glory* premiered at the American Place Theatre in New York City on November 1, 1964. This production, which included *My Kinsman, Major Molineux* and *Benito Cereno*, did not include *Endecott and the Red Cross*. Critics speculated about this truncated performance: Lowell felt *Endecott* was not ready to be staged in its first version (which underwent cutting and rewriting, but was dropped before first night); a performance of *Old Glory* in its entirety would have been too lengthy for an evening's entertainment. Lowell never gave an official explanation, but the publication and performance history of the trilogy seems to substantiate the speculation. *Endecott* was rewritten for the revised edition of *Old Glory*, which came out in 1968, and it was in this year that *Endecott* premiered alone (American Place, April 18). The three plays were performed as a unit in 1976; *Old Glory* was publicized as a Bicentennial showpiece about the nation in three of its crucial moments. It was an unlikely choice, since its vision of America was less than encomiastic. But Lowell the poet and Lowell the ancestor of a famous American family was a perfect author to market at the time.

After 1976, *Old Glory* gained more attention from literary scholars than from drama specialists. Seldom performed, it became the property of Lowell scholarship. Of the three plays, *Endecott* and *Molineux* commanded the least interest and, apart from university and amateur productions, were rarely produced. *Cereno*, which most critics considered the best one, had more visibility, and since it was filmed for television presentation, it is the least likely to fall into obscurity. It should be noted that Lowell liked *Cereno* best; he wryly commented that he wrote the other two "to go with it" (Hamilton interview). When Hamilton asked how he felt about his total dramatic output, he replied, "I wrote one play which I think well enough of, 'Benito Cereno.' "

*Old Glory* was a unique work; so critics had little to compare it with. But they were familiar with its sources and took refuge in lining up Lowell's text with the masters'. This was a convenient way to discuss it, although not the most judicious way. The general veneration of classics automatically put Lowell at a disadvantage, but there was a small benefit in comparing him to Hawthorne and Melville: it precipitated exploration into Lowell's poetics of imitation. Admittedly, the critics did not go far with this; no one thought to correlate *Imitations* with *Old Glory*, for example. But buried in the discourse was some awareness that a common principle was at work.

The most forceful statement on *Old Glory* was made by Robert Brustein in his Introduction to its first published edition (Farrar, Straus & Giroux, 1965). Brustein, who then headed Yale's drama department, called the work "an event of great moment" and predicted that it might "very well come to revolutionize the American theatre." In a sense, all subsequent criticism was a reply to his claim. Brustein did little with the concept of imitation. He restricted his observations on that to a broad compliment: Lowell had adapted tales by Hawthorne and Melville with a degree of fidelity, yet had made them unqualifiedly his own. Brustein raised the issue of using American historical material in a compelling manner; historical plays had grown unpopular because of the "lifeless high-school pageants" that Maxwell Anderson used to "grind out." But Brustein did not prolong his defense of historical verse plays; the reference to Anderson, who was already in decline, was largely a flourish of rhetoric. He was less interested in restoring a kind of play than in bringing major writers (like Lowell) into the theatrical orb.

According to Brustein, *Old Glory* brilliantly captured the American character at three periods in its history: colonial America, the eve of the American Revolution, the early nineteenth century. And in each play, violence is the order of the day; America resorts to violence in "moments of panic." Lowell's message is simple: Present-day America is merely repeating past behavior. When Brustein discussed Lowell's use of sources, he stressed Lowell's oneness of mind with Melville, but found Lowell more pessimistic about America. In *Benito Cereno*, Melville saw America's attitude toward slavery as a dark shadow; Lowell extracted this aspect of the novella and raised it to gigantic proportions. Brustein credited Lowell with fearlessness and respect for Americans by refusing to entertain them with complacent mundanities. Lowell was more than equal to the task of borrowing from Melville. Moreover, a large repository of historical material was waiting to be tapped and Lowell had shown us how to do it.

Brustein, then, found Lowell's dependence on other writers enriching rather than stultifying. Lowell's affinity with Hawthorne and Melville showed a continuum in American artists' thematic priorities. Lowell had suggested this himself in his conversation with Billington (*London Times*). He said that Melville had written *Cereno* on "the eve of the Civil War" and when *he* adapted or transformed *Cereno*, the "Civil Rights issue" was very much on his mind.

Brustein's flattering essay almost demanded an emphatic statement from an opposing critic, and John Simon was that critic. Carping with Brustein, he found nothing to admire in *Old Glory* (*Book Week*, February 20, 1966). After ridiculing Lowell's choice of the verse medium and adding that he was copying Eliot and Fry, Simon asked whether *The Cocktail Party* and *Venus Observed* were even "worthy of emulation." Poets might still have a place in the theatre, but poetry, "barring a miracle," did not. Simon used Brecht as an example of a twentieth-century playwright who kept his poetry off the stage, except in song interludes. Simon attacked the "highbrow" critics who welcomed *Old Glory* and the revival of verse drama "as if the world had become a better place." In their snobbery, they had refused to admit that the trilogy was riddled with obstacles: action which had no logical or natural justification, language which was inconsistent and often static. More importantly, Lowell's reliance on Hawthorne and Melville was a big mistake; he should have left them alone, since their tales transferred poorly to the stage. In *Molineux*, Lowell added a "kid brother" as confidant, a common device for dramatizing fiction. This was not only illogical, it destroyed Hawthorne's suggestion of isolation in the main character. Simon said that Lowell anticipated the pitfalls of changing genres and compensated by delivering "Hollywoodish, shoot-em-up" finales. He also quoted a passage from Lowell's *Cereno* to show how it was only a slight reworking of Melville's prose. Lowell was basically stealing and covering his theft by printing prose in stanzaic form.

In this withering review, Simon leaves no room to explore the positive qualities of *Old Glory*. Lowell had violated his sources, lifting what was useful, omitting what was not, and ending up with "rigmarole." Simon's extreme position tends to invalidate his legitimate observations. The trilogy *did* have flaws, and it did *not*, as Brustein had hoped, succeed in bringing about a renaissance in American drama. *Old Glory* enjoyed favor during the sixties, but so did many other texts with a political slant. Lowell had no real following among young playwrights; and historical plays—the few that appeared—came packaged as musical comedies (e.g., *1776*).

Between the polar views of Brustein and Simon stood a corpus of essays which made more moderate claims for *Old Glory*. Judicious analysis required expertise in both drama and poetry. Gerald Weales's "Robert Lowell as Dramatist" (*Shenandoah*, Autumn 1968) went far toward meeting this requirement. The essay, a balanced overview of the trilogy, gives equal attention to its dramatic and linguistic features. Weales realizes that verse in modern theatre requires a special pleading or "apologetics." He neither rejects nor advocates verse drama; there is no special virtue in the genre itself: each play must "go it alone." Weales reminds us that public taste controls the theatre industry with a stronger grip than it does other literary forms. Today's commercial theatre managements, with an instinct for survival, have discouraged poetic drama because of its financial riskiness. Consequently, Lowell was brave to write *Old Glory*, and it should come as no surprise if the trilogy receives less than its critical due. Theatre critics have their ear to the box office.

Weales seems to take Lowell's practice of imitation as a given. He gets quickly to *Old Glory*'s thematic structure. He says that Lowell's compatability with his sources proves how obsessed American writers are about their nation's violence. Lowell's preoccupation with American violence and tyranny gives the trilogy its unifying, albeit disturbing, tone. It also places him in a tradition known for its tragic vision. His transformation of Hawthorne and Melville reinforces a creditable archetype: the American character. Weales is one critic who considers the different flags in the plays a coordinating symbol. They have two functions: they are "worth fighting for (freedom) or against (authority)." But they are ultimately representative of evil; whatever nation or cause they stand for, they perpetrate violence. To Lowell, "both oppressor and oppressed, authority and usurper, are one." Weales finds the trilogy an unremittingly dark portrait of mankind.

The three plays, then, deliver the same message, says Weales, who was perhaps reductive in his interpretation. Other critics prefer to explain the different flags according to their episodic meaning in each play, but Weales's larger view has certain advantages for interpretation. He even makes a convincing argument that Brustein's reading of *Old Glory* as an "illumination of America" is too specific. To Weales, the work is about revolution in the abstract, about the process whereby the oppressed invariably becomes the oppressor. With time, all causes are corrupted, even noble ones. American history is just one example of a universal pathology. Particularized historical references increase, rather than reduce, proof of the trilogy's universality. Weales says that allusions to the French Revolution, in *Molineux*, underscore the irony about shifts of power and the inevitability of terrorism: "Under whatever flag, power demands action and that action is inevitably violent and tyrannical."

If Weales does not dwell on Lowell's departures from the original narratives, he detects a thematic progression in Lowell's use of his sources. In *Endecott*, the first play, the seeds of tyranny are sown; in *Molineux*, the second, this tyranny proliferates in a massive mob demonstration; in *Cereno*, the last, tyranny reaches its sinister extreme. In effect, Weales is demonstrating how strategically subtle Lowell's imitative process is. The vision in Hawthorne's "My Kinsman, Major Molineux" is darker than in his "Endecott and the Red Cross." And Melville's *Benito Cereno* is still darker than either of Hawthorne's tales. Tragedy magnifies with each play.

In order to appreciate Weales's comments, some background on Lowell's use of his sources would be helpful. *Endecott* is based on Hawthorne's stories, "The Maypole of Merry Mount" and "Endecott and the Red Cross" (Lowell changed Hawthorne's spelling of Endecott). This play essentially deals with the clash between Puritan authoritarianism (exemplified by Governor Endecott) and pagan hedonism (exemplified by Thomas Morton). As the colony's governor, Endecott is torn between the natural eroticism that abounds in Morton's Merry Mount community, his own pragmatic Puritan values, and the establishment Anglicanism which may overtake the colony. As a consequence of his actions, Endecott becomes both rebel and tyrant. He tears the red cross (representing the Anglican church) from the English banner to assert his freedom from England, but he also orders Merry Mount to be destroyed, because this community's principles differ from his own. He fits Weales's description of Lowell's character types: "oppressor and oppressed." As imitation, Lowell's play is generally faithful to the episodes in Hawthorne's stories. Hawthorne himself was generally faithful to the historical account; he made his changes to allegorize American Puritanism. Lowell's changes foreground Puritanism as an example of elemental tyranny.

*My Kinsman, Major Molineux*, also from Hawthorne, deals with the capture of Molineux, a Redcoat, by a mob on the eve of the American Revolution. In the course of the action, in which the major's nephew participates in the mob's violence, the colonists' rattlesnake flag is raised, signaling America's release from British rule. Lowell's play enlarges and more clearly outlines the political implications merely suggested in Hawthorne: the tyranny of a "democratic" mob. Hawthorne's story is faithful to historical account, but his characters are fictional. Lowell's changes occur in characterization: he gives the nephew Robin a confidant to externalize the tale's interior passages. Hawthorne's tales imitate history; Lowell's play imitates Hawthorne and history.

*Benito Cereno*, based on Melville's novella, is about an American captain, Delano, who offers assistance to the captain of a Spanish vessel. Delano discovers that the captain, Benito Cereno, is being held captive by his cargo of slaves, who have revolted. In this play the flag of Spain is walked on and used as a barber's bib, and the mutineers' skull-and-crossbones flag replaces it, signaling the "slaves'" victory. Melville's tale is based on an actual account (Amaso Delano's *Narrative of Voyages and Travels*, 1817), but Melville took liberties with the *Narrative*. He depicted Delano as an innocent who learns that evil exists not only in the world but in himself. Melville's Delano hesitates to act; Lowell's Delano does not. He kills Babu, the "slave" leader, showing that beneath his liberal facade is a hardened racist.

Of the three plays, *Cereno* has the most political overtones. Since poetry and propaganda generally make strange bedfellows, *Cereno* seemed slotted for the harshest criticism, but this was not the case; most critics preferred it to the other two plays.

Content change, therefore, was not in itself a basis for censure. To Weales, for example, the changes (or additions) were judged by their effect on staging potential. He cited passages which brought in contemporary political references for immediate satiric purposes—usually at an artistic loss. The most glaring instance was the mutiny in *Cereno*, which resembles the black nationalist activity in the sixties. The mutiny scene was closer to LeRoi Jones's drama *The Slave* than to Melville, Weales said. In another scene, Lowell converts Delano's assistance to the Spanish vessel to a critique on "our involvement in Vietnam and our general intention to save the world on our terms." These topical lapses damage the play, Weales thinks. Occurring in passages which deviate most from the original tale, they confuse meaning rather than re-create it. When he discusses the various characters, Weales argues that Lowell took more freedom with Melville than with Hawthorne. The American seamen in *Cereno* shoot the women, an act Lowell uses to signify America's indiscriminate selection of targets in Viet Nam. This episode reverses Melville: in his tale the women are among the cruelest mutineers, deserving punishment. These lapses notwithstanding, *Old Glory* manages to triumph, says Weales.

Weales gives a detailed defense of the style in *Old Glory*. Verbal effects grow directly out of the dramatic situation, especially in *Cereno*. He finds little bombast and, unlike Simon, doesn't mind Lowell's reproduction of Melvillean passages. The metaphorical constructs are central to the plays and heighten the visual counterparts on stage (banners, masks, armor). The metrical patterns in *Endecott* and *Cereno* are so subtle that only anaphora or repetition tell the audience they are hearing verse. And while *Molineux*, which has a strong four-stress line, is more mannered and artificial, its surreal characters and setting justify the metrical medium.

Weales's essay reflects the standard approach to *Old Glory*. He looks for symbols, unifying thematic devices, dramatic intensity, and lyrical moments. He likes what he finds and defends it in some detail, but apart from his lament on the prospects for modern verse drama, he says little about *Old Glory* in the framework of equivalent productions at the time. He elaborates on staging effectiveness only when it is handicapped by political material. Nevertheless, his high quality analysis compensates for the gaps.

How did *Old Glory* fare in contrast to other dramatic productions? When *Old Glory* played, the makeshift theatres in lower Manhattan were creating a furor, drawing attention away from Lowell's drama. This section of the city, known as off-off Broadway, became theatre's radical hub. Playwrights were working in new forms: "happenings," or impromptu scripts which called for audience participation; "transformations," or scripts which substituted acting devices for sets or large casts. Other types of entertainment defied classification. Going to the theatre meant encountering a strange spectacle rather than familiar reality. For example, in *Motel: A Masque for Three Dolls*, from the trilogy *America Hurrah* (1966), Jean-Claude van Itallie's giant-size dolls methodically destroy the set, an American motel, until the stage is a heap of ruins. And in Paul Foster's *Balls* (1964), nothing appears on stage but two white ping-pong balls which swing meaninglessly in the void. The play has no characters; its verbal content is delivered by tape recorder. Both public and critic were intrigued by these bizarre productions and came to expect them at the theatre. By comparison, *Old Glory* was tame. Some of the plays even made discussion of *Old Glory*'s verse structure seem a dead question; they, too, were written in verse, but of a kind more radical than Lowell's. *America Hurrah* was composed of long-line Whitmanesque speeches which catalogued the evils of America. Its vulgar imagery recalled Allen Ginsberg's "Howl." *Old Glory* and *America Hurrah* drew the same grim picture of America, but the latter made Lowell's text seem a sugar pill.

Thus *Old Glory* fell between two stools. It had none of the tedious realism Lowell deplored in "naturalistic" dramas, but it was far more conservative than the off-off Broadway fare. This limited the kind of audience it would draw. The cognoscenti (political liberals in those days) snubbed Broadway and flocked to Lower Manhattan. Political causes—feminism, civil rights, ecology, the Viet Nam War—did not just punctuate these plays, as they did *Old Glory*; they *were* the plays. *Old Glory* had a different quality. Its stage devices were also unusual, but because of their eclecticism. They looked back to classical, medieval, even nineteenth-century techniques: the neo-Elizabethan sets and dialogues of *Endecott*, the masked mummery in *Molineux*, the tableau and pageant-like mime in *Cereno*. The overlay of fantasy in *Molineux*, for example, was a far cry from the kind of realism Eliot gave *The Cocktail Party*. The trilogy was sufficiently different to be a risk for commercial managements, and Lowell's attempts to mount it at Lincoln Center failed. He finally found a home for it at American Place Theatre, which initially was established "to act as a forum for serious young playwrights who are unwilling, unable, or uninvited, to try Broadway." It tried to attract "novelists, poets, philosophers, to the theatre," and Lowell qualified perfectly.

The most reliable account of American Place is Richard Schickel's "New York's Best New Theatre Group?" (*Harper's*, November 1966). Schickel discusses the directors' standards and their refusal to pander to off-off Broadway's highjinks. American Place directors abhor sensationalism, he says, but despite their quality work they will go unappreciated. Schickel believes, with Weales, that Broadway's monopolistic hold will snuff out the publicity that productions like *Old Glory* sorely need. He predicted a brief life for *Old Glory*—in fact, for American Place itself; and he proved right.

*Old Glory* was championed, almost backhandedly, to point up the low caliber of other productions. In one instance, Robert Brustein argued that the production of *Molineux* and *Cereno* infinitely surpassed a show simultaneously running at Lincoln Center: Elia Kazan's version of Middleton's *The Changeling* (*New Republic*, November 21, 1964). To Brustein, the production at Lincoln Center "exposed itself to shock and ridicule." He blamed the newspaper reviewers for "monolithic mediocrity" and their inability to evaluate either production. What chance did Lowell have when critics could not recognize a dismal production of Middleton? Brustein attributed the reviewers' philistinism to the surfeit of "social-psychological" dramas which had conditioned audiences to sordid realism. Actors Studio, with its one-key Stanislavsky method, had atrophied taste.

To be sure, *Old Glory* did not give Lowell the kind of critical comfort he was enjoying as a poet during those years. *Union Dead* (1964) and *Near the Ocean* (1968) had brought him the title of America's foremost poet, but *Old Glory* was in the hands of a maverick director and his mounting at American Place was not everyone's cup of tea. Jonathan Miller, the director, wanted each play staged with a different tonal quality. This would enhance, rather than endanger, the trilogy's unity, he felt. (Since *Endecott* was not mounted with the others, Miller's total design was already hampered.) For the premiere, the actors in *Molineux* were painted chalk-gray and dressed in stiff, unbleached cotton. Miller felt that this play needed to be "put across with scintillating artificiality," that "the controlling image for all this was Alice-in-Wonderland" (Director's Note,

*Old Glory*, 1965 edition). On the other hand, he wanted the mood in *Cereno* to be "baroque and courtly." The actors in this play were ordered to move and speak as though they were "soloists in an oratorio." *Cereno* was a "new *Tempest*, in whose setting nature's and society's laws had been forgotten."

As performed, the play's political elements should have been swallowed up in the formal design, but the critics (like Weales) found them protruding anyway. Lowell approved of Miller's interpretation; he later spoke glowingly of him as a director (Hamilton interview). It is likely that Lowell recognized his inexperience in the theatre and gladly placed the text in Miller's hands. Miller merely remarked in his Note that Lowell was wonderful to work with, which suggests the director's hegemony.

The production made some critics uneasy. The *New York Times* review, which counted most at the box office, was "mixed" (November 2, 1964). Howard Taubman found both plays spotty, having potential but in need of revision. He preferred *Cereno* to *Molineux*. He added that dramatizing narrative was a chancy undertaking and that no amount of fine writing (which *Old Glory* possessed) could save an unstageable text. Taubman raised the standard argument about poets' place in the theatre. A rejoinder to this argument came from Lowell's fellow poet, W. D. Snodgrass. He said that narrowmindedness about genre had automatically damaged *Old Glory's* reception (*New York Review of Books*, December 3, 1964). Snodgrass' piece was sensitive and eloquent, but it showed a disinterest in theatre mechanics; it evaluated the text on literary terms. Between Taubman and Snodgrass, something resembling a favorable impression must have become evident to drama judges: when the 1964–65 season ended, *Old Glory* had captured five Obie awards. Lowell enjoyed a momentary triumph.

When the hoopla over the original production subsided, essays of a more literary orientation began to appear. M. L. Rosenthal published two fine pieces on the trilogy for *Spectator*; one examined it in the context of verse drama, beginning with Yeats, the other concentrated on its stylistic priorities. The first essay (November 26, 1965) emphasized the importance of Yeats and Eliot in modern verse drama, as well as their influence on Lowell. The "continuity" of Eliot was gloriously realized in *Old Glory*. Indeed, Rosenthal said that Lowell's work was comparable only to *Murder in the Cathedral*. Moreover, "Lowell's triumph was probably the greater" because Eliot's play had encountered less initial resistance. When *Murder* premiered in 1935, it had a setting suited to its contents (Canterbury Cathedral) and a sympathetic audience (those attending the Cathedral Festival). It was much harder for Lowell, and this might affect *Old Glory's* future. Rosenthal considered *Murder's* dramatic structure a model for *Old Glory*; Eliot had shown how to use historical material as a means of throwing light on "violent contemporary meanings." He did not object to Lowell's injection of topical material; he went right to the material and used it to explain Lowell's ideology. In connection with this, Rosenthal found Lowell to share Yeats's concept of history: "the impersonal character of fundamental historical change." But Lowell used this concept more successfully than Yeats, whose plays did not stage well. Rosenthal selected *Molineux* as the most Yeatsian of the trio. In this play, revolutionary fever was presented in a dreamlike abstraction, in which the crowd was a faceless mass moving in unison.

Rosenthal admired Lowell's ability to imitate great writers and to "reveal their revelance anew"; but he used the term "revision," not "imitation." A poet himself, Rosenthal was all too conscious of the difficulty of fusing borrowed texts with personal ideas. He guessed that the reason Lowell dropped *Endecott* from the first production was the improper balance between his "obsession with man's sadism" and Hawthorne's tales. He credited Lowell with sufficient objectivity to realize that his "murderous ending" was incongruous with the rest of the play. Lowell's reliance on Hawthorne, then, kept his own excesses in check.

In his analysis of *Cereno*, Rosenthal imputed to Lowell a far greater anti-Americanism than Melville's text contained. At no cost of admiration for the play, Rosenthal argued that Lowell's portrait of an "efficient and ruthless" America was a tad elementary. Comparing Lowell's and Melville's attitudes on racism, he said that Melville felt "the terrible irony of slavery," but was more trapped by the prevailing concepts of race and racial superiority in his time. Lowell was less complex; his depiction of blacks had a "revolutionary intensity and awareness" which threatened to unleash violence in the nation. Lowell's play was simple apocalypse. Rosenthal attributed the prophecy to the poet's personal guilt, which had surfaced in his early verse, but there it was correlated with his Puritan ancestors' massacre of the Indians. In *Cereno* it became American racism as a whole. Personal crisis, therefore, became the more engaging question of social and historical crisis. This explained Lowell's fierce political rhetoric.

Rosenthal's second *Spectator* essay (September 30, 1966) concentrated on the language and meter of *Old Glory*; in this area he found nothing to fault. The verse was at one time "ritualized and incantatory," at others, based on "racy common speech." The mixture was a boon rather than bane to the style. This time the problem of suitable speech for modern verse drama had been solved. Lowell was not, like Yeats, a "closet dramatist." The only unkind words in Rosenthal's essays were that Lowell was a "bit oversimplified" compared to Hawthorne and Melville, who delved deeper into the mysteries of the human spirit. But Rosenthal excused this as Lowell's need to be "burningly relevant." In its unmitigated integrity, *Old Glory* was a major work.

Lowell's oversimplification, however, troubled British poet Charles Tomlinson (*Critical Quarterly*, Spring 1967). He took this to be more the case when Lowell worked with Hawthorne than with Melville. He did not dun Lowell for borrowing texts; indeed, it was "well-meaning." Trying to traffic with giants was not the problem; it was (again) the verse medium, which forced Lowell to worry more about language than themes. Tomlinson· was far too gracious to hurl invective, as Simon had, but he ventured the idea that verse drama was a moribund mode. There was perpetual dislocation between a language of "bourgeois realism" and a medium which was essentially "one of recitative." Going through the plays, Tomlinson noticed that not until *Cereno* did the language resemble effective speech. He placed Lowell's text alongside the passages he took from the sources. Hawthorne's "Endicott" had a moving eloquence that, in Lowell's paraphrase, became embarrassing sentimentality. In Hawthorne's tale, Endicott, whose wife had died early in their marriage, observed a young bride at Merry Mount with stately nostalgia. The old Endicott "almost sighed for the inevitable blight of early hopes." Tomlinson found this passage notable for its understatement. He quoted Lowell's reconstruction of this, which becomes stilted dialogue; Endecott tells the bride:

You are almost as beautiful as my wife,
Misfortune has fallen too early on you and your husband.

But the language in *Cereno* markedly improves, he says. Lowell's violent rhetoric, a carryover from his early verse, is

appropriately implemented and sharpens the horrifying inci-
dents. Delano's observation about Benito Cereno and his supposed slave is fraught with verbal irony. Lowell accentuates the
master-slave relationship, "where the master *is* the slave, and
irremediably alone." He rhymes "unknown" with "alone" to
enforce the double meaning:

> The beauty of that relationship is unknown
> in New England. We're too much alone
> in Massachusetts.

A style analysis like Tomlinson's is a welcome addition to
the scholarship. Unfortunately, there is little of it. The critics
were more interested in Lowell's *thematic* fidelity to his sources,
and Alexander Laing made this the crux of his reading in *Nation*
(January 24, 1966). He, unlike Tomlinson, felt that Lowell did
an injustice to Melville. The novella was a darkly profound
examination of mankind, which Lowell reduced to a political
treatise on racism. But Lowell did more than justice to Hawthorne, Laing said; in fact, *Molineux* was "greater" than Hawthorne's tale. Lowell had turned Robin, Hawthorne's callow
adolescent, into an "American principle." The young man, who
in the tale seeks advancement through his prominent kinsman,
becomes a paradigm for the American Dream: youth can rise
by sheer native wit in the New World. The original Robin
was actually a "rite of passage" characterization of initiation
into manhood. Laing's reading is pitched to the readership of
*Nation*, a journal known for its sociopolitical orientation. He
limits stylistic appraisal to a few words on diction: the combination of "contemplative recitative with modern speech" to
give the effect of "generalized time." This rather arbitrary
summary has more potential than Laing allows it. The essential
tightness of the language supports the thematic schema of the
trilogy; Lowell's depiction of violence as native to the American character is even more horrifying when set loose in "generalized time."

Neither Laing nor Tomlinson is misleading in his analysis,
but at the same time neither critic grapples with the form-
content dualism in *Old Glory*. Tomlinson feels that Lowell
botches his language in *Endecott*, but he never shows how this
affects the trilogy's conceptual system. Laing praises the poetic
style of all three plays, but never demonstrates how this con-

tributes to the central vision—if indeed there is one. Each of their essays is prefatory.

There was surprisingly little interest in the autobiographical elements in *Old Glory*—certainly less interest than that shown in the poetry criticism. No one thought to question Lowell's choice of writers, or his possible identification with Hawthorne and Melville as men. Hawthorne, especially, interested Lowell; he carried the Puritan onus through his work in atonement for his ancestors' sins. Lowell felt similarly burdened. In his poem "Hawthorne" (*Union Dead*), Lowell had emphasized the implicit analogy between himself (or his tormented persona in the poems on mental illness) and Hawthorne:

> Even this shy distrustful ego
> sometimes walked on top of the blazing roof,
> and felt those flashes
> that char the discharged cells of the brain.

Clearly, this was an avenue for research in *Old Glory* scholarship, but it went untraveled.

But if autobiographical elements were ignored, psychological ones were not. There was little timidity about explaining motives (political or sexual) for certain episodes in the trilogy. The most unusual example of a psychological reading was Baruch Hochman's "Lowell's *Old Glory*," in *Tulane Drama Review* (Summer 1967). Hochman ranged from the far fetched to the plausible, especially in his reading of *Cereno*. This play was a morass of Freudian disorders, he said. The action was not a study in American racism or tyranny, but a full-cast dramatization of "civilization and its discontents." The relationship between Benito and Babu was not between master and slave, as Tomlinson had insisted; it was the "homoerotic communion" of two neurotic psyches. And the slaves' mutiny, foreshadowed in the hatchet-polishing scene, was not, as Weales thought, characteristic of the black nationalist activism, but of the "cannibalistic overtones" civilized man has suppressed.

Hochman's interpretation is intriguing, if bizarre; but its validity is questionable at best. It strengthens any argument about Lowell's generically bleak view of mankind, but apportions little insight into the play's literal meaning. It is self-serving discourse, squaring in no specific way with cause and effect in the action of the play. None of the later criticism picks up on Hochman's theory—or even troubles to challenge it. In the remainder of his essay, Hochman was more in step with standard readings, although his pitch remains psychological. He believes that at the heart of the plays is an "anguished conservatism," that Lowell's liberal ideas are forced. Lowell behaved like a liberal because, during the sixties, intellectuals were expected to do so. Although Hochman may have hit on an unflattering truth, he trivialized his case by giving no examples of this conservatism.

A far more responsible examination of *Old Glory* as an outgrowth of sixties politicism was Peter Shaw's "*The Old Glory* Reconsidered" (*Commentary*, June 1976). Shaw began with no presuppositions about Lowell's true political leanings. He took the text at its surface level and saw it primarily as a document of the decade. Lowell had exhibited the then-common syndrome of "espousing a cause." He anticipated the bitter anti-Americanism that dominated American literature for the remainder of the decade. Shaw's piece abstained, as such pieces did, from making aesthetic judgments on the work; instead, he demonstrated how politically provocative it was. Without blaming Lowell for the desecration of flags in the United States during those years, Shaw noticed the coincidence between Lowell's flag defilements and the flag burnings at draft headquarters and demonstrations. In each play a flag was debased: cut up (*Endecott*), replaced (*Molineux*), trod upon (*Cereno*). Shaw also said that *Old Glory* gave the "first shock of liberal guilt" to the nation—mostly about the black movement and the Viet Nam War, but tangentially about other American abuses. He believed that Lowell was more bent on raising our consciousness than on creating great drama. This freed Shaw from stylistic analysis, but, like Laing, he was satisfying the readership interests of the journal. By doing so, however, he focused on the extent to which Lowell imitated Hawthorne's and Melville's ideas. Hawthorne always presented American (Puritan) attitudes with a "questioning eye," while Lowell simply pointed a finger of accusation. Lowell's Puritans represented "greed and racism," pure and simple. By "racism," Shaw meant the Puritans' attitudes toward the Indians. Also, Lowell kept Hawthorne's plot details, but gave them a sixties context. For example, in *Endecott* he made the Merry Mount children fanatical; they resembled the contemporary "flower children" more than the original characters. Lowell portrayed these young people engaged in "innocent dancing" around the maypole, celebrating that segment of society which espoused slogans like "Make love not war." Hawthorne was much more critical of the young inhabitants at Merry Mount, Shaw argued. Their hedonism was just as rigid as the Puritan ordinances: "It was high treason to be sad at Merry Mount." Hawthorne intended Endicott's act of cutting the red cross out of the flag to be a symbol of the Puritans' religious bigotry. In Lowell's version the same act became "a single gesture of revolt."

Shaw finds the same ideological changes in the other two plays. Lowell turns a local episode into a national characteristic; uncritical of violence, Americans will sanction any means of overthrowing tyranny. Thus, in the original "Molineux," Hawthorne considers Molineux a representative of the establishment and the parade scene a routine ritual of the "transfer of power." In the play, the parade is reminiscent of the sixties youth marches, indulged in for the simple pleasure of "humiliating the establishment." Shaw's final example is from *Cereno*. Melville depicted Delano as a forthright, optimistic American whose naiveté actually saves him. In the play, Delano becomes a "smug bigot" who envies Cereno for owning a slave. Delano does everything for financial profit; as he brings provisions to the stricken crew, he worries that he will never be compensated for them.

Shaw's examples do not add up to a consistent argument about Lowell's political views. In disavowing the idea that we can actually know what Lowell truly believed in, and insisting that Lowell was merely depicting the values of the sixties, Shaw never resolves the contradictions and ambiguities of Lowell's vision. Is Lowell condoning the "flower children" in *Endecott* but not the young paraders in *Molineux*? Clearly, Shaw depicts Lowell as overly pessimistic about America. He glosses over the more hopeful moments in the plays—even *Cereno*. Delano's bosun, a young officer named Perkins, stands for the noble traits in Americans, for example; but Shaw's piece came out in the bicentennial year, when Americans wished to present a positive image of themselves. Works like *Old Glory* recalled a decade rife with violence.

Apart from evaluations of *Old Glory* as a whole, some stimulating essays were devoted to individual plays. Daniel Hoffman's "The Greatness and Horror of Empire: Robert Lowell's *Near the Ocean*" is an overview of Lowell's work up to 1967, but the best-developed section of his essay is an analysis of "Endecott" (*Hollins Critic*, February 1967). Hoffman undertakes a comparison between the tales and the play. "Endicott" and "Maypole of Merry Mount" make "ambiguous, even duplicitous" judgments about the Puritans. Hawthorne posed his condemnation of the Puritans against his "faith in equality and reason." To Hoffman, Hawthorne's Endicott is humanistic and realistic. Hawthorne halts the pagan celebration, which is actually a wedding of young lovers, with a sober aside:

> True love has its beginnings in an Eden of hedonistic joy, but in our unhappy world it must be brought under the discipline of human law.

Lowell's Endecott is more uncompromising. Nonetheless, Hoffman believes that the play's dramatization of this stern leader is adequately complex. And by creating Endecott's confidant, Elder Palfrey, Lowell was able to show the two strands of Puritanism, "baleful piety and worthy pride." Hoffman finds Lowell's imitation an enrichment of Hawthorne.

Milne Holton's study of *Endecott* takes Lowell's theory of imitation a little further. "Maule's Curse and My-Lai: Robert Lowell's 'Endecott,' " a contribution to the *Proceedings of a Symposium on American Literature* (Poznan, 1979), was written for a foreign audience. Holton prefaced his analysis with background on the American national character and its "experience in history," which was then put into the sixties' framework. He argued that Lowell's "act of reiteration" or "imitative impulse" informed his dramatic structure. Although his analysis of topical elements is similar to Shaw's (*Commentary*), the departures from Hawthorne are more carefully explained.

Holton emphasized that *Old Glory* opened two nights before Lyndon Johnson's election victory, and that just prior to that Lowell had refused to attend a White House arts festival—in protest against the war. The publicity surrounding his decision, and his subsequent disfavor with President Johnson, made Lowell uneasy about the political contents of *Endecott*. In the process of watering down the text he obfuscated the sources. But in the second version of *Endecott* (1968 revised edition of *Old Glory*), Lowell added Indian characters. He now came closer to Hawthorne's narrative, but at the same time was more overtly political in his indictment of racism. According to Holton, the murder of the innocent Assawamset and the violence done to the Indians became a historical parallel: American atrocities against the yellow Vietnamese were analogous to American atrocities against the red Indians in the nineteenth century. Flag colors and the color of dreams provide patterns of action which honor Hawthorne's darker meanings, says Holton: "Assawamset's white dream is supplanted by Endecott's black one." The tearing of the red cross from the white flag indicates that Endecott "cannot believe in doctrines of moral election," but must gratify his "impulse toward racial election." By this reading, Lowell's text attests to a race problem three centuries old. The second version of *Endecott* was more integrated with the thematic values of the other two plays. Lowell's diachronic survey of American history delivers synchronic verities. America in the sixties is little changed from colonial America, says Holton; here is Lowell's theory of history, all too sadly dramatized.

There is an essay on *Endecott* which finds greater discrepancies between Lowell and Hawthorne than Holton does. Richard Clark Sterne's "Puritans at Merry Mount: Variations on a Theme" (*American Quarterly*, Winter 1970) examines the shift in attitude toward the Puritan heritage in the more-than-a-century lapse between Hawthorne's and Lowell's versions. Sterne believes that Hawthorne ultimately assented to the Puritan way of life. His ambivalence about Merry Mount—the lost paradise, where revelry borders on the grotesque—eventually becomes a wish that a somber, harsh civilization could be humanized "by the same love which domesticates sexuality and shows the superficiality of hedonism." Hawthorne is as tolerant of Morton as he is of Endecott, says Sterne. Thomas Morton, an English barrister-adventurer who came to Quincy, Massachusetts and developed a Bohemian trading post at Merry Mount, negotiated with Indians, Puritans, and Anglicans alike. This is historical fact, as documented in Morton's account (*New England Canaan*) of his efforts to elude both Puritan and British (meaning Anglican) efforts to discipline. Hawthorne also believed that Endicott was not as shocked by the pagan maypole activities as history relates. Rather, they recalled his affectionate ties with old England and softened his "iron" Puritanism. Lowell, on the other hand, saw Endecott as the product of a "sick" Puritan civilization, which caused him great psychological conflicts. According to Sterne, Lowell's stage directions that the maypole be placed far to the side indicated that Endecott's "phallic vigor and gaiety" had ended, leaving him no alternative but to be cynical about the use of power. Thus, to

Lowell, the implications of this kind of psychic repression had radical results in American policy. Power had made America (like Endecott) violent.

Sterne's piece is astute and convincing. His interpretation is not susceptible to a Freudian reading because of his strictly scholarly approach. Others were more inclined to parallel Lowell, the man, with Endecott. Lowell's personal problems were greater than the play could dramatically withstand, said Peter Porter (*Listener*, September 8, 1966). Endecott was a dramatic projection of Lowell's ambivalence between stern morality and the more sensual side of his nature. Samuel Moon (*Poetry*, June 1966) and Peter Lewis (*Stand*, no. 4, 1968) voiced the same idea, but their treatment of *Endecott* was brief; both dismissed the entire trilogy as an emotional outburst, lacking in historical and artistic objectivity.

Jerome Mazzaro gave a more substantial psychological reading of Lowell, but he turned his attention to *Molineux* (*Western Humanities Review*, Autumn 1970). He argued that Lowell put himself more into the character of Robin than into any of the other characters in the trilogy. By his reading, Major Molineux becomes Lowell's grandfather, Arthur Winslow, and the nation's new consciousness (the spirit of the Revolution) is Lowell's declaration of independence from family authority figures. Thus *Molineux* repeats some of the themes in Lowell's poetry (especially *Land of Unlikeness* and *Lord Weary's Castle*): "verbal killing of a father image to accompany symbolic killings." Freedom and self-definition have historical and personal thematic parallels. Mazzaro sees strong Hawthornean duplication in this play, despite Lowell's subjectivity. The adolescent Robin's rite of passage—a motif critics tended to overlook—is strongly emphasized in both tale and play. Mazzaro sees a near-perfect resemblance between Hawthorne's and Lowell's adolescents.

Mazzaro continued his analysis of *Molineux* in a later essay (*University of Windsor Review*, Fall 1972). This time he placed it opposite *Endecott* and showed how it was a reversal of the id-superego phenomenon. The suppression of the "Jolly Merry Mounters by grey Puritans" stood for the repression of Lowell's id by his superego. *Molineux* reverses the earlier play, says Mazzaro; here, Robin's laughter at his uncle in the clothing parade scene becomes the repression of the superego by the id. Lowell's need to recall his own youth and his conversion to Catholicism in adulthood were more important than preserving historical accuracy. Mazzaro says this is proved by the nature of Lowell's elisions and addenda. For example, Lowell blurs the exact chronology in *Endecott* whereby Endecott comes to Merry Mount, when, in historical fact, Morton was in England. Hawthorne was aware of Morton's absence from the colony and kept to history in his "Endicott." Lowell put him in the play as a symbol of his own youthful freedom. Morton's fate in actual history was imprisonment in England; Robin's fate in Hawthorne is to participate in the American Revolution (as far as is known, Robin is not modeled after a historical figure). Lowell's psychic identification with both characters is darkened by the prospect of punishment (Morton) and violence (Robin). A far more reassuring self-image! Mazzaro's accent is, admittedly, strongly Freudian, but unlike Hochman, Mazzaro never loses grip of *Old Glory*'s relationship to literary and historical sources. He provides useful insights into Lowell's practice of imitation.

Treatments of *Cereno* were less inclined to find Lowell engaging in character identification. In fact, the *Newsweek* (May 3, 1976) coverage of *Old Glory* as a Bicentennial production failed to see a projection of Lowell's personality in *any* of the plays' characters. In *Cereno*, the *Newsweek* reviewer's favorite, Lowell was in sympathetic identification with all of the main characters: Benito, Babu, and Delano. This clash of sympathy gave the play its remarkable "dissonance," a tonal music that put other "so-called Bicentennial plays to shame."

Since *Cereno* in delivery was the most theatrical part of the trilogy, it got some coverage by drama specialists. David Knauf discussed its transference from novella to drama (*Educational Theatre Journal*, March 1975). Lowell altered the final action of Melville's story, thereby "activating the historical setting," and highlighting social implications which are barely significant in the narrative. Knauf believes that the dramatic form helps to make Delano a much more complex character than Melville's, who is shadowy and abstract. In Lowell's version, Delano exhibits a growing insensitivity in his efforts to understand the mystery surrounding the Spanish vessel. His initial encounter with the *San Domingo* crew has the spirit of friendship and formality, but his behavior slowly and subtly changes to cruelty and intolerance. In dramatic terms, Knauf identifies this as Lowell's "structure of suspense." Delano does not solve the mystery of the *San Domingo*, the mystery being conceptual ("the dark labyrinth of man's inhumanity to man"). This denouncement startles and shocks the audience. Delano finds the circumstances on board the ship merely "exotic." Babu's power derives from his careful arrangement of the "truth," so that it never exceeds the bounds of the audience's credibility. Strange figures march before Delano, some even scrubbing hatchets, but he remains remarkably slow of apprehension. The meal Delano shares with the Spanish captain (unlike Melville's frugal repast) is a "macabre banquet," whose ominousness Delano only dimly perceives. Ritual activities border on choreography, underscoring the concept that what is really happening remains a mystery.

Knauf says that this dramatic technique energizes guilt in the audience, but it is never isolated or ascribed. The linguistic reinforcement of the dramatic actions prevents us from tracing a "linear, rhetorical alignment upon specific issues." Knauf waffles a bit in this part of his analysis. He says that this is a controversial play about Negro suppression and an appeal for a compassionate solution to racism, but at the same time it contains arguments for supporting whatever position an audience may have toward suppression: "hostile, neutral or sympathetic." Knauf is evidently trying to prove that *Cereno* rises above literature of controversy through its "rhetoric of complicity." Delano is not so much haunted as hunted, and the audience should feel the same way by the end of the play. This is a sensitive aperçu, which Knauf could have developed a little further. The virtue of his essay, however, is that he discusses the play's language and action as a unit.

While it hardly does justice to *Cereno* to discuss it as a play about racism, *Cereno* unquestionably contained propaganda inserts. George Ralph's essay focuses on these inserts, but he defends their theatrical effectiveness (*Educational Theatre Journal*, May 1970). This effectiveness is accomplished through Lowell's changes from the novella, Ralph argues. Melville makes it clear, right from the beginning, that the blacks plan to take over the American ship and murder its crew. The crisis for Melville was to find a motivation for the delay and to retain an element of suspense. Lowell deliberately avoided this plot strategy, says Ralph. He had Babu and Delano act out a diabolic dialogue in which the final execution became a prophetic ritual: "The future relationship between the two races is clearly drawn." Given this reading, the formal and stilted atmosphere of the script is justified. The ornate costumes, chanting, and rhythmic manipulation of instruments project a ceremonial quality which is diametrically opposed to the realism audiences were encountering at the theatre.

Ralph compares *Cereno* with Arthur Miller's social-moral plays; he says that Lowell and Miller have similar views about the current state of society. Miller is "stronger in theory than in execution" and, because of his parochial realism, lacks Lowell's universal dimension. Lowell's exotic and remote setting for *Cereno*, for example, appeals to the audience's collective unconscious. In short, Ralph feels that poetry and propaganda do not make strange bedfellows. Poetry, with its mystical force, can turn propaganda into universal truth. Ralph's essay has its shortcomings. It is really a defense of Lowell's liberal position, with some appreciative remarks about theatricality thrown in. Ralph never really demonstrates how Lowell's play surpasses the novella.

A few critics picked up on Brustein's original praise of *Old Glory* as historical verse drama and evaluated *Cereno* in that category. Albert Stone said that, after researching the status of "historical literature," he found plenty of contemporary examples (*New England Quarterly*, December 1972). Moreover, he found some minor masterpieces in the pile: *The Sot-Weed Factor*, *The Confessions of Nat Turner*, *The Crucible*, and *Old Glory*. Stone disputes the premise that a "singularly antihistorical spirit," whether or not it was in reaction to Maxwell Anderson, has prevailed among the leading figures of American intellectual life. Stone numbers Lowell as the master of these writers who seek to engage the audience's historical imagination. Briefly comparing Miller's *The Crucible* with *Cereno*, for example, he finds the latter a more arresting achievement. Lowell transforms the mythical patterns of Melville's novella into "historicism," which defines and illuminates the ideological goals in American political philosophy. Lowell displays the innocent and "corrupt fulfillment" of American history. Civil War, dollar diplomacy, manifest destiny are offset by references to the Founding Fathers' noble precepts. The duality is embodied in Delano and his youthful, bosun, Perkins. Lowell has incorporated two Yankee characters in the place of Melville's one. Perkins is innocent idealism and Delano is the urbane, older American who has forgotten his liberalism.

Stone believes that Melville deals strictly with myth (the myth of American democracy) while Lowell transforms that myth into ideology. Although the difference is subtle, ideology is more clearly related to actual results of social conflicts. Thus, in Lowell's view, the economic gain so central to Delano's motive in rescuing the Spanish ship *had* to resolve in bloody violence. Stone acknowledges that Lowell's approach is less compassionate and complex than Melville's, but that Lowell is more faithful to historical realities. Admittedly, the mystery which so richly informs Melville's novella is lost in the topical specificity of *Cereno*. Stone chooses not to compare *Old Glory* with its sources to determine which is the greater work of art. He merely demonstrates how different artists interpret the same event in history.

Richard Howard also took an interest in what *Old Glory* said about history (*New Leader*, December 6, 1965). He talked mostly about *Cereno*, but his comments applied to the total work. The real source of the trilogy was the American psyche, not history, he said. In fact, there was "a deliberate emphasis on the non-historical view." The plays were not history plays, like *Richard III*, but romances, like *Pericles*. Of course, the problem with that statement is that scholars would quibble with Howard about classifying *Richard III* as a history play. Howard raised more problems than he solved. But aside from his genre label, Howard talked about the ethical tone of the trilogy. It had no uplift. At the end of each play "there is a violation of selfhood and a longing for rebirth." In each play "something is killed" (an ideal, an individual) but we are not told what has been saved. We are starved for "completion," Howard says, and Lowell leaves us nothing to hang on to.

Perhaps Howard pushed the idea about moral encouragement too far, but it is fair to say that *no* critic came away from *Old Glory* with his faith in America confirmed. They all remarked on Lowell's pessimism. *Endecott* and *Molineux* were confined to specific examples of corruption, but *Cereno* was America at its all-inclusive worst. This was Robert Ilson's argument in his essay on *Cereno* (*Salmagundi*, no. 4, 1966/67). Ilson focused on the transformation from Melville's Delano, a "person of a singularly undistrustful good nature," to Lowell's Delano, "a world cynic." In the Melville ending, Captain Delano returns to his own ship and sends his men out to capture the Spanish vessel. The slaves are taken alive and brought to Lima. Delano tries to avoid personal involvement with them. At the trial in Lima, Babu is judged guilty and executed; Delano plays no part in the sentencing. Lowell has Delano epitomize America and personally fire the bullets into Babu. Ilson attributes the plot change not so much to the difference between writers as to the difference in centuries. America has become so hardened since the nineteenth century that her policy for pacification is beginning to look more and more like fascism. In the novella, Captain Delano's ship is called *Bachelor's Delight*; Lowell changed the name to *President Adams*. This is not a reflection on Adams' integrity, Ilson argues; it is just a detail to suggest America's lost innocence.

Ilson was not the only one to bandy about the idea that Lowell saw America as fascist. W. D. Snodgrass got the same message from *Cereno* (*New York Review of Books*, December 3, 1964). He said the play was profound enough for tragedy. The repressive policy of the establishment has killed off all of America's healthy rebellious and energetic forces. The date of this piece helps to explain Snodgrass' attitude. The rebellious forces in America would become active in a very short time; by the mid-sixties, marches and riots became regular events in the United States. Lowell had actually anticipated them.

Richard Fein took Snodgrass' argument a bit further in *Robert Lowell*, but by then it was 1970 and the warnings in *Cereno* had been fulfilled. Fein could be more precise about Lowell's political meanings. He said that Lowell feared that, given the terms of slavery's constant presence in American history, rebellion was self-defeating. Babu engaged in his rebellion and his taunting of Delano with a sense of futility; real freedom was too much to expect. To Fein, this indicates Lowell's doubts about the success of the civil rights cause: Babu "senses his doom and that of his people; and the rebellion comes to be its own despairing end" (p. 131). History proved Lowell wrong, but when he was writing "Cereno," his fears seemed well founded.

When the critical statements on *Old Glory* are placed side by side, they show a similarity of interpretation. Admirers and detractors alike agree that, to Lowell, Americans' commitment to ideals perverts their humanity. Characters like Endecott and Delano, essentially decent men, are trapped by their moral righteousness. There is no doubt that Lowell is disenchanted with America. There is not such critical concord about the dramatic merit of *Old Glory*. The verse medium is called upon both in praise and blame, but it is not really the chief point of dispute. The truth is that no critic made a case for the trilogy as great drama. Lowell's efforts were deemed remarkable, but so were

Anderson's a few decades earlier. Lowell was to the new playwrights what Anderson had been to Lowell: a bit passé. But in
all fairness, a thorough and specialized study of Lowell as a
dramatist is yet to be done. At present, the idea holds that Lowell was primarily a poet, and *Old Glory* is the quirk of a poet
who, one day, decided to write a play.

## Imitations

*The Old Glory* was engendered by a variety of unusual circumstances; *Imitations* (1961) claimed an equally unusual origin.
It began when Lowell decided that he could write a better
version of Rilke's poem "Orpheus" than a parallel French version he had just read. After Rilke, he practiced translating other
European poets, intermittently over a ten-year period, usually
when he was unable to write his own poems. As the number of
"imitations" grew, he gathered them together for a volume. The
collection took the shape of a small anthology of European
poets in a chronological order, ranging from Homer to Pasternak. Lowell intended the work to be read as a sequence. In the
Introduction he explained his process of imitation: "I have been
reckless with literal meaning, and labored hard to get the
tone. . . . In poetry tone is of course everything." So he changed
lines, images, meter, even intent, in the originals. Everything
was subordinate to one objective: "to write alive English and
to do what my authors might have done if they were writing
their poems now and in America" (p. xi).

Although Lowell's rationale for *Imitations* generated lively
arguments in the scholarship, by and large the readings were
demonstrations of taste and personal preference: those who
found the Baudelaires the best and those who found the Baudelaires the worst; those who preferred the imitations of the
ancient poets and those who preferred the imitations of the
modern poets. The imitative act itself, however, was little investigated. Few critics thought in terms of "the anxiety of influence," a phrase coined by Harold Bloom in his volume bearing that title (1976). According to Bloom, modern poets are so
burdened by literature of the past—having to absorb it without
repeating it—that they suffer from fear of creative sterility. They
can, of course, produce masterpieces such as *The Waste Land*,
which structure a new poetics on former myths; but they can
also drift into mediocre repetition of former myths. Which of

these possibilities accounts for the composition of *Imitations?*

A question like this was not directly confronted, although scattered statements in the scholarship suggested an awareness of Lowell's "anxiety of influence." Nonetheless, the scholarship became more sophisticated with time. Critics became increasingly appreciative of the volume's large structural patterns, treating it as an entity rather than as a string of good or bad translations. They recognized the thematic inevitability in the order and choice of poems imitated. Indeed, *Imitations* could be analogized to *The Waste Land* as a modern epic-like composition built on discrete myths and fragments of Western history and culture. Like epic, *Imitations* contains a narrative structure (albeit a very loose one), and although there is no main character to parallel the epic hero, the dramatic figures (e.g., Achilles in the Homer imitation) metamorphose into a persona who changes from a warrior type to a representation of love and tolerance. Although the poems are placed in units according to their original authors (e.g., five poems from Villon, three from Leopardi, nine from Pasternak), "Pigeons" is taken from the Rilke group, where it belongs, and appropriated as the final selection. With this piece, Lowell uses the image of flight to recall the archetypal voyager, which in turn recalls the opening poem in the volume: a passage from the *Iliad*. The persona in "Pigeons" speaks as a Homeric hero would:

> What is home, but a feeling of homesickness
> for the flight's lost moment of fluttering terror?

The voyage is ended; the persona is heavy with humanity and wisdom. The volume has come full circle.

But while there is a greater understanding of the design of *Imitations*, its debt or kinship to works of the epic variety, such as *The Cantos* or Williams' *Paterson*, still needs to be researched. As Michael Bernstein said of *The Cantos* in *The Tale of the Tribe: Ezra Pound and the Modern Verse Epic* (1980):

> There is an underlying assumption, moral rather than anthropological, in presenting so many different cultural situations: the hope that seeing certain human experiences and institutions expressed in a wide variety of contexts will make us more open to the possibility for change and reform in our own sphere.

Bernstein credits Pound with shaping the idea of a collective heritage in contemporary values and language. Unfortunately,

Bernstein's text deals only with Pound's influence on *Paterson* and Charles Olson's *The Maximus Poems*; Lowell is not considered in the study. But it was with Pound, more than any other twentieth-century poet, that the concept of building modern poetry on ancient literature became legitimized. And when a full-scale analysis of *Imitations* is undertaken, it will have to discuss Pound's role in the development of the genre of imitation.

Pound started writing imitations because he knew that the poetry being written by his contemporaries had reached a dead end. He initiated a renaissance in order to counteract the power of Swinburne and Rossetti during the nineties decadent period. Their followers—Ernest Dowson, Lionel Johnson, even the early Yeats—had nowhere to go with the melancholy, dreamlike mode that had dissipated poetry into enervated, mannered archaism. Pound undertook to solve the problem and to answer the question Eliot had asked in the first decade of this century: "Where do we go from Swinburne? and the answer appeared to be, nowhere" (*Poetry*, 1946). Pound's mimetic genius allowed him to absorb the style and meaning of ancient poets, through masks and personae, into a unique kind of writing. He showed the modern poet how to transmit his apprehension of the past and make it available to the present as a civilizing force. Thus he went back to periods preceding the Pre-Raphaelites and multiplied the resources of literary imagination. Using Ernest Fenellosa's notes on ancient Chinese poetry, which gave him English equivalents for Chinese characters but no forms of meter or rhyme to follow, Pound could put the riches of an entire civilization into a modern vernacular. Thus was born *Cathay* (1915), his first major imitative work after the earlier adaptations of Tuscan and Provençal poets (*Canzoni*, 1911; *Ripostes*, 1912).

Although Pound's habit of imitation did not set a trend among American poets, it changed their perspectives on borrowing. Eliot and Wallace Stevens brought a new range of measures and diction to their verse by imitating French Symbolist poetry. But Stevens, particularly, seemed to prefer the exotic, almost foppish examples of the Symbolists (especially Verlaine) and, by doing so, continued the decadent nineties sensibility. Lowell's versions of Rimbaud and Baudelaire are closer to Pound's concept of imitation—the two poets are acclimatized to Lowell's native voice. And the voice in *Imitations* is one of its intriguing features. It bears a resemblance to the

Yeatsian or Poundian mask. Lowell used a form of self-translation which proceeded from immediate feeling to his sense of the social dialectic; by using other poets' works, he had a wider base for his synthesis of these two means of response.

The complexity of poetic voice was recently discussed by Merle Brown in *Double Lyric: Divisiveness and Communal Creativity in Recent English Poetry* (1980). Brown's application of his theory suggests ways in which *Imitations* may be more accurately interpreted. According to Brown, there is no "ego or individual" who does not have "an *alter* who is his essential *socius*." Interpretation in poetry, especially in translation, is a "mediating of antitheses as each person widens his inner community" (p. ix). When this idea is applied to *Imitations*, the double voice becomes the poet's struggle to overcome his self-pity and give objective form to his thoughts. What the reader must determine is how much of the vision is self-conscious and how much is the voice of society speaking through Lowell. Since, in *Imitations*, sober depiction of civilization derives most from voice, which is largely achieved through the diction and imagery of historical allusion, this doubleness has structural significance.

The issue of imitation, then, is replete with qualifications. It became a substantial topic of interest when Pound revived the practice in the early twentieth century. His creative versions of ancient Chinese poets and medieval troubabours reinvoked the Augustan debate about the *function* of a translator, which, as in the case of Pound's poetry, became the central critical approach to *Imitations*. But the growing interest in translation was also due to extraliterary matters such as the worldwide breakdown of cultural and linguistic barriers. When *Imitations* appeared, translation was one of those elusive factors of consideration in the political sphere: a potential tool to mitigate "cold war" tensions. Scholars like George Steiner and Noam Chomsky published studies on the science of communication, stressing the utility of language as a common human denominator. *Imitations* was a perfect specimen to study. Given Lowell's reputation as a politically minded and liberal thinker, critics wondered if *Imitations* would have a political tinge. Their curiosity was to prove unwarranted. Although the poems or passages selected by Lowell emphasized man's penchant for war, the text could hardly be called polemical.

Lowell was primarily interested in the artistic possibilities of imitation; his own statements on the subject were apolitical.

Happily, the flippancy of his remarks about writing plays was absent when he spoke about translation. (Lowell used the words "imitation" and "translation" interchangeably, except in his *Imitations* Introduction, where "translation" becomes a derogatory term.) His ideas about this art were fixed early on. A review he wrote on A. E. Watts's version of the *Metamorphosis* showed that by 1955 he had formulated his position on translation (*Kenyon Review*, Spring 1955). He spent less time evaluating Watts's rendition of Ovid than defending his own ideas. Aligning himself with the "risk-takers" in translation, he said that poetry takes precedence over literal accuracy. But there was another requisite: the successful translation necessitated that the original text have the potential to surrender some of its autonomy. He meant that the original must possess enough universality to be transposed to another period or culture. He said that it was equally important for the poet, in translating this text, to be willing to surrender something of himself (or herself). The truth of the original would then float free, since it had its own indestructible life.

Lowell further explained his translation theory in an interview with D. S. Carne-Ross, which was published in *Delos* (1968, vol. 1), a journal devoted to translation scholarship. Carne-Ross asked if he had a "method" and how it differed from other poets'. He also inquired if Lowell had turned to translation as a proof of America's cultural and political supremacy. The English during the Augustan period, for example, were so confident of their stature that they felt equal to ancient Rome. They could "meet Horace eye-to-eye." Lowell's reply to the first question was that he worked differently from someone like Pound. Pound virtually disappeared into the author he translated; he assumed the voice of the original, whether it was in *Homage to Sextus Propertius* or as *The Seafarer*. Lowell acknowledged that he was present in his own translations. He paraphrased what he had said in the *Imitations* Introduction: in his rendition of eighteen poets there was "one voice running through many personalities" (p. xi). With reference to the question about America's supremacy, Lowell said he had no illusions about himself or his nation. Moreover, he was not encouraging about the power of poetry to consolidate nations. Here, perhaps, he was showing the pessimism so characteristic of his personality. He suggested that international poetry conferences were providing a useful culture exchange, but only for the poets involved. Yet he conceded that, for the first time, there was an "openness of poets to poetry in other places." Even "in the thirties, Auden and Spender were not translating." Present-day poets were more inclined to cross linguistic borders.

Lowell indicated to Carne-Ross that he was more interested in translation as a means of enriching American culture than of bringing peace to the world. Here he was reflecting the liberals' contempt for national egotism during the sixties. Although Lowell made no direct accusations, poets during those years grasped any opportunity to chastise the government's self-righteous attitude. They felt that television clips of Southeast Asia, for example, made the world beyond our geographical borders seem a primitive place indeed. There was a deeper culture in those lands than scenes of peasants in rice paddies suggested. Lowell's ideas paralleled those of W. S. Merwin, a poet-translator, who felt that Americans should learn that they are not "the first person." On being awarded the Pulitzer Prize in 1971, Merwin said that Americans have assumed that they are the first persons, remaining ignorant that highly developed civilizations have existed for thousands of years. Translation was one way to avoid American chauvinism; Merwin said it kept him from being "too conscious of being an American" (*New York Review of Books*, June 2, 1971).

Lowell, who was of the same mind, said that he had become a classics major at Kenyon College in order to expand his understanding, and that the practice of translation should serve the same purpose: "I think we have the feeling of discovery of what we lack." Someone like Neruda, for instance, had "something that no North American poet" had. When asked if accuracy was a criterion, Lowell was noncommittal: "I wouldn't want to translate in any one way." Certain poets, like Juvenal or Dante, had to be faithfully rendered, while others, like Horace, allowed for more freedom. But all this was subordinate to his single responsibility: "to never destroy the original."

Lowell also insisted that he never worked with a poem that he believed he could have written himself. The idea had to be new; the imitation should "bring into English something that didn't exist in English before." So spoke Lowell, but several critics, as we shall see, felt that he deliberately chose poets whose sensibilities matched his own and that of his culture. They argued that, unlike Pound, who sought unfamiliar, exotic writers to translate, Lowell tapped into the hallmarks of Western literature: Homer, Sappho, Villon, Hugo.

Toward the end of the interview, Carne-Ross became less deferent in his questions. He asked why verse translators got away with more than prose translators, who were "stuck with this word-for-word thing." The verse translator could hide behind "inspiration." Lowell shied away from this note of condescension and Carne-Ross moved on to another topic. He had reservations about several of the Baudelaire renditions and asked Lowell why he had let the original language impose itself on a piece like "Le Cygne." He said this was one instance when Lowell did not dominate the original, but tried to reproduce French rhetoric in English. The finished product was "something marginally un-English." He quoted a passage in which the swan screams at the heavens:

> Its heart was full of its blue lakes, and screamed:
> "Water, when will you fall? When will you burst,
> oh thunderclouds?"

No English swan, even a Yeatsian one, would scream in such a grand way, he argued. In fact, though Carne-Ross did not note this, while English swans may not scream, neither did Baudelaire's swan. Baudelaire's operative verb for "scream" was *disait*, which is hardly histrionic:

> *Et disait, le coeur plein de son beau lac natal:*
> *"Eau, quand donc pleuvras-tu? quand tonneras-tu, foudre?"*

Carne-Ross's failure to note this makes his criticism more flamboyant than reliable. Moreover, Carne-Ross persisted in his badgering: Why was Lowell trying to bring the Latin rhetoric of emotion to English? Lowell's response was polite but unconvincing: He was trying to expand English. When Carne-Ross insisted that there was "a touch of absurdity" in these lines, Lowell finally confessed that he had felt "ragged" by critics, fearing they would accuse him of straying too far from the original. Thus the import of this brief exchange was that Lowell's lack of conviction was responsible for the failure of "Le Cygne." However, it is hard to tell to what extent Lowell's admission was caused by Carne-Ross's intimidating tone.

In the light of these statements, it is apparent that Lowell's theory of translation was far from what could be called a system, but it dovetailed with the current scholarship on the subject. In a seminal paper in *Comparative Literature Studies*,

Kimon Friar summed up the new approach: "All forms are valid, from the interlinear trot to the extreme paraphrase" (September 1971). Any method is admissible, Friar said; it is not how it was done, but *who* did it. To his mind, the best translation was by another poet, for he or she enriched both languages and altered the way the original poem was read. By this standard, the translator "tries through the letter to reach the spirit." Friar strengthened his postulate by stating that the translation process is common to both the original poet and his interpreter. The original poet never really presents his vision intact; language is as much a barrier to him as the foreign language is to the translator. It is even difficult to ascertain whether the vision is possible or even "exists without the words" in which it is apprehended. The embodiment in words, in itself, is a process of translation.

Friar admits that this idea is not new, but that it is easily forgotten when critics encounter a new translation. The system which views a series of marks or sounds as unchanging artifacts is, accordingly, obsolete. A poem, once created, becomes interpreted differently by the poet, his or her contemporaries, and readers in other cultures and epochs. Thus a translator's work is only one aspect of this general metamorphosis. Friar takes the translation process to be evolutionary, a way to break down barriers of customs and traditions and forge a relationship between two cultures. The translation flourishes "only after the other has preceded it and prepared the environment for it." Thus an original work is often the summation of an entire culture; works like the *Iliad* inject into the total knowledge of mankind a basis for understanding the particular civilization at hand.

Friar prefers to discuss the free adaptations of original poetry as a source of inspiration for a poet. He in no way undermines the "imitations" of Lowell—or Fitzgerald, Pound, or Yeats. Rather, they are the "authentic treasures of English literature." In the hands of such master craftsmen, the originals are even further enhanced. Also, "imitations" by these poets becomes a form of criticism. When the adaptation is of a famous work which has already become available in several translations, the process is even more estimable. The interplay of interpretations creates a legitimate genre of literature, Friar says.

Friar's essay is ardent and humanistic. Lowell's name is mentioned only in passing, but with respect. True to his premise, Friar values equally the methods of Lowell and Pound. No such tolerance was evident in John Simon's review of *Imitations* in *Hudson Review* (Winter 1967/68). Simon rode Lowell mercilessly. He questioned whether a translator has the right to change the mood, intention, or import of a poem: "At what point does an act of 'imitation' become an immoral act?" This time Lowell felt compelled to respond to Simon, who had so brutally dismissed *Old Glory*. In a subsequent issue of *Hudson Review* (Summer 1968), Lowell said that he resented being accused of immorality. But Simon was not to be intimidated and delivered a rejoinder to Lowell in the same issue. He expanded on his initial criticism. Calling a version of another's poetry an "imitation" changed nothing, said Simon. It only reinforced the charge that "to palm off one's own attitudes, sentiments, clumsiness on other poets under the guise of translating them is falsification and thus immoral."

Simon's words were so exaggerated as to sound humorous, but in fact Simon merely represented a different position: either reproduce the original with exact fidelity, or ignore it so completely that the new version is really new. Lowell's imitations fitted neither category. They needed a more exacting defense than that given by Friar, whose essay was sensitive but lacking in specifics. George Steiner's *After Babel: Aspects of Language and Translation* (1975), a historical survey of the phenomenology of translation, delivers a more systematic defense of translators like Lowell. Outlining the trends in current linguistics, Steiner justifies the new translation modes as part of man's recent discoveries about communication. Language itself is now understood to be "an immense body of shared secrecy," a device *not* to tell things but to *hide* them from outsiders. Steiner attempted to construct a model to explain the relationship between utterance and felt meaning, and to explore the problem of "constraint" in translation. He traces Lowell's—and Pound's—use of "imitation" back to Dryden, showing that its connotations go back to the Platonic theory of imitation, which saw *mimesis* as two removes from the reality and truth of Ideas. Aristotle conferred more positive value on the use of the word, since he stressed the didactic importance of imitative instincts. Nonetheless, says Steiner, the concept of imitation, in itself, retained a negative association.

In the eighteenth century the debate was reawakened when Dryden attempted to distinguish between "metaphrase" and "imitation." He found little difference between the two but decided that, in any event, neither was the suitable way to rework the classic poets. Rather, "paraphrase" was the more appropriate method: "the spirit of an author may be transfused, and yet not lost." Steiner considers Lowell's and Pound's renditions an attempt to hold the middle ground of translation. One must not forget that translation "extends far beyond the verbal medium." A translator is not only "making," he is "arguing out" a new meaning of his original; the dichotomy between letter and spirit remains the same throughout the centuries of translation. And Steiner, like Friar, found no ideal way to conjoin the two. Each translation must be judged (and respected) for its unique solution to this ancient and difficult practice. Steiner's liberalism allows for the appreciation of efforts like Lowell's and argues for an "underlying solidity and continuity" of a translation model. Steiner uses Lowell's imitation of Juvenal's Tenth Satire, which reconstructs imperial Rome, Augustan London, and modern New York City, as an example. He says this poem is a marvel of solidity and continuity. Lowell's accumulation of equivalences is a successive "rewrite of history," which expands, rather than reduces, his material. Substitution becomes a "mirror" of the self and the past at the same time. Therefore, the underlying deep structure of translation determines "the code of inheritance in our civilization." Additionally, it releases the writer from the trap of solipsism, to which Lowell was constantly and dangerously drawn.

Steiner stressed that translation's power to liberate a poet from narcissism has implicit political merit. His argument was ultimately analogous to Friar's: humanism and cultural evolution are the possible benefits of translation. But other critics were not so eager to impute such compliments to Lowell. They felt that Lowell did not venture far from narcissism because the poets he selected—especially the moderns—very closely resembled his own psychological makeup.

This was D. S. Carne-Ross's approach in his essay "The Two Voices of Translation" (*Robert Lowell*, ed. T. Parkinson, 1968). Carne-Ross did a one-to-one examination of the modern imitations in the text (Pasternak, Montale) and found them more satisfactory than imitations of earlier poets (Villon, Leopardi). He attributed this to a temperamental similarity between Lowell and modern poets in general. Lowell lacked Pound's ability to "make new the ancient or remote." He said that Lowell was best with poetry written in the last hundred years. Then he admitted to contradicting himself, because he felt that Lowell's Latin imitations (a few additions to his *Near the Ocean*) were good, but he quickly added that this could be attributed to the "modern sensibility" of Latin poetry. Actually, Carne-Ross kept changing his argument throughout the essay; his discourse was a string of personal reactions to individual poems. Moreover, he repeatedly used Pound as a model, which put Lowell at a disadvantage. Pound's "inspired ventriloquism," whereby he contrived to write as though he were Li Po, Propertius, or the anonymous Anglo-Saxon poet of *The Seafarer*, demonstrated a virtuosity which Lowell lacked. Delving into the problem of temperament in translation, he said that Lowell could not re-create a Leopardi poem because of the great difference between these two poets. The Montale versions, however, worked well because of Lowell's resemblance to Montale. Thus Carne-Ross disagreed with Lowell: his finest translations were precisely of those poems which he might have written himself.

This essay introduced more problems than it solved. Carne-Ross assumed that readers must be essentially bilingual to assume the proper literary perspective on *Imitations*, or the Latin pieces in *Near the Ocean*. How could one judge Lowell until he or she made sure that the rendition stood in a satisfactory relation to its original? Although a translation could be responded to independently, it was not, in itself, "ontologically complete." Carne-Ross then quibbled with Lowell's use of the term *imitation*. He said that Lowell was drawn to the Augustan term, but that, in fact, most of the versions in *Imitations* were really translations. Imitations, in the true sense, were Pope's reworkings of Horace and Johnson's *Vanity of Human Wishes*; "creative translations" were Pope's *Iliad* and Pound's *Seafarer*. Lowell's free reworkings were "imperfect translations." By classifying *Imitations* as translation, Carne-Ross narrowed his reading and never considered the volume's larger patterns. He ignored Lowell's directive that the book be read as a sequence, with "one voice" speaking. He both blamed and praised Lowell: blamed him for falling short of Pound's mastery, praised him for giving twentieth-century readers what Pope gave eighteenth-century readers: the spirit of the time rather than of the original. Carne-Ross was flattering only when he found examples of what he called "true translations." In this bracket he placed the versions of Villon's "Le Testament" and Montale's "Arsenio."

Carne-Ross goes far toward displaying his own facility with

languages, but he sheds little light on Lowell's process. The poet-translator Ben Belitt also regarded the volume as translation rather than imitation, but he was more laudatory than Carne-Ross (*Salmagundi*, 1, 1966/67). To Belitt, little was gained by defending *Imitations* on the ground that it was spared the "imputation of translation." The equivocation which derived from praising the book for *not* being a translation but, instead, a collection of "new poems," based on the work of European poets, actually served Lowell ill. This placed fabrication over mimesis, said Belitt, and disallowed the "inquiry" and "realism" ordinarily exercised in translation criticism. He reintroduced the debate about imitation and argued that Lowell had made himself a victim for the "purist" who would happily castigate him for taking liberties with masters. His argument was actually a defense of Lowell—or an effort to protect him from critics like Simon. Belitt felt that the poems (with very few exceptions) were brilliant "translations" and that Lowell should label them as such. The imitation rubric was an unnecessary defense mechanism; the poet, fearful of violating the originals by not reproducing something worthy of their beauty, shrank behind his terminology. What mattered most was that the product be excellent; Lowell need not fear to place himself in the pantheon of great translators. Belitt felt that Lowell failed with a few poets (especially Rilke and Baudelaire), but he more than compensated with his triumphs (especially Montale). He said that Lowell "re-orchestrates" the originals with consummate fidelity.

Thus Belitt delivered a limited approach to *Imitations*, but his insistence that "imitation" has been a centuries' old problem put Lowell's situation in an objective light. He was evidently uneasy with Lowell's statement that he had "taken liberties" (Introduction). He marveled at Lowell's brio of assault—cutting Hugo, unclotting Mallarmé, Ungaretti, and Rimbaud—but he did so more with wonder than admiration. He preferred to put Lowell's claims aside and make a case for him as a translator. Despite Lowell's formal admiration of Baudelaire or Pasternak, Belitt believed that he preferred the personal wretchedness of Montale. For this reason the Montale poems were the best in the volume. Moreover, the Montale pieces came the closest to true translations: they retained intact every sequence of Montale's thought. Every image had an English equivalent, every development of theme was laboriously followed. Belitt calls

Lowell's mimicry of Montale "a species of dramatism," a way to depersonalize his own persona and yet enact a persona native to his imagination.

Belitt's most penetrating insight is that *Imitations* was Lowell's way to move on to the province of drama, that his passion for transformation was more "theatrical" than "poetic." Belitt gives examples of Lowell's unsatisfactory diction equivalents. Two lines from the poem "Dora Markus" (Montale) prove his point: "*antica vita*" (meaning old life) becomes "old world's way of surviving," or "*i suoi riposi sono anche più rari*" (meaning its calms are even rarer) becomes "the let-ups are nonexistent." This not only fails as poetry, it obscures the interpretation. However, Belitt feels that Lowell captures something more essential, Montale's intentionality: the mystery of the poetic occasion itself," the "civilized tolerance of the ineffable."

He believes that in *Imitations* Lowell wanted to be a public rather than private poet, that he tried to create a European ambience by capturing the intonation of five languages. But what he really does is draw the reader's attention constantly to himself. Belitt's final diagnosis is that *Imitations* is a European version of *Life Studies*. Thus he incipiently notes that Lowell was retranslating his own poetic voice, but he stops short of developing this crucial point.

Too much of the commentary was devoted to generalizations about imitation. Lowell's directive that the collection be read as a sequence was seldom attended to. The critics became so obsessed with testing Lowell's versions that they did not consider the volume as a unit. Thom Gunn's essay "Imitations and Originals" illustrates this tendency (*Yale Review*, March 1962). Gunn is intrigued, though not impressed, with Lowell's technique. He acknowledged that Lowell is probably the most influential poet currently writing in America and that whatever he does is interesting. In this volume his "passionate struggle" accurately to render his subject matter in poetry has been turned to a new purpose. But the struggle to render some of the best European poetry of the past 3,000 years is more than he can handle, he says.

Gunn lists the three types of translation as *he* understands them, but they're really no different from the conventional categories: the "literal" translation, or trot; the "adaptation," or closer equivalent in one's own language than is achieved in a literal translation; and the "imitation," or rendition into topical

terms of the intention and subject matter of the original. Gunn
says that Lowell shifts between the three "procedures within a
single poem." Rather than preserving the tone of most of the
poets, Lowell merely tries to turn the original "into Lowell."
In short, the struggle which makes his personal poems so vivid
becomes a struggle with the three modes of translation. Gunn
uses Baudelaire for his examples because he feels that Baudelaire's temperament comes closest to Lowell's; but he finds that
Lowell's version of "Au Lecteur" fits none of the three categories: "it is not translation, adaptation, or imitation." Gunn
compares a passage from the poem with Lowell's "melodramatic" equivalent:

> *Ainsi qu'un débauché pauvre qui baise et mange*
> *Le sein martyrisé d'une antique catin,*
> *Nous volons au passage un plaisir clandestin*
> *Que nous pressons bien fort comme une vielle orange.*

> Like the poor lush who cannot satisfy,
> we try to force our sex with counterfeits,
> die drooling on the deliquescent tits,
> mouthing the rotten orange we suck dry.

Baudelaire could not have written "die drooling on the deli-
quescent tits," says Gunn; the line is closer to Allen Ginsberg.
The material of both quatrains is violent, but where Baudelaire
is able to comment on the experience with artistic control,
Lowell becomes helplessly immersed.

C. Chadwick's review of *Imitations* falls into the same camp
as Gunn's essay (*Essays in Criticism*, Summer 1963). Chadwick
says that these cannot be considered successful imitations, whatever worth they may have as original poems. Lowell is trying
to get the literal meaning, despite his insistence to the contrary,
but he fails to get the literal meaning as well as the tone; and
failure to grasp the former leads to failure to convey the latter.
Chadwick holds up the originals as absolute models. He suggests that Lowell doesn't know enough French to do Baudelaire,
Rimbaud, and Mallarmé justice. For example, the noise of a
hurricane in Baudelaire's "Le Cygne" refers to the rumble of
dustcarts, not the promise of rain. Lowell fails to realize that
Baudelaire was being metaphorical; he turns an image, intended
to evoke the dustiness of a Paris street, into an image of freshness: "a sprinkler spread a hurricane to lay the sediment" ("*la*

*voirie Pousse un sombre ouragan dan l'air silencieux"*). This method of ferreting out isolated lines and holding them up for ridicule makes Lowell seem the invariable amateur. Chadwick never balances them with examples of the finer moments in *Imitations*. But this is not Chadwick's worst fault; he refuses to consider the possibility that Lowell knows dustcarts from thunder, and that Lowell may wish to be as metaphorical as Baudelaire was.

The fact remains that the imitations were more complex than readings such as Chadwick's could appreciate. And while Lowell's deficiencies should not have been dismissed, neither should his self-imposed challenge have been underestimated. This was the stand taken by Robert Crick, who agreed with Chadwick that meaning and tone cannot be separate goals in translation (*Robert Lowell*, pp. 63–70). But Crick also argued that *Imitations* is "rarely dull" and that since Lowell had selected poets who are frequently translated, the originals would benefit from new versions. He said that, on the whole, Lowell had chosen poets who offer a "particular honesty of self-revelation," so that the volume extended into new fields of the "confessional impulse." By using another poet's work, Lowell was able to speak with greater directness than in his own poetry. This directness worked in some instances and not in others; it failed most with Leopardi and Baudelaire. Leopardi's nihilism and despair became too "highly-coloured" in Lowell's hands; the formal perfection of the Italian, especially its assonantal music, is hard to obtain in English.

Crick is even more disappointed with the Baudelaire renditions, but he adds that, historically, Baudelaire is at the juncture of traditional verse and the birth of modern poetry; this makes him extremely difficult to translate. His modern world-weariness is easily exaggerated by post-Freudian poets, while his traditional nobility, pity, and tenderness are forgotten. Crick says that Lowell fails to balance the two sensibilities, thereby sacrificing Baudelaire's sense of "firmly-maintained hope." Crick places Montale and Pasternak in the column of Lowell's successes. Lowell had said in his Introduction that Montale could be made "stronger in free verse," and Crick agrees. Pasternak works well because his conversational and prosaic strengths come naturally to Lowell. The "deeply-Russian, unallegorical and unromantic" view of nature is reproduced by Lowell with miraculous candor.

Crick's analysis is learned and objective. He shows only as much of his own erudition as is needed to compare the imitations with the originals. He also considers (albeit briefly) the poems as a sequence. Man's "senseless urge for butchery" is a recurring theme, dramatically expressed in images of pain, violence, and power. The first poem, "The Killing of Lykaon," sets the tone for all that follows. In this extract from the *Iliad*, Lowell depicts Achilles less as the Greek hero than as a "luster after blood." Crick is not entirely satisfied with the Homer and Sappho pieces. He would hold, in general, the earlier the original, the poorer the imitation. He also questions Lowell's omission of certain classical poets (Vergil, Ovid, Dante) and speculates that Lowell found them difficult to render in an "idiomatic voice." Ovid, especially, must have seemed "unrenderable" to Lowell. Like most of the critics, Crick devotes the bulk of his commentary to the twentieth-century imitations, which he prefers.

The mixed reception of *Imitations* was caused in some measure by the title of the book itself. Hayden Carruth was one critic to champion the volume, but he urged readers to skip Lowell's Introduction and to call the poems "translations," which is "what they are" (*Poetry*, January 1962). He was annoyed with the entire imitation debate and wished that the term *imitation* were completely forgotten. He blamed the terminology question on Pound, who had brought more attention to the term than it deserved. According to Carruth, Pound, a half-century earlier, had quarreled with the academicians and forced them to accept his radical compositions. At the time, he circumvented the issue by giving his translations such titles as *Homage to Sextus Propertius*. But, Carruth asked, aren't *all* translations, by definition, a form of homage? After dispensing with Lowell's title, Carruth selected his favorite "translations." They were all from the French, the language with which Lowell was "most at home," and in this group, the Baudelaires were the best. Carruth felt that even the deviations in meter and diction carried Lowell more toward Baudelaire than away from him. Carruth did not seem to realize his own inconsistency, for the very liberties he praised in Lowell's renditions were what qualified them as imitations. Apart from that, Carruth found the Montale pieces "tedious" because a certain flatness in the Italian gave Lowell little room for irony and elegance. He indirectly raised a critical question about the suitability of using different language sources in one text. Could Lowell use "one voice" through so many linguistic bases? But Carruth left the question unanswered.

Whatever the critics, or Lowell, meant by "imitation," there was general agreement that a convincing imitation could only come about when a poet has true sympathy with his original. But what was the basis for such sympathy? Crick implied that the distance of time between the original and the translation reduced sympathy; Carne-Ross believed that cultural similarities, irrespective of time gaps, cultivated sympathy; Belitt, Gunn, and Carruth said it existed only when the original poet's temperament resembled the translator's. Henry Gifford took a more conservative view of sympathy and the art of imitation (*Critical Quarterly*, Spring 1963). Chastising the modern poet's tendency toward self-centeredness, Gifford argued that literature—and civilization—must imitate to survive. Since the personal voice learns despair by repeating itself, it must reconstitute itself by going to the tradition; but the poet must listen attentively to the original, else he betrays both himself and the original. In Gifford's view, Lowell is a poor listener; his willfulness and failures of touch have resulted in "gross" renditions.

There are several critics, poets themselves, who disagree with Gifford. Self-centeredness can be a virtue in imitation, they claim. Reed Whittemore, for example, thinks it is important "to observe constant rhetoric and thematic resemblances between Mr. Lowell's Lowell verse" and his Villon, Baudelaire, Montale, or Rilke verse (*Kenyon Review*, Spring 1962). Whittemore aligns passages from *Lord Weary's Castle* with excerpts from *Imitations* and finds the same "voice" running through all. The same flat, staccato evocations of a scene appear in the following:

Roof-high, winds worrying winds
rake up the dust, clog the chimney ventilators,
drum through the bald distracted little squares,
where a few senile, straw-hatted horses wheeze
by the El Dorado of the rooming houses' windows in the sun.
                                        [From Montale]

I saw the sky descending, black and white,
Not blue, on Boston where the winters wore
The skulls to jack-o'-lanterns on the slates,
And Hunger's skin-and-bone retrievers tore
the chickadee and shrike.
                          [From *Lord Weary's Castle*]

Also, the passages from Baudelaire, Rilke, and Pasternak evince the same "preoccupation with lost souls" that one finds in the pieces from *Lord Weary's Castle*.

Finally, Whittemore observes that the vigor, life, and spirit Lowell finds in the world is born out of "involvement, immersion, blood." He is so impressed with *Imitations* that he predicts dozens of other poets will attempt their own conversions of "alien" literature, in imitation of Lowell. The prospect of that displeases Whittemore, who anticipates "seamy" results. In his view, *Imitations* is a superb book because Lowell is a superb poet.

When accolades are this easily conferred, it is generally because the critic feels that Lowell is a great poet *qua* poet. Lowell himself made the same point in a slightly different context: "Innumerable people for some reason want to be poets, and the only way they can be poets is by doing Virgil or Pasternak into English verse, and it's very bad, very dull poetry." He added that any translation must be a fine poem in its own right (Carne-Ross interview).

M. L. Rosenthal, who also took this position, exulted in *Imitations* (*Reporter*, December 21, 1961). This was no pedantic trot, he said; it was Lowell making extensions into his own brilliant effects and thoughts. Therefore, when it came to *Imitations*, the argument about "valid" translation was superfluous; a purist would always go back to the original anyway. The real importance of what Lowell was doing had to be understood in the light of modern poetic practice. Lowell had shown us how deeply rooted American poetry was in the French Symbolist tradition. Rosenthal noted that over a third of the selections are from Baudelaire and Rimbaud, and that Lowell had a common bond with them. In fact, his approach is less pedagogical than Pound's, less stylistically absorbing than Eliot's. In effect, Lowell is closer to the Symbolists in character and temperament than Pound or Eliot. Rosenthal's assessment of the non-French imitations was equally flattering. With Montale and Pasternak, Lowell shared "an ultimate heaviness of spirit that goes hand in hand with a dazzling keenness of response to sense impressions." Rosenthal was also eager to note that Lowell could express the gaiety of love (which critics seldom noticed), as in the following version of Pasternak:

Beneath a willow entwined with ivy,
we look for shelter from the bad weather;

one raincoat covers both our shoulders—
my fingers rustle like the wild vine around your breasts.

["Wild Vines"]

There was joy as well as grief in this volume, he argued. By
turning his attention to foreign poets, Lowell had temporarily
abandoned his "tremendous inwardness" and "agonized use of
his literal self." Lowell knew that he must somehow free himself from the solipsistic persona of *Life Studies*. To Rosenthal,
this proved Lowell's artistic integrity and courage. The prediction was that Lowell's unique undertaking could only expand
and strengthen his poetry. This was a refreshing approach; few
critics talked about how the translation process might change
Lowell's verse.

Among the critics interested in Lowell's temperamental affinity with his sources, Louis Simpson offered a unique point
of view (*Hudson Review*, Winter 1961/62). He felt that Lowell expended great imagination when he worked with a poet
whose temperament was far from his own (e.g., Leopardi). Lowell was prevented from falling into the excesses of identification; moreover, he worked best when translating passages that
did not lend themselves to shock or exaggeration. Thus Simpson preferred the Leopardi imitations to the Baudelaires. Baudelaire, with his "confessional air," encouraged Lowell's faults.
Like Crick, Simpson argued that Baudelaire was a touchstone
for evaluating translators. But while he granted that Lowell fell
short of Baudelaire, he found the Rimbauds "splendidly joy-
ous." What is more, Lowell had resolved in Rimbaud the "difficulties of sound and meaning." Simpson closed with a generous
tribute: *Imitations*, in its gentility and urbanity, had taught us
something about the "tact of poetry." In essence, he was com-
menting on the mood which pervaded the text. From mood, it
would have been one short step to a consideration of "voice,"
but Simpson did not advance in that direction.

It is interesting to speculate on the reception of *Imitations*
if it had not included Lowell's Introduction. His three-page defense seemed to trouble the critics more than the poems. Critics
felt obliged to address their remarks to Lowell's statement of
purpose. For example, William Cookson challenged Lowell's
suggestion that *Imitations* be read as a sequence (*Agenda*, Sep-
tember/October 1962). He noted the choice of poets and asked

if Lowell had made any attempt to trace a recognizable stylistic or thematic coherence among them. Cookson thought not.

Failing to find a sequential structure, Cookson followed the usual procedure and delved into the individual renditions. One could easily predict his response; without the unifying element of "sequence," the work was just a collection of hits and misses. Thus Homer was better done than Sappho, Villon was better done than Baudelaire, the first part of the volume was better done than the second, and so on. But Cookson was less interested in the excellence of individual selections than in "a more important matter": could Lowell have achieved the same effects with the poems by just working within the discipline of "correct translation"? Cookson believed Lowell could, and concluded that the whole imitation process was unnecessary. After all, Lowell had not created something that did not exist in the language before. Why not use the traditional method? In his free adaptations of Rilke, Montale, Pasternak, which were put into *vers libre*, Lowell proved himself a poor metrist. Cookson added that the only good *vers libre* translator was Pound, largely because he was a "musician." If Lowell had tried to find the equivalent of these poets' meters in English, rather than reducing them all to a standard loose rhythm, the results might have been better.

Were there any critics who found *Imitations* successful as a sequence? Yes, but they were few. Richard Fein was one such defender, and devoted a chapter of his volume *Robert Lowell* (pp. 72–92) to a discussion of this subject. He refused to ask of each poem "How close is it to the original?" Rather, he stressed that *Imitations* had no literary analogue; it was the finest example of Pound's pioneering translation theory: to render the "tale of the tribe" in modern temper. Fein also keenly noted that *Imitations* was an imitation of the themes in *Life Studies*, especially the third part, which is devoted to dead or dying writers who meant so much to Lowell. In *Imitations*, the following poems become the correlatives of his earlier pieces on Ford Madox Ford, Hart Crane, and George Santayana: "Villon's Epitaph," "Heine Dying in Paris," "At Gautier's Grave." This was just one example of how Lowell had linked the two volumes; the larger link was the confessional impulse which ran through both.

After establishing that Lowell's imitative habits were mostly diverted toward his earlier work, Fein discussed the volume as a sequence. There was an order and emphasis of major motifs which gave the work an "inevitability." The Homer extract introduces a military motif which continues in the poems of Hugo, Rimbaud, Valéry, Rilke, and Montale. From Homer's Achilles to Montale's Hitler, Lowell traces the "terrifying vision of the military hero in Western culture." Other reconstructions develop out of this military motif, and their sources may be found in Lowell's poetry. For example, the Mary symbolism of *Land of Unlikeness* is now replaced by Helen (in the Valéry poem "Hélène"), who begins her sonnet by claiming Mary's color: "I am the blue!" The gesture of a Marian supplication becomes a gesture of violence in Helen, who is "the inspiration of poets whose art means consciousness of war." Fein also notices that certain poems in *Lord Weary's Castle* are "reimitated" in this book; thus his earlier version of Rimbaud's "War" becomes "Evil" in *Imitations,* the thematic thrust of "The Soldier" (one of his pieces in *Lord Weary*) is repeated in his Homer extract on Lykaon, and Hugo's "Russia 1812," in Lowell's hands, sounds remarkably like his own "For the Union Dead."

While the war motif runs through *Imitations*, it is not the only unifying thread, says Fein. He classifies "the compassionate self" as a motif ancillary to the war poems. It is primarily represented by the Villon section of the volume. In these imitations, Lowell returns to his own religious poetry: "Villon's Prayer for His Mother" is a variation on his "A Prayer for My Grandfather to Our Lady" (*Lord Weary*). Fein, then, eschews the idea that Lowell chose poets for their temperamental affinity to him. He says that Lowell grasped originals, which permitted him to rewrite his standard themes. Unlike critics who fail to see a similarity between Lowell and Leopardi, Fein detects in both poets a mutual "theme of infinity." Thus the Leopardi imitations explore the mind flourishing within a "larger sense of nothing," or within an awareness of the self-annihilation that will end identity. This is carried to modern expression in the Montale poems, which seem to take place in a void. These Italian imitations return us to *Life Studies*, which is about the release man finds when he submits himself "to the given reality." At the same time, the themes of the compassionate self and infinity are intertwined with Lowell's keen consciousness of man's proclivity toward war. Each of these obsessions is intensified by the other.

When Fein turns to the Baudelaire imitations, which he considers the most significant in the volume, he finds Lowell mirroring Baudelaire's "voyaging out" theme. For example, "The Swan" ("Le Cygne") uses the city as a place of heroic revery and present despair, which is remarkably similar to Lowell's poems about the death of a city ("For the Union Dead"). Indeed, because Lowell is "one of our major poets of the city," Fein says that the Pasternak poems are the most puzzling in the collection. Lowell is not a nature poet. Why does he have nine imitations of Pasternak, a poet who saw nature as a "return to himself"? Attempting to justify Lowell's choice, Fein suggests that Pasternak offered an alternative to the death-oriented "longing for infinity." Pasternak, in other words, becomes Lowell's conscience, forcing him back to the "burdens of awareness." The interplay of these ideas adds fugal variations to an already thematic design. Finally, all the elements are brought together in Rilke's "Pigeons," a poem about going beyond one's territory and the risks involved. In this poem, flight becomes a metaphor for the artist's need to transcend his familiar boundaries; but in terms of the entire volume it becomes the imaginative embodiment of Lowell's concept of imitation. Thus, to Fein, *Imitations* triumphs as a sequence, a harmonic synthesis of tradition and the vision of a major poet.

Fein's chapter is a responsible addition to the scholarship, but its very resourcefulness proves how far the study of Lowell's imitation process has to go. Even Fein neglected to indicate that the poet Lowell imitates more than any other poet in *Imitations* is himself. For instance, while he ably discusses Lowell's version of "Pigeons," he overlooks the connection between this poem and Lowell's imitation of Elizabeth Bishop's "The Armadillo" in "Skunk Hour" (*Life Studies*). Lowell's parade of the skunks at the close of "Skunk Hour" is modeled after the flight of Bishop's armadillo during a fire. The skunks are not as pathetic or benign as her armadillo, which retreats "head down, tail down," but the instinctual drive to live is a core theme in both poems. In "Pigeons," which is dedicated to the famous Holocaust scholar Hannah Arendt, artistic survival becomes as crucial as physical survival. The "same old flights" cannot sustain the poet, who needs to throw his imagination "almost out of bounds." Thus there is a contiguity between "Skunk Hour" and "Pigeons" which adds dimension to both poems.

Those who have followed Lowell's work from its beginnings know that imitation was one of his most fruitful methods of composing. *Land of Unlikeness* (1944) contained loose paraphrases of early Christian poems. *Lord Weary's Castle* (1946) included phraseology taken directly from eighteenth-century Calvinist writings ("Mr. Edwards and the Spider") and from Thoreau's *Cape Cod* ("The Quaker Graveyard in Nantucket"). Even *Life Studies* (1959), a purportedly autobiographical volume, contains a poem which began as a translation of Catullus ("To Speak of Woe That Is in Marriage"). In later years he reworked his *Notebook*, which had its earlier version, as three volumes (*History, Dolphin, For Lizzie and Harriet*).

*Imitations*, then, was not an anomaly; it was simply a variation on a habitual process. It was Lowell European style. Admittedly, a few critics identified this trait in Lowell's writing, but they did so in random or desultory fashion. A revisionist approach to *Imitations* must address itself to certain questions: How does acknowledgment of this process change our artistic evaluation of the work? In his penchant for imitation, did Lowell's rationale succumb to rationalization? And doesn't every poet imitate himself and others to some degree? If so, does Lowell's technique constitute a major poetic? When critics confront these questions more categorically, *Imitations* will likely cease to have ancillary status in the canon. At present, it is shelved with *Old Glory*; indeed book-length studies, such as Axelrod's *Robert Lowell* (1978), completely pass it by.

There are other lacunae in the *Imitations* scholarship. Lowell stated in his Introduction that the work should be read as a sequence with "one voice running through many personalities, contrasts and repetitions." With the exception of Whittemore's brief words on the univocality in *all* Lowell's writing, voice in *Imitations* drew little notice. Critics talked about affinity of temperament (or its lack) between Lowell and his sources, but they fragmented the text by doing so. Besides, it would be impossible to discuss temperament in ancients like Hower, Sappho, or Der Wilde Alexander, an obscure thirteenth-century poet. Moreover, critics' discussion of "temperament" in modern poets is too impressionistic to be authoritative. They seldom distinguish between the temperament of the persona in Montale—or Baudelaire or Rimbaud—and that of the poet. Nor do they distinguish between the persona in *Imitations* and the temperament of Lowell himself. Perhaps there is no useful purpose in making such distinctions between a poet's temperament and that of his persona—if it is possible. But by questioning this critical approach we may learn more about Lowell's use of voice. The fact remains that the elegiac voice in his verse volumes is noticeably present in *Imitations*. Lines in the source poems which do not have a lamenting quality become passages of gloom in Lowell's versions. In the Sappho imitation, "Three Letters to Anaktoria," Lowell reconstructs fragments (all that remains of Sappho) so that the persona appears suicidal:

> A woman seldom finds what is best—
> no, never in this world,
> Anaktoria! Pray
> for his magnificence I once pined to share . . .
> to have lived is better than to live!

Even the titles Lowell gives the poems (when they are altered from the original or there is a fragment from a large work) suggest the dark side of life: "Black Spring," "The Ruined Garden," "The Old Lady's Lament for Her Youth." There is the same preoccupation with death and the past that one finds in Lowell's other verse:

> Oh quickly disappearing photograph
> in my more slowly disappearing hand!
> [From Rilke's
> "The Cadet Picture of My Father"]

While critics were not absorbed with Lowell's "voice," neither were they interested in the French Symbolist tradition in *Imitations*. Lowell was ambivalent about the Symbolist structure of *The Waste Land*; he wanted to go beyond its formal elegance and learned allusions, which he imitated in his own early volumes. He considered *Life Studies* his release from Eliot's grip, but his Baudelaire renditions in *Imitations* demonstrate that his release was far from complete, or even fully desired. His version of Baudelaire's "Le Voyage" is not only dedicated to Eliot, it contains stanzas so reminiscent of "Prufrock" and *The Waste Land* that they seem parodic:

> The worn-out sponge, who scuffles through our slums
> sees whisky, paradise and liberty
> wherever oil-lamps shine in furnished rooms—
> we see Blue Grottoes, Caesar and Capri.

But what is even more important about the "French connection" is the compatibility of theme in Baudelaire's and Rimbaud's poems with that in *Lord Weary* or *Life Studies*.

Of course, a few studies dealt with the consistency of tone in Lowell's work as a whole. Geoffrey Hill made tentative efforts to correlate all of Lowell's writing as elegiac (*Essays in Criticism*, 13, 1963). He noted that, beginning with *Land of Unlikeness*, Lowell borrowed motifs and images from the Puritan tradition; some overtly, as in "Mr. Edwards and the Spider," others covertly, their sources less easy to determine. Hill said that *Imitations* was a triumph of tone because it represented the apex of Lowell's technique. He was a master at merging his voice with that of other poets. Hill was impatient with critics who called Lowell an amateur translator. On the contrary, Lowell could enjoy the "ultimate in selfhood" and remain engaged in a "full-time and self-abnegating task." His moral, aesthetic, and psychological energies coalesced in the imitative process. Hill spoke of *Imitations* as a sequence, but only in passing. What he observed about it as a sequence was its deathward direction. He said that the dominant subject was "force," the force of destiny (exemplified in "The Killing of Lykaon") and the force of gravity ("Pigeons"); in essence, the two were the same. A dark and disturbing mood hovers over *Imitations*, concludes Hill.

Jerome Mazzaro would agree. His brief coverage, in *The Poetic Themes of Robert Lowell* (pp. 120–22), takes the "past forms of state" to be the sequential thread which runs through the poems. The work resembles Ovid's *Metamorphosis* as a world view of moral decay. From one period to another, men are destroyed by "hate, anger, love, war, hope, dreams, nature, and time." Man's will is powerless against the process, says Mazzaro, and Lowell selects isolated moments in history to illustrate this. The unifying principle in *Imitations* is not so much the collage of poets throughout history as the tonal unanimity of their themes. Mazzaro agrees with theorists like Steiner and Friar, that all literary forms are transmutations of a cultural repository. That the poems are translations is as insignificant as the fact that Ovid's tales are not his own. Ovid's fables, which are mainly translations, are a series of contrasts and repetitions which include many personalities. This is exactly what Lowell gives us in *Imitations*.

Thus war and man's dark history seem to be the modifying strands for Lowell's sequential structure—at least this was the conclusion of those who searched for evidence of a sequence. But Lowell made no references to war or moral decay in his Introduction; he merely talked about his technique and the importance of making his authors "ring right." The critics extrapolated from Lowell's verse, which is concerned with the struggle of the self in the flux of history, and charted this theme as a sequence in *Imitations*. Their readings were generally convincing, especially Fein, Hill, and Mazzaro; and Daniel Hoffman's essay should be added to the list (*Hollins Critic*, February 1967).

Putting *Imitations* on a par with *The Waste Land* and *The Cantos*, which also present a world view of moral decay, Hoffman argues that Lowell's use of different sources is analogous to the collage units of Eliot's and Pound's works. All three are organized as a modern synthesis of Western literature. *Imitations* is no gathering of "garbled" mistranslations, any more than are Eliot's or Pound's masterpieces. Hoffman then argues that Lowell selected poets whose themes related to a passage or quest. He did not take poets of great passion, erotic or otherwise, but those whose knowledge of love, war, and death freed them from illusions of innocence. The hero in his poems understands his subjection to history and his own corruption. Lowell, then, has deviated little from the vision in his own verse. The Paris of Baudelaire's "The Swan" strongly suggests the Boston of Lowell's "For the Union Dead." Hoffman takes his analysis just one step further than other critics by noting that the most potent poems are from poets who specialize in "self-disgust." Villon, Baudelaire, and Rimbaud are his central examples. Because of Lowell's deep attachment to such writers, *Imitations* has none of the past's "humane balance." There is no room for the comic side of life in this book. By going one step further than other critics, perhaps Hoffman goes too far. His generalization cannot be correctly applied to the Pasternak imitations, which take up a substantial portion of the volume. Although the nine Pasternak selections do not brim with gaiety, they capture the enduring mellowness of life. The seasons' changes are viewed nostalgically, but always with an expectation of what will follow:

> The much-hugged rag-doll is oozing cotton from her
>     ruined figure.
> Unforgetting September cannot hide its peroxide
>     curls of leaf.
> Isn't it time to board up the summer house?
> The carpenter gavel pounds for new and naked
>         roof-ribs.                                       ["September"]

Indeed, allusions to the seasons are often made throughout
the volume. Stephen Yenser, whose analysis of *Imitations* as a
sequence is even more ambitious than Fein's, sees the return to
spring as the linking motif (*Circle to Circle*, pp. 165–99). His
direct reversal of other critics' commentary rests on the notion
that *Imitations* ends in optimism and hope. Fein and Mazzaro
are wrong, says Yenser; this is not a pessimistic view of history.
The order of the poems thematically parallels the cycle of the
seasons. About halfway through the collection the mood swings
upward and stays up. The Rilke imitations, especially, instruct
Lowell that, by "laboring in earnest," one can abolish despair
and accommodate faith, hope, and creativity to his life. The
volume has a plot, which is demonstrably of the epic genre. As
such, it includes events and settings which one would expect to
encounter in a heroic poem. The first poem, "The Killing of
Lykaon," with its invocation to the muse, constitutes a micro-
cosm of the whole. Homer is Lowell's guiding spirit for his
"ghost of a plot." Yenser divides the book into seven sections;
the choice of poets for each section relates more to the stage
of a psychic journey than to the particular poet. From Homer
to Rimbaud, the vision is one of spiritual descent. With Mallarmé's "At Gautier's Grave" ("Toast Fenebre"), Lowell discovers the means to combat nihilism. Finally, with Valéry's
"Hélène," he finds a way to bring the past to life, thereby
accepting the transience of all mortal things.

There is something too pat about Yenser's reading, I feel, but
it offers a good balance to the somber analyses that dominate
the scholarship. Its greater virtue, however, rests with the fact
that Lowell's volume is apprehended as a unit—calculatedly
forethought and designed. Yenser does a careful exegesis of
certain diction equivalents and shows how Lowell keeps re-
turning to words or images to punctuate his cyclical motif.
Thus the first line in the first poem is "Sing for me, Muse, the
mania of Achilles." Midway through the volume the word
"mania" appears in the Rimbaud imitation "Les poètes des sept
ans." However, the line in which Lowell incorporates it ("Ver-
tige écroulements, déroutes et pitié") is semantically unrelated
to this word ("dizziness, mania, revulsions, pity"). Yenser suspects that there is a connection between this line and the volume's initial line. He then turns to the last line of Rilke's "Die
Tauben," which ends the book. Here again, Lowell has transfigured the original "miraculously multiplied by its mania to

return." This Rilke piece, discussed as "Pigeons" by other critics, returns the reader to the first poem. The circle is complete.
Is the elusive use of one word at three points in the book enough
evidence for Yenser's "circle" theory? Perhaps. (Surely critics
like Cookson would find it far fetched.) Lowell never indicated
that "mania" is a pivotal word; but, as was remarked earlier, he
said nothing about thematic elements in *Imitations*.

When we review the reception of *Imitations*, it is obvious
that its appeal was far from universal. The volume appeared
at the beginning of a turbulent decade, yet it lacked the kind
of political topicality that drew readers. Pound's name was invoked when the imitation question arose, but Pound was declining in popularity in these years. His alleged fascist leanings
made his former reputation for urbanity and cosmopolitanism
seem anti-American. Did the translation "game" draw poets
who lacked the democratic spirit? To a degree, critics associated Lowell with Pound, which may have diminished the success of *Imitations*. Between 1948 and 1950 Lowell had made
news as a participant in the Bollingen Prize controversy over
Pound. As one of twelve judges who debated honoring a "turncoat," Lowell defended Pound on purely artistic grounds.
Years later, in the *Paris Review* interview, he expressed no re-
grets over his stand. It was simply a matter of voting for the
best book of the year. According to Lowell, Pound represented
no threat to democracy: "He had no political effect whatso-
ever and was quite eccentric and impractical." But the two
names remained linked. To say this is not to search for a
nemesis; Lowell's book must stand on its merit. However, cultural attitudes determine the popularity of translation. Other
languages suggest other countries, and in times of national crisis
we tend to alienate ourselves from other countries—and their
literatures.

Before concluding this survey of *Imitations'* reception, we
should mention several essays which restrict their analyses to
a single poet in the volume. They are all negative, and consequently beg the question about judging *Imitations* purely as
translation. In "Rilke in Translation," Roger Hecht carefully
analyzed the six Rilke selections (*Sewanee Review*, 71, 1963)
but was far from laudatory. He said that Lowell made a "curious hodge-podge" of all six poems, but that "Pigeons" was the
worst. This was a curious reversal; "Pigeons" was one of the

other critics' favorites. Hecht found its metaphor so dislocated
that the finished product was not sufficiently Rilke, not sufficiently Lowell, but a mixture of both and spoiled:

> Back in the dovecote, there's another bird,
> by all odds the most beautiful,
> one that never flew out, and can know nothing of
>     gentleness. . . .
> Still, only by suffering the rat-race in the arena
> can the heart learn to beat.

Hecht concluded that when a poet tries to "sieve" other
poets' sources through his sensibility, the results can be disastrous. Robin Fulton made the same point about Lowell's
Ungaretti imitations (*Agenda*, 6, 1968). He agreed with Lowell's assertion in the Introduction that "tone" is everything—
that, in fact, it is the only course open to the verse translator.
But how does one define tone? Fulton chose to define it in terms
of the connotations of words. Ungaretti's style was "economi-
cal, elliptic, resonant." Why did Lowell try to "unclot" it
(Lowell's term)? Fulton did a line-by-line reading of "Tu Ti
Spezzasti," which Lowell entitled "You Knocked Yourself Out."
The very title was inappropriate: it sounded comical; it was
too closely associated with boxing; it was irrelevant to Ungaretti's poem. A child is killed in the original poem, but the circumstances surrounding the death are not specified. Thus the
references to crushing stones re-create a sense of implacable
destiny, not the destructiveness of nature:

> *I molti, immani, sparsi, grigi sassi*
> *Frementi ancora alle segrete fionde*
> *Di originarie fiamme soffocate*
> *Od ai terrori di fiumane vergini*
> *Ruinanti in implaceabili carezza:*
> *—Sopra l'abbaglio della sabbia rigidi*
> *In un vuoto orizzonte, non rammenti?*

> Those unnumbered, ruthless, random stones,
> tense, vibrating still, as if slung
> by the smothered abysmal fire;
> the terror of those Amazon cataracts cascading
> down miles to the chaos of implacable embraces;
> the rock's lockjaw above the sand's
> detonating dazzle—do you remember?

What are we to understand by the "rock's lockjaw," asks Fulton. And isn't "detonating" a once-only event, "a sudden perfective occurrence, not continuous like the 'dazzle' "? Lowell's diction fails to establish the urgency of the narrator's tone because he loads Ungaretti's elemental nature imagery with extraneous associations.

Marjorie Perloff devoted an entire chapter to Lowell's Rimbaud imitations in her *Poetic Art of Robert Lowell*. She, like Hecht and Fulton, felt that Lowell did justice neither to his original nor to himself. But she made a far more substantial case about the aesthetic value of the finished product. Recalling Simon's extravagant attack on *Imitations*, she claimed that to speak of Lowell's method as an immoral act was irrelevant. She selected one poem, "Nostalgia" (Rimbaud's "Memoire"), and explained the bases for its failure. The poem is about childhood and is a fuzzy cross between the visionary mode of the original and Lowell's naturally more concrete imagination, as represented in the childhood poems of *Life Studies*. Lowell cannot capture the "purposely vague, dreamlike, hallucinatory" texture of "Memoire." His compromise is to psychologize Rimbaud's imagery. Restricted by Rimbaud's tone, Lowell cannot "break loose enough to find his own," says Perloff. Lowell also turns Rimbaud's lyric utterance into sequential narrative. Exclamatory noun phrases, such as *"L'assaut au soleil des blancheurs des corps de femme,"* become declarative sentences: "His eyes were blinded by white walls." The reader expects something to happen in the Lowell version, but the story does not take shape. Perloff attributes this confusion to Lowell's inability to reproduce Rimbaud's fragmentary vision. In the original, "the memory calls up successive images, often seemingly disconnected." Lowell, with his "historical" rather than "visionary" imagination, cannot give the piece a satisfying tone. His translation is at once too free and not free enough.

There the case rests. Perhaps the word "mania," which is repeated in the volume, is its most important word. Lowell's overreaching task must have been executed in a sort of madness. The creative frenzy may, at times, have sacrificed elegant workmanship for haphazardness.

## References

Axelrod, Steven Gould
  1978. *Robert Lowell: Life and Art*. Princeton: Princeton Univ. Pr.
Belitt, Ben
  1966/67. "*Imitations*: Translation as Personal Mode." *Salmagundi*
  no. 4, pp. 44–56; reprinted in *Robert Lowell: A Portrait of the
  Artist in His Time*, ed. Michael London and Robert Boyers. New
  York: David Lewis, 1970.
Bentley, Eric
  1946. *Playwright as Thinker*. New York: Harcourt Brace Jovano-
  vich.
  1961. (editor) *The Classic Theatre, Volume 4: Six French Plays*.
  Garden City, N.Y.: Doubleday.
Bernstein, Michael André
  1980. *The Tale of the Tribe: Ezra Pound and the Modern Verse
  Epic*. Princeton and London: Princeton Univ. Pr.
Billington, Michael
  1967. "Mr. Lowell on T. S. Eliot and the Theatre." *London Times*
  Mar. 8, p. 10; reprinted in *Profile of Robert Lowell*, ed. Jerome
  Mazzaro. Columbus: Merrill, 1971.
Bloom, Harold
  1973. *The Anxiety of Influence: A Theory of Poetry*. Oxford:
  Oxford Univ. Pr.
Brown, Merle E.
  1980. *Double Lyric: Divisiveness and Communal Creativity in Re-
  cent English Poetry*. New York: Columbia Univ. Pr.
Brustein, Robert
  1964. "We Are Two Cultural Nations." *New Republic* Nov. 21,
  pp. 25–30; reprinted in his *Seasons of Discontent: Dramatic
  Opinions*. New York: Simon & Schuster, 1965.
  1965. "Introduction." In *The Old Glory*, pp. xi–xiv. New York:
  Farrar, Straus & Giroux; also London: Faber, 1966.
Carne-Ross, D. S.
  1968. "Conversation with Robert Lowell." *Delos* no. 1, pp. 165–75;
  reprinted in *Profile of Robert Lowell*, ed. Jerome Mazzaro.
  Columbus: Merrill, 1971.
  1968. "The Two Voices of Translation." In *Robert Lowell: A
  Collection of Critical Essays*, pp. 152–70. Englewood Cliffs, N.J.:
  Prentice-Hall.
Carruth, Hayden
  1962. "Toward, Not Away From . . ." *Poetry* Apr., pp. 43–47.
Chadwick, C.
  1963. "Meaning and Tone." *Essays in Criticism* Oct., pp. 432–35;
  reprinted in *Critics on Robert Lowell*, ed. Jonathan Price. Coral
  Gables, Fla.: Univ. of Miami Pr., 1972.

Cookson, William
1962. Review of *Imitations*. *Agenda* Sept./Oct., pp. 21–24.
Crick, Robert
1974. *Robert Lowell*. New York: Harper & Row.
Fein, Richard
1970. *Robert Lowell*. New York: Twayne.
Fergusson, Francis
1949. *The Idea of a Theatre*. Princeton: Princeton Univ. Pr.
Friar, Kimon
1971. "On Translation." *Comparative Literature Studies* Sept., pp. 197–213.
Fulton, Robert
1968. "Lowell and Ungaretti." *Agenda* Autumn–Winter, pp. 118–23.
Gifford, Henry
1963. Review of *Imitations*. *Critical Quarterly* Spring, pp. 94–95.
Gilman, Richard
1968. "Life Offers No Neat Conclusions." *New York Times* May 5, sec. 2, pp. 1, 5; reprinted in *Profile of Robert Lowell*, ed. Jerome Mazzaro. Columbus: Merrill, 1971.
Gunn, Thom
1962. "Imitations and Originals." *Yale Review* Spring, pp. 480–89 [480–82].
Hamilton, Ian
1971. "A Conversation with Robert Lowell." *Review* Summer, pp. 10–29.
Hecht, Roger
1963. "Rilke in Translation." *Sewanee Review* Summer, pp. 513–22 [516].
Hill, Geoffrey
1963. "Robert Lowell: 'Contrasts and Repetitions.'" *Essays in Criticism* Apr., pp. 188–97; reprinted in *Critics on Robert Lowell*, ed. Jonathan Price. Coral Gables. Fla.: Univ. of Miami Pr., 1972.
Hochman, Baruch
1967. "Lowell's *The Old Glory*." *Tulane Drama Review* Summer, pp. 127–38.
Hoffman, Daniel G.
1967. "Robert Lowell's *Near the Ocean*: The Greatness and Horror of Empire," *Hollins Critic* Feb., pp. 1–16; reprinted in *The Sounder Few*, ed. R. H. W. Dillard, George Garrett, John Rees Moore. Athens: Univ. of Georgia Pr., 1971.
Holton, Milne
1979. "Maule's Curse and My-Lai: Robert Lowell's Endecott." In *Proceedings of a Symposium on American Literature*, pp. 175–86. Poznan, Poland: Uniwersytet im Adama Mickiewicza w Poznan in Seria Filologia Anzielska.

Howard, Richard
1965. "A Movement Outward." *New Leader* Dec. 6, pp. 26–28.
Ilson, Robert
1966/67. "*Benito Cereno* from Melville to Lowell." *Salmagundi* no. 4, pp. 78–86; reprinted in *Robert Lowell: A Collection of Critical Essays*, ed. Thomas Parkinson. Englewood Cliffs, N.J.: Prentice-Hall, 1968.
Knauf, David
1975. "Notes on Mystery, Suspense and Complicity: Lowell's Theatricalization of Melville's *Benito Cereno*." *Educational Theatre Journal* Mar., pp. 40–55.
Laing, Alexander
1966. "The Knack of Doing Double Duty." *Nation* Jan. 24, pp. 103–5.
Lewis, Peter
1968. "Robert Lowell as Dramatist: 'The Old Glory.' " *Stand* no. 4, pp. 59–74.
Lowell, Robert
1955. "The Muses Won't Help Twice." *Kenyon Review* Spring, pp. 317–24.
1961. "Introduction." In *Imitations*, pp. xi–xiii. New York: Farrar, Straus & Cudahy; also London: Faber, 1962 and 1971; also New York: Noonday, 1962.
1968. "Letters to the Editor." *Hudson Review* Summer, p. 248.
Mazzaro, Jerome
1965. *The Poetic Themes of Robert Lowell*. Ann Arbor: Univ. of Michigan Pr.
1970. "Robert Lowell's *The Old Glory*: Cycle and Epicycle." *Western Humanities Review* Autumn, pp. 347–58.
1972. "National and Individual Psycho-History in Robert Lowell's 'Endecott and the Red Cross.' " *University of Windsor Review* Fall, pp. 99–113.
Merwin, W. S.
1971. "On Being Awarded the Pulitzer Prize." *New York Review of Books* June 3, p. 41.
Miller, Jonathan
1965. "Director's Note." In *The Old Glory*, pp. xv–xix. New York: Farrar, Straus & Giroux; also London: Faber, 1966.
Moon, Samuel
1966. "Master as Servant." *Poetry* June, pp. 189–90.
*Newsweek*
1976. "New Glory." *Newsweek* May 3, pp. 83–84.
Perloff, Marjorie
1973. *The Poetic Art of Robert Lowell*. New York: Cornell Univ. Pr.
Porter, Peter
1966. "Lowell's Kinsmen." *Listener* Sept. 8, p. 359.

Prior, Moody
1947. *The Language of Tragedy*. New York: Columbia Univ. Pr.
Ralph, George
1970. "History and Prophecy in *Benito Cereno*." *Educational Theatre Journal* May, pp. 155–60.
Rosenthal, M. L.
1961. "Found in Translation." *Reporter* Dec. 21, pp. 36–38.
1965. "The New Lowell." *Spectator* Nov. 26, pp. 699, 702.
1966. "Blood and Plunder." *Spectator* Sept. 30, p. 418.
Schickel, Richard
1966. "New York's Best New Theatre Group?" *Harper's* Nov., pp. 92–100.
Seidel, Frederick
1961. "Interview with Robert Lowell." *Paris Review* Winter–Spring, pp. 56–95; reprinted in *Robert Lowell: A Portrait of the Artist in His Time*, ed. Michael London and Robert Boyers. New York: David Lewis, 1970; in *Robert Lowell: A Collection of Critical Essays*, ed. Thomas Parkinson. Englewood Cliffs, N.J.: Prentice-Hall, 1968; in *Writers at Work, Second Series*, ed. Malcolm Cowley. New York: Viking, 1963; in *Modern Poets on Modern Poetry*, ed. James Scully. London: Collins, 1966.
Shaw, Peter
1976. "*The Old Glory* Reconsidered." *Commentary* June, pp. 64–67.
Simon, John
1966. "Strange Devices on the Banner." *Book Week* Feb. 20, pp. 4, 12; reprinted in *Robert Lowell: A Portrait of the Artist in His Time*, ed. Michael London and Robert Boyers. New York: David Lewis, 1970; in *Critics on Robert Lowell*, ed. Jonathan Price. Coral Gables, Fla.: Univ. of Miami Pr., 1972; in his *Singularities*. New York: Random House, 1975.
1967/68. "Abuse of Privilege: Lowell as Translator." *Hudson Review* Winter, pp. 543–62; reprinted in *Robert Lowell: A Portrait of the Artist in His Time*, ed. Michael London and Robert Boyers. New York: David Lewis, 1970.
1968. "Letters to the Editor." *Hudson Review* Summer, p. 248.
Simpson, Louis
1961–62. "Matters of Tact." *Hudson Review* Winter, pp. 614–17.
Snodgrass, W. D.
1964. "In Praise of Robert Lowell." *New York Review of Books* Dec. 3, pp. 8, 10.
Steiner, George
1975. *After Babel: Aspects of Language and Translation*. New York: Oxford Univ. Pr.
Sterne, Richard Clark
1970. "Puritans at Merry Mount: Variations on a Theme." *American Quarterly* Winter, pp. 846–58.

Stone, Albert E.
  1972. "A New Version of American Innocence: Robert Lowell's *Benito Cereno.*" *New England Quarterly* Dec., pp. 467–83.
Taubman, Howard
  1964. "Theatre: Lowell, Poet as Playwright." *New York Times* Nov. 2, p. 62.
Tomlinson, Charles
  1967. Review of *The Old Glory. Critical Quarterly* Spring, pp. 90–91.
Weales, Gerald
  1968. "Robert Lowell as Dramatist." *Shenandoah* Autumn, pp. 3–28; reprinted in his *Jumping Off Place.* London: Macmillan, 1969.
Whittemore, Reed
  1962. "Packing Up For Devil's Island." *Kenyon Review* Spring, pp. 372–77 [372–74].
Yenser, Stephen
  1975. *Circle to Circle: The Poetry of Robert Lowell.* Berkeley: Univ. of California Pr.

# CHAPTER 3

# *The Puritan Burden*

On April 12, 1639 Percival Lowle, a citizen of Bristol, sailed from London on the *Jonathan* for Boston. After a nine-week voyage, Lowle and his family reached the New World. For three centuries the descendants of this aristocratic family would figure prominently in the pages of American political and cultural history (their story is documented in Ferris Greenslet's *The Lowells and Their Seven Worlds*, 1946). Percival and his sons spelled their surname in diverse ways: Lowle, Louell, Lowel, Lowell; and in the early eighteenth century the spelling was standardized. The heritage associated with this name became an obsession to Robert Lowell and, in turn, to his critics. The critics, largely unfamiliar with the particulars of this family tree, limited their "name dropping" to just two of its members, James Russell and Amy. Even less was said about Lowell's mother's ancestors (the Winslows), one of whom had arrived on the *Mayflower*. But there was, and remains, much general reference in the scholarship to Robert's Bay Colony ancestry. He became known as the "Puritan" poet. In that framework his tone and imagery could be conveniently explicated. What more solemn tribute could critics confer upon a poet of such high seriousness? The designation seemed appropriate.

To a degree, Lowell himself reinforced the Puritan label. He projected an image of the conscience-stricken, morally earnest citizen. His poems, especially the early ones, abounded in religious allusion, and when he wrote about other poets he emphasized the religious thought in their verse: "My own feeling is that union with God is somewhere in sight in all poetry, though it is usually rudimentary and misunderstood" (*Sewanee Review*, Summer 1943). In effect, he facilitated a formulaic reading of his canon as fraught with vestiges of Puritanism. But there the easy classification ends. Lowell's religious and ethical beliefs were contradictory and constantly changing. It took an attentive critical intelligence to chart these beliefs and define their function in the poetry. It also took some understanding of the Puritan tradition in American literature. Perhaps the most amusing portrait of Lowell as "Puritan" is in Norman Mailer's *The Armies of the Night* (1968), wherein Mailer described Lowell at a political rally, about to deliver a speech attacking the government's policy on Viet Nam. Mailer is a bit self-indulgent, but he mirrors standard impressions about Puritanism in the American character:

> As he sits on the floor with his long arms clasped mournfully about his long Yankee legs, "I am here," says his expression, "but I do not pretend I like what I see." The hollows in his cheeks give a hint of the hanging judge. Lowell is of good weight, not too heavy, not too light, but the hollows speak of the great Puritan gloom in which the country was founded—man was simply not good enough for God [p. 43].

Was this the true Lowell or was he posturing for the public? What matters when we decipher the criticism is that this was Lowell as the critics saw him.

Before we advance the discourse pertinent to this chapter, it would be helpful to comment on the acknowledged Puritan influences in American literature. Literary history reveals a pattern of thought in American writers, not—as might be thought —of materialism, but of self-questioning and tragic awareness. Instead of the American Dream, heuristically enunciated in the Founding Fathers' documents, we have the American Nightmare, vividly depicted by Melville, Hawthorne, Poe, and others. The nightmare version retains the residue of Calvinist teachings: the doctrine of election, the notion of evil unleashed in the world. As Harry Levin noted in *The Power of Blackness* (1958), the Puritans were fond of invoking "the primal darkness, the void that God shaped by creating light and dividing night from day" (p. 29). The prospect of doom was never far from their thoughts. To the critics, Lowell's sensibility was compatible with this strain of thought, for he bore the Puritan Burden. It was present in his themes, prosody, imagery, even his choices of genre. The last of these became the most challenging category for analysis; critics had constantly to adjust to Lowell's new modes.

The seventeenth-century transplantation of Puritans from Old to New England, in theocratic and economic terms, was a perilous undertaking. In a wilderness atmosphere, men of class (or at least, burgess) distinction had to prove their mettle; potential capitalists, they were intent on acquiring ample land-holdings. Endow such men with religious zeal, a sense of righteousness, and the vestiges of stern Calvinism, and the results were predictable. The tyrannies charged to the New England leaders are explained by ambition reinforced with rigorous discipline. The church-state established in the Massachusetts Bay Colony would in time substitute an economic for a theocratic basis of authority, which succeeded largely because of its rationale of "divine sanction." Lowell was fond of injecting Bay Colony history into his poems.

Accounts of Puritan literary practices, in Kenneth Murdock's *Literature and Theology in Colonial New England* (1949), Perry Miller's *The New England Mind* (1953), or Sacvan Bercovitch's *The Puritan Origins of the American Self* (1975), suggest analogues for discussing Lowell's poetry. The Bay Colony Puritan, rather than hating literature, was quite devoted to it:

> He read some classic poets, he read Spenser, he read the French poet DuBartas as translated into English by Joshua Sylvester; he dipped into other "holy poetry"—including that of the Anglican, George Herbert—and rejoiced in what he read [Murdock, p. 141].

But this early New Englander felt that he should compose poetry only as a means of serving God and developing his virtue. Hoping that he might be one of a small number of souls chosen for salvation, the Puritan poet searched for evidence about his fate, and lived with the desperate tension of learning that fate. He also believed that, as he made history—whether in war with the Indians or in building his mercantile empire—evidence of God's pleasure or displeasure would present itself. His interpretation of justice was therefore more personal than communal, and his secularism was tempered by the certainty that all he said and did revealed the divine plan. The literary modes which best appropriated his nature were the diary (or diary-like) poem and the elegy. In each, the dialogue with a spiritual presence could be undertaken. The poet could justify his composition as a form of meditation rather than as an egocentric pastime. Because he believed that the Word was transmitted through signs, he filled his verse with elaborate codes and complex meters. His poetry was often intense and obscure.

One could easily object that these formal characteristics

apply to a large block of modern poetry besides Lowell's (Roethke's, Jarrell's, Berryman's or, earlier, Hart Crane's), an objection which makes the "Lowell as Puritan" rubric less exclusive. And indeed, modern poetry *has* been extensively analyzed in this context, for example, in Roy Harvey Pearce's *The Continuity of American Poetry* (1961) and Hyatt Waggoner's *American Poets: From the Puritans to the Present* (1968). But Lowell parts company with other modernists by consciously invoking Puritan history for thematic purposes. He was not consistent, however, in his appraisal of that history; he vacillated between praise and censure.

A qualification must be made when we link Lowell's work with the Puritan tradition. That tradition has become as familiar as a myth (Mailer, for example, fully expected his readers to grasp the meaning of his Lowell description), but when critics discuss the dark strain of Puritanism in Lowell's poetry, they are really recalling the Separatist, or Plymouth Pilgrim, part of the background. The Plymouth Pilgrims, as we know, established the first New England colony. Initially exiled in Holland, their temporary haven from England, they were more fanatic than the Bay Colony settlers who came directly from England in the later part of the century. Because the Plymouth Colony leaders lacked the experience to develop a primitive terrain, the community of inhabitants acquired a somber, gloomy outlook. But the large and prosperous Bay Colony, centered at Boston, boasted a different breed of settlers. Their pragmatic, commonsensical approach to living reconciled the ways of God with the values of the marketplace. Their cultural history was less solemn. Thus when a critic like Waggoner makes the following observation and attributes it to Puritanism, he is telling just part of the story:

> The sense of evil, of the darkness of experience, of the alien unknown and uncontrolled in which man is immersed, has been expressed for us, in our times and our terms, by most of the finest poets [*American Poets*, p. 4].

What interests us is whether Lowell had internalized this side of the tradition. There is little information in Lowell's interviews or essays about his familiarity with Puritan history or religion; in fact, his comments about religion refer mostly to Catholicism. Whatever he felt or understood about Puritanism surfaced in the poetry, which, for familial or psychological reasons, reflected the dark vision.

The assessment of Lowell as a "Puritan" poet is filled with ambiguity, largely because of vague terminology. It is hard to know what aspect of Puritanism a critic may have in mind: the religious, aesthetic, or cultural. Nevertheless, it is accurate to say that nearly all of the scholarship considers faith a crucial factor in Lowell's thought; and when faith is mentioned, there is usually a reference to Puritanism. The scholarship divides into two units: that which deals with Lowell's religious ideas in a general way and that which interprets these ideas as they surface in specific texts. The latter is best presented chronologically. In both units there is a critical consensus: whatever religious affiliation Lowell assumed, it brought him more grief than joy. A few months after his death, Robert Fitzgerald published a eulogistic essay in the *New Republic* (October 1, 1977). A long-time friend of Lowell, he had often witnessed the poet's spiritual crises:

> After his first grave manic attack in '49, after his first hospitalization, all concerned grew wary on his behalf, as indeed he did himself, of excitements religious, political or poetic. He no longer could be a Catholic because, as he told me, it set him on fire.

Fitzgerald, elaborating on this subject at a memorial service at Harvard University (March 2, 1978), commented on Lowell's emotional fragility. His religious imagery alone, he said, revealed a mind "close to madness." For example, the description of Mary with "scorched blue thunderbreasts of love" ("A Prayer for My Grandfather to Our Lady," *Lord Weary*) proved that he had gone beyond even "the extremes of the baroque." Problems of faith undermined his psychic health.

In his overview of Puritanism, Lowell was close to William Carlos Williams. Puritanism was a "malaise," said Williams, and its tradition had stifled America's greater potential. In *In the American Grain* (1925) he indicted the Puritans: "They are the bane, not the staff. Their religious zeal, mistaken for a thrust up toward the sun, was a stroke in, in—not toward germination but toward the confinements of a tomb" (p. 66). Williams, in turn, was echoing the views of other writers during the twenties. Dreiser, H. L. Mencken, and Van Wyck Brooks believed that Puritan values, tools to advocate gentility, were destroying the literature. For example, Mencken blamed the prolixity of bad American fiction on Puritanism: "the delusion that a work of art is primarily a moral document, that its purpose is to make men better Christians and more docile cannon-fodder"

(*The Idea of an American Novel*, p. 120). This climate of disfavor in the early twentieth century had moderated by the time Lowell became engaged in composition; but it had not entirely disappeared. No doubt, it exacerbated his efforts to reconcile his familial conflicts. After converting to Catholicism in 1940, Lowell thought his personal battle with Puritanism had been won, but the critics were not so confident. For three decades they focused on his dilemma, deeming it alternately beneficial and injurious to his creativity. Marius Bewley called it a "head-on collision between the Catholic tradition and an Apocalyptic Protestant sensibility" (*The Complex Fate*, 1952).

While most observers were content to accept Lowell's changing religious beliefs as he announced them in his verse (e.g., Catholic in *Lord Weary's Castle*, agnostic in *Life Studies*), Herbert Leibowitz insisted that Catholicism had no place in the poetic vision (*Salmagundi*, 1966/67). He said that Lowell wrote *only* as a Puritan, in the company of such "kindred souls and fellow sufferers" as Hawthorne and Jonathan Edwards. He had assumed the Puritans' obsession with death and imitated their penchant for elegiac poetry: "Lowell excels at funerary art, at epitaph-making." Lowell's dalliance with Catholicism was not really congenial to him; even in the poems which use Catholic terminology, the imagination is operant in other areas. Although the early poems focus on the mercy of Jesus or the Virgin Mary, "Lowell's poetic imagination is empirical, concrete, not transcendental; the pain rather than the resolution convinces the reader. The hands are the hands of Jesus but the voice is the voice of John Calvin."

In effect, Leibowitz's assumption is a bit simplistic. It panders to a fallacy about the Puritan mythos; English poetry, written by Puritans, is hardly sexually repressed (*pace* Milton!). Leibowitz comes closer to historical accuracy when he treats Lowell's condemnation of American abuse of power, which, as the poet saw it, was fostered by the Puritans' fanatic will and ambition, by their religious and commercial zeal, and by an individuality carried to the extremes of unreason and arrogance. Thus Leibowitz's analogy between Ahab's horrific mission in *Moby-Dick* and Lowell's derision of violence in "Quaker Graveyard in Nantucket" is well taken. Both Melville and Lowell are preoccupied with their demonic heritage. Leibowitz, then, understands Lowell's Puritanism in moral rather than spiritual terms.

It is easier to separate moral from spiritual values than to separate spiritual from theological values. The Puritans' moral judgments can be measured by their actions, some of which Lowell pointedly condemned, but the distinction between Lowell's spiritual and theological convictions is harder to draw. In *American Poets*, Waggoner made an effort to separate the two. Arguing that Roethke and Lowell are the two modern poets who most (and best) renew the mystical tradition in frankly personal lyrics, Waggoner reviews their specific influences. Roethke's spiritualism stems from the Emerson, Thoreau, and Whitman side of the tradition, while "no major poet writing today is further from the spirit of Emerson and Whitman" than Lowell. But Waggoner is careful not to drop Lowell into the Puritan slot. Lowell is too cognizant of the decline of Puritanism into Unitarianism and of Unitarianism into secularistic accommodation. Waggoner says that Lowell's Catholic conversion was a dramatic acting out of the awareness that Puritanism had long been bankrupt. He was not exchanging one set of theological beliefs for another; rather, he was like T. S. Eliot—another convert—accepting historical reality. His new faith did not condemn Protestanism. In "Waking Early Sunday Morning," written as late as 1967, the Protestant ethic gives ground for hope, and Lowell recalls his family's Bible hymns with a note of nostalgia:

> Yet they gave darkness their control,
> And left a loophole for the soul.

To Waggoner, Lowell's constant objective was to have "faith," defined by the critic as a kind of humanistic hope rather than as religious conviction. Waggoner's most convincing example is in the poems that offer tribute to four writers in *Life Studies* "who got along without [religious] faith." Ford Madox Ford, George Santayana, Delmore Schwartz, Hart Crane—these were the modern writers Lowell wished to emulate. They clung to "spars" on their modern spiritual journeys "though faithless." Although Lowell never stated what those spars were, his very imprecision proved that his system (philosophical, ethical, theological) was a broad, amorphous form of humanism. This is Waggoner's contention and it is persuasive, though, at the time, most critics were not content to take Waggoner's position. Humanism, a term both too imprecise and philosophical for the then-dominant New Critical school, implied an "intentional fallacy" that such critics could not justify in the verse itself. Critics who felt most comfortable approaching literature

from the point of view of intellectual history found religious
themes of special interest. They took up a kind of existential
Christianity.

## General Religious Commentary

Naturally, Lowell's poetry had an attraction for critics whose
primary interest was religious; their responses were, expectedly,
parochial. They searched for affirmation in his verse, and were
disappointed when it failed to appear. Will Jumpers' essay
"Whom Seek Ye?: A Note on Robert Lowell's Poetry," which
appeared in the *Hudson Review* (Spring 1956), exemplified this
sort of reaction. Jumpers was oblivious to Lowell's strategy of
the mask or use of persona; if the speaker in *Lord Weary's
Castle* or *Mills of the Kavanaughs* exhibited despair, then Lowell had failed his readers. Thus "Lowell is a serious, intelligent,
gifted and powerful—albeit sometimes misguided—poet. In his
denial of Calvinistic total depravity, predestinarianism, and
faith without works, he does not reach the affirmation of
Aristotelian-Thomistic reason, freedom and individual responsibility." But the blandishments were equally absurd. For example, Mother Anita Von Wellsheim was delighted that Lowell
used "Marian" imagery in the same volumes Jumpers had condemned (*Renascence*, Summer 1958). She found the allusions
to Mary an indication of Lowell's new-found affirmation. Both
Jumpers and Von Wellsheim felt that Puritanism had been de-
leterious to Lowell's poetic vision; however, they regarded
only its thematic priorities and were oblivious to its aesthetic
properties. This was usually the case with general religious
commentary.

Vincent Buckley offered a more penetrating approach to the
topic in *Poetry and the Sacred* (1968), which concentrates on
the poets in English and American literature who wrote mystical verse. The pantheon includes Blake, Hopkins, Wordsworth,
and (among the moderns) Eliot. Buckley found Lowell a problematic example, but included him nonetheless. He selected
Lowell's most uniformly acknowledged "religious" poems and
argued that their 'iconography" gives little more than passing
significance or a "flimsy frame" to what is really an unrelated
"psychic conflict." By Buckley's criterion, the common denominator in religious poets is a self-yielding; that is, the poet
gives in, if not to God, to some mystic power of his perceptions

and to his perceptions' capacity to utter what may be termed
"the transcendent." Oddly enough, Lowell often showed the
same tendency:

> In certain of the early poems we find the remarkable blend of self-
> yielding to individual perceptions with an over-assertive pattern-
> ing of experience which apparently serves to point up the arbitrar-
> iness and violence of those perceptions. In other words, Lowell's
> struggle is often with his own spontaneity [p. 72].

Then, selecting one of Lowell's more "Christian" poems,
"Quaker Graveyard," Buckley described it as "religion as myth
and myth as ejaculation." Begging the question, he found
"something wrong" with it as religious poetry; the result of the
procedure in most of this poem, and in many other well-known
poems from the early books, is that "confusion *becomes* his
meaning." The cries to God are really desperate appeals for
release from the horrors and boredoms which Lowell has created himself. Buckley's position derives from orthodoxy; he
expects Christian poems to espouse specific dogma. He also believes that religious poets keep their imaginations outside of
history, a restriction that Lowell was incapable of observing.
Buckley concludes that Lowell had a nervous persistence that
there *be* belief. Lowell's faith was that he *needed* faith.

Leslie Fielder would disagree. Central to his essay "The Believing Poet and the Infidel Reader" (*New Leader*, 1947) is the
conviction that Lowell is rooted in dogma and sees the world
"in terms of original sin and grace." Indeed, Lowell is regarded
as a singular anomaly: a believer sending out messages to a
world of agnostic readers. His popularity originates from this
particular ability: "He presents singly, once and for all, the
believer's uncongenial doctrine in a manner available only to
a group (one has, I think, to say clique) that has not made his
leap to belief." Concerning the poetry, Fielder says that its
aesthetic properties are baroque, or Catholic. Fielder finds little
of the Puritan influence in Lowell's writing. He says that the
baroque style, which has been the traditional expression of
Catholic faith in a "broken environment," has a disjunct center.
It makes a "shrill assertion that complication is the essence of
pattern" and that human will is the "spring of creation." These
qualities, along with a profusion of "free detail," are found in
Lowell's verse.

Fiedler's essay is unique and brilliant. It does not insist on

labeling Lowell's religious ideas. Lowell is neither Puritan nor
Catholic; he is a poet whose *style* is Catholic. Of course, Fiedler
wrote this essay during Lowell's early period, when the verse
was at its most flamboyant. If we applied his argument to Lowell's late verse, would we conclude that his plain style resembled
the hymn-like meters of certain Puritan poets? Most likely not.
None of the scholarship on his late verse discussed Puritan
prosodic modes. This may be due to several factors: that Puritan American verse, being both plain and intricate, was too
varied to serve as paradigm; that critics searched for Puritanism
in Lowell's themes but not in his formal structures. Fiedler's
thesis, consequently, had no rejoinders.

Jerome Mazzaro, a constant and ardent follower of Lowell,
wrote several studies on the poet's spiritual vision. In 1965 he
published his most extensive (though not his best) treatment of
the subject, *The Poetic Themes of Robert Lowell*, in which
only the "mystical" elements in Lowell's work are considered.
There is little or no stylistic analysis. He begins by explaining the artistic failure of *Land of Unlikeness:* Lowell had a
superficial grasp of Protestant theology. The poet dogmati-
cally believes in apocalypse, but "he cannot imagine the events
in terms which are vivid enough for good epical poetry." To
Mazzaro, he seems merely a young man in a library, using the
Bible as a source book for poetry. But he says that Lowell is
absorbed in the New England mercantile system, which evolved
to the present-day national economic structure. Lowell is also
absorbed in the Puritans' massacres of the Indians and colonists
with different religious doctrines. Mazzaro says that Lowell
renders the Puritans as "Faust-Cain prototypes" whose obsession
was power. In addition to the Faust-Cain figure, who dominates
the volume, the "Christian Pilgrim" figure, based on Bunyan's
*Pilgrim's Progress* and representing the modern American's conscience, makes an appearance. Pilgrim's realization of his lost
condition produces fears, doubts, and discouragement. Mazzaro
identifies Pilgrim with Lowell, but asserts that while Lowell
uses Protestant morality to enforce his theme, he is moving in
the direction of Catholicism as a condition for salvation. In a
world of fading Christianity, Rome is still the Eternal City.
This conviction becomes the foundation for *Lord Weary's
Castle.*

Mazzaro, who is knowledgeable on Catholic types of mysticism, finds the work after *Unlikeness* suffused with them, but his
argument has one shortcoming: neither Lowell's recorded state-

ments about religion nor the poems themselves allude to such
types of mysticism. The thesis is interesting nonetheless; it sets
up a hypothetical pilgrimage and persuasively charts the poems
along the route. Thus Lowell's quest parallels the quest described in St. Bonaventure's *Meditations on the Life of Christ.*
As Mazzaro sees this quest:

> There are in the active life two parts. The first part is that in
> which a soul exercises herself chiefly in correcting herself. The
> second part of the active life is spent in doing good actively to
> the neighbour. . . . Between these two parts of the active life is
> the contemplative life! The active life is possible, then, only after
> the "union with God" of the contemplative life. To achieve it,
> Lowell must first seek an escape theology [p. 34].

In *Lord Weary*, which fully uses a Catholic framework, the
"notional assent to vision has been replaced by a closer approxi-
mation to mystical vision." Although Mazzaro does not equate
the excellence of specific volumes with the triumph of a mystical vision, he correlates this mysticism with poetic inspiration.
He offers provocative premises. For instance, in "Mills of the
Kavanaughs," a poem more weighted with plot and character
than the typical Lowell poem, the transition is "an anthropo-
centric rather than a theocentric one." Although Mazzaro insists that the poem reflects the "contemplative tradition of St.
Bernard and St. Bonaventure," he designates the poem's "real
tragic vision" as a removal of the deity from drama (since the
poem is decidedly dramatic), at which point "ritual becomes
motivated human action."

But Mazzaro's thesis can lead into dangerous waters, which
occurs when he discusses the later volumes, when Lowell's
"mystical" voice had been silenced. *For the Union Dead* is assessed as follows:

> His work still "grits" instead of resolves, especially as it no longer
> contains both a view of corruption and a pattern of salvation; it
> has only the corruption [p. 135].

Mazzaro retreats from scholarly observations and makes moral
judgment: *Union Dead* shows Lowell's lapse into self-pity and
a loss of grace. This is a disappointing conclusion to a stimulating study.

In truth, Mazzaro never appears convinced of Lowell's mysticism. The knowledge of Lowell's conversion to Catholicism

seems to provide Mazzaro with a *donnée*, or procrustean bed.
Indeed, one year after *The Poetic Themes* was in print, Mazzaro
published an essay which substituted a humanistic approach for
the former religious approach (*Salmagundi*, Winter 1966). This
essay more organically integrates Lowell's ideas with his experiments in genres, and those in turn with the poets he imitated.
Mazzaro enlarges his argument about religion to include historical determinism and links Lowell's dramatic monologues
with Browning's: "The protagonists of both Lowell and Browning poems assume the poses of a Calvinistic God working his
wrath and caprice upon the helpless world." Drawing from the
"Cal" persona in Lowell's poems (signifying Calvin and Caligula) and Browning's "Caliban at Setebos," Mazzaro says that
both poets attempt to exact a faith in what has become an evolutionary universe: "man's origins are nature and chance, unhampered by Christian charity." Man's alternative, in Browning's and Lowell's systems, is "to extend his dominion over
nature and chance so as to insure continued survival." Mazzaro
says, however, that in Lowell's personal poems in *Life Studies*,
"absurdism is offered."

In all, Mazzaro insists on a Christian teleology for Lowell's
work. The sentimentality and absurdism of the later volumes
are the result of failed Christian experience. Lowell's only resort is to advocate Christian charity as the basis for his new
sociopolitics; but the major point is that Mazzaro does not consider Lowell a Puritan poet. He puts Lowell in an older spiritual
and literary context than seventeenth-century New England.
He ascribes more eclecticism and a wider background to Lowell, and this commendable breadth of vision more reliably accounts for Lowell's changing conceptual patterns. Ultimately,
Mazzaro is not misguided into forcing a doctrinal exegesis of
the poems, but it is paradoxical that the *one* book written on
Lowell's religious themes is immersed in Catholic doctrine.

Lowell's comments on his religious symbolism are instructive:
"I won't say the Catholicism gave me subject matter, but it gave
me some kind of form, and I could begin a poem and built [*sic*]
it to a climax" (*Paris Review* interview, 1961). It helped his
stylistic "arrangements," he said. When asked about his spiritual
condition while he was composing *Lord Weary*, he replied:

> Then there is a question whether my poems are religious, or
> whether they just use religious imagery. I haven't really any
> idea. . . . I'm sure the symbols and the Catholic framework didn't

make the early poems religious experiences. Yet I don't feel my experience changed very much. It seems to me it's clearer to me now than it was then, but it's very much the same sort of thing that went into the religious poems—the same sort of struggle, light and darkness, the flux of experience [pp. 75–76].

The last sentence of this quotation is the most telling. Lowell was not being evasive; he was honestly rejecting the idea of doctrinal commitment. This is the view Hugh Staples takes in *Robert Lowell* (1962). He says that Lowell's rebellion is not against his Puritan legacy, but a "total" one. His "war is not with a time, a place, the fabric of a specific society or a particular political system, but against the pressures of reality itself." His satirical analysis of the deficiencies of early New England rulers is countered by an admiration for their achievements, and a knowledge that they, too, were rebels. Lowell is really modifying tradition "within its own framework." His outcries against order are themselves ordered by rigid formalism. Staples here joins with Fiedler, who saw the effect of religion on Lowell as a baroque style, in transcending the notion of doctrinal content to a perception of the effects of doctrine on the dynamics of the verse. This fits well with the poet's own statements, at least in the 1961 *Paris Review* interview.

Several critics who emphasized the Puritan background concluded that its impact on Lowell was restricted to furnishing particular historical figures, the heroic types Lowell needed to emulate. Richard Fein takes one of these to be Jonathan Edwards (*Robert Lowell*, 1970). New England is important to Lowell's poetry and Boston is Lowell's "Babel," but rising above all of this region's corruption is Edwards, whose "full belief is linked to death." According to Fein, Lowell respects and fears Edwards' absolute capacity for belief. To Lowell, full belief results in the inability to stand life; man's capacity to tolerate the fierce contradiction fascinates him. Edwards makes no compromises; his vision is so intense that it becomes a force for survival. Thus Fein believes that Lowell was attracted to the irony which explains Edwards' greatness. Unfortunately, Fein does not extend this premise about religious contradictions to Lowell's Catholic figures, thus leaving unexplored the influence of Lowell's conversion on his poetry. If Fein had made the extension, he would have realized that Lowell shows no such admiration for Pope Pius XII in "Beyond the Alps" (*Life Studies*). Indeed, "Mother Marie Therese" (*Mills of the Kavanaughs*) is the only Catholic persona Lowell presents in a flattering way; and she is characterized in pagan splendor as one devoted to politics and hunting.

Another critic who considers Jonathan Edwards Lowell's chief influence in Puritan theology is Patrick Cosgrave (*The Public Poetry of Robert Lowell*, 1972). Cosgrave argues that, in the early volumes, only the poems on Edwards ("Mr. Edwards and the Spider," "After the Surprising Conversions") establish a "continuously harmonious relationship between personality, forms, resources, doctrine, and insights." Here Lowell is able to probe the mystery in the relationship between God and man. In "Mr. Edwards and the Spider," which is based on Edwards' writings, the "real and unvarnished content of Lowell's theology" is presented:

> The gulf between the majesty of God and the insignificance of man is too great to be understood, or, in any significant way, acted upon. It can, however, be illustrated by comparing man to a spider. This illustration, however, conceals as much as it reveals. For the nature of man and the nature of the spider are quite different, particularly in the way in which they understand death [p. 67].

Cosgrave says that Lowell's doctrines are "narrow" and that he uses Edwards' "Predestinarian" theology because his own is limited. But it is *Cosgrave* who is limited. Lowell took Edwards' essay "The Habits of Spiders" (*Of Insects*) and transformed it into a profound religious-philosophical lyric. The following excerpt from stanza III aptly demonstrates this:

> A very little thing, a little worm,
> Or hourglass-blazoned spider, it is said,
> Can kill a tiger. Will the dead
> Hold up his mirror and affirm
> To the four winds the smell
> And flash of his authority? It's well
> If God who holds you to the pit of hell,
> Much as one holds a spider, will destroy,
> Baffle and dissipate your soul.

Cosgrave does, however, offer several thoughtful observations about Lowell's spiritual concepts. He says that it is difficult to establish where Lowell drew the line between evil in human nature and the evil manifested in New England history. Although Lowell never questions the deeply evil tendency in man, he never clearly explains the "basic nature and effect of the central Puritan impulse." One could quibble with Cosgrave—that Lowell had no responsibility to do so, in the poems or elsewhere—but his insight explains why the early poems are difficult to interpret.

Glauco Cambon's treatment of Lowell and Puritanism proves how broad the category can be. In *The Inclusive Flame: Studies in American Poetry* (1963), a thesis-ordered book, Puritanism is understood as a "frontier" phenomenon rather than as a religious one. In Cambon's view, the American writer is shaped by the geographic and cultural spaces he feels must be conquered; the "horizon of unknown possibilities" dictates his experimental, prophetic approach to language. This pervasive frontier mentality fosters a demonic drive in all American writers. In Lowell's case, the constant need to push toward the edge becomes a flight from the "deprivations" of America. The extremism of his quarrel with Puritanism is manifested at "a declamatory pitch" that would prove dangerous to a lesser imagination. Lowell's tense and complex relation to the past is a futile quarrel, since the past is unchangeable. His Puritan ancestry explains his conversion to Catholicism: just as the New Englanders had to secede from Europe, so Lowell's secession from his secessionist forebears continues their attitude. This action is unrelated to any motivating ideology. Cambon says that Rome becomes Lowell's Walden, and when Rome no longer holds its ideological significance, a new way to rebel must be found. Lowell's moral tension and his proclivity toward apocalyptic statement, then, have nothing to do with religious searching. They are part of the cultural syndrome. In short, Cambon believes that the Puritans' legacy to Lowell was the "fever" always to go further. His argument becomes most palpable when he examines Lowell's genre experiments.

When we consider the response that Lowell's religious themes have elicited, it is a long leap from the Christian existential attitudes of the fifties to the more austere Heideggerian concerns of the seventies' critics. From this school of the seventies, the most brilliant survey of Lowell's religious concepts is Charles Altieri's "Robert Lowell and the Difficulties of Escaping Modernism," a chapter in his *Enlarging the Temple: New Directions in American Poetry during the 1960s* (1979). Altieri finds few theological bases for the poetry, but he does not rule out the presence of a Christian order, which includes small-scale Puritanism. Granting Lowell an extremely cultivated sensibility, he says that Lowell integrates secular echoes, from Freud's theory of *thanatos* to Hannah Arendt's notion of public and private evil, with Calvinist ideas of doom and evil. The incompatibility of the secular and spiritual produces the tension and tragic wisdom in Lowell's poetry, an incompatibility which has not surfaced in the younger, less religiously committed poets who are writing today. Lowell's is the last eloquent expression of this sensibility, says Altieri. His importance derives from the integrity with which he dramatized this sensibility through a new poetic. The early poetry is imbued with the "incarnational" metaphor, the basis for the irony which defines the poles of tension in great poetry. Altieri explains the incarnational metaphor as a device to reconcile particulars with universals in poetry:

> Incarnation provides a doctrinal basis by which an essentially symbolist poetic can assert the value of the mind's orders while insisting that universals are not mere fictions but contain the actual structure and meaning of particular experiences.

A poet who employs this metaphoric mode has a moral vision, for the opposition of the universal and the particular is ascribed, in some tentative way, to the polarity of flesh and spirit. Unfortunately, Altieri does not offer examples of this practice in the early volumes. He merely indicates that it helped Lowell "reach a middle ground which is the interrelationship of objects as experienced by men." As such, it is "humanist," a term Altieri is not afraid to use. Thus, for Altieri, the dense, obscure symbolic structures of *Unlikeness* and *Lord Weary* are not Puritan in origin; they are Lowell's meeting point for the subjective and objective poles of his experience.

Altieri says that the leap from the incarnational circle to the realistic, "domestic context" of *Life Studies* is a philosophical one. Lowell's conversion to Catholicism and his subsequent apostasy created a void he was compelled to fill. He filled it with "self-consciousness," the "only imaginative force and locus of materials one can employ to achieve some basis for value." *Life Studies* was the text through which he attempted to resolve his spiritual, artistic, and psychological crises. After *Life Studies*, the intensity and anguish subsided. In *Near the Ocean* the "self-pity" changed to "cosmic pity." With the transition "from God to the landscape," Lowell was freed from the constraints of myth and other generic structures which now seemed escapist. From *Notebook* on, he used the novel as poetic model, since the realism of a prose mode allowed him "freedom of possibility." Altieri finds the later, more prosaic style the vehicle for Lowell's "freedom of tragic vision."

Not only does Altieri deemphasize the Puritan legacy; he believes that Lowell finds in his ancestry the symbol of failed authority. Jonathan Edwards—or Pope Pius, for that matter—did not inspire him. Altieri notably departs from other critics here. Lowell's brand of morality, in the poetry at least, is too unique to be pigeon-holed as Puritan, Catholic, or otherwise. In effect, Altieri discovers in Lowell the "imposing egotism" which makes him a truly modern poet. If Lowell is trapped, tragic, elegiac, it is his present world and not his heritage that makes him so.

## Religious Commentary on Specific Texts

When Allen Tate wrote the Introduction to *Land of Unlikeness* (1944), he called it a "consciously Catholic work." He meant that Lowell wrote it to reflect a distinct tradition in literature, more British than American. But the poems were drawn from the history of New England ("Children of Light," "The Park Street Cemetery") and Europe ("Napoleon Crosses the Beresina"); they also dealt with World War II (e.g., "Christmas Eve in the Time of War," "Scenes from the Historic Comedy," "Leviathan"). Even the Catholic poems are not decidedly doctrinal (e.g., "On the Eve of the Feast of the Immaculate Conception, 1942"). They adduce such subjects as warfare, family relations, the secularism of Boston's Beacon Hill; but the title, which is from St. Bernard's writings, and refers to souls living in a land alienated from the mind of God, suggested that this was a Catholic tome. And that was how it was initially received. Only later did critics (like Staples and Ehrenpreis) point out how much Puritanism it contained. But, given the initial responses to its religious elements, it took Randall Jarrell to understand that Lowell had rendered a sociohistorical depiction of Catholicism (*Partisan Review*, Winter 1945). Lowell had presented a frightening view of the Catholic world and creed, replete with a "violent company of martyrs and leaders." The church was an awesome wielder of political and economic power throughout the centuries. Jarrell traced the stylistic sources for the volume to a Puritan (Milton) as well as to a Catholic (Hopkins). His attribution implied that Lowell was still using models, having not yet found his own poetic voice. He did not correlate the models' doctrines with the contents of *Unlikeness*.

Other critics looked less deeply at Lowell's assessment of Catholicism. They talked about its richness of religious rhetoric (C. F. Flint in *Virginia Quarterly Review*, Spring 1945; D. Devlin in *Sewanee Review*, Summer 1945). Others, like Conrad Aiken (*New Republic*, October 23, 1944) and Arthur Mizener (*Accent*, Winter 1945), found Lowell's Catholic framework an intellectual limitation. To use Catholic thematic material was old fashioned, naive. Mizener even called it "a vehicle for hysteria." None of these critics realized that the Catholic imagery was a vehicle for other areas, not a thematic source in itself. John Frederick Nims, in a coupling which shows how Lowell was perceived at the time, reviewed *Unlikeness* with Thomas Merton's *Thirty Poems* in an essay entitled "Two Catholic Poets" (*Poetry*, 65, 1944–45). Nims was displeased with *Unlikeness*, which weighted religious themes with political ones. He said that this gave the poems too much "diversity of material." Genuine religious poetry is rare and difficult to write; and Merton had done a better job than Lowell. Nims confined his commentary on the imagery (which he called "figures") to one observation: in certain poems a single figure overwhelmed the total effect of the poem, and its emphasis detracted from its artistry. He concluded that the figures were not "organic," an insight that later critics more fully expounded.

Some of the obscurity in the religious readings of Lowell's early volumes came from critics' failure to define the proper "religious" relation a poet bears to God in his poetry, a failure Lowell had noted himself in his *Sewanee* essay (see above). Even Buckley's *Sacred and the Profane* skirted this problem. Clarification, however, has been offered by Louis Martz, who said that a poet who is fundamentally Christian tends to draw distinctions between nature and supernature; he also draws distinctions between himself (the "I" in the poem) and nature (*The Poetry of Meditation*, 1962). Donne and Eliot, who belong to this category of religious poets, are direct in their petitions to God. They think in terms of the sacred and the profane. They are unlike the poet of romantic mysticism (Whitman, Stevens, or Roethke, for example), who breaks down the differences between subject and object and senses a oneness with nature and God. This latter species of religious poet identifies the "I" with surrounding objects. In American literature, this represents a resurgence, or continuum, of the transcendental sensibility. Catholicism fits into the former category. Lowell used the formal features of the former category: a cerebral language of conceit and paradox, as opposed to the natural language of ecstasy used by the tradition of romantic mysticism. However, once this distinction is made, a hard line cannot always be drawn. Wallace Stevens, for example, seems to bridge both sides. In Lowell's case, even after his break with Catholicism he continued, in his poetry, a sharp separation of God from world. Unlike Roethke or Stevens, he did not see divinity in nature.

Since definitive studies of Puritan theology and literature had not appeared till the forties—Murdock's *Literature and Theology* set the precedent—*Unlikeness* did not benefit from the critical distinctions just suggested. Lowell's language of conceit and paradox fit perfectly the New Critical standards, which held Metaphysical poetry in high esteem. By this curious twist, Lowell was compared with Donne and Herbert, but R. P. Blackmur contended that Lowell lacked true mysticism (*Language and Gesture*, 1945). Lowell's violent and fractious imagery in this early volume indicated "mere fanaticism of spirit and of form." The verse was a therapeutic outlet, a verbal thrashing out of Lowell's conflicts about leaving his familial religion for Catholicism. His "faith compels him to be fractiously vindictive, and in dealing with faith his experience of men compels him to be nearly blasphemous." Had critics paid attention to an essay Lowell published the same year that *Unlikeness* appeared (*Kenyon Review*, Autumn), they would have been apprised of his devotion to Hopkins in those years. The essay celebrated Hopkins' "sanctity" and its manifestation in his stunning meters. More importantly, critics overlooked Lowell's complex attitude about the Puritans in *Unlikeness*. "Children of Light" told of crimes against the Indians in King Philip's War:

> Our Fathers wrung their bread from stocks and stones
> And fenced their gardens with the Redman's bones

while "The Park Street Cemetery" contrasts the bright ideals of the Puritans with decadent present-day Boston, "Where the Irish hold the Golden Dome." The "Irish" in this line represent the heavily Catholic population in Boston. Hence the indictments cross denominational lines.

Later assessments were more conscious of these complexities.

In "The Age of Lowell," Irvin Ehrenpreis credited the Puritan
heritage with the thematic problems of *Unlikeness*: "Lowell
saw in the ideals and motives of his ancestors the same contradictions, the same denial of a Christ they professed to worship,
that made his own world a land of unlikeness" (*American
Poetry*, 1965). Ehrenpreis found the volume's erratic rhythms
and blasphemous images "arbitrary." But in those years it was
not public information that Lowell's religious turmoil was taking its toll on his creativity. This might have illuminated, if it
did not excuse, his "fractious" style.

In 1970 Mazzaro delivered a more informed analysis of *Unlikeness* (*Modern American Poetry: Essays in Criticism*), cor-
relating its ideas with the content of the books Lowell was
reading at the time. In 1941–42 Lowell had worked as a reader
at a Catholic publishing house, Sheed & Ward, and among his
reading assignments were Christopher Dawson's *Religion and
the Modern State* (1935) and *Progress and Religion* (1938), and
T. S. Eliot's *The Idea of a Christian Society* (1939). A topic
commonly addressed in these books was the failed vision of
American millennialism. Dawson and Eliot attributed the per-
version of American aspiration toward evolutionary perfection
to Puritanism, which had substituted materialism for a reign of
humanism on earth. At the same time, they maintained that
radical Puritanism, far from representing the antithesis of
Roman Catholicism, shared that tradition of medieval Catholicism which conjoined church and state.

According to Mazzaro, Lowell viewed the Puritan intention
to restore Godly virtues to government as a transposition of
Catholic principles. Mazzaro considers *Unlikeness* a "shrill"
apocalyptic statement on the failure of both religions. Although
he makes only tenuous correlations between Eliot's and Dawson's studies and specific poems in *Unlikeness*, there is a fundamental soundness in his argument that Lowell found more similarity than dissimilarity between Catholicism and Puritanism.
Finally, Mazzaro notes that in 1943, one year before *Unlikeness*
appeared, Lowell had resisted going into military service, and
that his written statement of that decision echoed in ethical
terms what Eliot and Dawson had propounded in historical
terms.

When *Lord Weary's Castle* made its appearance in 1946,
Lowell had incorporated some of the *Unlikeness* poems into the
text. He discarded those poems which had, in his words, "a
messy violence." Archetypal seasonal patterns prevail in *Cas-*

*tle*: the promise of spring becomes a search for redemption in poems like "The First Sunday in Lent." The book's title refers to a ballad story on the theme of man's ingratitude and the rejection of Christ's teachings. The strictly religious poems have the aura of public pronouncement; the devastation of the war had been the inevitable outcome of man's fall from grace. The allegorical character of *Castle* was a carryover from the Puritan practice of interpreting historical events as prophecy. In *Puritan Influence in American Literature* (1979), Emory Elliot suggested that the obsession with the relationship between sacred and temporal history was the Puritans' legacy to American literature. It persists in writers as diverse as Twain, James, Melville, Faulkner, and even such seeming anti-Puritans as Fitzgerald, Mailer, and Hemingway. History had a special cosmic significance:

> The relationships . . . between the individual and God constituted public as well as private issues. If the individual fell, the community might follow him into apostasy and destruction. . . . The pressure of this divinely imposed errand, which crushed the spirit of some individuals, might finally crumble the emerging society, as changing fortunes would cause the people to shift in mood from exuberant self-assurance to self-castigating guilt. [p. xiv].

*Castle* contains this system of thought. Lowell saw World War II as a fulfillment of prophecy and, like the Puritan, searched for evidence of personal guilt in this global catastrophe. Yet this spirit of anguish was expressed in a Catholic framework. Few critics at the time cogently handled this combination of disparate ideas in the volume. Peter Viereck recognized, at least, that Lowell's imagery had transmuted event into allegory; he was moving in the right direction (*Atlantic*, July 1947), but Viereck was more concerned that the poems revealed a deeply troubled mind. He predicted that if Lowell resolved his religious crises, he would become one of America's major poets. In the meantime, *Castle* suffered from "crammed and blazing metaphors," which were overwhelming for such short poems. The gist of other reviews was that Lowell's faith caused him great suffering; his tough rhythms were his device for grappling with his misery. He was compared to Christ. An essay in *Renascence* (Fall 1949) placed him in the company of Dante and Claudel; his central experience embodied the "Christ-Form." Journals with a predominantly Catholic—or at least Christian—editorial policy were wild with enthusiasm. *Com-*

*monweal* (December 27, 1946) hailed his importance as a Catholic. *Christian Century* (December 4, 1945) and *Catholic World* (January 1947) were pleased that a modern poet reminded men that they possess a conscience.

As time passed, and with the aid of Staples' extensive glossary (in *Robert Lowell*), critics fretted less over the obscure passages in *Castle*. This left them freer to plot the difficult passages in Lowell's mythical world, or cosmography. They became more cognizant of the volume's Puritan elements. Thomas Vogler said that *Castle* is an exemplum of the "dissolution of American Puritan ideals." He linked the mythic echoes in *Castle* with the Vergilian myth of melancholy: the *Aeneid* was an exemplum of the loss of early Roman heroic stature (*Iowa Review*, Summer 1971). Robert Crick said that the characters in *Castle* either personified or were victims of some form of corruption (*Robert Lowell*, 1974), but he felt that Lowell was more convincing when examining the "endemic corruption of Puritan stock" than when examining present-day corruption. His argument was in direct opposition to Altieri's (*Enlarging the Temple*)—but this debate should be examined in the chapter on Lowell as historian.

Later readings of *Castle* tended to relate Puritanism to Lowell's familial problems rather than to his spiritual ones. M. L. Rosenthal's discussion of the poem "Between the Porch and the Altar" is a biographical interpretation, despite the fictive nature of the persona: "He [Lowell] is sick with the burden of his mother and of the crushing family traditions and 'New England Conscience' associated with her" (*Robert Lowell: A Portrait of the Artist in His Time*, 1970). *Castle* is now regarded as a testimony of Lowell's strong sense of psychic and religious exile. During its composition, Lowell was on the brink of collapse, and shortly after its completion he underwent his first confinement in a mental hospital. By the 1950s he had entered a new cycle; he had become divorced from his first wife, his Catholicism, and his early poetic mode.

*Mills of the Kavanaughs* (1951) elicited little critical discourse on the Puritan elements in Lowell's poetry. Since its title poem, a variation on the dramatic monologue, departed stylistically from Lowell's earlier verse, critics concentrated on stylistics. The most overtly religious poem in the volume, "Mother Marie Therese," drew plaudits from Jarrell (*Poetry and the Age*, 1953). He said it was the "best poem" Lowell had ever written;

its topoi were rendered in elaborate patterns, which now had "organic unity." He was also delighted that Lowell could now see and appreciate the hedonistic side of Catholicism. The drab asceticism of the priest in the poem is unfavorably compared with the nun's sensuality. Lowell, it seemed, was beginning to take his religious concerns more lightly. But certain critics found this change unsettling. Katherine Bregy wished that Lowell would deliver a less cynical message (*Catholic World*, October 1951), while Frank O'Malley said that, despite the new attitude, the poet was moving toward the "clarity" of God (*Renascence*, Autumn 1951).

*Mills* came to be regarded as the volume in which Lowell had begun to remove religion from his thematic repertory. Staples (in *Robert Lowell*) noticed the absence of a Christian cosmos in the title poem. "Mills" was printed in two versions; the first appeared in *Kenyon Review* (13, 1951); the second, just a few months later, was used in the title volume. Wyatt Prunty compared the two versions and showed how the deletions in "Mills" indicate Lowell's changing ideas (*Agenda*, 18, 1980). The first version was posited on a Christian cosmology; it contained references to the Virgin Mary and St. Patrick. These were deleted in the second version and replaced by epigraphs from Arnold's "Dover Beach" and William Carlos Williams' *In the American Grain*. To Prunty, this is Lowell's rejection of myth—for Christianity had become just another myth to Lowell. This left him only empirical means to explain truth. He had to explain events through a series of "representations of the past," thereby replacing religious allegory with causality. Thus Anne Kavanaugh, the central character in "Mills," interprets the present through revery rather than through the divine sign or Word. Prunty concludes that Lowell's only solution to his dilemma was to explain "truth" by spotlighting his "isolated, subjective self." Thus it is a short step from *Mills* to the secularism of *Life Studies* (1959).

Now the critics had no alternative but to use the term "humanist" when they discussed *Life Studies*. If they mentioned Puritanism, it was merely a recycling of old commentary, and the conclusion was that Lowell had become, like the Puritans themselves, disenchanted with the "American Eden" (Samuel Hazo in *Commonweal*, October 28, 1960). Glauco Cambon looked for Christian elements in the poems, particularly "Beyond the Alps" (*Accent*, Winter 1960). He was nonjudgmental, which was a welcome change from reactions to *Mills*, in which

critics had still expected Lowell to play spiritual leader. But
Cambon regarded Lowell's apostasy from Catholicism as moving toward the role of humanist and to a more deeply historical
vision: "It is a plea for completeness versus onesidedness, for
the wholeness of imagination and reason, science and faith. It
protects our minds from the death of wonder, and keeps a
breathable atmosphere available." Ian Hamilton went so far as
to say that Lowell's dalliance with Catholicism showed a lapse
of taste (*Review*, August/September 1962). He said that "Lowell's Catholicism has been well described as simply a way of
abusing Calvinism." His religious conflicts gave no cure for the
ills they helped to diagnose. Indeed, his recondite Christian
references were "thoughtlessly vulgar and sensational."

Thus the criticism had taken on a new cast. "Skunk Hour,"
one of the most praised selections in *Life Studies*, drew elaborate
religious commentary from John Berryman (which will be discussed later in a survey of the major "religious" poems). But
the later commentary began to use sociopolitical perspectives
instead. Part of this was due to the change in the poetry. Lowell had tuned into the political furor of the sixties and left his
personal debate with God out of his verse. This generated a
kind of fuzzy "moral" commentary, which in more astute critics was termed "neo-Christian." But by and large, Lowell's
morality was linked not to ideological scruples but to his attitude toward war, marriage, racism, and other social issues.

For all intents and purposes, *Union Dead* (1967) was the last
volume which critics pumped for evidence of Lowell's Puritanism. The setting for the title poem, "For the Union Dead,"
is Boston and its monuments: the "old South Boston Aquarium,"
the "tingling Statehouse," "St. Gauden's shaking Civil War relief." Since nature is not an underlying metaphorical tool for
this volume, critics found in Lowell's depiction of modern Boston the equivalents of the Puritans' apocalyptic reading of the
natural world. Urban images symbolized the Bostonians' spiritual
malaise, which delivered not so much a prophetic message as a
grim reminder that faith was dead. When references *are* made
to nature, they evoke images of landscaped gardens in Renaissance England. In "The Public Garden" the park is full of dead
leaves and empty fountains; the moon is a "stranger," which
"lies like chalk/over the waters." The old world order is gone.
Although several critics believe that "The Public Garden" is

about the dying union of two lovers (e.g., Fein, p. 94), the scriptural imagery also suggests spiritual death:

> Remember summer? Bubbles filled
> the fountain, and we splashed. We drowned
> in Eden, while Jehovah's grass-green lyre
> was rustling all about us in the leaves.

In another example, "Jonathan Edwards in Western Massachusetts," the persona (Edwards) enjoys a reverie of "designed" gardens whose *"breath of flowers"* came and went *"like warbling music"* (Lowell's italics). Since the Puritans often equated the American wilderness with the Devil, Lowell was here projecting his sacramental (or Catholic) reading of nature onto a Puritan divine. The historical Edwards yoked wild nature with the evil in human souls.

Modern Boston, then, is Lowell's modern Babylon. Lowell had announced his departure from another city, Rome, in *Life Studies* ("Beyond the Alps"): "Much against my will . . . I left the City of God where it belongs." Now his spiritual residence is Boston, where "Faith is trying to do without/faith." Thus both the urban and the natural worlds are correlatives for loss. In *Pity the Monsters*, however, Alan Williamson argued that no opposition between Catholic and Protestant religious experience is dramatized in *Union Dead*. The major change in this volume, he said, was Lowell's new perception of Edwards ("Jonathan Edwards in Western Massachusetts"). In the early Edwards poems (*Lord Weary*), the preacher spoke in his own voice; now, Lowell spoke in his own voice, which was conspicuous proof of the poet's alienation: "The power of identification that enabled the young Lowell to breathe freely, though with fierce antitheticalness, within the very words and cadences of Edwards' mouth, is gone" (p. 84). Lowell has grown less absolute and more relativistic in his appraisal of Edwards. Paradoxically, they are now of a single mind: both see the Promised Land (America) in a dream of the past, "a Renaissance England where body and spirit, nature and grace, action and ideals were reconciled" (p. 86).

Lowell retraces the contradictions of Edwards' life more lovingly than before; Edwards' obsession with Calvinist depravity is now softened by references to his courtship of Sarah Pierrepont. Lowell also finds Edwards' vacillation about be-

coming president of Princeton University an act of wisdom
rather than passivity. In *Lord Weary*, Edwards had surrendered
his will and personality to his religious system ("After the Surprising Conversions") in *Union Dead*, Lowell explained Edwards' behavior in psychological terms :"paralytic melancholy"
and "a fear of life." Williamson concludes that the later characterization demonstrates Lowell's "mature detachment," which
may have liberated Lowell the man but may have stultified
Lowell the poet. Indeed, Williamson is right; the early Edwards
poems are superior to the one in *Union Dead*.

Whatever Puritan roots remained in *Union Dead*, they were
the adaptation of symbolism and emotional fervor to the service
of political commentary. The enlivened language of the Puritan
sermon was Lowell's metier here. It differed from his Catholic
rhetoric of *Lord Weary*—ornate and involuted. Now the message was clearer, more personally self-questioning; and when
Lowell questioned himself, he followed a Calvinist tradition:

> The Puritans had been taught to search for the enemy within
> rather than to attack the intruding evil directly. The logic ran
> this way. If there is trouble from without, it must be because the
> community's weaknesses have invited difficulties; instead of wast-
> ing energy and time ranting against the external threat, be it Satan
> or the wrathful God, the King or hard times, it is far wiser to
> expose and purge the inner evils and eventually triumph over ad-
> versity through private labors [Elliott, *Puritan Influences*, p. 110].

Thus, in "For the Union Dead" Lowell does not accuse the
nation's racists, but hints at his own discomfort and shame over
the plight of blacks:

> When I crouch to my television set,
> the drained faces of Negro school-children rise like
> balloons.

The strategy of obsessive self-examination, which evoked
strong emotional responses in colonial audiences, works similarly for Lowell, who subtly manipulates his readers. This is
not to say that critics always recognized the similarity between
Lowell's self-flagellating persona and Puritan rhetoricians. They
were more inclined to notice the *objects* of his social criticism
than his manner of transmitting that criticism. Geoffrey Hartman came closest to recognizing this (*Partisan Review*, Spring
1965). Focusing on the title poem, which he considered the best

in the book, Hartman said that the ideal of service, of "dying into life," was Lowell's message now. It was delivered in a "quieter and naiver" style than the accusative rhetoric of earlier works. Lowell's ideas, however, had not changed. He had inverted a Christian paradox with a "parody of Revelation," but was still using the Puritan concept of tension between "trivia and magnalia," in which life becomes a "satanic 'going to and fro' in the earth." The basic change between this volume and *Lord Weary*, said Hartman, was that Lowell had come to resist "methodical darkness." The poet no longer set scriptural typology against daily events, but the precarious motion of his verse showed an unchanged "prophetic" mind.

Hartman correctly eschewed consideration of Catholicism in *Union Dead*. Thomas Parkinson went further and said that the poems took the "whole matter out of the hands of any god at all" (*Robert Lowell: A Collection of Critical Essays*, 1968). Man himself had become the god of his environment at all levels; the world had reverted to a prelapsarian state in which men and beasts act alike. Animal metaphors dominate the volume. Parkinson is troubled by *Union Dead* and blames Lowell for failing to convert his sense of guilt and futility into art: "when they become the poem, the entire process breaks down." But his aesthetic criticism covers a deeper displeasure—with Lowell's moral torpor. Thus it is appropriate for Lowell to depict "collapsed morale, lost heart, gone mind," but he should do so in "structured language," as did Eliot and Yeats. By selecting these models, Parkinson was playing Puritan to Lowell! Eliot's or Yeats's moral order, while perhaps germane, was too conservative for Lowell's attitude in the sixties.

Stephen Axelrod had just the opposite reaction to *Union Dead* (*Robert Lowell*). His analysis strongly connects Lowell the man with Lowell the poet; and since the second half of the volume depicts Lowell gradually recovering from his "suicidal crisis," Axelrod rejoices in Lowell's movement toward affirmation. This is a humane way to interpret *Union Dead*, and one wants to share Axelrod's concern for the poet, but Axelrod uses the same criterion Parkinson used, the "intentional fallacy." By Axelrod's reading, Lowell had searched for outlets in "mystic oblivion," which failed. His apocalyptic quest was implicitly suicidal, until he learned how to connect with other egos: "first by sympathetically identifying himself with great writers of the past (in poems about Hawthorne and Jonathan Edwards) and finally by rediscovering his love for his wife,

Elizabeth Hardwick" (p. 142). Thus, to Axelrod, *Union Dead* is about recovery from mental collapse.

Lowell thought of Hawthorne and Edwards as "great writers," rather than for their obsession with Puritanism. This is where Axelrod's argument breaks down, for there was a gallery of writers whom Lowell could have written poems about, if he were simply seeking "great writers." His notebooks are filled with copies of poems by Donne, Herbert, Dickinson, Crane, Eliot; but their presence—either conceptual or stylistic—is not felt in *Union Dead*. Edwards and Hawthorne had a special importance for Lowell.

Stephen Yenser also argued that Lowell admired Edwards and Hawthorne as writers, but that they gave Lowell something more than literary inspiration (*Circle to Circle*). They had taught him "to meditate upon the commonest things in the hope that they are true as well as insignificant." This, curiously, was the legacy of Puritanism. Edwards' and Hawthorne's shocking and exhausting visions had taught them (and in turn Lowell) how to survive. Yenser's premise is that the very darkness of Puritanism engenders its own light. Lowell's penchant for irony seized upon this phenomenon. At the same time, the similarity between Edwards and Hawthorne cannot be pushed too far. Hawthorne, like Lowell, was reviewing a past; Edwards was living it. Yenser did not address the difference.

Richard Fein did (*Robert Lowell*, pp. 96–99). He recognized Lowell's relentless self-exploration as a Puritan characteristic and found the poems on Edwards and Hawthorne—and even the elegy on Alfred Corning Clark—exempla of this ethos. In fact, "Alfred Corning Clark" was a more subtle example. In this poem, about a dead playboy friend, Lowell tried to find some meaning in Clark's life. He was attracted to the dead man's "triumphant diffidence" and "refusal of exertion," an inversion of the Puritan ethic. This is less contradictory than it appears, for Corning's vacant life had "the odd honor of withdrawal." It indirectly recalls the Puritan sense of inevitable helplessness before God. Fein sees the link between this poem and "Hawthorne": "Lowell's Nathaniel Hawthorne is but Alfred Corning Clark taken fire with his sense of his own mind's voiding itself through its strategies of awareness." The next poem to link this idea of valorous consciousness is "Jonathan Edwards in Massachusetts." Edwards kept faith in his own ideas, although the world left him far behind. Thus these three figures' self-loyalty, however idiosyncratic, represents the better part of our national ethos.

## The Major Religious Poems

The chief difficulty with this category is definition: Which of Lowell's poems may be correctly termed "religious," and of these, which "major"? In isolating the major poems, we might consider the selections in the most-used anthologies: *The Norton Anthology of American Literature* (vol. 2, 1979), *Contemporary American Poetry* (Houghton Mifflin, 3d edition, 1980), and *Anthology of American Literature* (vol. 2, Macmillan, 1980). Among their Lowell selections, these volumes offer "Mr. Edwards and the Spider," "The Quaker Graveyard in Nantucket," "Skunk Hour," and "Waking Early Sunday Morning" —all documents of Lowell's religious attitudes at pivotal points in his career. In addition to these better-known texts, a few important poems (like "Dea Roma" and "Beyond the Alps") have prompted comment on their religious content. Finally, as we make up the corpus for this section we must acknowledge several distinguished "religious" poems from *Lord Weary*, some of which fall into a thematic unit.

As the previous section demonstrated, Lowell was classified as a post-Christian poet whose poetic force was not doctrinal but surged, nonetheless, from religious impulse. His work did not drive critics to theological exegesis or elicit in readers recognition of a traditional God. In fact, critics who wrote after the sixties decided that Lowell had demythologized theology and domesticated God, even in his early volumes. His persistent self-consciousness and candor suffered from a touching vulnerability; he never achieved the elevated state of mysticism that Eliot had reached, for example. Yet when critics searched for a predecessor to Lowell, Eliot's name was the one most frequently invoked.

Lowell and Eliot were descendants of New England colonists. Eliot's ancestors came to America in the mid-seventeenth century. Andrew Eliot emigrated to Massachusetts at the time when Michael Wigglesworth's *The Day of Doom* (1662), a fire-and-brimstone epic poem, held sway over the populace. Andrew served as a juror at the Salem witch trials, a role he later publicly regretted. (Josiah Winslow, Lowell's maternal

ancestor, was commander-in-chief in King Philip's War against
the Indians, a role Lowell denounced in an early poem, "Children of Light.") Thus T. S. Eliot, like Lowell, was no stranger
to the Puritan Burden. At the same time, he appeared to be less
traumatized than Lowell by religious experience, and derived
more solace from his conversion to Anglican Catholicism than
Lowell did from Roman Catholicism. But he shared with Lowell a distaste for the bigotry and hypocrisy of Puritanism, as
well as dismay at twentieth-century secularism. Eliot believed
that, after the seventeenth century, passion and intelligence
could not work together in commitment to a Christian God; a
"dissociation of sensibility" had taken place. He wrote in 1933
that "the chief clue to the understanding of most contemporary
Anglo-Saxon literature is to be found in the decay of Protestant-
ism" (*After Strange Gods*, p. 41). Lowell, like Eliot, went back
to pre-Reformation Christianity for his models, to the poets
and philosophers of the Middle Ages; and Eliot's dictum that
the Christian scheme seemed the "only one which would work"
(*Listener*, March 16, 1932) might well have been written by
Lowell.

Eliot's attitudes about Puritan theology and ethics, which
bear mention here, are succinctly summarized in this passage
from Charles Berryman's *From Wilderness to Wasteland: The
Trial of the Puritan God in the American Imagination* (1979):

> Despite Eliot's deep concern about "the misery of man without
> God," he did not care much for evangelical crusades. He doubted
> the value of faith that was not the result of slow and painful dis-
> cipline, and he felt distaste for any exaggerated public display. He
> was highly suspicious of the extreme behavior generated by the
> Great Awakening in the eighteenth century, and he could never
> fully appreciate the theological genius of Jonathan Edwards.
> Nevertheless it is probable that Eliot had more in common with
> the last of the great Puritans [Edwards] than he generally cared
> to admit [p. 196].

These words inevitably remind us of Lowell, as does Berryman's following remark on Eliot's disdain for the political
ideals of the American Enlightenment: "With his conviction of
original sin, Eliot could not share Jefferson's optimism about the
essential goodness of human nature. With his belief in authority
and hierarchy, Eliot was not convinced that democracy was
either possible or desirable" (p. 197).

Despite these shared attitudes, there has been little scholarly interest in comparing Lowell's and Eliot's poetry. Critics paired the poets' names, but went no further. No one, for example, has examined such corollaries as the following: *The Waste Land*, like *Land of Unlikeness*, was a search for religious security, inspired by the devastations of war; "Ash Wednesday" and *Four Quartets* are echoed in *Lord Weary* and *Near the Ocean*; the thematic crux in both poets' works was a nostalgia for more heroic and ordered ages.

"Dea Roma" (*Unlikeness*) was Lowell's first serious effort to depict the antithetical forces of Christianity. It gains importance primarily as a precursor to the more noted "Beyond the Alps" (*Life Studies*). In both poems Lowell extols the Rome of faith, not the Rome of power politics. By the time he had written "Beyond the Alps" he had left the church, but, as stated in the poem, "much against my will." The essay which best explicates the variations between the two poems is Glauco Cambon's "Dea Roma and Robert Lowell" (*Accent*, Winter 1960). The earlier poem is an impersonal recapitulation of the history of Rome, says Cambon, a "judgment of Western history as a lost chance." Lowell looks at the city, as Hawthorne's Count Donatello did in *The Marble Faun*, with a Puritan's fiery judgment. He asks in line 11: "How many roads and sewers led to Rome?" Despite his conversion, Lowell cannot forget that Rome's legions "soldiered through this world/Under the eagles of Lord Lucifer." In "Beyond the Alps" modern Rome retains the empire image, but now Lowell blames a disintegrating civilization for the pope's ineffectuality when he proclaims Mary's bodily assumption as dogma:

> The lights of science couldn't hold a candle
> to Mary risen—at one miraculous stroke,
> angel-wing'd, gorgeous as a jungle bird!
> But who believed this? Who could understand?

Even Mussolini was not an adversary, for he was, like the rest of mankind, "pure prose." The modern age lacks the understanding for such visionary dogma. Indeed, the phrase "couldn't hold a candle," which recalls the traditional offering of votive candles, punningly expresses this inadequacy. Hence Lowell poetically relates his departure from Catholicism to a train ride from Rome in which he crosses the Alps:

> I watched our Paris pullman lunge
> mooning across the fallow Alpine snow.

Cambon associates Switzerland with ancestral Calvinism, since Calvin's theology was strongly established in Geneva. Lowell *crosses* the Alps, signifying his departure not only from Rome but from his Puritan heritage as well. Cambon then compares the details in "Dea Roma" with those in "Alps" and concludes that the latter are gentler. Lowell has made an affectionate farewell to Rome, a city that "knows the value of time as passive endurance." Now a fuller human being, he has come to understand, if not to believe, what she represents. Cambon's metrical and imagistic examples give weight to his argument that the suppler, "gentler" style of "Alps" promises a more "breathable atmosphere," or, in philosophical terms, the compromise of Christian existentialism.

By the time book-length studies on Lowell started to appear, "Dea Roma" had fallen into obscurity. "Alps," however, continued to intrigue critics. It was the first poem in the *Life Studies* volume, a prologue announcing a new order. To M. L. Rosenthal it was a "historical overture to define the disintegration of a world" (*The Modern Poets*, 1960). Now that Lowell had forsaken the heights of ancient myth, he experienced contemporary life as a "violent contradiction." Rosenthal saw "Alps" as the appropriate introduction to the confessional poems which dominate this volume—a public analogue for his personal hell. His point was well taken. The poems' order of appearance produced a dramatic structure of growing intensity. While Rosenthal played down the religious elements in "Alps," Staples emphasized them: "Is it too much to assume that this poem is Lowell's reluctant valediction to the Catholic mysticism that informs *Land of Unlikeness?*" (*Robert Lowell*, p. 69). Staples did not share Cambon's conviction that Lowell's apostasy brought him greater understanding. Rather, Lowell was trying desperately to "arrest the flux of the actual," to bring a measure of order and meaning into a vacuum. Thus the keynote in this poem (and in the entire volume) is stasis.

Later readings disagreed with those of Staples; critics focused on other images in the poem besides the Alps: ideological images of heights (Mt. Everest, the Acropolis). Decidedly secular ideologies were questioned in the poem, or so argued Williamson, Yenser, and Axelrod, each of whom had his favored theme to press. Williamson said that Mussolini, not Pope Pius, was the focal subject in the poem (*Pity the Monsters*). Claiming that Lowell saw in Western civilization a sexual basis for the drive to power, Williamson concluded:

> The extent of Lowell's moral claim on behalf of humanity as a crude, warmth-loving flesh-mass can be seen in his sympathy for Mussolini, the man of "pure prose" who seems somehow better than the idea he follows and renders ridiculous [p. 94].

Given Lowell's abhorrence of tyrants—of any ilk—Williamson's interpretation is not convincing. But there is a textual basis for discounting it; references to Mussolini take up four lines in a forty-two-line poem, and their function is tonal rather than factual:

> There the skirt-mad Mussolini unfurled
> the eagle of Caesar. He was one of us
> only, pure prose. . . .
> The Duce's lynched, bare, booted skull still spoke.

While "Alps" may not be unanimously apprehended as a religious poem, neither is it a paean to Mussolini. Yenser, taking a different approach than Williamson's, agreed with Staples that the poem announced Lowell's split with Catholicism; but for him this was as important as its "linear theory of history" (*Circle to Circle*). There is, says Yenser, a "hint of the Renaissance theory of the 'running down' of history which is not easily combined with a cyclical theory" (p. 124). Therefore, the speaker's disillusionment with present religious and political forces suggests the progressive breaking up of culture and the isolation of modern man. If Williamson banks on too isolated a detail for his interpretation, Yenser banks on a too general collocation of details. Yenser fails to acknowledge that Lowell's leap from "Hellas" to modern Rome is a subtle tribute to Western culture. Because Lowell felt that religion, whether pagan or monotheistic, often provided the rationale for political action, he stressed its importance. But the reference to "Hellas, when the Goddess stood" is no more or less glorious than the reference to "the crowds at San Pietro." Rosenthal's argument that the images of external disintegration provide a metaphor for Lowell's personal collapse is closer to the mark.

In all, critics found "Alps" a complex and, in some sections, incomprehensible poem. No one gave a coherent explication of the lines:

> Tired of the querulous hush-hush of the wheels,
> the blear-eyed ego kicking in my berth
> lay still, and saw Apollo plant his heels
> on terra firma through the morning's thigh . . .
> each backward, wasted Alp, a Parthenon
> fire-branded socket of the Cyclops' eye.

Lowell's religious allusions were less obscure than these classical ones. In the lines on Pope Pius, Lowell clearly implied that science and technology had replaced the religious miracle; but it was hard to render a logical paraphrase of the lines just quoted. Cosgrave was the only critic who insisted that the poem's ambiguities strictly applied to Catholicism:

> He leaves open the question of whether he is now denying the essential truth of Catholic doctrine or whether he is leaving Rome in disgust at the failure of the Church on earth to live up to that doctrine [*Public Poetry*, p. 123].

When we consider the framework of the entire poem, of the volume, and of the poetry after *Life Studies*, Cosgrave's distinction becomes irrelevant. Doctrinal quibbles never dominated Lowell's poetry. Staples, Yenser, and even Williamson understood this.

Axelrod found an interesting allusion to Puritanism in "Alps," but it was generically more cultural than religious (*Robert Lowell*). He postulated that Lowell was familiar with a letter written by Henry James which contained the following remark: "I shall probably not . . . be beyond the Alps. . . . That way Boston lies, which is the deadliest form of madness" (p. 104). The connection is not as loose as it seems. James's letter, which had been written to William Dean Howells, showed an ironic understanding of the Bostonian tradition. The phrase "beyond the Alps" encapsulated the story of New England's rebellion against the Old World.

Whoever the critic, there was uniform agreement on one point: the speaker in "Dea Roma" and "Alps" was Lowell himself. There was no talk of a persona; the poems were confessions. This was especially surprising since this position was taken by "New Critics," who ordinarily were disposed to ignore the author and his biography in their analyses. The distinct disadvantage of this approach was that structures of meanings were overlooked; the advantage was that as early as 1944, when "Dea Roma" appeared in *Unlikeness*, critics recognized the beginnings of a unique poetic mode. By the time "Alps" appeared, the mode was known as confessionalism.

Wedged chronologically between "Dea Roma" and "Alps" are two poems from *Lord Weary* which critics numbered among Lowell's best verse: "Mr. Edwards and the Spider" and "The Quaker Graveyard in Nantucket." Since the first of these contains excerpts from Edwards' writings, altered by an occasional word or phrase, the poem is something of a treatise on Calvinism. Edwards' words, which literally are youthful observations on the flight of spiders, deal analogically with the human soul. When Edwards saw a spider thrown into a fire, it reminded him of God casting souls into hell. Lowell extracted this simile from Edwards' essay and used it in the poem to express his attitudes—toward Puritanism and Edwards. Critics were mixed in determining what those attitudes were. Staples, usually thorough at explication, made a brief and, for him, impressionistic statement about "Mr. Edwards": "He [Lowell] intensifies the satire on the morbid fantasies of extreme Calvinism by hoisting Edwards by the petard of his own phraseology." (*Robert Lowell*, p. 35). Staples never showed how or where the poem's formal elements were satirical. He praised Lowell's stylistic fusion of Edwards' words with his own and concluded that Lowell had invested Edwards' character with "subtlety and sophistication." This was a compliment to Lowell, but it shed little light on the poem.

Dallas Wiebe (*Contemporary Literature*, 3, 1962) wrote a penetrating analysis of "Mr. Edwards," claiming it as part of a sequence. Along with "After the Surprising Conversions," "The Slough of Despond," and "The Blind Leading the Blind," it formed a dramatic narrative on Edwards as a preacher. As background for these poems, Wiebe recalls Edwards' famous sermon which so terrified a parishioner (Josiah Hawley) that he went home and slit his throat. Wiebe says that most readers wrongly respond to these poems as an attack upon Edwards and Calvinism, and that a close look reveals a more lenient view of Edwards.

He is "eventually cruel in his effects, but Mr. Lowell does not let his character become over-simplified. Edwards is allowed to have admirable qualities." Lowell's defense of Edwards turns on the principle that it is better to commit suicide than to exist outside God's grace. Moreover, Edwards was vindicated. In the poem, his sermon (where nature imagery converts horrifying events into a strangely bucolic fantasy) had defeated spiritual sloth in the congregation, even if it cost a human life. Wiebe is the first critic to emphasize Lowell's attraction for the fierce, authoritative aspects of Calvinism. His view of Lowell as a deeply conservative man ran counter to the "liberal" image other critics had conjured of the poet. In the seventies, Wiebe's view began to gain popularity.

There were several other stimulating interpretations of "Mr. Edwards." Richard Fein drew a relationship between Hawley's "conversion" (and subsequent death), as a result of the sermon, and Lowell's conversion to Catholicism:

> Intense belief and conversion create their own extremes which show up the laxity and unconcern of the usual pedestrian belief. Josiah Hawley and Lowell's poem show us that conversion is taking our life into our hands [*Robert Lowell*, p. 12].

According to Fein, the underlying poetic energy in this poem arises from the urge to be extinguished, to suffer no longer. The vivid nature imagery heightens and enhances life at the same time it heightens a longing for death. An important difference between Wiebe's and Fein's analyses is that Wiebe thinks Lowell identifies with Edwards, while Fein thinks he identifies with Hawley. Is Lowell, then, thinking as a Puritan, as a Catholic, or as neither?

The scholarship after Fein's book (1970) does not continue or resolve the debate. Axelrod describes the poem as merely Lowell's exercise in self-knowledge, wherein Lowell recognizes in Edwards an "ideological enemy" or "human brother" (*Robert Lowell*, 1977). But what is more disappointing is that Axelrod never justifies the anomaly between these two means of identification (p. 69). In contrast, Williamson delivers a laborious analysis of the poem, in which he aligns Edwards' prose with Lowell's poetic rearrangement (*Pity the Monsters*, pp. 23–29). Williamson says that although the persona who is speaking in the poem is Edwards, Lowell is actually "addressing" Edwards by subtly altering the preacher's words. The poet foregrounds Edwards' morbid imagination by incorporating words like "mildewed" and "creaking" into the source:

> I saw the spiders marching through the air,
> Swimming from tree to tree that mildewed day
> In latter August when the hay
> Came creaking to the barn.

Thus Lowell creates a distance between himself and the preacher. By using these negative epithets (e.g., "mildewed day"), Lowell confers more dignity on man than Edwards does. Had Williamson pursued this idea a bit further and provided some background on the Puritans' apprehension of nature, he might have strengthened his argument. In their cosmic hierarchy, the Puritans gave man a status comparable to lower forms of life. Williamson's observation, though cursory, was correct. He also suggested another way in which Lowell created a distance between himself and Edwards, a "last retreat" that Edwards could not have accepted: a state of *acedia* (sloth) in which the soul has given up its moral struggle. Thus, in the poem, Lowell concludes that there is a stalemate between the soul and God. According to this premise—if it is correct—Lowell no longer hoped to find faith through conventional religious channels when he wrote "Mr. Edwards." Williamson steers clear of drawing such a conclusion, but his analysis implies a certain secularization in Lowell.

The debate on Lowell's judgment of Edwards remains open, yet when analysis of "After the Surprising Conversions" (a companion piece to "Mr. Edwards") is added to the argument, the picture becomes clearer. But "Conversions" is poetically less distinguished than "Mr. Edwards," and has generated little critical commentary. A careful analysis has helped clarify the Lowell-Edwards issue—Carolyn Allen's "Lowell's 'After the Surprising Conversions': Another Look at the Source" (*Notes on Modern American Literature*, Summer 1979). Using Edwards' *Narrative of Surprising Conversions* (1737), Allen shows how Lowell changed the text ever so slightly and, by doing so, depicted an egotistical, callous Edwards persona. Her findings directly contradict Wiebe's more generous characterization. In the poem, the persona's casual tone, as he reports Hawley's violent death, makes him oblivious to his responsibility for the suicide:

> He mediated terror, and he seemed
> Beyond advice or reason, for he dreamed

That he was called to trumpet Judgment Day
To Concord. In the latter part of May
He cut his throat.

Allen says that Lowell was horrified by the story, and indicates
this through a coldly clinical diction. Moreover, the poetic
account of the suicide is just part of Lowell's "continuingly
judgmental attitude toward New England history," which
helped create the "messiness" of his own life. Hence we encounter, once more, the Puritan Burden theory, but this time
the critic finds Lowell's shoulders tired.

"Quaker Graveyard," a long, seven-section elegy on Warren
Winslow, is considered Lowell's prototypical (and to some
critics his finest) New England poem. Its harsh, questing religious drive is clearly that of the Lowells of Massachusetts and
that of the tormented modern world, which—to the poet—
could probably use a little Lowell blood. Nantucket, perhaps
the area's most aristocratic summer resort (reached by steamer
from Woods Hole, which is referred to in line 91 of the poem),
serves as locus where summer sailors sport for a Sunday race;
where the whaling boats, leaving for New Bedford, pass (whal-
ers are heightened, in their majestic force, by Lowell's references to *Moby-Dick* and, through this leviathan, to other biblical echoes). The place of nineteenth-century Quaker sailors is
also the place of twentieth-century submarines, rising (like the
whales) and dispatching sailors (like Warren Winslow) to their
graves. Whether or not it is entirely successful, this is clearly
a major poem. It is also a religious poem, although—in its sweep
through the Bible, Quakerism, American transcendentalism,
existential doubt, and an English Catholic shrine—it would be
hard to say *what* religion it is based on.
Marius Bewley sensed the vitality with which Lowell used his
Nantucket setting. In Bewley's words, "there is an immediacy
of relation between his sensibility and the old New England
of shipping and the sea that comes off with great distinction"
(*Scrutiny*, 17, 1950). The poem's final line, "The Lord survives
the rainbow of His will," embodies the entire mystery and contradiction which Lowell perceived to be the Puritan tradition.
The poem's critical reception was not as polemical as that of
"Mr. Edwards." Staples' chapter on it (in *Robert Lowell*) is
seminal and the later scholarship, with an occasional detraction,
builds on his reading. Despite the enigmatic final line, the poem's

meaning is fairly clear. The greatest difficulty is its esoteric
Catholic diction and biblical allusions; but Lowell does not use
the poem to debate his religious uncertainties. At the same
time, or perhaps because of this, it is considered one of Lowell's
most mystical poems. It eulogizes Lowell's cousin, Warren
Winslow, a sailor who drowned in the Atlantic during World
War II. In Staples' estimation, it is Lowell's attempt to move
away from the excited, dramatic tone of religious revelation to
a subdued, personal tone. He considers the poem a modern
equivalent of "Lycidas"; as in the Miltonic model, Lowell goes
beyond personal lament to larger spiritual issues. And also like
Milton, Lowell uses place names to localize and domesticate his
classical and biblical sources.

After the diatribe against Quakerism in the early sections of
the poem, the late sections settle down to meditative peace and
calm. This time Lowell uses Quakers, rather than Calvinist
Puritans, to symbolize spiritual alienation and economic greed.
The alteration gives the poem a more general New England
context. Staples argues that Lowell regards Winslow's death as
a late and indirect effect of Quakerism. Lowell follows Melville's concept of the Nantucket Quakers in *Moby-Dick*, where
they are described as "the most sanguinary of all sailors and
whale-hunters" (chapter 16). Thus the Quakers divorced themselves from the meaning of Christianity and deprived themselves of the possibilities of grace. In contrast, the Virgin, who
is at the heart of the poem (stanza VI, "Our Lady of Walsingham"), has transcendental wisdom and

> knows what God knows,
> Not Calvary's Cross nor crib at Bethlehem.

To Staples, the reconciliation at the end is a manifestation of
Catholic mysticism. In a sense, however, Staples contradicts
himself. He attributes both domesticated theology and ascetic
mysticism to Lowell's tone, but never explains how, or indeed
whether, the presence of both constitutes a philosophical system.

Irvin Ehrenpreis both disputed and agreed with Staples, finding the poem less accomplished than Staples did but sharing
Staples' emphasis on its Catholic mysticism ("The Age of Lowell," *American Poetry*, 1965). Ehrenpreis compared the poem
with Eliot's "Dry Salvages," but only to say that Lowell's lines
had a more "posed air" and "willed simplicity." Eliot, he said,
was more at ease with his beliefs, as his style indicated. Ehren-

preis' paraphrase of "Quaker Graveyard" is one of the most cogent in the scholarship:

> The world, he keeps saying, exists as a moral order in which separate men are not masters but participants: both the sea slime from which we rose and the whale that we plunder lie beneath the same law that subsumes humanity. To sectarian arrogance he opposed the innocence of the humbler orders of creation, for whom cruelty is an accident of their nature. As the solvent of arrogance he offers the Catholic compassion of Christ embodied in Mary his mother [p. 82].

Unlike Ehrenpreis, Mazzaro did not find Lowell's line "posed" or "willed," but a successful demonstration of the "contemplative voice" (*Poetic Themes*). However, contemplation had its ideological disadvantages, which in turn became poetic disadvantages. For Mazzaro, Lowell's pursuit of truth, which was the *true* subject of the poem, was limited by the poet's tendency to ignore social and moral incentives to action. Mazzaro's argument is clear only in the thematic context of his book. The poem is so richly allusive that critics fare better when they first address standard readings (such as Staples', Ehrenpreis', or Jarrell's) as a groundwork for discourse. Jarrell considered Lowell's Catholicism a crucial factor in the poem, but he said it was the Catholicism of a convert, "one of those heretical enthusiasts" (*Poetry and the Age*, 1953). There was little serenity in "Graveyard," except in the Walsingham stanza (here he and Staples agree). The last line, "The Lord survives the rainbow of His will," does not open out into liberation, said Jarrell, but into "infinite and overwhelming possibility." This produces something of the terror, but none of the pity, of Blake's visionary poetry. Jarrell's impression is that Lowell's Catholicism ("literary, emotional, anthropomorphic") is suited to literature. Nonetheless, he apprehends Lowell's sensibility as Calvinist; hence the violence and joylessness of "Graveyard."

The poem, then, has a triad of possible meanings: that Lowell concludes with mystical fervor after having rejected several alternatives (Staples); that Lowell has the knowledge "one has of one's damned kin," which leaves him no peace (Jarrell); that Lowell never established a religious foundation and merely juxtaposes views of saving grace (Ehrenpreis). Patrick Cosgrave said that the poem embodies all three possibilities and is, consequently, a failure (*Public Poetry of Robert Lowell*). Its multilevel structure, to which Staples attributed its greatness, gives it too many meanings. To Cosgrave, this reduces the possibility

of consolation its speaker so willfully asserts in the final section
(he echoes Ehrenpreis).

The term "consolation" turns our attention to the poem as
an elegy and its status within the elegiac mode. Marjorie Perloff
examines "Graveyard" as elegy, stating her case in terms of
stylistics (*English Literary History*, March 1967). She agrees
with Mazzaro that the poem is a retreat from action, but dis-
agrees with Staples that it matches "Lycidas." Unlike "Lycidas," which has a contrapuntal structure, moving from lament
to consolation, "Graveyard" neither laments nor consoles. The
poem is so complicated, by discrete allusions and images, that
the speaker never directly deals with the force or meaning of
death. Although Perloff does not sort out the doctrinal passages, her exhaustive analysis reveals that the poem has no coherent system. Her commentary implies that where there is
no definable philosophical structure, there cannot be classical
elegy. Instead, later "personal" poems, such as "My Last After-
noon with Uncle Devereux" (*Life Studies*), approach the universality of classical elegy that "Graveyard" strains to achieve.
Perloff's essay brilliantly demonstrates that form *is* meaning.
Within the parameters of our present subject, she verifies Ehrenpreis' position.

There are several other (less successful) efforts to substantiate the three approaches to "Graveyard." Philip Cooper reiterated Staples' ideas, then appended his own observations (*Autobiographical Myth of Robert Lowell*, 1970). He said that the
poem is not a supplanting of Puritanism by Catholicism, but a
counterpointing of the two which accommodates both the violence and serenity which inhabit the lines. Cooper's view reflects the tendency among later critics to gloss over Lowell's
contradictions. They argue that the poems, being personal, do
not lend themselves to classifiable or objective explication and
are best understood as shards in an autobiographical mosaic.
The drawback with such an approach is that the poetry receives
little formal analysis.

Most later treatments of "Graveyard" are incorporated into
book studies and are subdued—indeed, almost perfunctory. Fein
(1970), Crick (1974), Yenser (1975), and Axelrod (1978) discuss
the poem as though the major arguments have been exhausted.
Each of these scholars defers to "Graveyard," but tempers def-
erence with the reservation that it lacks some quality necessary
to great verse. This is easily explained by the truism that taste
and standards change. The intricate symbolic patterns in "Graveyard" do not stupefy readers, as they did several decades ago.

Finally, a word about the politically oriented commentaries. Alan Williamson (*Pity the Monsters*) attributes the poem's marginal success to Lowell's frustration with his spiritual quest. Lowell is moving toward the abstraction of Christian existentialism, says Williamson, which is the only compromise left. The poem evolves as an unconscious review of alternatives, which are wistfully rejected. Robert Hass (*Salmagundi*, Spring 1977) is not sure that Lowell finds even the comfort of Christian existentialism. According to Hass, the poet viewed "the whole of human life" as "sterile violence" and despaired of finding a "saner social order."

"Graveyard," then, has had a checkered reception. Critics have dubbed it both religious and nonreligious, with reasonable arguments on each side. Eliot is mentioned once or twice as a model for the poem, but no one thought to compare Lowell's repeated allusions with those in *Waste Land*. Both poems use quotations and borrowed language to enrich their textures and to create a bridge with the past. Now that Eliot's and Lowell's modes are a closed chapter in literary history, their resemblance emerges more distinctly.

It is remarkable that *Lord Weary*, which houses "Mr. Edwards" and "Graveyard," imparts a nervous intensity that is consistently channeled into religious images; yet the importance seems to belong elsewhere. Religion is like a thematic trapping to disguise what Lowell really wants to say. Perhaps this is why his interest in Edwards or Puritanism cannot be completely accounted for. Did Edwards (1703–58), the last great defender of Puritanism before its decline, become Lowell's champion of lost causes? Was Lowell identifying with him, and if so, what was Lowell's lost cause? Lowell did not seem interested in other Puritans as literary models or subjects, as, for example, John Berryman was ("Homage to Mistress Bradstreet"). Lowell's obsession with Catholicism is equally perplexing. His conversion had all the qualities of the brief, tempestuous love affair. His passionate apostrophes to Mary in *Lord Weary* are matched only by his erotic sonnets to Caroline in *The Dolphin*. It is hard to mistake the sexual inference in this address to the Virgin:

> Mother, my bones are trembling and I hear
> The earth's reverberations and the trumpet
> Bleating into my shambles
>
> ["The Dead in Europe"]

or the phallic fantasy in "Colloquy in Black Rock":

> Here the jack-hammer jabs into the ocean;
> My heart, you race and stagger and demand
> More blood-gangs for your nigger-brass percussions,
> Till I, the stunned machine of your devotion,
> Clanging upon this cymbal of a hand,
> Am rattled screw and footloose.

Yet Staples, in an opinion as yet unchallenged, said that "Colloquy" is "an anthem celebrating the miracle of the Eucharist, expressed in terms of a personal awareness of Divine Immanence symbolized by the feast of Corpus Christi" (p. 41). The reactions to *Lord Weary's* Catholic poems changed with time, as a sampling from the early (Eberhart), middle (Parkinson), and late (Axelrod) criticism will demonstrate; but they all took the religious avowals at face value. Richard Eberhart (*Sewanee Review*, Spring 1947) contrasted Lowell's Catholicism with Thomas Merton's, and though he never directly trounced Merton, one could see that he preferred Lowell's anguished spirituality:

> In one sense the two poets are striking at the same goal, a universal hymn of praise, the glory of the Lord. When Merton is unconvincing it is because he is so sure, when Lowell is unconvincing it is because he is so unsure. . . . Lowell is not altogether out of Hell; he convinces us that he is human, bodied [p. 326].

With the passage of time, Lowell's uneasiness with Catholicism was less sentimentalized by critics. Thomas Parkinson astutely observed that Lowell could not reconcile his poetic technique with his sense of Catholicism: "the poetry could not cope with the generosity of the Church and forced that many-mansioned house to a very restricted tenement" (*Robert Lowell: A Collection of Critical Essays*, 1968). Here, at least, was an inkling that the religious ideas in *Lord Weary* covered up other concerns. But the later scholarship retreats from the challenge of discovering them; and it fails to associate the persona in the overtly religious poems (e.g., "The Holy Innocents," "The Crucifix") with the persona in the personal ones (e.g., "Rebellion," "In the Cage"). Axelrod takes the entire volume to be a journal of "exile," a word that appears in the first and last poems: "Lowell feels exiled from the contemporary world because of his faith; and in another sense he feels exiled *in* the

contemporary world" (*Robert Lowell*, 1978). Doomed godless-
ness paralyzes the poet's psyche, says Axelrod. There is something spurious about this view. Granted its relevance to Lowell, it is also relevant to a host of other poets. Axelrod, who *did*
note the Eliotic "myth of apocalypse" in *Lord Weary*, should
have pursued that more promising idea instead. Thus *Lord
Weary*, the volume which brought Lowell his first Pulitzer
Prize and ample critical attention, still needs to be probed.

The next poem to present problems in religious interpretation is "Skunk Hour" (*Life Studies*), for it is hard to hang doctrinal analysis on this work. A dramatic monologue, it presents
the thoughts of a troubled man, alone, at night. The one literary
echo in the poem, occurring in the line "I myself am hell," is
taken from a Puritan work, *Paradise Lost*. In book IV, Lucifer
cries out: "Which way I flie is Hell; my self am Hell." Staples,
ordinarily quick to detect sources, especially those with religious content, did not mention this one. He said that the entire
poem was a "startlingly candid revelation" of Lowell's mental
illness, and that the following lines impart "explicit naturalism":

> a mother skunk with her column of kittens swills the
>     garbage pail.
> She jabs her wedge-head in a cup
> of sour cream, drops her ostrich tail,
> and will not scare.

But a few critics correlated these lines with sacramental communion. The skunk, as man, was searching for nourishment.
Theirs were the most interesting treatments of "Skunk Hour"
and have remained, to date, the standard interpretations.

Three essays on the poem were published as part of a symposium in *The Contemporary Poet as Artist and Critic* (1964).
Richard Wilbur, John Frederick Nims, and John Berryman
presented their impressions and Lowell replied to them. His response was not defensiveness, for the readings were flattering.
What Lowell *did* say however, was that although he was not
misunderstood, he was "seen through," revealing that he brought
more unconscious material to the poem than he had perhaps
intended. Both Wilbur and Nims picked up the Miltonic echo.
Wilbur says the poem has a pattern similar to many poems in
*Lord Weary*, which close with a prayer for man's regeneration.
What now replaces the prayer is the poet's contemplation of a

mother skunk and her kittens. "Are they the equivalents of a prayer?" Wilbur rhetorically asks; but he does not think this poem shares the earlier ones' prophetic vision. The skunk image refers to a diseased society which the poet inhabits; the self is not so much Lucifer's self as the one which the world has thrust upon him. What Wilbur really admires in "Skunk Hour" is its great range of feeling—not necessarily religious, but not devoid of religious feeling. Nims is inclined to see more doctrinal references in the poem. Focusing on the following lines, he reminds us that "the famous hill in our tradition was named for a skull: Calvary, from the Latin *calvaria*":

> One dark night,
> my Tudor Ford climbed the hill's skull;
> I watched for love-cars. Lights turned down,
> they lay together, hull to hull

This is some kind of emotional crucifixion for the speaker, says Nims. The "love-cars" recall the mechanical, debased love scene in *Waste Land* (Nims is one of few critics to catch this). Nims makes an inventory of all the sterile images (the avid heiress, the fairy decorator, the lewd lovers, the church's chalky spire); but, unlike Staples or Wilbur, he says that the skunk image translates the entire poem into a benediction of life. The skunks appear "in the softest and dreamiest of natural light—light with its many connotations of hope and truthfulness." These ordinarily despised creatures engage in a natural quest, foraging for food (albeit in garbage pails) with a noble obstinacy. In short, Nims argues that Lowell ultimately celebrates life—not a Christian existentialist celebration but a humble, primitive one. Lowell's reply to Nims suggests that Nims's reading is too affirmative. Although the skunks search "in the moonlight," Lowell stresses that the scene takes place at the end of day:

> This is the dark night. I hoped my readers would remember John of the Cross's poem. My night is not gracious, secular, puritan, and agnostical. An Existentialist night. Somewhere in my mind was a passage from Sartre or Camus about reaching some point of final darkness where the one free act is suicide [p. 107].

Of the three essays in the symposium, Berryman's was the most incisive. Berryman would not call the poem friendly to Christianity, but "heavy with spiritual despair." The skunks

swilling sour cream are a "greedy parody of the Eucharist."
They represent a "small counterpoise to the poem's terror," an
effort to stave off the dark night of the soul. Berryman finds
distant allusions in the poem, which go back to the Old Testament, Ovid, and Marlowe. On the surface, his discourse seems
objective and academic, but one cannot fail to note that when
he harps on the "poem's terror" he is bringing much of his
*own* terror into the reading. He recognizes Lowell's synthesis
of Marian imagery: the poem begins with one mother (of a
bishop) and ends with another (of a column of little skunks),
and the latter is fiercely nurturing. Lowell has finally come to
understand the Freudian implications of his Mary obsession.
Berryman, through sheer instinct and identification, touches on
the core of the poem. His is the best essay yet to appear on
"Skunk Hour." Lowell showed satisfaction with it, remarking
that Berryman had "hit a bull's eye."

In Lowell's later work, the poem which critics were most
inclined to label religious was "Waking Early Sunday Morning" (*Near the Ocean*). An intensely introspective work, "Waking" is a free-associative meditation on spiritual atrophy. Since
the meditation takes place on a traditional day of worship, it
subtly satirizes the convention of churchgoing in America. Axelrod aptly summarizes the poem's contents:

> The poem centers first on the apparent departure of the Christian
> God from the human scene, and then on the political violence
> occupying the empty space that remains. Lowell has awakened
> this Sunday morning to a world grown old and dark—a world
> where a "remorseful" sun can produce only enough light to equal
> a "blackout," where "vermin" confidently continue their obses-
> sive night activities unaware that day has ever dawned [*Robert
> Lowell*, p. 184].

Apart from topical political commentaries on "Waking" (discussed in the next chapter), several essays compared it with
Stevens' "Sunday Morning," to which it bore obvious relation.
Elizabeth Lunz's "Robert Lowell and Wallace Stevens on Sunday Morning" (*University Review*, Summer 1971) demonstrates
that Lowell's poem is not only a grim rejoinder to Stevens, but
a censure of Stevens' philosophy. Stevens' hedonistic delight
was immune to the realities of war and political corruption,
says Lunz, while Lowell's ever present tendency toward despair was intensified by it. Stevens anticipated an age of har-

mony and understanding, wherein the chaos, though it signaled the death of God, would bring new myths and the revival of the imagination. To Lowell, who anticipated only "incipient madness," such a position was thoroughly untenable; Stevens' "death of God" did not herald freer worship, but the opposite. The result of Lowell's reflection, according to Lunz, is recognition of loss: "What, after all, is there to do on Sunday mornings anymore, with the era of chaos already come? There can be none of Stevens' complacencies in 1967."

The lessons of war only stiffened Lowell's aversion to the "excessively playful, suave and careless" detachment of Stevens' aesthetic. While Lowell recognizes in the traditional Sunday morning church ritual the same hypocrisies which Stevens had rejected, he still cherishes the contact with order and divinity. When Lowell had reviewed Stevens' *Transport to Summer* in 1947, he expressed his disapproval of Stevens' flippancy: "The detachment and flexibility of a poet who can say in one place that Christianity is too nebulous, in another that it is too rigid, and in another that 'the death of Satan is a tragedy/for the imagination' are disarming" (*Nation*, April 1947). There is no little irony here: critics leveled the same indictment at Lowell with respect to "Waking."

Mary Kinzie selects the emblems of Adam, Christ, and Noah in the poem and says that Lowell gives them a "characteristic skewing" (*Salmagundi*, Spring 1977). The references to "the thorn tree" and the "tree of breath" turn into dead wood, says Kinzie, but she cannot ascribe Lowell's dark vision to an objectifiable theory. She can only conclude that Lowell is in a psychic deadlock: "The prophet may be a fool, but the hatred and iniquity are commandingly perverse." Lowell, then, is as irresponsible as Stevens.

Axelrod is less accusatory toward Lowell than Kinzie is, but he has a similar impression of "Waking" (*Robert Lowell*, p. 184). He says that Lowell's persona is the mirror image of Stevens' woman, but he has wakened *early* Sunday morning, "glimpsing reality coldly and clearly." In effect, Lowell is baring his Puritan nature, expressing annoyance at God's withdrawal. Axelrod is correct here; the tone in "Waking" is trenchantly Puritan. The following couplet sounds as though it were lifted from an Edwards sermon:

> When will we see Him face to face?
> Each day, He shines through darker glass.

Other critics who brought up Stevens in their discussion of
"Waking" bore down on Stevens' hedonism. Richard Howard
defended Lowell's monumental effort to reflect the times in a
kind of classical way and still relate this to the torment of his
private spiritual life (*Poetry*, September 1967). Lowell could
not afford Stevens' "pleasure," said Howard; Stevens was too
escapist for the troubled sixties. In depicting the nation's condition, Lowell achieved the right proportion of "outward impulse and horrified withdrawal." And Michael London said that
Stevens' poem was inferior to Lowell's because Stevens sought
the supreme fiction in poetry as a replacement for the fiction of
God. Lowell's intelligence was too "skeptical of fictions" (*Robert Lowell: A Portrait of the Artist in His Time*, 1970).

We must remember that Howard's and London's essays appeared during years of crisis in America. Critics were eager to
applaud Lowell's woeful prophecies. They were not so interested in matching the imaginative poetic powers of Stevens and
Lowell as in appreciating the message of "Waking." These lines
in the final stanza became as familiar as a prayer:

> Pity the planet, all joy gone
> from this sweet volcanic cone;
> peace to our children when they fall
> in small war on heels of small
> war

After some time had lapsed, critics returned to theoretical
and formalist analyses of the poem. Williamson carefully explored the religious elements and found them "Edwards-like"
and Freudian (*Pity the Monsters*). This was no contradiction,
argued Williamson, for the "chinook salmon" (the poem's opening image) represented sexualized violence as well as unimagina-
ble innocence. The fish in Christian iconography is both
Leviathan and Christ; in archetypal psychology, it is both the
phallus and the embryo in the womb. The opening lines,

> O to break loose, like the chinook
> salmon jumping and falling back,
> nosing up to the impossible
> stone and bone-crushing waterfall

give an "Edwards-like view of our biological nature: that it is
'really' a trap or a mechanism." Like Edwards, Lowell "holds

no consolation for the individual consciousness that has done the acting and suffering" (p. 116). Thus we are back to the Puritan doctrine, which Williamson insists is still a major obsession to Lowell. "Waking" is more humane than "Quaker Graveyard," but it is just as metaphysically pessimistic.

Yenser takes the same view as Wiliamson, but he finds the structural and prosodic elements in "Waking" very Eliotic (*Circle to Circle*). Lowell's religious passages sound like Eliot in a "meditative mood," but Lowell's poem is a "parody of the benediction at a church service," which in *Four Quartets* is most sincere. As an antisermon, "Waking" is nonetheless as devotional as *Four Quartets*, says Yenser.

But he might also have recalled a much earlier Eliot in a Sunday morning mood, playing with Greek-derived words and highly sexual references: "Mr. Eliot's Sunday Morning Service." Sweeney, in the Eliot poem, is quite different from the persona in "Waking." To Eliot, contemporary man without faith is little more than an animal: "Sweeney shifts from ham to ham/ Stirring the water in his bath."

This survey of the reception of the major religious poems thus returns to a consideration of Eliot, and acknowledges itself as, in part, a reflection of the elder poet, in the sense that Lowell received and transmitted Eliot's influence. Lowell criticism embraced a period in which Eliot loomed as the great figure to be judged against, then sank, in the sixties and seventies, to the reactionary from whom Pound and Williams had "saved" American poets (including Lowell), and now stands clearly in need of a balanced review. But Lowell, born twenty-nine years after Eliot, wrote his early poetry in a second world war and tuned his artistic consciousness to the military and political futilities of Korea and Viet Nam, not the wasteland of *entre deux guerres* culture. Aside from contextual differences, there were obvious differences in the ways the two poets dealt with religion: Lowell seems rarely to place a specific sect at the center of his work. As the critics have shown, it is difficult to find a consistent creed that governs the thought and imagery of even the major religious poems. They are clearly, however, the work of an American who carries the double burden of the Puritan inheritance and its related—and democratized—version of *noblesse oblige*. Thus, from off the coast of Massachusetts (the location of "Dry Salvages") or of Maine, Lowell will ponder a secular hell never completely "tamed by Miltown" or saved by Mary's grace. The graveyards, the ancestors, in-

evitably evoke a teleological sense which is ultimately, if un-
specifiably, religious. Edwards, Thoreau, Melville; the whale,
the salmon, and perhaps the skunk, whirl about in these poems,
catching in the record of critical responses a host of interpretations as mixed as the poems which inspired them. Finally, we
must bear in mind that a sense of pastness and death, as close
as the loss of a Winslow or as distant as Troy, can on the one
hand inspire religious searchings and, on the other hand, a sense
of history. Both Lowell and his critics never seem sure which
is which but it is to this record of the historical-cultural sense
that we turn in the next chapter, "The Custodian of Culture."

## References

Aiken, Conrad
   1944. "Varieties of Poetic Statement." *New Republic* Oct. 23, pp.
   528–30 [530].
Allen, Carolyn
   1979. "Lowell's 'After the Surprising Conversions': Another Look
   at the Source." *Notes on Modern American Literature* Summer,
   item 17.
Altieri, Charles
   1979. *Enlarging the Temple: New Directions in American Poetry
   during the 1960s.* Lewisburg, Pa.: Bucknell Univ. Pr.
Axelrod, Steven Gould
   1978. *Robert Lowell: Life and Art.* Princeton: Princeton Univ.
   Pr.
Berryman, Charles
   1979. *From Wilderness to Wasteland: The Trial of The Puritan
   God in the American Imagination.* Port Washington, N.Y.: Ken-
   nikat.
Berryman, John
   1964. "On Robert Lowell's 'Skunk Hour.' " In *The Contemporary
   Poet as Artist and Critic*, pp. 99–106. Boston: Little, Brown.
Bewley, Marius
   1950. "Aspects of Modern Poetry." *Scrutiny* Apr., pp. 334–52
   [339, 342–48]; reprinted in his *The Complex Fate.* London:
   Chatto & Windus, 1952; in *Robert Lowell: A Portrait of the
   Artist in His Time*, ed. Michael London and Robert Boyers. New
   York: David Lewis.
Blackmur, R. P.
   1945. "Notes on Seven Poets." *Kenyon Review* Spring, pp. 339–52
   [347–49]; reprinted in his *Language as Gesture.* New York: Har-

court Brace Jovanovich, 1952; in his *Form and Value in Modern Poetry*. Garden City, N.Y.: Doubleday, 1957.

Brégy, Katherine
1947. Review of *Lord Weary's Castle*. *Catholic World* Jan., pp. 374–75.
1951. Review of *The Mills of the Kavanaughs*. *Catholic World* Oct., pp. 76–77.

Buckley, Vincent
1968. *Poetry and the Sacred*. London: Chatto & Windus.

Cambon, Glauco
1960. "Dea Roma and Robert Lowell." *Accent* Winter, pp. 51–61.
1963. *The Inclusive Flame: Studies in American Poetry*. Bloomington: Indiana Univ. Pr.

*Christian Century*
1946. Review of *Lord Weary's Castle*. Dec. 4, p. 1473.

Cooper, Philip
1970. *The Autobiographical Myth of Robert Lowell*. Chapel Hill: Univ. of North Carolina Pr.

Cosgrave, Patrick
1972. *The Public Poetry of Robert Lowell*. New York: Taplinger.

Crick, Robert
1974. *Robert Lowell*. New York: Harper & Row.

Devlin, D.
1945. "Twenty-four Poets." *Sewanee Review* Summer, pp. 457–66 [459–60].

Eberhart, Richard
1947. "Four Poets." *Sewanee Review* Spring, pp. 324–36 [328]; reprinted in *Robert Lowell: A Collection of Critical Essays*, ed. Thomas Parkinson. Englewood Cliffs, N.J.: Prentice-Hall, 1968.

Ehrenpreis, Irvin
1965. "The Age of Lowell." In his *American Poetry*, Stratford-upon-Avon-Studies no. 7, pp. 65–95. New York: St. Martin's; reprinted in *Robert Lowell: A Portrait of the Artist in His Time*, ed. Michael London and Robert Boyers. New York: David Lewis, 1970; in *Robert Lowell: A Collection of Critical Essays*, ed. Thomas Parkinson. Englewood Cliffs, N.J.: Prentice-Hall, 1968; in *Critics on Robert Lowell*, ed. Jonathan Price. Coral Gables, Fla.: Univ. of Miami Pr., 1972.

Eliot, T. S.
1932. "Christianity and Communism." *Listener* Mar. 16, pp. 382–83.
1934. *After Strange Gods: A Primer of Modern Heresy*. London: Faber & Faber; also New York: Harcourt Brace Jovanovich.

Elliott, Emory
1979. *Puritan Influences in American Literature*. Urbana: Univ. of Illinois Pr.

Fein, Richard
    1970. *Robert Lowell.* New York: Twayne.
Fiedler, Leslie
    1947. "The Believing Poet and the Infidel Reader." *New Leader*
    May 10, pp. 10, 12.
Fitzgerald, Robert
    1977. "Robert Lowell: 1917–1977." *New Republic* Oct. 1, pp.
    10–12.
Flint, F. Cudworth
    1945. "Comments on Recent Poetry." *Virginia Quarterly Review*
    Spring, pp. 293–301 [294].
Freemantle, Anne
    1946. Review of *Lord Weary's Castle. Commonweal* Dec. 27, pp.
    283–84.
Greenslet, Ferris
    1946. *The Lowells and Their Seven Worlds.* Boston: Houghton
    Mifflin.
Hamilton, Ian
    1962. "Robert Lowell." *Review* Aug./Sept., pp. 15–23; reprinted
    in *Modern Occasions* Winter 1972, pp. 28–48; in his *The Modern
    Poet.* New York: Horizon, 1969.
Hartman, Geoffrey
    1965. "The Eye of the Storm." *Partisan Review* Spring, pp. 277–
    80; reprinted in *Robert Lowell: A Portrait of the Artist in His
    Time*, ed. Michael London and Robert Boyers. New York: David
    Lewis, 1970.
Hass, Robert
    1977. "Lowell's Graveyard." *Salmagundi* Spring, pp. 56–72.
Hazo, Samuel
    1960. "Poetry of Contact." *Commonweal* Oct. 28, pp. 116–18.
Howard, Richard
    1967. "Fuel on the Fire." *Poetry* Sept., pp. 413–15; reprinted in
    *Robert Lowell: A Portrait of the Artist in His Time*, ed. Michael
    London and Robert Boyers. New York: David Lewis, 1970.
Jarrell, Randall
    1945. "Poetry in War and Peace." *Partisan Review* Winter, pp.
    120–26 [124–26].
    1953. *Poetry and the Age.* New York: Knopf.
Jumpers, Will C.
    1956. "Whom Seek Ye?: A Note on Robert Lowell's Poetry."
    *Hudson Review* Spring, pp. 117–25.
Kinzie, Mary
    1977. "The Prophet Is a Fool: On 'Waking Early Sunday Morn-
    ing.' " *Salmagundi* Spring, pp. 88–101.
Leibowitz, Herbert
    1966–1967. "Robert Lowell: Ancestral Voices." *Salmagundi* no. 4,

pp. 25–43; reprinted in *Robert Lowell: A Portrait of the Artist in His Time*. New York: David Lewis, 1970.

Levin, Harry

1958. *The Power of Blackness: Hawthorne, Poe, Melville*. New York: Knopf.

London, Michael

1970. "Wading for Godot." In his ed. *Robert Lowell: A Portrait of the Artist in His Time*, pp. 101–5. New York: David Lewis.

Lowell, Robert

1943. "A Review of *Four Quartets*." *Sewanee Review* Summer, pp. 432–35.

1944. "A Note." *Kenyon Review* Autumn, pp. 483–86.

1947. "Imagination and Reality." *Nation* Apr. 5, pp. 400–02.

1964. "On 'Skunk Hour.'" In *The Contemporary Poet as Artist and Critic*, pp. 107–10. Boston: Little, Brown.

Lunz, Elizabeth

1971. "Robert Lowell and Wallace Stevens on Sunday Morning." *University Review* Summer, pp. 268–72.

Mailer, Norman

1968. *The Armies of the Night*. New York: New American Library.

Martz, Louis

1954. *The Poetry of Meditation*. New Haven: Yale Univ. Pr.

Mazzaro, Jerome

1965. *The Poetic Themes of Robert Lowell*. Ann Arbor: Univ. of Michigan Pr.

1966-1967. "Lowell After For the Union Dead." *Salmagundi* Winter, pp. 57–68; reprinted in *Robert Lowell: Portrait of the Artist in His Time*, ed. Michael London and Robert Boyers. New York: David Lewis, 1970.

1970. *Modern American Poetry: Essays in Criticism*. New York: David McKay.

Mencken, H. L.

1961. *The Idea of an American Novel*, ed. Louis D. Rubin and John Rees Moore. New York: Crowell.

Mizener, Arthur

1945. "Recent Poetry." *Accent* Winter, pp. 114–20 [116–17].

Murdock, Kenneth

1949. *Literature and Theology in Colonial New England*. Cambridge: Cambridge Univ. Pr.

Nims, John Frederick

1945. "Two Catholic Poets." *Poetry* Feb., pp. 264–68 [266–68].

1964. "On Robert Lowell's 'Skunk Hour.'" In *The Contemporary Poet as Artist and Critic*, pp. 88–98. Boston: Little, Brown.

O'Malley, Frank

1949. "The Blood of Robert Lowell." *Renascence* Fall, pp. 3–9; reprinted in *Renascence* Summer 1973, pp. 190–95.

1951. Review of *The Mills of the Kavanaughs*. *Renascence* Autumn, pp. 105–6.

Parkinson, Thomas

1966–1967. "For the Union Dead." *Salmagundi* no. 4, pp. 87–95; reprinted in his ed. *Robert Lowell: A Collection of Critical Essays*. Englewood Cliffs, N.J.: Prentice-Hall, 1968.

1968. "Introduction." In his ed. *Robert Lowell: A Collection of Critical Essays*, pp. 1–11. Englewood Cliffs, N.J.: Prentice-Hall.

Pearce, Roy Harvey

1961. *The Continuity of American Poetry*. Princeton: Princeton Univ. Pr.

Perloff, Marjorie

1967. "Death by Water: The Winslow Elegies of Robert Lowell." *English Literary History* Mar., pp. 116–40; reprinted in her *The Poetic Art of Robert Lowell*. Ithaca, N.Y.: Cornell Univ. Pr., 1973.

Prunty, Wyatt

1980. "Allegory to Causality; Robert Lowell's Poetic Shift." *Agenda* Autumn, pp. 94–103.

Rosenthal, M. L.

1960. *Modern Poets: A Critical Introduction*. New York: Oxford Univ. Pr.

Seidel, Frederick

1961. "Interview with Robert Lowell." *Paris Review* Winter–Spring, pp. 56–95; reprinted in *Robert Lowell: A Portrait of the Artist in His Time*, ed. Michael London and Robert Boyers. New York: David Lewis, 1970; in *Robert Lowell: A Collection of Critical Essays*, ed. Thomas Parkinson. Englewood Cliffs, N.J.: Prentice-Hall, 1968; in *Writers at Work, Second Series*, ed. Malcolm Cowley. New York: Viking, 1963; in *Modern Poets on Modern Poetry*, ed. James Scully. London: Collins, 1966.

Staples, Hugh

1962. *Robert Lowell: The First Twenty Years*. New York: Farrar, Straus & Cudahy.

Tate, Allen

1944. "Introduction." In *Land of Unlikeness*. Cummington, Mass.: Cummington Pr.

Viereck, Peter

1947. "Poet Versus Readers." *Atlantic* July, pp. 109–12 [110].

Vogler, Thomas

1971. "Robert Lowell: Payment Gat He Nane." *Iowa Review* Summer, pp. 64–95.

Von Wellsheim, Mother Anita

1958. "Imagery in Modern Marian Poetry." *Renascence* Summer, pp. 176–86.

Waggoner, Hyatt H.

1968. *American Poets: From the Puritans to the Present*. Boston: Houghton Mifflin.

Wiebe, Dallas E.
1962. "Mr. Lowell and Mr. Edwards." *Wisconsin Studies in Contemporary Literature* Spring–Summer, pp. 21–31.
Wilbur, Richard
1964. "On Robert Lowell's 'Skunk Hour.'" In *The Contemporary Poet as Artist and Critic*, pp. 84–87. Boston: Little, Brown.
Williams, William Carlos
1925. *In the American Grain.* New York: Albert & Charles Boni.
Williamson, Alan
1974. *Pity the Monster: The Political Vision of Robert Lowell.* New Haven & London: Yale Univ. Pr.
Yenser, Stephen
1975. *Circle to Circle: The Poetry of Robert Lowell.* Berkeley: Univ. of California Pr.

# CHAPTER 4

# The Custodian of Culture

A nineteenth-century ghost seems to haunt twentieth-century criticism of Robert Lowell. Sometimes the presence is evoked by name, sometimes only by implication; but the figure of Matthew Arnold prompts many comparisons. Trying to find a place for religion in an increasingly secular world—as the world was in Arnold's day, as the world was in Lowell's day—Arnold and Lowell assigned poetry the task of perpetuating morality and culture.

Other parallels may be drawn. Both men had distinguished careers as educators: Arnold held the professorship of poetry at Oxford from 1857 to 1867; Lowell served as visiting professor at distinguished institutions such as Harvard, Kenyon College, Iowa University, Essex University. Both were respected public figures: as an inspector of nonconformist schools, Arnold wrote papers on educational reform; as a political "inspector," Lowell advocated pacifism and civil rights. On the personal side, both were melancholic individuals whose poetry voiced a conflict between Puritan conscience and the appeal of pleasure. They were equal in their effort to overcome painful subjectivity by diligently studying and imitating the classics; but the mode proper to each poet's temperament was elegiac and nostalgic, nonetheless. Perhaps Lowell, richer in sense endowment than Arnold, was more successful at verse making. Arnold's poetry has not stood the test of time as well as that of other Victorians, although no Victorian prose critic has worn better than he. Time alone will decide Lowell's permanence.

The greatest similarity between Arnold and Lowell, at least as perceived by the critics, is in the realm of values. In *Culture and Anarchy* (1869) Arnold criticized English social and political life, attacking middle-class complacency and materialism. In his books on religion (especially *Literature and Dogma*, 1873) he spoke for a Christianity which finds theology unimportant and consigns to religion the power to inspire charity and dignity in man. But even in these texts he was unable to rise above his wistful outlook.

Critics, then, could not wisely ignore the resemblance between the two poets, a resemblance Lowell himself cultivated. Indeed, Lowell's admiration for Arnold is revealed in an unpublished essay on Eliot's religion, written about 1967 and first printed in Axelrod's *Robert Lowell*:

> Eliot's faith seems almost willfully crooked, dry, narrow and hard in comparison with what I would like to describe as the toleration, hope and intuition of Matthew Arnold's tragic liberalism [Ms., Harvard Houghton Library].

Clearly, Arnold was on Lowell's mind, and if he was on the critics' minds too, this could create, if handled with the restraint due any such imputation of influence, a broad base for the critical discourse whereby Lowell's ideas, especially in the historical and political poems, could be explicated within a familiar context.

It would not be an overstatement to say that Arnold had more readers in America than he had in England. His explicitly nonmetaphysical, commonsense approach to literature appealed to Americans, while, as a school inspector, he knew and understood the middle class better than most intellectuals. However, the irony about Arnold's posthumous reputation in America lies in the complex interrelations between himself, Irving Babbitt, Paul Elmer More, and T. S. Eliot. Despite objections to aspects of Arnold's thought (Babbitt called him a fuzzy thinker; More said he avoided first principles), these men were Arnoldians. Eliot, too, said that "Arnold was neither thorough enough, nor comprehensive enough, to make any fundamental alteration of literary values," but he was quick to applaud Arnold's "discrimination of the values and relations of the components of the good life" (*Criterion,* January 1925). And in "Matthew Arnold and American Letters Today," Norman Foerster implored American writers to emulate Arnold's respect for the past ("Our writers must be made aware that there is no dead past") and encouraged them to "make sure [the past] is not lost" (*Sewanee Review,* July 1927). There are moral heresies in art, Foerster continued, but there is also a place for morality in art. Arnold had taught us that "the aesthetically right involves the morally right." Ethical and aesthetic standards are indissolubly united, said Arnold, although the end of art is not moral edification. Relying on Aristotle's *Poetics*, he maintained that poetry is an imaginative imitation of reality, however sordid.

In Foerster's view, Arnold had taught us that smug morality must no longer be defended by responsible writers. Arnold, then, had returned us to the human condition, at no cost to Christianity. In a position piece, "Orthodoxy and the Standard of Literature," Allen Tate made a similar pronouncement: "What Catholic literature in America needs today is a Catholic Matthew Arnold. His critical dialectic would come to something like this: *Always ask questions!*" (*New Republic*, January 5, 1953). If we are going to have a modern literature in which Christianity exhibits a certain reality, Tate argued, writers must find that reality in the depths, as well as the heights, of the human situation.

Such, then, were the points Arnold scored with the New Humanists and New Critics, those writers to whom Lowell apprenticed himself during his college years. For Lowell, who began his awareness of social action in the thirties, magazines were alive with warnings of civilization's decline. It was easy to accept Arnold's prophesy that literature, in its quasi-religious function, would serve as a social savior. Indeed, when *Lord Weary's Castle* appeared, Lowell was considered an agent of that prophesy. Reviewing *Lord Weary* in *Poetry in Our Time* (1956), Babette Deutsch hailed Lowell for his "revolutionary humanism." Using epithets which had been customarily applied to Arnold, she continued: "The poetry of Robert Lowell is eloquent, of a religiosity founded . . . on tortured sympathy for his fellows" (p. 346).

To be sure, critics linked Arnold's and Lowell's names less frequently as time went by, but the connection still held. As late as 1971, Lowell, reiterating his sense of the Arnoldian influence during an interview with Ian Hamilton, described "Near the Ocean" as his version of "Dover Beach" (*Review*, Summer). "Near the Ocean," which opens with a scene of marital discord, closes with an exhortation similar to that in "Dover Beach":

> Ah, love, let us be true
> To one another! for the world, which seems
> To lie before us like a land of dreams,
> So various, so beautiful, so new,

> Hath really neither joy, nor love, nor light,
> Nor certitude, nor peace, nor help for pain;
> > ["Dover Beach"]

> Sleep, sleep. The ocean, grinding stones,
> can only speak the present tense;
> nothing will age, nothing will last,
> or take corruption from the past.
> A hand, your hand then! I'm afraid
> to touch the crisp hair on your head—
> > ["Near the Ocean"]

The Lowell poem is more fierce than Arnold's, less idealized in its apostrophe to the lover (Lowell compares her to a Medusa); but the belief that human love is man's only salvation is the theme common to both texts.

There is, inevitably, some overlap between the commentary in this chapter and that in "The Puritan Burden." For example, Foerster's appreciation of Arnold for denouncing smug morality recalls the campaign undertaken by writers in the twenties (Mencken, Dreiser) to rid fiction of "Puritan gentility." Lowell's views on morality and sociopolitics were molded from two sources: his New England upbringing and his intellectual and artistic tutelage at Harvard and Kenyon College. The Arnoldian influence derives from the latter, though sometimes the effect of indoctrination from the two sources was identical. As a consequence, a failure among some critics to separate the influences on Lowell of Puritan family and humanistic education has marred a portion of the commentary, particularly that which addresses Lowell's "moral" precepts. The scholarship markedly improves when concrete topics, like war and Christianity, Lowell's ethical position on war, and Lowell's theory on history, engage the critics. These topics may be used to form a thematic dividing line within the Lowell canon: *Land of Unlikeness* and *Lord Weary's Castle* are concerned with the turbulent American past; *For the Union Dead*, composed midpoint in Lowell's career, pays attention to contemporary social, political, and moral ills, as do *Near the Ocean* and the *Notebook* series.

Another overlap occurs in the critics' discussion of Arnoldian influence, specifically in the Eliotic link between Arnold and Lowell. Eliot's dictum that our culture had made a "religion of poetry" reminded critics of Arnold's legacy. In several instances, the *critics* behaved as Arnoldians when they chastised Lowell for not being scrupulous enough. The weariness and resignation which colored his late work irritated the moral sentinels of the profession, as it did A. L. French, whose "Robert Lowell: The Poetry of Abdication" (*Oxford Review*, 1968) is the best example of this attitude. Lowell derived a certain pleasure from being a prophet of doom, says French; the poet neither dramatizes ethical conflicts nor puts up any resistance in his form, "because it [conflict] is not present *as* form." Just as Lowell the man surrendered, "so the life with which the poem deals surrenders without putting up more than a token fight." French does little to describe the "form" he so adamantly belittles, thereby weakening his case, but more seriously, he forces a criterion on Lowell, rather than inductively exploring the possibility that Lowell was recasting a poetic expression on morality.

The most balanced approach to Lowell's Arnoldian qualities is R. K. Meiners' *Everything to Be Endured: An Essay on Robert Lowell and Modern Poetry* (1970), a monograph which indirectly replies to French. By using historicist methodology, Meiners exempts Lowell from the charge of abdication. Lowell's work is the inevitable outgrowth of the modernist sensibility, with its painful representation of human experience. Had Arnold lived in Lowell's period, he would have been less sure of his convictions, Meiners suggests. There was in Arnold's time the beginning of a descent to "poetry of passive suffering." Arnold saw it and censured it, although he was not always exempt from it in his poetry. The substance of this new mode was a poor substitute for what Arnold called the "eternal objects of poetry and the representation of human action, preferably heroic action." Meiners believes that the kind of personal, self-conscious, "breaking point" poetry that Arnold witnessed in its burgeoning stage reached its culmination in *Life Studies*. Thus Lowell was the poet most like and unlike Arnold.

Meiners constructs an image of Lowell which is "more or less religious," in which Lowell encounters the same crisis Arnold encountered; however, since Arnold was closer to the "classic-Christian" tradition, his effort to overcome despair was easier. Rather than attributing Lowell's elegiac tone to a "growing unhappiness with his city, his family, and their involvements in New England's theological and mercantile past," Meiners argues that Lowell is the most articulate spokesman of the progressive decline in belief in a post-Christian culture. Arnold's longing for the "classic" return was echoed by Tate, says Meiners, but Tate could not sustain it. From there it was a short step to Lowell's predicament: "Where Lowell begins as a poet is approximately where Allen Tate had arrived by the time of *The Winter Sea*: with the same sense of the loss and perhaps even the new irrelevance of the traditional religious-humanistic view of man and culture." Lowell, then, is reduced to being "rhetoric haunted," asking "Shall poetry move out into the world and can it?" By Meiners' formula, Tate is the fulcrum between Arnold and Lowell: Tate had less conflict than Arnold but more conflict than Lowell.

So far so good; but when Meiners couples "For the Union Dead" with Tate's "Ode to the Confederate Dead," he becomes less persuasive. In the process of linking Lowell to Arnold through Tate, Meiners himself sounds like Arnold. He revives the nineteenth-century cultural-anthropological concept of the study of literature, and ignores the stylistic and tonal differences between the Tate and Lowell poems.

Charles Altieri builds on Meiners' general theory about the irrelevance of belief in modern culture, but his conclusion is both more authoritative and more applicable to Lowell's poetics (*Enlarging the Temple*, 1979). First, he doesn't stress the Lowell-Tate relationship any more than is warranted: Tate introduced Lowell to formalism, but Lowell learned as much from other Fugitive poets. Altieri parallels Lowell with Arnold without resorting to an intermediary figure. Like Arnold, Lowell is "condemned to nostalgia" because he cannot integrate his humanism with the secular, prose world. This trait is so reprehensible to the younger poets, says Altieri, that they are determined to find a new poetics. Poets who wrote in the sixties and seventies, a period "rife with conflict, hope and demands for action," could not adjust to Lowell's "nervous egotism."

Concentrating on personal agonies, Lowell was insufficiently interested in public issues, his confessional mode being purely narcissistic. The mode was, admittedly, a transitional necessity (the transition from Symbolism to Postmodern poetics), but it could not solve the younger poets' problem: to restore confidence in "the social and epistemological powers of the imagination." To Altieri, this lack of rapport between the new poets and Lowell is not unflattering: "One basic measure of his greatness is the intense energies other poets put into creating alternatives to his imposing egotism." Nonetheless, if Altieri overlooks the younger poets' somewhat callous obliviousness to Lowell's political activism, his discussion of the stylistic manifestations of Lowell's "nostalgia" and their subtle, almost imperceptible change from *Unlikeness* to *Near the Ocean* completely eclipses other shortcomings.

Falling somewhere between Meiners' and Altieri's analysis is Denis Donoghue's seven-page analysis of Lowell's Arnoldian morality, especially as it affects "authority and the self" (*Connoisseurs of Chaos: Ideas of Order in Modern American Poetry*, 1965). Donoghue reaches his position from a different direction than Altieri, but their conclusions are remarkably similar. Donoghue rejects the idea that Lowell's poems are "acts of violence directed against all the forces of constriction wherever the poet feels them—especially those associated with his own New England ancestors, guardians of a deadly law." If this were the case, he argues, the poetry would dramatize little more than the sentimental image of a tender poet traumatized by his immediate family and dark ancestry. Rather, Lowell should be credited with those intellectual talents which deliberate the limited choices of modern man. Donoghue says that the crucial conflict falls somewhere between authority and the self; the poems emerge as dialectical "counters" of this conflict. Loss of belief leaves Lowell several alternatives:

> The individual self can rely upon its own resources—such as they are—or it can accept the order provided for it by a compelling, totalitarian force, of whatever kind, or it can spend a lifetime searching for a more benign, more personal order, sufficiently firm to make its edicts persuasive if not legal.

Like Altieri, Donoghue regards the changes in the work as components in a growing ideology. He eschews that species of commentary which singles out volumes for their "falling off or crowning triumph" of moral conviction. Rather, certain texts dramatize a "benign" order: in the autobiographical poems this order is in emblems, such as the crucifix, which "sets off 'Mammon's unbridled industry.' " When the order is authoritarian (or totalitarian), the self squirms, cowers, or yields. Donoghue says that Lowell's most remarkable poems were written to express the latter, where there is no middle term, no gentle order, no Christ, and no hope of finding him.

Donoghue's essay was written during the mid-sixties, when Lowell had newly relinquished all religious affiliations and was on the threshold of a major ideological transition. It proved prophetic, for the dominant concern in Lowell's forthcoming volumes (*Notebook, History*) was the prolixity of totalitarianism throughout history. The tension that dominates these volumes arises from absence of hope for self-autonomy in a world of tyranny (here Lowell includes even those nations which espouse parliamentarianism or democracy). According to Donoghue, Lowell truly sought a divine authority, but his modern sensibility and cognitive powers would not permit him to find it. In effect, he always wanted a "mediator" (another word for God). Lowell considered self-autonomy, that purportedly desirable psychological state, too vulnerable to chaos, loneliness, and despair. Donoghue concludes that the elegiac tone in the poems, the nostalgia for something lost, was Lowell's effective disguise for his conservatism. Thus, although Donoghue never mentions Arnold by name, his portrait of Lowell resembles Arnold.

Not all critics endorsed the view that Lowell's nostalgia was generated from exhaustion, passivity, or moral torpor. Because Lowell's "morality" was an elusive topic for critical analysis, the essays were equally elusive. Often there were opposite readings of the same text. For example, we can see the inconsistency by aligning Christopher Ricks's "Robert Lowell at 60" (*Listener*, March 10, 1977) with French's and Donoghue's essays. All three assess *Union Dead*, among other works. Like French and Donoghue, Ricks brings a set of expectations to the poetry: a search for a moral position. Far from detecting a passive "abdication" (French) or choice between "orders" (Donoghue), Ricks finds that violence—national, supranational, domestic, personal—is Lowell's constant resort, "terrible in its variety (of time, of place, of motion, of nature) and terrible in its unchangingness." Ricks's essay typifies the late criticism, which rejects the notion of Lowell as liberal pacifist: "Isn't Lowell famous for the violence of his ways with language, with understandings? And how can there be an art which preaches non-violence and practices violence?"

French does not think in terms of liberalism as such; Donoghue does not chart Lowell on a political spectrum. Of the three, Ricks's position carries most weight because he dissects form in specific poems, finding structural examples of violence in the meter itself. Nonetheless, like French and Donoghue, Ricks uses an *a priori* standard, applying the Horatian rule that poetry should teach as well as delight.

We should pause for bearings here, noting our awareness of what must be apparent to the reader: a certain lack of direction in the criticism. Because time seems to have had little effect on the critics' way of perceiving the subject, this survey of "moral" criticism is not chronological. We have instead a theme which —rather than analyze the components of culture, religion, and morality—we have chosen to associate with a man, Arnold, whose thought embodied the whole, impossible tangle of ideas. (We want to remind the reader that Arnold serves here *as a reference*, not a "key," to the Lowell canon.) Morality, cut loose (for Arnold and later writers) from the anchors of religion, became extremely hard to define. The poet, the world, and love all seemed to elude each other. National culture, especially in its primitive aspects, beckoned postindustrial man as the Rhine maidens did Wagner. The intellect, honed at Oxford or Kenyon, was strained with the tuggings of loneliness, despair, primitive seduction, *and* the aristocratic responsibilities of leadership in crisis. We meet all of these concerns, usually not clearly separated from one another, in the criticism of Lowell.

In the early pages of this chapter we were able to identify a fairly central moral concern. As we return to our examination, we must deal with a set of works in which the just-mentioned aspects are more intricately tangled. Although we are largely concerned with tracing specific themes of Lowell criticism, we must not forget formal concerns. Those critics have seemed most helpful who have most carefully aligned, say, the violence they find in the themes of moral chaos with the prosodic violence, and have shown specifically how Lowell has stood apart from many of his contemporaries who have attempted the same thing.

We may well resume where we left off, with the question of morality—but seeing the problem as morality begins to be bound (not always with strictest logic) to a personal angst. What did the critics mean by "morality"? Since no twentieth-century critic could safely retreat behind doctrinal standards, some observers measured Lowell's morality by the degree to which he suffered, or gave evidence of doing so, in the poetry. Morality = Suffering. This formula was considered absurd by yet another group of critics, who simply attributed the suffering to mental disturbance. While the latter group may have made the former seem naive, at best, it offered little coherent explanation of how Lowell's mental suffering forged a cultural vision. The former group, at least, credited Lowell with historical awareness and a lugubrious concern for the future. It was at times too generous in its assessment (e.g., Babette Deutsch), but it was able to site Lowell's brand of suffering on the literary map—as well as the sociocultural one. It was hard to suggest a single provenance for Lowell's "moral" sensibility; indeed, it might not have been prudent to do so. However, had these critics postulated that Arnold's "Marguerite" poems and Lowell's *Dolphin* poems are unnerving documents of self-condemnation, each dramatized through complex sea motifs, the Arnoldian connection would have been more apparent, for it is on the subject of eroticism that the poems evince a curious mixture of impassioned ecstasy and impossible alliance:

> In the void air, towards thee,
> My stretched arms are cast;
> But a sea rolls between us—
> Our different past!
>
> [Arnold]

> Glad to escape beguilment and the storm,
> I thank the ocean that hides the fearful mermaid—
> like God, I almost doubt if you exist.
>
> [Lowell]

Something in both poets wishes, out of fear, that the love not exist. By glorifying the love object, Arnold and Lowell succeed in denying it. When extrapolated to extrapersonal themes, this characteristic converts both poets into outsiders, their self-division separating them from their times and cultures.

In 1950 Marius Bewley started a trend in interpretation which identified Lowell's disordered life and thought with the American "ruined man" (*Scrutiny*, April 1950). Although broad in generalization, Bewley's interpretation is as plausible as any. Bewley's book deals with the unique, eccentric nature of American literature, his title repeating Henry James's argument that it is "a complex fate" to be an American. To Bewley, Lowell depicts the American background as "alive with the sense of responsibility," but assumes this responsibility with a sense of strain, which is noticeable in his "feverishly tortuous" prosodic structure. Moreover, though Lowell feels that his thematic structures must be logical and highly ordered, they emerge as "slippery and concealed." Handicapped by his complex moral sense, Lowell felt an obligation to observe the standards of logic and rhetoric and to confer dignity on the American heritage; by doing so, he ran into "dreary territory." Bewley is sympathetic to Lowell's earnestness, but he is not merciful about the poetry (*Poems 1938–1949*), which never "transcends the dreary materials he builds them with." Bewley describes and evaluates selected poems, which is all that his premise permits him to do.

Patrick Cosgrave tries to stretch the same moral premise, adding that Lowell was searching for "the unblemished Adam" (*The Public Poetry of Robert Lowell*, 1970). He goes far afield but never uncovers the basis for, nor the import of, Lowell's "unblemished Adam" obsession. The thrust of his text is that Lowell's central ambition had always been to function as a public poet, in the manner of Alexander Pope; but Pope could share his cultural resources with his readership in a way that Lowell could not.

Two general points are made about the canon: "Firstly, an inherent violence—moral in appearance, probably partly psychological in origin—is inseparable from Lowell's work at its fullest stretch." Few would quibble with Cosgrave on this point, but when he moves to his second point, that Lowell's true ambition is public and "burns to judge men and affairs against an immutable and objective standard," his persuasiveness is diminished. Since Lowell's moral concern is always regarded in terms of public performance, private moralities are judged by public attitudes and actions. By this principle, says Cosgrave, Lowell's "assertion of life is often tangential, while the main energy is employed for the purposes of annunciation." Using this thesis as a scale, Cosgrave scores the volumes for their level of incantation, ritual, and violence; the less these are in evidence, the more successful the volume.

There are obvious weaknesses in such an approach, and Cosgrave succumbs to them. This is especially true of his chapter on *Life Studies*, which, in his opinion, has "ambiguous" stanzas, and "though ambiguity of a high order is a necessary element in poetry, it here represents evasion." But the implausibility increases! Cosgrave attributes Lowell's ambiguity to inability to find resources for judgment; in other words, *Life Studies* is an example of moral disintegration. In this volume, especially, Lowell uses "personal intervention" to assess public events and issues, wherein the poems lack balance between "personality and resources." I would complain less about Cosgrave's book if he had chosen specific public events, or issues referred to in the poems, and showed how Lowell dealt with them.

The fact remains that Lowell, both in his lifestyle and in public appearances, cultivated an image of anarchy and irreverence (despite Mailer's solemn portrait in *Armies of the Night*). This seemed to have had little impact on the critics. Indeed, when Lowell "misbehaved" and shocked academia—his third marriage was one instance of unacceptable behavior—critics searched even more ardently for signs of "guilt" in his verse (especially *For Lizzie and Harriet*). They wanted to believe that while he shook the foundations of morality, he did so with much misgiving. They also ignored the anecdotes about the heavy-drinking, often violent Lowell, who put the finishing touches to his first marriage by closing his Maine house and drowning the family cat and her litter in the lake (documented in Heymann's *American Aristocracy: The Lives and Times of James Russell, Amy and Robert*, 1980). Moreover, the notion of Lowell as upright preceptor became more pronounced after his death. In "The Morality of Form in the Poetry of Robert Lowell" (*Ariel*, January 1978), William Bedford carried that approach to its sentimental extreme, repudiating the idea that there were negative values in the verse. The essay is predominantly a defense of *Notebook*, which, in its fragmentary and casual structure, seems to enact the moral and political fragmentation Lowell saw around him. Bedford shuns such an explanation:

> It [Lowell's morality] is an order as fragile as the form of the poems themselves; but equally, just as the liberal and pastoral values mourned in "Waking Early Sunday Morning" and "Fourth of July in Maine" are a permanent measure of what man can achieve, so Lowell's verse reminds us that such order is possible.

Bedford finds Lowell's conflict between formalism and free verse—and the tentative prosodic solutions which characterized each new volume after *Life Studies*—his most significant contribution to contemporary moral consciousness. Thus "For the Union Dead" presents a form "whose very gracefulness is almost representative of New England liberalism, and by virtue of its quiet arrangement of horror, articulates a vision of contemporary American society that has the breadth of a much larger-scale work." Pretty sentiments, but little substance.

Too frequently, Lowell's suffering is so vaguely identified

that it might be the "property" of any number of contemporary poets. Charles Molesworth's "Republican Objects and Utopian Moments: The Poetry of Robert Lowell and Allen Ginsberg," a chapter in his *The Fierce Embrace: A Study of Contemporary American Poetry* (1979), is a case in point. Ginsberg and Lowell are depicted as "the best poets of their generation who knew how to survive their own publicity"; both are "commentators" of the public occasion, their private musings determined by the course of public events. But Molesworth says that Lowell regards the present, as well as the past, with a gloomier outlook than does Ginsberg. His sense of history is like a failed republicanism, which relays a series of long-distance recriminations and broken promises. Lowell is tempted to read history as the record of exploding vanity and of power justified by more power. Arguing that the nexus of thought synthesized in Marxism, Freudianism, and Darwinism produced in Lowell a "devolutionary" view of man, Molesworth attempts to outline the poet's moral vision. In doing so, he stretches the limits of credence: Lowell's reactions to the public scene show determinism, intermittent savage irony, an undercurrent of pathos—yet these qualities do not detract from his tragic and heroic image!

One is prompted to ask how such a description differs from that of other politically committed poets—to wit, Eliot's or Pound's savage irony, Frost's sense of determinism, the pathos in lesser contemporary poets like Bly or Levertov. Molesworth paints an all-too-familiar portrait: Lowell gives us "a language dense with phrases and broken sentences, chipped and scarred by a nervous allusiveness, a learned poetry made even more cluttered by diffidence." His description of the poems' linguistic features is applicable to much current poetry: "the twisting of phrases, the buckling of syntax till it yields the curves, however gnarled, of his sensibility." Molesworth fails to explain the qualities by which Lowell surpassed the work of most poets of his generation, or how his moral vision forged a poetic.

There is, admittedly, some correlation between the critics' obsession with Lowell's "morality" and the changes in the American political arena. If one were to graph the contour of criticism, the increase in Lowell sanctification would be most noticeable during the sixties, with vestigial hagiography continuing through the seventies. When Seamus Heaney delivered a memorial address on Lowell at St. Luke's Church in London (October 5, 1977), he compared him with Christ:

He did not pitch his voice at "the public" but he so established the practice of art as a moral function within his own life that when he turned outward to make gestures against the quality of the life of his times, those gestures had been well-earned and possessed a memorable force.

The occasion, of course, demanded a eulogistic statement, but it is doubtful that Lowell's poems were founts of spiritual nourishment. Too many of them are cynical; there are even hostile pieces about his son, his second wife, his parents, critics, himself (his nickname in the poems, "Cal" for Caligula, is symptomatic). Thus when Heaney says the voice in the poems is "oracular and penitential" and that Lowell's purpose was "redemptive," we are inclined to shrug.

The tormented search for a personal—and national—morality was not the only area in which critics chose to link Lowell and Arnold. They credited Lowell with possessing Arnold's intellectual and cultural sophistication, though they were divided about the extent to which Lowell had adapted Arnold's "tragic liberalism." Alan Williamson (*Pity the Monsters*) said that Arnold preserved the mental and moral security of the world by affirming "adult" qualities over vitality and imagination. Self-restraint, reasonableness, social and familial responsibility—these were the virtues of the old order. Lowell echoed this, says Williamson, especially in *Life Studies*, in which poems like "Grandparents" produce a "cultural allegory." These lines from "Grandparents" reveal Lowell's nostalgia for protective figures:

the nineteenth century, tired of children, is gone.
They're all gone into a world of light; the farm's my own.

Stephen Yenser compared Arnold's and Lowell's respective views on the ascetic life, tracing Lowell's "Mother Marie Therese" back to Arnold's "Stanzas from the Grand Chartreuse." Lowell is "ambivalent about the ascetic life; but whereas Arnold was skeptical of its philosophical foundations, Lowell is convinced of the corruptibility of its adherents" (*Circle to Circle*, p. 108). Thus Yenser shares with Williamson the belief in Lowell's conservative bias; institutions (familial and religious, in their examples) are fallible but necessary.

When critics turned to Lowell's political-historical views, his "tragic liberalism" was strenuously contradicted. One of the most knowledgeable essays in this category is in Thomas R. Edwards' *Imagination and Power: A Study of Poetry on Public Themes*. Edwards acknowledged that his analysis, which appeared in 1971, was necessarily inconclusive because, since Lowell's political vision was characterized by "idiosyncratic complexities," predictions about future work would be spurious. Edwards' caution later proved unwarranted, for the position in the essay brilliantly speaks for the canon, now that it is complete. According to Edwards, Lowell typifies the modern poet who takes public events seriously, yet longs to retain an impartial, disinterested intelligence. Liberalism becomes the position (or nonposition) that poets of Lowell's sensibility will assume; in effect, it is an openness to conflicting interests and ideologies which somehow accommodate each other. Lowell's case is further compounded by his circumstances: his aristocratic heritage with its attraction toward traditional religious authority. Thus he assumes several poses in the poetry. In "The March" (*Notebook 1967–68*), for example, he mocks his activist self even as he depicts his participation in the 1967 Pentagon March. In this poem, Edwards argues, Lowell too easily accepts the poet's public role as one of weakness:

> Consciousness of ineffectuality leads to taking action without really committing yourself to the outcome, except for the *personal* outcome, which can be bravely, even cheerfully endured as suitable punishment for having abandoned your high-minded detachment [p. 73].

At the same time, Lowell, in his effort to avoid total commitment, assumes a self-mockery; he plays the "buffoon" to keep from fully believing in the seriousness of the event. This has the paradoxical effect of heightening the value of politics at the expense of the imagination. Lowell continually wrestled with the dilemma, since it pitted his political against his artistic conscience. According to Edwards, he sought solutions in various ways; for example, in "Inauguration Day: January 1953" (*Life Studies*) Lowell suppressed his speaking self into the texture of the verse, "so that the poem and not the poet" registered the significance of the event. Symbols of enclosure and stasis satirically conveyed the political significance of this public ceremony, installing Eisenhower as president. Lowell plays the augurer in this poem, and if "his auguries are clouded and uncertain, they all the more truthfully express the uncertainty of public actions." Edwards argues that in "July in Washington" (*Union Dead*) personal and political meanings are successfully merged; the poem keeps important subjects from being reduced to the scale of the mind that contemplates them, and that mind, while it knows its limitations, "refused the consolation of pretending to be *more* limited and weak than it really is."

There is, therefore, no consistent direction in Lowell's poetry. "The March," written later than "July in Washington," is for Edwards an example of regression. While each poem provides a different perspective on the interaction between the poet and his public role, it is clear that Edwards sees Lowell at his poetic best when he is not "succumbing to the Liberal Vice of overvaluing public 'realities' and its resultant undervaluing of one's own participation in public acts." Balanced appraisals such as Edwards' are hard to come by in this unit of criticism.

There are several admirable studies on the scope of Lowell's thematic treatment of war and history. Tate, Bewley, and Jarrell, among others, had noticed the almost perverse intermingling of religious imagery with war imagery in the early volumes; but it was not until the sixties that substantial efforts were made to explain such a conjunction. Richard Fein's "Mary and Bellona: The War Poetry of Robert Lowell" (*Southern Review*, Autumn 1965) indirectly attributes this conjunction to Lowell's need to attach some redemptive meaning to war. Put in such a way, Fein's premise sounds like rationalization, but the essay is a fascinating foray into the texts. Fein places Lowell among the post–World War II group of poets, claiming that his is the only religious poetry arising out of the holocaust. His poetry demonstrates a wartime Christianity, which, as portrayed on the title page of *Land of Unlikeness*, "cannot conceive of the cross without a horrendous gargoyle clutching it." In essence, Fein proverbializes one of Lowell's major themes: "war is a distortion of religious experience." Lowell displays this anomaly with sarcastic and uncompromising intelligence.

Fein says this anomaly dominates "On the Eve of the Feast of the Immaculate Conception, 1942" (*Unlikeness*), in which "war becomes a kind of ghastly human eucharist, a rekilling of Christ in the form of dead soldiers." Moving to later volumes, Fein discovers a surprisingly frequent combination of poems in which war themes and religious holidays are merged (i.e., "Christmas Eve under Hooker's Statue," "Cistercians in Germany"). In the later volumes, a growing number of military leaders populates the verse (Napoleon, Charlemagne, Charles the Fifth, Caesar, Colonel Shaw). To Fein, this makes it increasingly apparent that Lowell views all wars as one, that his vision of destruction is a composite which ultimately refers to the present. References to religion in poems about war offer no relief; instead, they intensify the horror and our perception of it. Or more correctly, in placing the horror within Christian terms of experience, Lowell "tries to measure and plummet the violation and at the same time, through the Christian knowledge, prevent the awareness from falling into the abyss."

Fein, therefore, gives a modified psychological interpretation of the yoking of religion and war. Since war is part of man's permanent earthly condition, Lowell must domesticate it "to save consciousness from going under." This is not only a tantalizing premise, it explains Lowell's need to justify the unsavory aspects of the Christian culture. If Fein, who does not bring Arnold into his discussion, reads Lowell correctly, he is endowing Lowell with Arnoldian principles. In "Sweetness and Light" (*Culture and Anarchy*, 1869), Arnold linked the production of good literature to the health of society, thus making value judgments about both society and literature. The nation that knows its besetting faults may transform its vices through culture (or poetry). Arnold said that the impulse toward self-conquest and moral development was still in its beginning stage:

> But the idea of beauty and of a human nature perfect on all its sides, which is the dominant idea of poetry, is a true and invaluable idea, though it has not yet had the success that the idea of conquering the obvious faults of our animality, and of a human nature perfect on the moral side,—which is the dominant idea of religion,—has been enabled to have.

At first sight, this kind of preaching seems far removed from Lowell's way of proselytizing, as Fein understood it. Not so. The same mental activity is at work. By carrying the tragedies of civilization into his poetry, Lowell attempted to unite reason and the will of God.

War and history fascinated Lowell, especially as they affected the American past and presaged the future. The most thorough study of this topic is Alan Holder's "The Flintlocks of the Fathers: Robert Lowell's Treatment of the American Past" (*New England Quarterly*, March 1971). Holder's essay appeared before *History* (1973) was published; however, since many of the selections in *History* are revisions from the *Notebook* volumes, which were available to Holder, the discussion stands with some authority. (Also, *History* covers the span of Western civilization, while Holder's interest is limited to Lowell and American history.) Holder goes through the volumes chronologically, looking for literal evaluations, on Lowell's part, of events. He does not begin with a thesis, but accumulated evidence points to the idea that Lowell viewed Puritanism with abhorrence. Holder maintains that Lowell "did not so much turn to the past as turn *on* it. The nodal points of our history are, in his poems as well as in his dramatic trilogy *Old Glory*, the unjust use of collective violence against men or nature."

Indeed, the American story has been repeatedly that of antagonism and brutal exploitation between man and man, and man and nature. In early poems, such as "Children of Light," the Puritans' callousness toward the Indians is depicted as a kind of "casual, domesticated violence." The moral smugness of the Puritans as Indian killers, who conceive of themselves as "the elect of God," has of course been noted by other scholars—Staples, Bewley, Tate. Holder differs from them in showing how Lowell castigated even the admirable moments in American history. Therefore, the epigraph to his poem "At the Indian Killer's Grave" employs a reference to King Philip's War which was found in a story by Hawthorne, "The Gray Champion." Holder notes that Hawthorne's story is basically a tale that *praises* a historical event (defiance by some colonists of the British authorities in Boston), but Lowell changes the priorities, focusing on an inconsequential passage in "The Gray Champion" which casts a shameful light on the colonists. Another instance of Lowell's deep pessimism is his disagreement with Emerson: "Where the earlier writer [Emerson] could take pride in the rebellious colonial energies that culminated in the War of Independence, Lowell's references to the Revolution are generally no more admiring of the victors than are his treatments of those who triumphed over the Indians." Holder says that critics mistakenly believe that Lowell admired Emerson; those critics who thought he admired Jonathan Edwards were also mistaken. Lowell saw in Edwards' pastoral life (and sermons) another instance of the American compulsion for violence. In Edwards' case, it was a "violence of the imagination directed against his listeners." That Edwards never admitted his role in causing Hawley's death exemplifies the standard American rationalization of its violence.

When Lowell observes the American present, says Holder, he regards it (with disdain) as a continuation or repetition of the past. However, as he moves closer to the present, Lowell becomes more contradictory in his attitudes. He combines a "pacifist's hatred of violence with an armchair general's fascinated regard for combat." Holder is most original when he undertakes an explanation of such paradoxes. Moreover, he finds Lowell's practice of revision generated not so much by a desire to improve style as to reflect his changing point of view. Thus Lowell's different versions of poems illustrate his growing ambivalence. For example, in the early piece, "Concord" (first published in *Partisan Review*, July–August 1943), both Emerson and Thoreau are regarded with hostility because their Transcendentalism "sponsored Unitarianism with its debased theology." In its second version (*Unlikeness*), Lowell dropped explicit reference to Thoreau. Lowell had separated out Thoreau as a pacifist, a role that Lowell played at the time (the year was 1944, when heavy air strikes and Allied invasions of the Continent stepped up the tension of battle). By the third version (*Lord Weary*), Thoreau was restored to the poem and treated as a pacifist role model. Holder offers just a few examples of poetic revision as instance of political conversion, but he heightens the importance of establishing the chronology of textual versions. Holder concludes that the most contradictory feature of Lowell's historical vision is his Calvinist rigidity working against his humane liberalism. Thus in "Mr. Edwards and the Spider" Edwards is depicted as harsh; at the same time, the poem indulges the notion of man as a "creature whose puny exertions of force, attempts at dominion, are laughable when seen against the power of the Lord." Holder's reading of "Quaker Graveyard" uncovers an even crueler Lowell:

> Lowell's own picture of the Quaker sailors drowned at sea would seem to partake of an Edwardsian satisfaction in the contemplation of sinners properly punished. Like Edwards' portrayal of the spider cast into the flames, Lowell's poem provides a grand spectacle of destruction.

With Holder, the religious interpretations we noted in the last chapter become secularized, part of an almost Darwinian sense of historical violence. To call attention to and thus (hopefully) correct such a fault is surely in Arnold's pattern, yet Holder's "spectacle" is hardly a carryover of Arnold's "tragic liberalism." Holder softens his conclusion by emphasizing that

Lowell tried to interact with the historical event, as did major writers of the past: Hawthorne, Emerson, Thoreau. Although he quarrelled with this triumvirate, he shared with them the challenge of reconciling American political ideals with historical events, which in turn had to be reconciled with a religious doctrine, whether Calvinist, Unitarian, or Catholic.

Holder's position is not popular; commentators tend to regard Lowell the historian as one who exploits the subject merely to sound his personal crises. In *Modern American Lyric: Lowell, Berryman, Creeley and Plath* (1978), Arthur Oberg argues that Lowell moves through history in order to find private meaning; thus there is a private, rather than public, poet in Lowell's work. Yet the distinction blurs, and Holder and Oberg merge when we consider that the strict generic limits of Latin— and Augustan—public poetry are not observed by modern authors. We are reminded that, before Lowell, Arnold considered the historical moment (the withdrawal of the "sea of Faith") from a personal and erotic point of view. Indeed, the very nature of imaginative literature suggests that, unlike the historian, the poet typically personalizes his subject (a trait which Lowell acknowledges in the Naipaul interview noted below).

These cautions having been registered, we nevertheless acknowledge that there are degrees of public and private concern which it is the legitimate business of criticism to delineate. Oberg's sense of Lowell is personal and lyrical. He says that "Lowell's sense of history, like that of Yeats and Pound, is lyric and elegiac rather than narrowly philosophical or historical. When Lowell turns to history or pre-history, it is biography which interests him." Oberg also says that the figures in history which interested Lowell are frequently pairs of sad, tragic, sometimes violent lovers (e.g., Antony and Cleopatra). As Lowell arched through the epochs, most extensively in *Notebook*, he changed his priorities: "from a Marxist (man is what he makes) to an Existentialist or Nihilist-Existentialist (man is what he does) to a lyrical (man is what he loves) sense of man." Oberg quotes a line from *Notebook*, "What you love you are," to support his premise—a poor choice, for as Holder and others have demonstrated, Lowell loved and hated according to his shifting moods. Moreover, Oberg's treatment is dictated by the thesis of his book: the contemporary lyric is ultimately what the lyric had always been, a love poem. Despite Oberg's sensitive précis of the late poems ("to live is to love;

therefore, to love is to change—this is one of the syllogisms operative in the sonnets"), his reading is inappropriately romanticized.

O. B. Hardison provides a more reliable evaluation of Lowell's comprehension of history. He argues that the deficiency of *Imitations*, which consists of adaptations of other poets' works, stems from Lowell's need to incorporate self into his poems. Lowell's special ability is the capacity to "recover what Ransom and Tate have agreed to call the world's body—by introspection to create the image of a particular man at a particular moment in history" (*Shenandoah*, Winter 1963). The "imitations," in which Lowell transformed himself to another poet's sensibility and culture, prevented Lowell from exercising this capacity. Hardison had discovered a requirement vital to the poet's creativity. Lowell himself would later suggest that, for a writer, political events acquire significance in terms of the personal acts the writer experienced. In an interview with V. S. Naipaul, he recalled his participation in the 1967 Pentagon March: "It was mainly the fragility of a person caught up in this situation" (*Listener*, September 4, 1969).

Did Lowell ever evolve a system for interpreting history? Critics were inclined to think not. Some, like Louis Simpson (*A Revolution in Taste*, 1978), patronizingly observed that Lowell was too elitist to understand the masses. Others, like Jerome Mazzaro, presented an elaborate inventory of the sources he felt contributed to Lowell's changing concept of history ("Robert Lowell's Early Politics of Apocalypse," *Modern American Poetry: Essays in Criticism*, 1970). Prior to delving into what he calls Lowell's "deterministic" outlook on Western history, Mazzaro remarks on the pervasive Arnoldian slant to Lowell's view: "In the manner of Arnold, Lowell is intent in his art to show his readers what 'morality' is." Lowell's poems about history and culture suggest that he was familiar with this passage, quoted by Mazzaro, from Arnold's "The Study of Poetry" (1880):

> We should conceive of poetry worthily, and more highly than it has been the custom to conceive of it. We should conceive of it as capable of higher uses, and called to higher destinies than those which in general men have assigned to it hitherto. More and more mankind will discover that we have to turn to poetry to interpret life for us, to console us, to sustain us.

Mazzaro then outlines the background for Lowell's apocalyptic grasp of history. Lowell's view is not far from what Yeats devised in *A Vision* (1917), whereby history, being cyclical, is a process outside of human control and causes civilization's decline. Yeats's work was followed a year later by Oswald Spengler's *The Decline of the West*, which upheld a similar theory. Richard Dawson's *Beyond Politics* (1939), which Lowell undoubtedly read (Mazzaro speaking), was more explicit about those constrictions of political institutions which make history deterministic. Arguing that dictatorship and democracy were not opposites but "twin children," Dawson instructed Lowell to distrust democracy (Mazzaro again):

> Anyone who studies the history of the First French Republic in the light of recent political developments cannot fail to be impressed by the way in which the Jacobins anticipated practically all the features of the modern totalitarian regimes.

Fascism, communism, and democracy offered the world the "comings" of Benito Mussolini, Josef Stalin, and Franklin Delano Roosevelt. In the early forties, it was not always easy to distinguish between the three ideologies, says Mazzaro. Mazzaro aside, it is hard to know how Lowell felt about these ideologies. All we have on record is his comment to A. Alvarez: "My first book was written during the war, which was a very different time from the thirties. . . . The world seemed apocalyptic at that time, and heroically so. I thought civilization was going to break and instead *I* did" (London *Observer*, 1963). Mazzaro says that Lowell's fears were fixed by the war, leaving him thereafter in constant anticipation of doom. Such a premonition prompted in him the compulsion, similar to Arnold's in the nineteenth century, to warn his society.

Mazzaro's encyclopedic compilation of the sources which purportedly helped to synthesize Lowell's view of history is just that—encyclopedic. Lowell is never credited with sorting *out* these sources. Mazzaro suggests, though never forthrightly declares, that Lowell reacted emotionally to an onslaught of impressions, dizzying events, and the provocative Yeatsian and Spenglerian theories. The main problem with this position is that we fail to learn precisely what the texts and events meant to Lowell. As we asked of Molesworth's essay, In what *special* way did Lowell convert what was, after all, information common to poets other than himself?

Frances Ferguson's "Appointments with Time: Robert Lowell's Poetry through the *Notebooks*" (*American Poetry since*

*1960: Some Critical Perspectives*, 1973) is an attempt to explain Lowell's view of history as a modern poet's struggle with time. No mention is made of Arnold, nor does Ferguson judge Lowell in an Arnoldian manner. Citing Emerson's dictum that "there is no history; there is only biography," she finds Emerson's contemporary equivalent in Lowell. Lowell's "anti-historical subjectivity" is his way to avoid temporal disjunction; that is, he uses the poem as a "mediator" between personal and historical time. Ferguson's argument, to this point, resembles Hardison's; then it veers, unsteadily, toward the abstruse. For example, she says that *Life Studies* mediates between the Robert Lowell who wrote in the present and the "past Robert Lowells, his own past selves." Even in personal pieces, like "Home after Three Months Away," the Lowellian speaker moves into and out of the consciousness of literary characters while devising an identification with them (e.g., *Richard II:* "Is Richard now himself again?"). Through this projection, "his and Richard's disorders *create* an order, salvaging them from the surrender to time."

Ferguson makes an interesting contribution to the growing effort to explain Lowell's revisions: they are a kind of repetition which constitutes "re-vision"; therefore all previous literature is an index to a "once-living consciousness which can be renewed by an altering re-vision." Unfortunately, Ferguson does not enlist examples from the poetry to support her theory. She shrinks from the challenge by pigeon-holing Lowell's method as Hegelian: "In Hegelizing his poetry, Lowell attempts to yoke the passage of personal historical time with a growth analogous to the development of the phases of World-History." This may or may not be true; but a few examples might have helped us decide.

What we *do* know from accounts of Lowell's interest in philosophers is that Hegel's mind never greatly intrigued Lowell. Hegel's name appears in one of Lowell's early poems ("Sublime Ferian Sidern Vertice," *Hika*, 1940) and refers to the philosopher's awareness of governments' power to plunge nations into global conflicts. But as Heymann noted in *American Aristocracy*, Lowell was no more fascinated by Hegel than by other philosophers. Heymann's statement is one of delimitation: "He [Hegel], like other great humanist visionaries—Aristotle, Aquinas, Erasmus, and Voltaire—simultaneously addressed philosophical and political issues" (p. 483). Moreover, nowhere in the interviews, or in the commentary by Lowell's colleagues and friends (e.g., Jarrell, Tate, Berryman), is Hegel given any consideration. If Ferguson had developed her Emersonian correlation beyond its use as an introduction to her essay, she might have unearthed a more dependable basis for Lowell's theory of time.

Scattered references to Lowell's historical and political views in the standard reviews accompanied his volumes' publications. Starting with *Union Dead*, these references are more frequent and detailed. Prior to surveying this part of the scholarship, I would like to mention two other treatments of Lowell's historical theory—one brief, the other book length—which represent the furthest points of polarity. Walter J. Ong apprehends Lowell's theory as traditional and orthodox (Arnoldian, in other words, although Arnold is not named). He says that Lowell felt compelled to "build poetry around historical events which have been felt by him as a part of his own life world" (*In the Human Grain*, 1967). Lowell evinces a distinctly open-end or linear view of history, but incorporates his concepts of justice into his interpretation, says Ong. This is a reasonable way to summarize Lowell's thought process; it does not contradict the by now standard view that self was a primordial concern in all of the poet's speculation.

In contrast, Alan Williamson, whose *Pity the Monsters* proceeds on the notion that Lowell's poetic vision was entirely "political," has little patience with readings such as Ong's. To begin with, Williamson states a hypothesis about Lowell's ideology:

> [Lowell] harbors within himself an Eliot-like conservative's insistence on forms of integrity lost in historical "progress"; yet he exemplifies a revolutionary's vision of apocalyptic community and hunger for poetic justice, and at times a liberal's sharp, impersonal scruples.

This statement, because it includes so many possibilities for analysis, sounds like an unpromising introduction to Williamson's project: to synthesize all the political elements in Lowell's poetry into a coherent vision. Not so. Williamson is a cogent interpreter who, by refusing to be judgmental and by remaining committed to his inquiry, gives us an excellent work of scholarship. He demonstrates that Lowell has indeed played the conservative, the revolutionary, and the liberal—sometimes

all at once. This means, for our purposes, that it would be inappropriate to apply the Arnoldian stamp to Williamson's
book. Williamson departs from Cosgrave's argument that Lowell's work is divided into public and private brackets. Rather,
there is an interaction between the personal and the public
Lowell: "He is almost continuously being both, and more deliberately so as his work advances."

It should be noted that *Pity the Monsters* followed shortly
upon the publication of *Notebook* and *History*, so that it
seemed as though the political forum was Lowell's only interest.
*Day by Day* reversed that to some degree, yet there is enough
emphasis on politics in this volume (published three years after
*Pity the Monsters*) to sustain Williamson's thesis. "Fetus," a
poem about a convicted abortion-surgeon, takes a dim view of
law courts:

> The court cannot reform the misstep
> of the motionless moment . . .
> So many killers are cleared of killing,
> yet we are shocked a fetus can be murdered

And in "Domesday Book," a poem about taxation practices in
English history, Lowell defines justice in one acerbic line: "If
they have you by the neck, a rope will be found."

Lowell may not have become the "modern epic poet of history" that Williamson had predicted in 1974, but he diagnosed
the contemporary scene with deep awareness of the factors
which produced society's present condition. Building on Lowell's interview remarks, that Freud was his favorite theoretician
on the subject of civilization, Williamson stated that Lowell
himself was "concerned with the cost of civilization to instinctual satisfaction and even instinctual awareness." At the
same time, Williamson found that on occasion, as in *Near the
Ocean*, Lowell questioned Freud's assumption that human aggression is an instinct, growing out of animal greed or out of
*thanatos*. Rather, Lowell *wanted* to find the causes for aggression in social ills or neurotic distortion (proof of his liberal side).

In reviewing the canon up to 1973, Williamson says that the
acme of Lowell's career begins with *Union Dead*; from that
volume on, Lowell reaches an epic scale and his poetic voice
becomes less ironic, more passionate and authoritative. The conscious grandeur of tone and use of compelling meter, temporarily abandoned in *Life Studies*, are now restored to his poetic

range, vividly dramatizing his new vision. *Lord Weary* is not completely discredited; Williamson believes that its excessive and strained symbolism and meters were necessary transitional elements that a "young visionary political poet" had to utilize before reaching a mature mode. *Life Studies* is a rich and emotionally moving book, yet it does not seem to embody Lowell's complete voice, says Williamson. The reasons are technical: "The verbal elements are restricted, the prophetic dimension reduced, the public judgments rendered more difficult and relativistic."

Williamson's appraisal of *Life Studies* is one of the most original treatments of this volume. Although Williamson does not regard it as Lowell's major work, thereby departing from the critiques of Ehrenpreis, Rosenthal, Altieri, and Perloff, his case is convincing. *Life Studies* is a "political book," says Williamson, which deals with the socialization of the individual by family, class, and law. The speaker in the volume often seems less a whole man than the embodiment of a man's search for objectivity, for acceptance of himself through self-knowledge. In this sense, then, the volume is *less* personal than earlier texts (Williamson is the first to convicingly argue this; most others find in *Life Studies* the apotheosis of confessionalism). It is also a transitional text, leading away from the exclusively personal "toward a shared world of sophisticated discourse which provides methods of analysis, historical and cultural contexts for even the most delicate issues of sensibility." After *Life Studies* a new self emerges in *Union Dead*, a self which has cultivated a social awareness that Williamson, at any rate, believes is here to stay; but his argument becomes a little unsteady. One might easily reply that this new self is nowhere in evidence in *The Dolphin* or *Day by Day*, where Lowell regresses to unhappy introspection in poems about his family, his unhappy marriages, his nervous breakdowns. But Williamson dismisses these topical thorns by giving them an extrapersonal dimension. *Life Studies*, then, is a book about rebelliousness against social oppression. As opposed to the large-scale oppression of Puritan mercantilism, the pervasive evil in early volumes, now the oppression is caused by families and class codes.

When Williamson applies his thesis to *Near the Ocean*, he again proves provocative. He relates Lowell's sociological perception to the late, radical Freudians, Herbert Marcuse and Norman O. Brown. "Near the Ocean," the title poem, is "an explicit, two-edged, comparison between sexual and political cycles." Its nearly surrealistic disjunction and montage of images suggest that historical and technological progress manifests a "repetition neurosis, a collective sexual anxiety that drives man to create constantly grander, but never fully reassuring, aggressive simulacra of the phallus." To be sure, Williamson overassigns the Freudian influence on Lowell, but he refreshingly complements an already pluralistic scholarship with vitality, sympathy, and (his most appealing quality) no slurring of other interpretations.

Conservative, revolutionary, liberal. Was Lowell a curious combination of all three, as Williamson insisted? The neo-Freudian slant to Lowell's ideas, if Williamson was right, would qualify him as conservative; the view of man as an aggressive, instinctual creature in need of constant check is centuries old. Freud had merely prescribed therapy as the check to replace the earlier one, religion. Actually, the drift in the criticism was toward labelling Lowell a conservative, a view which concretized after his death.

Heymann's *American Aristocracy* (1980) is the ultimate example of this position. Heymann says that Lowell was conservative, regal, and even deferent before tyrants: "The common man was the bane of civilization, not its crowning glory. . . . The Few were the good, intelligent, the independent, the Many were the barbaric, ignorant and the easily swayed" (p. 484). Citing instances in Lowell's interpersonal relationships as well as in the poems, Heymann silhouettes a man who was far from a "democratic spirit." Lowell would have turned in his grave. Even more devastating was William Barrett's imputation that Lowell was too dumb to be either conservative *or* liberal. In *The Truants: Adventures among the Intellectuals* (1982), a memoir about the New York circle of writers in the post–World War II years, Barrett imparts his and Delmore Schwartz' impressions of Lowell:

> Delmore used also to complain about Lowell as "dumb"—not "stupid," that was reserved for Berryman. Delmore had in mind particularly what he thought were Lowell's naiveté and gullibility on political ideas. Lowell did seem to move slowly in intellectual conversation, as if he had to assimilate each point at the deliberate pace of his own more solemn pentameters [p. 27].

While Barrett's comment has the virtue of contributing to the biographical literature on Lowell, it sheds little light on our inquiry into Lowell's political ideas. All the more disappointing, when we learn that Barrett was an editor of *Partisan Review* in the forties and had endless conversations with that handful of intellectuals who figured in the political-literary scene: Mary McCarthy, Edmund Wilson, Lionel Trilling, Philip Rahv, and of course Lowell.

When we turn to the survey of the volumes insofar as they espouse Arnoldian values, we encounter another set of problems. The vague "moral" commentary is, happily, dropped but is replaced by a compulsion on the critics' part to elicit Lowell's responses to newspaper headlines. Rather than subordinating Lowell's topical references to some kind of philosophical or even aesthetic context, critics tended to look for Lowell's political message. Moreover, there was some blurring in their notions of Lowell's historical and political perspectives. Yet one fact clearly emerges: if we use Williamson's trio of affiliations (conservative, revolutionary, liberal), we find that no critic saw fit to label Lowell as revolutionary. There is a toss-up between the other two.

With the exception of Williamson, who addressed *Life Studies* as a political work, critics believed that Lowell's political and historical poetry began with *Union Dead*. Yet, might not the real source of this response be found not in the poetry but in the readers whose consciousness about the national political climate had been heightened, causing them to expect the same of Lowell? While some of the poems in *Union Dead* are overtly political (e.g., "Fall 1961"), others are as domestic and personal as the selections in the final section of *Life Studies* (e.g., "Myopia: A Night"):

> All autumn, the chafe and jar
> of nuclear war;
> we have talked our extinction to death.
> I swim like a minnow
> behind my studio window.
>
> ["Fall 1961"]

> What had disturbed this household?
> Only a foot away,
> the familiar faces blur.
> At fifty we're so fragile,
> a feather . . .
>
> ["Myopia: A Night"]

It is well to recall, however, that both the overtly political
"Fall 1961" and the overtly personal "Myopia" share an almost
surreal combination of familiar household details contorted by
a dread of evil forces. As usual in Lowell, the political and the
personal are never far apart. Critics were more accustomed to
"Myopia," which repeated the sentiments of *Life Studies*. So
the criticism focused on pieces like "Fall 1961" and the title
poem, which was singled out as the volume's crowning achievement. Here Lowell had merged the personal ("Once my nose
crawled like a snail on the glass") with the political ("There are
no statues for the last war here") with eloquence. There is an
Arnoldian allusion in the elegiac piece "Soft Wood," which
critics might have exploited, but none did so:

> Sometimes I have supposed seals
> must live as long as the Scholar Gypsy.
> Even in their barred pond at the zoo they are happy,
> and no sunflower turns
> more delicately to the sun
> without a wincing of the will.

This elegy, dedicated to and about Lowell's relative, Harriet
Winslow, recalls Arnold's longing to escape the fever and fret
of modern life ("The Scholar Gypsy," 1853). Stephen Yenser
likened this passage to Schopenhauer's emphasis on the self-
preserving instincts of man:

> If the seals are "happy," it is their ignorance that is their bliss;
> and if they "live as long as the Scholar Gypsy," it is their brute
> instinct that assures their immortality [*Circle to Circle*, p. 234].

The limpid melancholy of "Soft Wood" is about the closest
Lowell ever came to Arnold's voice. But the critics searched
for Arnoldian echoes in a conceptual rather than tonal context.

In the broader reviews of *Union Dead*, John Wain expressed
slight disappointment that the realism and soul-baring of *Life
Studies* were not repeated with "stabbing pathos" (*New Republic*, October 17, 1964). While the title poem, with its studied
irony, was "perfectly realized," a poem like "July in Washington" moved from detailed observation to generalized truth but
"did not quite get there." Never the twain, says Wain. I disagree; what better synthesis can we find than in the following
excerpt?

On the circles, green statues ride like South American
liberators above the breeding vegetation—
prongs and spearheads of some equatorial
backland that will inherit the globe.
The elect, the elected . . . they come here bright as dimes,
and die, dishevelled and soft.

There is even a throwback to the Puritan doctrine in the pun
"the elect."

With the passage of time, critics were less inclined to regard
*Union Dead* as just a muted sequel to *Life Studies*. Indeed,
*Union Dead* is one text whose interpretation has benefited by
the objectivity of time. This becomes evident when we compare a sampling of essays written over the span of a decade.
Richard Howard's review, which was couched in the martial
jargon of the sixties (*Nation*, October 26, 1964), referred to the
speaker in the poems as a "survivor," to the poetry as a "campaign of survival," to the text as the "site" of life's battle.
Howard did not enlarge upon the reasons for Lowell's em-
battled vision. He was, characteristically, caught up in the
fervor of the day; as such, Howard as critic played the Arnoldian.

Richard Poirier took a less martial approach to *Union Dead*:
Lowell had shown himself to be "our truest historian" (*Book
Week*, October 11, 1964). The poet had combined his personal
breakdown with his visions of public decline. The past exerted
a control over Lowell's imagination, especially in poems like
"Caligula" and "Union Dead." Poirier's position was similar to
Hardison's (and of course to Staples, the originator of the position that every subject Lowell chose "ultimately becomes himself"). Lowell evoked the past as if the only important element
in history were himself. Poirier recalls that Hawthorne also experienced this paradoxical entrapment in a past which eluded
him yet took in him "some special shape." This is a legitimate
way to discuss *Union Dead*. The only problem with Poirier's
essay is that everything he says of *Union Dead* is equally true
of *Lord Weary* (a good illustration of the necessity for stylistic
analysis, for no two books are more stylistically dissimilar).

There were several readings of *Union Dead* which became
platforms for antiwar propaganda. Some, like the *National Observer* review (unsigned, January 4, 1965), were accolades:
Lowell was a great poet because he wanted us to stay out of
Viet Nam. Others, like Robert Bly's essay (*Sixties*, Spring 1966),

were not. Although Bly agreed with Lowell's antiwar leanings, he said that Lowell had the right ideas for the wrong reasons. Lowell had been contaminated by both left and right influences (he condemned in Lowell what Williamson praised), and had elevated alienation by being "intellectual about it." Bly claims that Lowell's ideas are "decrepit." Unfortunately, Bly's essay delivers no ideas at all. This is one reason his essay is such an interesting cultural specimen: it reflects the new sixties proclivity toward meditation and withdrawal. Activism, whatever its program, was beginning to be censured as establishmentarian. Bly is extreme both in language and indictment. Lowell's ideas are "banal" and "journalistic"; Lowell cannot make a poem live inside a certain emotion without "becoming counterfeit." Then, in a travesty of Arnold's "The Function of Criticism," Bly turns the essay into a diatribe against American readers: they are so far from "the center of themselves" that they cannot recognize Lowell's counterfeit!

There was, however, an Arnoldian reading of *Union Dead*, by Thomas Parkinson, which made Bly's essay sound like a love letter (*Salmagundi*, 4, 1966/67). Parkinson faulted Lowell for presenting a "human condition to which there is no solution." Lowell mirrored the demoralization that was gnawing at American ideological principles. The poet's sense of futility and guilt was alarming to Parkinson, who demanded that the artist today move beyond "the drag toward individuality." (Where have we heard that before?)

Although it was not apparent at the time, Parkinson's essay was one of the first to signal a disenchantment with the confessional mode. Lowell was indulging in personal anguish, even though he addressed public issues while doing so. Toward the end of the sixties, *Union Dead* was treated to more incisive textual analysis. For example, Paul Doherty discussed the details in the title poem and showed that nearly every historical observation was inaccurate (*Concerning Poetry*, Fall 1968). Actually, what Doherty demonstrated was that the poems *did* go beyond sheer confessional anguish, that historical truth had been sacrificed to an artistic, ethical truth. Thus in "Union Dead" the wording of the epigraph had been changed from "*He* leaves all behind to serve the country" to "*They* leave . . ." (my italics). This universalized the sacrifice, Doherty argues. Also, the bracing of the Shaw Memorial (a bas-relief by Saint-Gaudens in a corner of Boston Common) or the State House was *not* done because of the excavations for the Boston Com-

mon garage; contrary to verisimilitude, Lowell fabricated for
a higher truth. Perhaps the movement away from topical readings of *Union Dead* originated with Lowell's denial that he
wrote with polemicist intentions. In a printed exchange with
Diana Trilling (*Commentary*, April 1969), Lowell refuted her
accusation that he was trying to "draw applause from the
young." Contending that controversy was bad for the mind
and heart, he swore that he had never been "New Left, Old
Left, or Liberal." Trilling was, he said, preoccupied with petty
violences, such as student uprisings, while indifferent to the
larger threats to humanity. Lowell denounced the extremism of
students (who at that point were taking over presidents' offices
at universities) as potentially as totalitarian as the causes they
denounced. Lowell's rejoinder to Trilling sounded very Arnoldian: sorrowful and wise. Yet we must not confuse the quiet
eloquence of his public statements, which impart a sense of
ethics and concern for mankind's future, with what is actually
said in *Union Dead*. The poems are still products of an exacerbated psyche and the strain of a turbulent domestic life which
led the poet to create brutal portraits—mostly of himself, even
when nominally about another:

> Animals
> fattened for your arena suffered less
> than you in dying—yours the lawlessness
> of something simple that has lost its law,
> my namesake, and the last Caligula.
>
> ["Caligula"]

There were critics who pounced on the idea that the volume
was the work of a crazed mind, but their comments were just
as limited as the politically motivated ones. Their reviews
sounded less like literary criticism than diagnoses of Lowell the
"patient." A. Alvarez (*London Observer*, March 14, 1965) and
Peter Dale (*Agenda*, Summer 1966) found Lowell grown more
tormented; *Newsweek* (October 12, 1964) said that he was
closer to the breaking point than he had ever been; Peter
Davidson (*Atlantic*, January 1965) said that the poems saw life
"unsteadily and far from whole." And to the critic in *Southern
Review* (unsigned, Winter 1965), Lowell was neither serene nor
tormented but "totally evasive."

In fairness to the critics, *Union Dead* was a testy work to
interpret. The poems go forward and backward at the same

time: to the private and obscure style of earlier years ("The
Sacred Head"); to the confessionalism and free rhythms of later
years ("Middle Age"). It was easier for critics to ferret out
political and psychological elements in the work than to un-
tangle the stylistic potpourri. The issue of Arnoldian elements
got lost in the shuffle, only to be found again in later scholarship. For example, Williamson dealt with the title poem as an
instance of "moral resolution" (*Pity the Monsters*). Focusing on
the characterization of Colonel Shaw, who persisted with his
Negro regiment, Williamson argues that, to Lowell, Shaw's
death was a "moral success." Shaw's triumph, the "power to
choose death and live," shows that Lowell had superseded "political abstraction." Lowell no longer read history as black or
white; he now thought in terms of mass psychology and of
historical repetition. And yet he still brought his elegiac touch
to "Union Dead," this time to mourn the closing of the aquarium: "Lowell mourns the loss of a curiosity about other living
beings that made people want aquariums." Even in what would
seem an unrelated reference, Lowell pits an idealized past—
when men acknowledged kinship with the animal world—
against a mechanical present.

Where the question of Lowell's identification with Jonathan
Edwards absorbed critics in earlier years, now they posed the
same question about Colonel Shaw. In "Private Poet, Public
Role: Lowell's 'For the Union Dead,' " Steven Hoffman suggests that Lowell imaginatively identifies with Shaw, both as
monument and man (*Notes on Modern American Literature*,
Summer 1979). As young men, both embarked on moral cru-
sades: Shaw at the head of the Union's first black regiment,
which was decimated at the futile charge on the Confederate
stronghold at Fort Wagner; Lowell as the incarcerated conscientious objector during World War II. According to Hoffman:

> Both men, as well as the moral imperatives that incited them, live
> on through the timeless configurations of art: Shaw in the dura-
> ble bronze of St. Gaudens' sculpture; Lowell in the persona of
> "For the Union Dead."

The familial link between the two men—Shaw's sister married
Robert Lowell's ancestor, Charles Russell Lowell, another Civil
War hero—reinforces the identification. When Lowell empha-
sized the vastly different circumstances which confronted the

two men (face-to-face confrontation during a cavalry charge and modern, impersonalized devices of destruction), the irony of similarity–dissimilarity gains full force. Lowell's persona (himself) adapts to a passive heroism because it is no longer possible to imitate Shaw's active heroism. Hoffman says that in the poem Lowell does not minimize his self-doubts, yet he manages to present "an image of compassionate survival, in humanistic rather than theological terms." Hoffman's essay, with its emphasis on the humanistic power of poetry to effect what war or theology had in the past, is a classic example of Arnoldian temper.

Axelrod responded differently to "Union Dead" (*Robert Lowell*). While he, too, believed that Lowell harkened to the past in order to expose the moral squalor of the historical present, Axelrod found the dramatization of Shaw less than flattering:

> The circumstances of Shaw's brutal death and burial, in what Lowell called "the first modern war," suggests that Fort Wagner and Hiroshima are both part of the same historical curve of increasing technological barbarity. Equally disturbing, the hidden homicidal or suicidal strain that Lowell detects in Shaw himself . . . corresponds to the Ahab-like spirit he finds deep in the American character, a spirit of "violence and idealism" capable in our day of producing nuclear holocaust [pp. 170–71].

By this reading, Lowell is far from elegiac—or Arnoldian. Axelrod, like Holder ("The Flintlocks of the Fathers"), says that Lowell is too dissatisfied with America, both past and present, to be encomiastic.

Thus we find that the title poem of this, Lowell's first distinctly political volume, remains a source of controversy. In one of the earliest reviews of *Union Dead* (*New York Times Book Review*, October 4, 1964), G. S. Fraser had called the poem a "song of praise" for the indomitable spirit of man. Since then, critics have qualified Fraser's words. As we have tried to show in the last few pages, criticism of both "Union Dead" and the volume enclosing it matured considerably from the single-minded concentration on psychological and martial violence, which was the initial response to the more balanced late treatments of critics like Hoffman and Axelrod. When we turn to the reception of texts written after *Union Dead*, we find that the critics continue to argue about Lowell's political beliefs.

Three years after *Union Dead*, Lowell presented his readers a new work (in another genre) to grapple with: his "imitation" of Aeschylus' *Prometheus Bound*. It was first printed in the *New York Review of Books* (July 13, 1967), a tabloid which had come into being as a result of a long-term strike by employees of the *New York Times*. A temporary replacement for the newspaper's book review section, the *New York Review* was managed and contributed to by a politically minded group of writers. Elizabeth Hardwick, Lowell's wife, was one of its editors. The essays, plays, poems, reviews which filled its pages imparted noticeably anti-administration sentiments, especially about its Viet Nam policy. *Prometheus* fit the pattern.

Although the play is a translation, it is at a second remove from Aeschylus; Lowell worked *from* a translation. He chose the "dullest" he could find in order to pique his own originality. Lowell retained the plot of the play as well as its dramatic structure: a series of conversations that Prometheus has with his friends and enemies, all of whom attempt to persuade him to surrender to Zeus. Since the *Prometheus* is one surviving play from the original trilogy, we do not know how Aeschylus resolved the Zeus–Prometheus confrontation. Lowell extracted and enlarged upon one theme from the original: the conflict and consequence of the passage and exchange of power. In Lowell's version it is made clear that neither submission nor rebellion is the winning strategy against Zeus. Both Atlas, the submissive one, and Typho, the rebel, are punished: one doomed to carry the world on his shoulders, the other to lie buried beneath Mt. Etna. In his confrontations with the main characters, Prometheus debates the efficacy of rebellion. This is where Lowell departs most from the spirit of Aeschylus; a kind of despair consumes Lowell's hero, who has such prophetic power that he envisions even the futility of evolution and its inevitable decline.

The play is weighted down with long speeches, and would not seem a likely prospect for effective performance, yet its premiere at the Yale Repertory Theatre (1966/67 season) was startingly well received. Robert Brustein's account of his years as head of Yale Repertory, *Making Scenes* (1981), includes a detailed description of the production of *Prometheus*, a play which, according to Brustein, Lowell had written with the assistance of a grant from the National Endowment for the Arts. President Johnson, furious that a government agency had given money to an artist who had directly censured his Viet Nam war policy, had demanded that the award be withdrawn. The endowment panel refused to comply. While the decision was a triumph for Lowell, it placed the production in a political maelstrom; the reviewers mostly disagreed about the choice of Jonathan Miller as its director. Miller's highly mannered production of *Old Glory* (see chapter 2) had been too eccentric for some critics' tastes; Miller's *Prometheus* was equally eccentric.

The play was set in what resembles seventeenth-century Inquisition Spain, although the actual locale was undesignated. The correlation between Spanish brutality during the Inquisition and the implied brutality of the Johnson administration made Johnson's partisans uneasy. In *Making Scenes*, Brustein insists that Miller was "anxious to let the action resonate in the minds of the spectators without urging them toward any single interpretation." He said that the play echoed all forms of tyranny, one of which could conceivably be identified as America's treatment of the Vietnamese, but that a "certain historical distance" had been maintained, nonetheless. Brustein discouraged the New York press from coming to the opening of *Prometheus* (May 9), since he expected "arrogant proclamations" and faintly patronizing tones to surface. And they did. Walter Kerr (*New York Times*, May 11) commended the production as a "perfect project for a serious university theatre." When a respected critic, such as Kerr, delivered a verdict in the nation's most powerful newspaper, the die was cast. The image of *Prometheus* as a fledging drama (although brilliant in concept) was never erased. Brustein himself found the production an example of the "resourceful intelligence" he had hoped to see applied to the classics. In his tally of the plays produced at Yale while he headed the drama department (1966–1979), he numbered *Prometheus* among the few in which he took the most pride. In the face of a culture indifferent to humanity and art, efforts like Lowell's reminded us of the "important values."

Despite the noble motives of Yale Repertory Theatre, Kerr's opening-night review, and Lowell's artistic courage, the play has not since enjoyed a good critical reputation, either as a text to be read or as a performance to be seen. Even enthusiasts of *Old Glory*, such as Gerald Weales, could not warm up to *Prometheus*. Weales speculates that Lowell has "a kind of apology tucked away" in his Author's Note when he calls it "the most undramatic" of the Greek tragedies (*The Jumping-Off Place*). Weales's response is that *Old Glory* has similar "undramatic" qualities (e.g., endless speeches), yet it succeeds as a theatrical work. The failure is not so much in the limited stage action of *Prometheus* as in its characterizations; the characters suggest, but never become, men. The paradox, says Weales, is that characterization is limited by Lowell's artistic virtues: intellectuality, irony, sense of language, emphasis on theme, preoccupation with major current political and cultural concerns.

Weales then gives *his* summary of the play's basic theme: power leads to violence. Thus, "in a thermonuclear age, the absolute power is the last to rule because it leads to final destruction." If this is what Lowell is saying, Weales continues, then there is a contradiction between the idea of a final end and the recurring pattern suggested in the play's dominant images, power and force. The closing speeches make the action seem historically cyclical: "the pattern of tyranny-rebellion-tyranny-rebellion symbolized in the endless punishment of the gods." Is Lowell predicting civilization's doom or a continuation of the tyranny-rebellion pattern, asks Weales. Weales does not trouble to sort out the ramifications of his question, but the question indicates that, to Weales, Lowell did not idealize the past.

There were a few favorable reactions to the Yale production of *Prometheus*, and they came from critics who approved of Lowell's political posture. The British were hostile to the United States' Viet Nam policy and consequently regarded Lowell as a comrade in spirit (*London Times*, June 17, 1967); *Nation's* editorial policy was in groove with the political attitudes voiced in *Prometheus* (June 26, 1967). In America, Francis Ferguson admitted to being confused by the jumbled ideas in the play, especially those that were merged in the character of Prometheus (*New York Review of Books*, August 3, 1967). I should add that the ambiguity Ferguson referred to recalled the critiques leveled at the characterization of Colonel Shaw—or Edwards, for that matter. Lowell had a penchant for making his heroes (mythical and historical) a composite of nobility and ignobility, goodness and evil, arrogance and humility. If we put these characters together, we would find that they form a unifying archetype. In the case of *Prometheus*, critics bypassed the challenge of explicating this archetype by claiming that Prometheus was reduced to a caricature whose speeches were misted over with similes (*Newsweek*, May 22, 1967; *New Leader*, June 19, 1967). While the preponderance of similes is a distraction, the content of those speeches and the nature of the character whom Lowell had shaped to deliver them were never clearly viewed.

Once the reception history of *Prometheus* had passed the level of performance reviews, critics paid more attention to its thematic and literary appurtenances. Jonathan Price considered the play a self-examination in the guise of philosophy (*Works*, Autumn 1967). This explained why it was "dry, difficult, metaphysical"; but these ordinarily unflattering terms exemplified its virtues, said Price. As with dialectic in philosophy, *Prometheus* proceeds by opposites. Price guesses that by the time Lowell wrote this play he had given up his search for truth, yet created in Prometheus a hero who continues to search for it; hence the play's ambiguity and internal conflict. The text clears away anyone's doubts about Lowell's continuing belief in God or any form of established religion, proving that for Lowell God is dead. After making this absolute pronouncement, Price moves on to the politically topical inferences in the play. Cronus, the old god, is compared with "aspects of Eisenhower, Chamberlain or Macmillan"; when Zeus and Prometheus overthrow him, "they fell like the new frontiersmen sweeping into Washington." The promise of liberalism is aborted, however: "Kennedy gave way to Johnson and what had seemed like an exciting overthrow" had become almost a worse tyranny. To Price, Prometheus is a projection of Lowell, as someone who threw himself before the gods (Johnson, on a political level; his family or lovers, on a personal level) and continually rebelled but never found his freedom. Unlike Weales, who finds the inconsistency at the end of the play a flaw, Price regards the inconsistency the true meaning of the play. That *Prometheus* raises questions is its value.

One of the virtues of an admiring critic is that he often places the work he admires in the pantheon, leading him to compare a text with its antecedents. M. Byron Raizis performs this service for *Prometheus*, which he considers equal to former versions of the myth (e.g., Shelley's *Prometheus*). His comprehensive essay in *Papers on Language and Literature* (Summer 1969 supplement) examines the cultural values expressed in Lowell's play, values which are distinctly modern. The schematic structure of *Prometheus* includes the three levels of importance in the Aeschylus original, but Lowell reverses their order of importance. Thus Aeschylus' theme is the suffering individual:

(a) at the hands of an omnipotent and arbitrary enemy; (b) as part of a citizenry at the mercy of tyrants; (c) at the mercy of an intransigent new deity. By reversing this order of suffering, Lowell enhances his appeal to a modern audience. To Raizis, the theme of alienation is dominant in Lowell's version, with the alienation of the intellectual becoming the dominant focus. Lowell is, therefore, closer to the Romantics' notion of the Promethean myth than to the Victorians', who saw the fall of Zeus as ushering in a new era of social justice, peace, and progress. The fierce idealism of the Romantics, who resisted any imposition of power on the individual, is what really informs Lowell's play, says Raizis. Prometheus' story is "the story of his [Lowell's] own self"; Lowell has made the original "ring right" for him. The merit of this essay is that it grounds Lowell's cultural theory in the context of literary history.

While Raizis calls *Prometheus* the story of Lowell's "own self," he stops short of enlisting biographical material for his argument. Mazzaro translates the play's speeches about freedom and individualism to realistic equivalents (*Comparative Drama*, Winter 1973/74). The play expresses Lowell's difficult recognition and acceptance of his "public role," says Mazzaro. Lowell recognized the need for movement from intellectualism to activism in the final years of the Johnson administration. Thus Lowell is Prometheus, the thinking man who may never be free but must act. In Lowell's rendition, Prometheus "is a rebel in defeat," who has to consider what it was that brought him into isolation. He does this by reexamining his options in the form of "visitors." Consequently, the play proceeds through a round of dialogues in which Prometheus learns that "as his power is silence, his weakness has been one of expression." But, as he discovers all those who have betrayed him (Alcyone, Ocean, Hephaestus, Hermes, Zeus), he moves to a final perception: one must strive to act. Mazzaro interprets Prometheus' final appeal to his mother (Earth) as an admission that "his acts will continue to be humanly directed." Concluding his analysis, Mazzaro explains that Lowell had called *Prometheus Bound* the most lyrical of the Greek tragedies because it is "revelatory of man's inner workings"—not, as we might suppose, because it is "musical" or "choral." Therefore, the structural device Lowell used was "an interiorization of action," a dramatization of Prometheus' emotions and of the objective reality that produces these emotions. Lowell's triumph is in taking a play with a definite technical handicap—its main character is immobile from the start—and creating a dynamic "state of intellect" that is as vital as traditional dramatic action.

I would offer an addendum to Mazzaro's fine analysis: the freedom and individualism Prometheus (Lowell) pines for, and despairs of achieving, recalls Arnold's failed expectations. In his poem "A Wish" (1867), Arnold laments what he has lost, or more correctly, never found:

> I ask but that my death may find
> The freedom to my life denied;
> Ask but the folly of mankind
> Then, then at last, to quit my side.

Lowell's decision to enter the public forum is the subject of another worthwhile essay, Milne Holton's "I Think of Fire: Robert Lowell's *Prometheus Bound*" (*Proceedings, Symposium on American Literature*, Poznan, 1979). Holton also views the play as an externalization of Lowell's inner debate about entering the public life. But Holton bolsters his essay with a recapitulation of the political events which clouded American history during the sixties and then explains the analogues between the characters in the play and the national leaders (Eisenhower, Kennedy, Johnson). He also discusses those passages which most clearly establish Lowell's identity with the hero (such as Prometheus' speech to Ocean's daughters: "I was born higher and had less chance"). As Holton points out, many contemporary news items are transposed into classical dramatic imagery, making the play (on one level) a vivid synthesis of the American political scene. For example, the mud and fire imagery which pervades the text is central to Lowell's "apocalypic impulse," but the sixties audiences associated mud with "the rice-fields and wetlands of Southeast Asia." Holton agrees with Mazzaro that *Prometheus* demonstrates Lowell's shift of sensibility from the "frustration and powerlessness" that colors *Notebook 1967–1968* to resolution and purpose.

Before we conclude this section on *Prometheus*, account should be taken of John Simon's conservative warning that Lowell had no right to tamper with Aeschylus (*Hudson Review*, Winter 1967–68). Simon does not find all the political allusions that Mazzaro and Holton found; *Prometheus* "is not as a whole about anything identifiable." Simon feels that "there is not a great deal in Aeschylus, but at least we know what the issue

is"; in Lowell, there is only "generalized violence" and in-
dulgence in a "thin, clotted prose full of headstrong, runaway
images." Simon is so uniformly negative that any authentic
claims about the play's artistic weakness—and Simon does make
a few—lose their authority. He prompted others to run to Lowell's defense, as did Daniel Hoffman (*Hollins Critic*, February
1967). Hoffman argues that a poet must feed on the past, use
it, and renew it. Critics like Simon do not understand that the
lines between imitation and creativity, originality and adaptation "are not in fact separated by the chasm Simon would throw
down between them." There, by and large, the dispute ends.

*Prometheus* has not stimulated a proliferation of commentary.
For those who are interested in the Arnoldian strain in Lowell's
work, *Prometheus* offers still untapped possibilities for analysis.
For example, Lowell's drama has much in common with Arnold's *Empedocles on Etna* (1852), a poem about Empedocles,
the ancient Greek philosopher, who flung himself into the vol-
cano after discovering that his life (for metaphysical and political reasons) was of no worth to him. I would add that Arnold
temporarily removed *Empedocles* from his canon because he
felt that it represented a "continuous state of mental distress,"
which might depress his readers' spirits. We might shudder to
think how many texts Lowell would have to eliminate from his
canon for this reason. But this indulgent aside reinforces what
was said earlier in this chapter: Arnold, living in an earlier epoch,
found it easier to battle the pathos of nostalgia and self-pity;
Lowell surrendered.

*Prometheus* was essentially a dramatic statement of the ideas
that filled Lowell's poetry volume of the same year, *Near the
Ocean*. *Ocean* gave the critics a surprising and mixed bag to
deal with: surprising in that it abounded in regular iambic feet
and rhyming couplets; mixed in that half its contents consisted
of translations, ranging from Horace to the sixteenth-century
satirist Quevedo. Lowell had completely abandoned his jaunty,
natural, *Life Studies* style in this volume, after partially doing
so in *Union Dead*. City images, especially of Rome, dominate
*Ocean*.

In *Dionysus and the City* (1970), a study of the thematic significance of the city in modern literature, Monroe Spears observes that all the city images in Lowell's work represent failed
departures from the "city of traditional culture." His generalization is particularly germane to *Ocean*, for, as Lowell says in
its prefatory Note, the theme which runs through the volume

is "Rome, the greatness and horror of her Empire." According
to Spears, each of Lowell's city images provides "a bitter sense
of contrast" between the professed ideals of civilization and the
realistic history of a "highly specific city." Indeed, a hidden
symbolism runs through all place references—and the symbol is
corruption. In *Ocean*, Rome, as archetypal city, represents all
that taints Western civilization. To develop his theme, Lowell
engages some "collaborators," literary and artistic. Half of this
somewhat slender volume is comprised (as we said) of translations, mainly of Roman poets. As artistic collaboration, Sidney
Nolan's drawings run through the text, creating what Lowell
calls "the bridge" between Rome and America. To some reviewers the drawings were fillers for this "coffee-table" book,
but the stir created by the elaborateness of this edition occurred
mainly at the time of publication. Later commentary ignored
the drawings.

Were Arnoldian criteria applied to *Near the Ocean*? Yes, but
in a curious fashion. Since Lowell had returned to traditional
meters, some critics felt that this signaled a return to his tendency toward didacticism and that the poet of the early volumes
had resurfaced. This was incorrect, argued other critics, like
G. S. Fraser (*New York Times Book Review*, October 4, 1964).
Fraser said that *Union Dead* proved that Lowell could go beyond the free-wheeling "brute particulars" of *Life Studies* to
a new manner, which had been "earned" by the more impersonal and formal discipline of the early poems. Lowell's rhetoric
had been loosened in the way that Pound's extremely formal
"Sestina Altaforte" (1909) was superseded by the supposedly
"off-the-cuff" casualness of "Hugh Selwyn Mauberly" (1920).
Now Lowell was able to combine historical range with a passionate exactness that condensed "miraculously what it would
take a historian many pages to say." Moreover, the fact that
Lowell could now expose himself so nakedly to the times and
to his own experience endowed him with the "voice of a
prophet." This was quite different from labelling him "didactic."

Fraser was being prophetic himself, for *Notebook* and *History* were the full-scale documents of a poet-historian. Fraser
would later do a retrospective piece on Lowell and claim that
*Ocean* was the most satisfying collection Lowell had produced
"so far" (*Salmagundi*, Spring 1977). This essay preceded Lowell's death and the appearance of *Day by Day* by just a few
months, which made Fraser's summation practically all inclusive. Fraser compared the title poem, "Near the Ocean," with

a sonnet from *The Dolphin*, which, while it was a happier poem
than "Ocean," had serious structural difficulties. For our purposes, this meant that Fraser preferred Lowell when he acted as
spokesman for a culture. Fraser welcomed the fact that Lowell
had used the confessional mode only as a transitional solution,
where it had become a terminal one for other poets. "Hysterical
self-exposure" had reached a dead end. Lowell, happily, had not
forgotten his public responsibility. The better for his readers,
since his personal and ancestral history had turned him into a
"distinctly symbolic personage." As an Englishman, Fraser was
conscious that Lowell's "aristocratic" tradition made anything
that happened to him of interest to the reader—simply because
it happened to *him*. By the time of *Union Dead*, it had become
obvious that Lowell was not a "committed" public poet or a
"party man of any sort." He was simply an objective observer
of the public scene and a scholar of history. In *Ocean*, Lowell
sees the United States as a new Roman empire, but also as the
"last Empire" on earth. What makes Lowell's vision even more
horrifying is its contrast with the Arcadian or Edenic world of
the New England coastline. The title poem's ocean imagery
bespeaks an eternal present and redeems the speaker, who, as an
American, remains "uncorrupted by the past." With a slight
stretch of time limits, we could apply Fraser's interpretation of
"Ocean" to "Dover Beach":

> The sea is calm to-night.
> The tide is full, the moon lies fair
> Upon the straits—

And when Fraser says that "Ocean," despite its use of terrifying
Greek myths, transforms to "triumph and bliss" because of
Lowell's great feeling, these lines from "Dover Beach" leap to
mind:

> Sophocles long ago
> Heard it on the Aegean, and it brought
> Into his mind the turbid ebb and flow
> Of human misery . . .

In both poems the lyrical quality of the prosody injects a
sublime feeling into an otherwise despairing work. Fraser goes
into some detail about the eight-line tetrameters of "Ocean" and
notes that the metrical trick in the last line of the quatrains—
the use of duple against single stresses to slow down the lines

and give them gravity—makes this one of Lowell's most technically adroit compositions.

Reviewers liked to dwell on "Waking Early Sunday Morning," another distinguished poem in "Ocean"; some of them compared its version in the 1967 edition with an earlier version printed in the *New York Review of Books* (August 5, 1965). Peter Davison (*Atlantic*, October 1967) felt it was time to name Lowell the likely successor to Frost and Williams, but he was troubled by the feeling that the "patrician" in Lowell had begun to reassert itself. He said this was demonstrable if we lined up the early version of "Waking," which dealt with Lowell's disappointment in his personal life, with the later version, which hid personal grief in alleged grief over public ills. Dubbing *Life Studies* Lowell's highest achievement, Davison argued that *Ocean* was a regression to "the custodian of culture" voice. Finally, Davison warned that constant reworking of poems did not necessarily improve them. The revisions were simply Lowell's transfer of personal lyrics to public poems. And it was this process, said Paul Zweig, that brought a "curiously impersonal mood" to the poetry (*Nation*, April 24, 1967).

Zweig criticized Lowell's meters, his "doggerel couplets," which belong in satire or the neat epigram, but which develop into neither mode in *Ocean*. Indeed, for this critic, Lowell was veering in the direction of satire in this volume, but he was not consistently skilled at this art. Satire, which requires total control of the persona, with no retreat to the personal gripe, eluded Lowell. Zweig concluded (correctly) that rather than sustaining effective satire, Lowell brought in a "self-revealing violence" which merely made the poems "unsettled."

Louis Martz also noticed that *Ocean* aspired toward satire, but did not quite carry if off (*Yale Review*, Summer 1967). Lowell's sense of pity, according to Martz, was disintegrated by a deep cynicism and "grinding" images of misery. Martz, incidentally, insisted that Lowell's true voice was elegiac and that when he departed from it he was unconvincing.

David Kalstone was less harsh about the volume and considered Lowell "canny about public motives" and the individual's way of adjusting to these motives by skillfully deceiving himself (*Partisan Review*, Fall 1967). Kalstone defended Lowell against the accusation that he could not equal the objective critical temper of the Roman poets. Although the volume was intended as an abridgment between the two cultures (Lowell's Preface indicates this), Kalstone said that Lowell never really

desired the "easy command" of a Juvenal. Both Lowell and the
times were more troubled; what Lowell really wanted to capture was the Romans' "heroic resolve." Kalstone's adumbration
of the historical context gave his argument more solidity than
other critics'. He understood that the span of 2,000 years inevitably wrought changes in the satiric temper; he focused on
what Lowell *presented*, not on what was expected—even by
Lowell. Kalstone elaborated on the voice adjustments in the
title poem, which showed the inner resources by which the self
deals with daily tensions and issues. And contrary to the claim
that Lowell lacked drama, Kalstone charted the "overheard
stage directions" to the self ("Stop, back off". ."Look up". .
"Sing Softer") which culminated in public address. There was
a highly dramatic strategy in Lowell's movement of voice from
invocation to question to command.

*Ocean* presented a handicap to critics: it required that they
have expertise in both comparative/classical literature and modern poetry in order satisfactorily to judge the entire volume.
F. H. Griffin Taylor was one critic with expertise in both, and
he determined that the translations fell short of the original
poems, especially "Waking Early" (*Sewanee Review*, Spring
1969). His approach centered on morale and how this affects a
poet's work. Thus the Roman poets (Horace, Juvenal) had
a different grasp on their times, which were "no easier than
ours." Though Taylor never quite faults Lowell's poetry, he
implies, through comparison, that Lowell is not equal to the
task he has created for himself: to serve as spokesman and guide
to the people in troubled times. (There is of course some question as to whether Lowell actually felt that to be his task; the
Preface to *Ocean*, Lowell's only statement of his intentions
there, was elusively worded.) Taylor's premise would imply
that a poet like Lowell was incapable of dealing with Roman
satire. His emotional reserves were too slender; consequently,
he searched the past "without comfort" and the present "without understanding." Poets like Juvenal celebrated the struggle
and did not vacillate in their positions, whether they were ultimately on the side of victory or defeat. Taylor found Lowell
too frail of spirit. Moreover, Lowell didn't "seem to be in any
place," despite the Maine-coast suggestions in the volume, nor
did he seem to *want* to be in any place. Thus even in his translation of Juvenal, which is considered the best in the group,
Lowell never quite captures the sweep and energy of the original. Taylor takes an Arnoldian view of the role of the poet:

duty comes before self-indulgence when the welfare of humanity is at stake. There is something decidedly orthodox in this, but
Lowell made himself vulnerable to this standard.

America was becoming another Rome, said *Ocean*, repeating
the premonitions of college students, journalists, civil rights advocates, and liberal politicians. Therefore, it was not surprising
that *Ocean* struck a responsive chord with newspaper and journal reviewers, who found it relevant and topical. Although most
of the reviews reflected the exigencies of deadlines and immediate impressions, their preferences are still interesting to record.
For example, British newspaper accounts were predominantly
favorable, a curious reaction when one considers that Lowell
indicts America for its "empire" mentality. The subject was a
natural sore point for the British, but they seemed to relish
Lowell's castigation of American colonialism in Southeast Asia.

Another reason for British approval of *Ocean* related to the
volume's use of traditional meter and myth. The *Times Literary
Supplement* (unsigned, August 3, 1967) called the book a reward of discipline, whereby nothing had been lost in Lowell's
confessional disgressions and free-verse experiments of recent
volumes. Lowell's idiom was now "weighty in an Augustan
sense," a qualification for automatic approval.

Donald Davie was highly complimentary (*Manchester Guardian Weekly*, July 20, 1967). He said that Lowell had written a
Freudian interpretation of the Orestes and Perseus myths in the
title poem, and that the bizarre sexual fantasy constructed from
these myths was a "way of understanding America." Davie's
reading was seminal but he did not develop it. It led the way for
such psychopolitical interpretations as Williamson's in *Pity the
Monsters*. Another eminent British critic to applaud *Ocean* was
Julian Symons (*New Statesman*, July 21, 1967). He acknowledged Lowell's grasp of history and the skill with which he
turned public fact into the private drama of statesmen—especially President Johnson.

A few British critics were not enraptured by *Ocean* as a
whole, but could not deny the majesty of the title poem (*Listener*, September 7, 1967; *Agenda*, Spring 1968). The *Agenda*
critic felt that perhaps Lowell was not ready to publish another
book and succumbed to the pressures of bookmaking. But in all,
the British were pleased that Lowell had gone "public" after
his stage of "picking fluff from the navel." Indeed, the *Manchester Guardian Weekly* put *Ocean* on its end-of-the-year list
of recommended books.

In the United States, there was delight that Lowell had written another winner, but this delight, among the newspaper reviewers, was less aesthetic than didactic, and Lowell was most
praised for bringing the national scene into his poetry (*Chicago
Tribune Magazine of Books*, February 5, 1967; *New York
Herald Tribune Book World*, January 29, 1967). The *Christian
Science Monitor* (January 26, 1967) was happy to note that this
poet never fell "into the groove." And in the literary journals
he was praised for finding "new technical strength and order"
(*Contemporary Literature*, Spring 1969), as well as for being
the only American poet who could put our horror into a grand
style (*Massachusetts Review*, Summer 1967). Whether or not
Lowell liked it, *Ocean* had elevated him to the role of leader and
judge. Lines in the title poem referred to President Johnson's
swimming naked in a pool "sick/of his ghost-written rhetoric!"
This exposure of power in such a vulnerable and pitiable state
enthralled readers.

Together, the reviews just mentioned were little more than
nominal bouquets for a poet who had put into meter what men
were saying in the street. Headier scholarship came with Patricia Meyer Spacks's "From Satire to Description" (*Yale Review*, Winter 1969), an analysis of one of the translations in
*Ocean* (Juvenal's Tenth Satire). In an argument which indirectly rejoins Martz and Zweig, who considered Lowell a failed
satirist, Spacks views Lowell as the quintessential modern poet
who can only translate Juvenal in existential terms. She proceeds
by demonstrating the difference between Samuel Johnson's imitation of the Tenth Satire ("The Vanity of Human Wishes")
and Lowell's poem, which adapts Johnson's title.

Although Johnson's is a "meticulous" translation, it is nonetheless an eighteenth-century one. As such, it is judicious and
authoritative; but more importantly, it is essentially a Christian
poem, fired by an energy of purpose: to reform! Although the
universe of his poem is confusing and chaotic, some solution for
man is desired—and indirectly suggested. To Spacks, Lowell's
"blazing scorn" is nearer to Juvenal's tone than to Johnson's,
yet Lowell is so involved in corruption that he cannot summon
the satirist's traditional authority. Unlike Johnson's "convoluted" presentation, which distances him from the immediate
situation and makes him a "personified figure of Observation,"
Lowell's version merely makes flat assertions in a state of "passive endurance." He can only half-heartedly suggest the possibility of prayer in a modern scene which is insane, whose chief

symptom of madness is "obsessive sexuality." In terms of merit, Spacks does not choose between Johnson's and Lowell's renditions of Juvenal, but she implies that it is meaningless to expect a modern poet to espouse philosophical values from another century. Lowell may not master the conventional elements of satire, but he better captures the Juvenalian belief in man's inordinate—and unchangeable—folly and blindness. While Spacks does not discuss the other poems in *Ocean*, her generalizations fit them as well.

As we traverse such commentary as Spacks's, we might ask: What does she tell us about Lowell and "culture"? Indeed, what does the corpus of commentary on the late volumes tell or instruct us about this topic? It would seem that if Lowell was intent on preserving values in a society, he was most circumspect—except when he pitched at the theme of political authority and the state. And it is in his regard for the welfare of the nation that he duplicates Arnold's concept of "culture." This is how the *Oxford Anthology of English Literature* explains Arnold's use of the word:

> He does not use it, as anthropologists and sociologists later came to do, to refer to the totality of a society's institutions, beliefs, arts, and modes of behavior. Nor does he use it in the more restricted sense in which it signifies the general intellectual and artistic activity of a society . . . it is the ideal response to the fact that the world in modern times is moved by ideas to an extent never known before and that the welfare of humanity and of any particular nation depends upon reason, to bear upon social and political life.

Lowell, like Arnold, was not absorbed in the "general intellectual and artistic activity" of his society. Portraits of his fellow artists (Schwartz, Jarrell, Peter Taylor) place emphasis on how these men coped with their personal dilemmas. And when we turn to *Notebook*, despite its overlay of topical allusions, we find that Lowell's role as observer is indirect and unprogrammatic.

*Notebook 1967–68*, a peculiar combination of fragment and finished poetry, became a preliminary version of *Notebook* (1970). If reviewers did not pounce on the former volume when it was released, they had the confusing option of reviewing both volumes as independent compositions or of regarding the first volume as a draft of the second. In the Afterword of *Notebook*

*1967–68,* Lowell inserted a list of dates which record tragic public events during 1967 and 1968, such as the Viet Nam War, black riots in Newark, the assassinations of Martin Luther King and Robert Kennedy, the Russian occupation of Czechoslovakia. The poems form a grim backdrop to these events, although they are not specifically about them. The book had the tentative original title *Notebook of a Year* and was intended to be a seasonal account of the interaction between Lowell the man, living from day to day, and the political background suggested by the chronology. It eventually extended beyond an annual cycle, became the product of three years' jottings, and accumulated to nearly 300 sonnets. Although politics is the shaping theme, Lowell concentrated on his favorite subjects: old writer friends, relatives, the art of writing poetry, the mythos of history. The focus of interest constantly shifts, so that the volume, taken as a whole, imitates the disorder of life. Lowell's elusiveness was not lost on the critics. If they felt kindly toward him, they attributed his elusiveness to a generalized sorrow about society.

F. M. Kuna did *not* feel kindly (*English Studies,* December 1971). He deplored Lowell's ambivalent attitude toward historical figures like Hitler or Stalin, and his "spinelessness" about current tyranny. By using objective psychological terminology and detachment, Lowell evinced the unforgivable trait of "contemporary American intellectualism." A few British critics regarded *Notebook* with contempt. John Bayley (*Review,* December 25, 1970) and Douglas Dunn (*Encounter,* March 1971) objected to Lowell's arrogance and Olypianism about his nation's crises. Ian Hamilton (*A Poetry Chronicle,* 1973) and Dannie Abse (*Review,* Spring/Summer 1972) deplored his self-indulgence, which brought with it sentimentality and self-parody. Clearly, none of these critics considered Lowell a "custodian of culture."

Wedged between these hostile studies of *Notebook* were a few incisive essays which withheld judgment and tried to isolate the informing idea in the volume. Stephen Moore's "Politics and the Poetry of Robert Lowell" (*Georgia Review,* Summer 1973) expressed doubt that politics was good for Lowell. Claiming that "the 'right' feelings can produce some very bad verse," Moore selected the most successful examples of political verse. He concluded that "Lowell registers his revolt mainly by withdrawal." Citing the poem "Election Night," Moore argued that Lowell's abstention from voting in the Humphrey–Nixon presidential election is effectively realized in the poetic structure. Lowell was not proud of his action, and this is conveyed in a conversation with his daughter, which is reproduced in the poem:

> My daughter telephones me from New York,
> she talks *New Statesman*, "Then you're a cop out. Isn't
> not voting Humphrey a vote for Nixon and Wallace?"
> It's funny-awkward; I don't come off too well.

Many readers, likely, would disagree with Moore that this is successful political verse, or doubt that it is verse at all. But *Notebook* was all that its title conveyed and was intended to catch the flurry of trivial details which surrounded important events like elections.

In Dwight Eddins' "Poet and State in the Verse of Robert Lowell" (*Texas Studies in Literature and Language*, Summer 1973), Lowell was placed in the company of poets—Milton, Shelley, Yeats, Eliot—who found that human destiny is always immanent in crises of the state, Lowell was the opposite of Wallace Stevens, who retreated from the public scene and advised poets to avoid the "pressure of reality," yet Lowell was never able to become the activist. *Notebook*, said Eddins, dramatized the difficulty of positive commitment: "The individual realizes moral power by psychological victories—by doggedly refusing to offer his approval to bloodshed, on the one hand, or to acquiesce in public corruption on the other." The direction of Lowell's political thought moved in a straight line: from early zeal to growing passivity. From the past, Lowell had selected ancient Greece as his ideal state, "where government, art, religion . . . formed a dynamic, coherent whole." In Lowell's view, no modern state, the United States notwithstanding, approached this sort of balance.

With regard to formal preferences, Eddins said that "epic lamentation" was Lowell's favorite vehicle for political poetry. Thus, despite their Juvenalian overtones, the poems in *Ocean* or even *Notebook* were executed in a heroic-elegiac, rather than satirical, mode. Eddins also cited examples of how figures in history (e.g., Lincoln) were treated differently at different times in Lowell's career. Historical objectivity was obviously not Lowell's dominant interest; he interpreted history according to his changing view about violence and its justification for ultimately moral causes.

The thread of this argument was picked up by John Peck,

who devoted an essay to the analysis of a single poem, "Domesday Book" (*Day by Day*), and showed how it exemplified Lowell's views on culture (*Salmagundi*, Spring 1977). On a literal
level, "Domesday Book" is about the so-called second taxation.
For Lowell, the ancestral practice, by which landowners taxed
peasants, has been turned against them in this modern period of
the "welfare state." Peck argues that on one level the poem is
a "cultural elegy" of modern conservatism, but that the collage
structure of imagery delivers a more important meaning. Lowell
is imitating not the form of a "historical argument" about this
subject, says Peck, but of a "certain turn of mind." In other
words, the poem proves itself to be a false analogy, in which
the decline of a tradition is *not* the theme but is a phenomenological expression of the restless repetition and helplessness a
poet experiences *with* this theme. Lowell is neither praising nor
deploring the ethics of either form of taxation. Peck argues that
nothing is resolved in the poem, but that this is precisely the
point. In the final analysis, Lowell uses history for its "seizures
of significance," for its "quotability" in poetry.

Peck's thesis is interesting and provocative. It cries out for
exploration in two interdependent directions: Could the thesis
be convincingly sustained in a close reading of an entire volume, say *History*, and can the thesis itself stand the test of logic?
As to logic, Peck's thesis that the poems express *process*, the
phenomenological experience of argument, rather than the
*product* of argument, was frequently on the lips of literary
theorists of the day. To the extent that this thesis emphasizes
the *experience* of the aesthetic experience, it is clearly cogent;
but where it serves only to mask an author's inability to resolve
his themes, it obfuscates the work.

Another aspect of the appeal to "process" as content, relevant
to the criticism of the sixties, is that this popular theory, which
could laud a poet for neither praising nor deploring, for *not*
resolving an issue, ran counter to the slogan hurled at the intellectuals of the day, "If you're not part of the solution, you're
part of the problem." Can there be any wonder that so much
confusion surrounds Lowell's political life and political poetry
of the time, as well as the criticism of both?

Lowell extracted more than a hundred poems from *Notebook* and later inserted them—substantially revised—into *History*
(1973). Although the organization of this chapter suggests that
*History* should command our attention here, the volume is best
understood as a work of revision, for the thematic content varies

little from that already discussed in the earlier work. Thus *History* is reserved for the next chapter, which concentrates on Lowell's stylistics. We leave the matter of Arnold's legacy to future Lowell scholars. Some of the analogies drawn between the two poets have seemed tenuous at best, others indisputable. Whatever direction scholars take hereafter, they would do well to recall these lines from Arnold's "Bacchanalia; or, The New Age":

> The world but feels the present's spell,
> The poet feels the past as well—

## References

Abse, Dannie
> 1972. "The State of Poetry—A Symposium." *The Review* Spring/ Summer, pp. 3–73.

Altieri, Charles
> 1979. *Enlarging the Temple: New Directions in American Poetry during the 1960s*. Lewisburg, Pa.: Bucknell Univ. Pr.

Alvarez, A.
> 1963. "Robert Lowell in Conversation." London *Observer* July 21, p. 19.
> 1965. "Poetry in Extremis." London *Observer* Mar. 14, p. 26.

Arnold, Matthew
> 1960– . *Complete Prose Works*, ed. R. H. Super. Ann Arbor: Univ. of Michigan Pr.

Axelrod, Steven Gould
> 1978. *Robert Lowell: Life and Art*. Princeton: Princeton Univ. Pr.

Barrett, William
> 1982. *The Truants: Adventures among the Intellectuals*. Garden City, N.Y.: Doubleday.

Bayley, John
> 1970. "The King as Commoner." *The Review* Dec. pp. 3–7.

Bedford, William
> 1978: "The Morality of Form in the Poetry of Robert Lowell." *Ariel*, Jan. pp. 3–17.

Bermel, Albert
> 1967. "Shaky Footholds." *New Leader* June 19, pp. 27–29.

Bewley, Marius
> 1950. "Aspects of Modern Poetry." *Scrutiny* Apr., pp. 334–52 [339, 342–48]; reprinted in his *The Complex Fate*. London: Chatto & Windus, 1952; in *Robert Lowell: A Portrait of the Artist in His Time*, ed. Michael London and Robert Boyers. New York: David Lewis, 1970.

Bly, Robert
1966. "The Dead World and the Live World." *Sixties* Spring, pp. 2–7 [4].
Brustein, Robert
1981. *Making Scenes: A Personal History of the Turbulent Years at Yale, 1966–1979.* New York: Random House.
Cosgrave, Patrick
1970. *The Public Poetry of Robert Lowell.* New York: Taplinger.
Dale, Peter
1966. Review of *For the Union Dead. Agenda* Summer, pp. 76–78.
1968. "Review of *Near the Ocean.*" *Agenda* Spring, pp. 93–95.
Davidson, Peter
1965. "Madness in the New Poetry." *Atlantic* Jan., pp. 90–93.
1967. "Difficulties of Being Major." *Atlantic* Oct., pp. 116–21.
Davie, Donald
"A Judgement on America." *Manchester Guardian Weekly* July 20, p. 11.
Davis, Douglas
1965. "In the New Poetry, Lowell's Stature Grows." *National Observer* Jan. 4, p. 17.
Deutsch, Babette
1956. *Poetry in Our Time.* New York: Columbia Univ. Pr.
Doherty, Paul
1968. "The Poet as Historian: 'For the Union Dead,' by Robert Lowell." *Concerning Poetry* Fall, pp. 37–41.
Donoghue, Denis
1965. *Connoisseurs of Chaos: Ideas of Order in Modern American Poetry.* New York: Macmillan.
Dunn, Douglas
1971. "Snatching the Bays." *Encounter* Mar., pp. 65–71 [65–67].
Eddins, Dwight
1973. "Poet and State in the Verse of Robert Lowell." *Texas Studies in Literature and Language* Summer, pp. 371–86.
Edwards, Thomas R.
1971. *Imagination and Power: A Study of Poetry on Public Themes.* New York: Oxford Univ. Pr.
Eliot, T. S.
1925. "A Commentary." *Criterion* Jan., p. 162.
Fein, Richard
1965. "Mary and Bellona: The War Poetry of Robert Lowell." *Southern Review* Autumn, pp. 820–34.
Ferguson, Frances
1973. *American Poetry Since 1960: Some Critical Perspectives.* Cheshire: Carcanet.
Fergusson, Francis
1967. "Prometheus at Yale." *New York Review of Books* Aug. 3, pp. 30–32.

Foerster, Norman
1927. "Matthew Arnold and American Letters Today." *Sewanee Review* July, pp. 298–306.

Fraser, G. S.
1964. "Amid the Horror, A Song of Praise." *New York Times Book Review* Oct. 4, pp. 1, 38–39; reprinted in *Profile of Robert Lowell*, ed. Jerome Mazzaro. Columbus: Merrill, 1971.
1977. " 'Near the Ocean.' " *Salmagundi* Spring, pp. 73–87.

French, A. L.
1968. "Robert Lowell: The Poetry of Abdication." *Oxford Review* Michaelmas, pp. 5–20.

Gilman, Richard
1967. "Securing the Beachhead." *New York Herald Tribune Book World* Jan. 29, pp. 4, 12.
1967. "Still Bound." *Newsweek* May 22, p. 109.

Gullans, Charles
1965. "Edgar Bowers' *The Astronomers* and Other New Verse." *Southern Review* Winter pp. 189–209 [200].

Hamilton, Ian
1971. "A Conversation with Robert Lowell." *Review* Summer pp. 10–29.
1973. *A Poetry Chronicle*. London: Faber.

Hardison, O. B., Jr.
1963. "Robert Lowell: The Poet and World's Body." *Shenandoah* Winter, pp. 24–32.

Heaney, Seamus
1978. "On Robert Lowell." *New York Review of Books* Feb. 9, p. 37.

Heymann, C. David
1980. *American Aristocracy: The Lives and Times of James Russell, Amy and Robert Lowell*. New York: Dodd, Mead.

Hoffman, Daniel G.
1967. "Robert Lowell's *Near the Ocean:* The Greatness and Horror of Empire," *Hollins Critic* Feb., pp. 1–16; reprinted in *The Sounder Few*, ed. R. H. W. Dillard, George Garrett, John Rees Moore. Athens: Univ. of Georgia Pr.

Hoffman, Steven
1979. "Private Poet Public Role: Lowell's 'For the Union Dead.' " *Notes on Modern American Literature* Summer, item 18.

Holder, Alan
1971. "The Flintlocks of the Fathers: Robert Lowell's Treatment of the American Past." *New England Quarterly* Mar., pp. 40–65.

Holton, Milne
1979. " 'I Think of Fire': Robert Lowell's *Prometheus Bound*." In *Proceedings of a Symposium on American Literature*, Seria Filologia Anzielseca. Poznan, Poland: Universytet Adama Mickiewicza w Poznan.

Howard, Richard
    1964. "Voice of a Survivor." *Nation* Oct. 26, pp. 278–80.
Kalstone, David
    1967. "Two Poets." *Partisan Review* Fall, pp. 619–25 [622–25].
Kermode, Frank, et al.
    1973. (editor) *Oxford Anthology of English Literature.* New
    York, London, Toronto: Oxford Univ. Pr.
Kerr, Walter
    1967. "Theatre: 'Prometheus Bound' Performed at Yale." *New
    York Times* May 11, p. 52.
Kuna, F. M.
    1971. "Current Literature 1970–II, New Writing: Poetry." *Eng-
    lish Studies* Dec., pp. 573–79.
Lowell, Robert
    1943. "Concord." *Partisan Review* July–Aug., p. 316.
    1967. "Note." In his *Near the Ocean,* unpaged. New York: Farrar,
    Straus & Giroux; also London: Faber.
    1969. "Afterthought." In his *Notebook 1967–68,* pp. 159–60. New
    York: Farrar, Straus & Giroux.
    1969. "Liberalism and Activism." *Commentary* Apr., p. 19.
Maddocks, Melvin
    1967. "A Poet's Dialogue with Himself." *Christian Science Moni-
    tor* Jan. 26, p. 5.
Martin, Graham
    1967. "Wastelanders." *Listener* Sept. 7, pp. 311–12.
Martz, Louis
    1967. "Recent Poetry: Fruits of a Renaissance." *Yale Review* Sum-
    mer, pp. 593–603 [595–97].
Mazzaro, Jerome
    1979. *Modern American Poetry: Essays in Criticism.* New York:
    David McKay.
    1973/74. "Prometheus Bound: Robert Lowell and Aeschylus."
    *Comparative Drama* Winter, pp. 278–90.
Meiners, R. K.
    1970. *Everything to Be Endured: An Essay on Robert Lowell and
    Modern Poetry.* Columbia: Univ. of Missouri Pr.
Molesworth, Charles
    1979. *The Fierce Embrace: A Study of Contemporary American
    Poetry.* Columbia: Univ. of Missouri Pr.
Moore, Stephen C.
    1973. "Politics and the Poetry of Robert Lowell." *Georgia Review*
    Summer, pp. 220–31.
Naipaul, V. S.
    1969. "Et in America Ego." *Listener* Sept. 4, pp. 302–4; reprinted
    in *Profile of Robert Lowell,* ed. Jerome Mazzaro. Columbus: Mer-
    rill, 1971.
*Newsweek*
    1964. "In Bounds." *Newsweek* Oct. 12, pp. 120–22.

Oberg, Arthur
1977. *Modern American Lyric: Lowell, Berryman, Creeley and Plath.* New Brunswick: Rutgers Univ. Pr.

Ong, Walter J.
1967. *In the Human Grain.* New York: Macmillan.

Parkinson, Thomas
1966–67. "For the Union Dead." *Salmagundi* no 4, pp. 87–95; reprinted in his ed. *Robert Lowell: A Collection of Critical Essays.* Englewood Cliffs, N.J.: Prentice-Hall, 1968.

Peck, John
1977. "Reflections on Lowell's 'Domesday Book.'" *Salmagundi* Spring, pp. 32–36.

Poirier, Richard
1964. "Our Truest Historian." *Book Week* Oct. 11, pp. 1, 16; reprinted in *Critics on Robert Lowell,* ed. Jonathan Price. Coral Gables, Fla.: Univ. of Miami Pr.

Popkin, Henry
1967. "Lowell's Alternative to Aeschylus." *London Times* June 17, p. 6.

Price, Jonathan
1967. "Fire against Fire." *Works* Autumn, pp. 120–26; reprinted in *Critics on Robert Lowell,* ed. Jonathan Price. Coral Gables, Fla.: Univ. of Miami Pr.

Raizis, M. Byron
1969. "Robert Lowell's *Prometheus Bound.*" *Papers on Language and Literature* Summer, pp. 154–68.

Ricks, Christopher
1977. "Robert Lowell at 60." *Listener* Mar. 10, pp. 314–15.

Sheehan, Donald
1969. "Varieties of Technique: Seven Recent Books of American Poetry." *Wisconsin Studies in Contemporary Literature* Spring, pp. 284–301 [286].

Simon, John
1967/68. "Abuse of Privilege: Lowell as Translator." *Hudson Review* Winter, pp. 543–62; reprinted in *Robert Lowell: A Portrait of the Artist in His Time,* ed. Michael London and Robert Boyers. New York: David Lewis, 1970.

Simpson, Louis
1978. *A Revolution in Taste: Studies of Dylan Thomas, Allen Ginsberg, Sylvia Plath, and Robert Lowell.* New York: Macmillan.

Spacks, Patricia Meyer
1969. "From Satire to Description." *Yale Review* Winter, pp. 232–48.

Spears, Monroe
1970. *Dionysus and the City: Modernism in Twentieth-Century Poetry.* New York: Oxford Univ. Pr.

Stafford, William
   1967. "Critical Involvement of the Poet." *Chicago Tribune Magazine of Books* Feb. 5, p. 5.
Symons, Julian
   1967. "Cooked and Raw." *New Statesman* July 21, p. 87.
Tate, Allen
   1953. "Orthodoxy and the Standard of Literature." *New Republic* Jan. 5, pp. 24–25.
Taylor, F. H. Griffin
   1969. "A Point in Time, A Place in Space." *Sewanee Review* Spring, pp. 300–318.
*Times Literary Supplement*
   1967. "Open Sores." *Times Literary Supplement* Aug. 3, p. 705.
Vendler, Helen
   1967. "Recent American Poetry." *Massachusetts Review* Summer, pp. 541–60 [559–60].
Wain, John
   1964. "The New Robert Lowell." *New Republic* Oct. 17, pp. 21–23; reprinted in *Robert Lowell: A Portrait of the Artist in His Time,* ed. Michael London and Robert Boyers. New York: David Lewis, 1970.
Weales, Gerald
   1968. "Robert Lowell as Dramatist." *Shenandoah* Autumn, pp. 3–28; reprinted in his *Jumping Off Place.* London: Macmillan, 1969.
Williamson, Alan
   1974. *Pity the Monsters: The Political Vision of Robert Lowell.* New Haven and London: Yale Univ. Pr.
Yenser, Stephen
   1975. *Circle to Circle: The Poetry of Robert Lowell.* Berkeley: Univ. of California Pr.
Zweig, Paul
   1967. "Murderous Solvent." *Nation* Apr. 24, pp. 536–38.

CHAPTER 5

# "A Small-Scale Prelude": Lowell's Stylistics

In an essay he wrote shortly before his death, Lowell compared the practice of his craft with a journey:

> Looking over my *Selected Poems*, about thirty years of writing, my impression is that the thread that strings it together is my autobiography; it is a small-scale *Prelude*, written in many different styles and with digressions, yet a continuing story—still wayfaring [*Salmagundi*, Spring 1977].

Lowell admitted to having tried "discordant things" and hoped that his progress from one style to another had proved to be more than just a "series of rebuffs." Few of us would balk at these words. Lowell was known for his easy dissatisfaction with forms and his constant experimentation. The "satiation and disgust" he felt with his poems was often matched by the critics' annoyance, especially with *Notebook* and *Day by Day*, Lowell's least admired volumes.

*Lord Weary's Castle* signaled a return to traditional meters at a time when poets like Williams (in *Spring and All*) and Pound (in *Cantos*) were beginning to win respect for nonmetrical verse. That is, when critics conceded that it *was* nonmetrical, for, upon encountering a good poem, they swore that some kind of metrical pattern contributed to its excellence. When Eliot wrote (in 1942) that "only a bad poet could welcome free verse as a liberation from form," he was warning poets to observe constraint in their use of open forms ("The Music of Poetry"). Indeed, *Lord Weary's* appeal was in part attributable to its standard meters, which created no problems for critics during the forties. Later critics were not only less appreciative of its regular meters but conscious of the volume's conformity to a coterie style, as we learn from an interview conducted by Harvey Gross with poet-critic Stanley Kunitz:

Gross:    When Robert Lowell published *Lord Weary's Castle* in
          1946, right after the war, he seemed to have set a pro-
          sodic fashion. His book set me to writing rhymed coup-
          lets, *terza rima*, etc. Very often the impact of a major
          poet will establish the prosody of a creative age. Simi-
          larly, in 1959 when *Life Studies* appeared, we experi-
          enced a rerun of freer forms.

Kunitz:   I don't think that Lowell, with *Lord Weary's Castle*,
          really set anything because he derived his style out of
          the Southern traditionalists: Ransom and Tate in par-
          ticular. I don't think it was a novelty in that epoch
          [*Antaeus*, Spring 1977].

(I should point out that this exchange between Gross and
Kunitz is one of the few which centers on Lowell's prosody;
most of the stylistic criticism yokes prosodic analysis with
analysis of diction and imagery.)

Without much effort, critics noticed a stylistic constant:
poems couched in elevated diction and obscure symbolism employed traditional meters; poems couched in natural speech and
a paucity of symbolism employed free forms. This was neither
a startling discovery nor an exclusive ascription to Lowell's
verse; it was the formula with which critics distinguished "modern" from "postmodern" poetry, the free-form pattern representing the "postmodern" category.

Lowell's early style began to acquire a bad name when the
Postmodern poets dissociated their philosophical as well as literary ideology from that established by the Modernists. The new
generation (e.g., Ginsberg, Creeley, Ashbery, O'Hara, Merwin,
Snyder) recoiled against Allen Tate's injunction that "formal
versification is the primary structure of poetic order, the as-
surance to the reader and to the poet himself that the poet is in
control of the disorder both outside himself and within his own
mind" (*Essays of Four Decades*, 1968). The Postmodern poet
David Antin offered a witty redefinition of Tate's formal versification: "It is the pathetic hope of a virgin for an experienced
lover whose competence (detachment) is sufficient to lead her
to an orgasm, and all to be achieved by the mere maintenance
of a regular rhythm" (*Boundary 2*, Fall 1972). Meter, for the
Modernists, had an inherent symbolic force which represented
moral order, or resembled (for John Crowe Ransom) the reading of "an ecclesiastical service by the congregation."

The idea of a metrics as a moral or ideal order, says Antin,
is "a transparently trivial paradigm worthy of a play by Racine

and always yields the same small set of cheap musical thrills." When Lowell, for example, attempts to "energize" a poem, he enacts this paradigm and succeeds in producing pathetic or vulgar results. These iambic lines from "Colloquy in Black Rock" (*Lord Weary*), which seek to reach "some contrived peak of feeling," sound, to Antin, merely mechanical: "My heart you race and stagger and demand/More blood-gangs for your nigger-brass percussions." Antin's brassy accusation (I should add that he refers to Lowell's meter as "a kind of pornography") does not minimize its seriousness or importance, however.

In a more conventionally toned, but similarly focused, analysis of metrics, Anthony Easthope associates the pentameter line with the championship of "bourgeois culture" (*New Literary History*, Spring 1981). The very use of pentameter, says Easthope, stands for the claims of society, against which a poet's variations stand for the claims of the individual. While the closure of forms may seem repressively rigid, it delivers another kind of autonomy:

> Pentameter aims to preclude shouting and improper excitement; it enhances the poise of a moderate yet uplifted tone of voice, a single voice self-possessed, self-controlled, impersonally self-expressive, a tone which has retained its dominance in British culture since the Renaissance.

Easthope, unlike Antin, bears no animosity toward the idea of metrics as a tool for culture, which, paradoxically, makes Antin the greater moralist.

When we turn to the dispute over Lowell's metrics, we find the criticism is made up of brief skirmishes rather than full-scale battles. Some critics are firm in their conviction that Lowell is a proficient prosodist, whatever his form; others predict that the only enduring part of his canon is the verse written in open form—primarily *Life Studies*. A few test the validity of the notion that Lowell's changing styles were a function of his changing values. Since the critics employ the word "style" in such a variety of ways, it is difficult to survey their commentary schematically. As far as is possible, however, I will observe the following categories: the background in American poetry which spawned Lowell's stylistics; theoretical as well as *ad hoc* approaches to Lowell's stylistics; the dispute over the definition of Lowell's "confessional" mode (which, by any other name, appears to be his only mode); the critical interest in Lowell's practice of revision.

When we place a poem from *Lord Weary* alongside a poem from *Day by Day*, we find the difference startling. Lowell's style changed gradually over the years, becoming looser and more direct—a shift which was, of course, not unique to Lowell. In its stylistic aspect, Lowell's poetry exemplifies what we have come to recognize as "modern." It has its most immediate precedent in the short lyric or meditative poem of the Romantic period. In effect, it is a reflective poetry, yet conveys the feeling of conversation, usually dealing with actual or familiar experience. While not primarily narrative, it often contains narrative elements: incident, character, setting. It is generally inimicable to the *art pour l'art* philosophy; and though symbolism may be present, the Symbolist aesthetic never really gains a stronghold—as David Perkins claims in his encyclopedic *History of Modern Poetry* (1976). According to Perkins, British *and* American poets are still writing in the "typically English way," a reflective mode common to the eighth-century poem "The Seafarer" as well as to Coleridge's "Frost at Midnight"—and, by extension, to virtually all of Lowell's poetry. This generalization is crucial to our discussion of the Lowell criticism, for in some camps Lowell was labeled a Symbolist poet, especially when his early work was the object of examination.

When Lowell started to write, American poetry was struggling to reestablish its credibility. Subsequent to the nineteenth-century renaissance, when poets like Whitman, Dickinson, and Emerson installed a heritage at once "native" and "classic," there was an interim in which originality was replaced by a sentimental but fashionable verse, such as that produced by Bryant, Whittier, and Longfellow. But during the decade between 1910 and 1920 the unique voice that characterizes our national literature was reawakened. The new generation boasted a roster including such names as Frost, Eliot, Pound, Wiliams, Stevens, and Moore. Imagism was the most publicized movement at the time and its practitioners advocated a departure from the salon type of poetry that filled the magazines. Its duration as a movement was brief, however, and the body of verse known as Imagist was never as memorable as the poets (Pound, Cummings, Moore, Williams) who had once subscribed to its manifesto. Although the Imagists had a great deal to do with promoting free-verse composition, Imagism as such did not demand its use. It was still possible to present concrete images in traditional meters. Moreover, Imagism's first theorist was an Englishman, T. E. Hulme, whose aesthetics emanated from a group of Cambridge intellectuals, anxious to erase the lingering traces of Georgian verse. The movement was not sufficiently American to gain impetus in the United States. Lowell was not the direct offspring of a particular Imagist poet, although critics tossed about Pound's and Williams' names when they discussed stylistic influences in his verse. In any case, critics had a penchant for identifying Lowell as a successor to their chosen progenitor rather than as a successor to a movement or school.

When, as a student in the thirties, Lowell started to contribute poems to university-based journals (like *Kenyon Review*), there were two poets whose works commanded attention for their decidedly American qualities: E. A. Robinson and Robert Frost. Robinson, for all his bombastic rhetoric, wrote verse which was inhabited by convincing characters. Robinson brought to the realm of poetry the believable portraits that were then found only in fiction. The realism and pathos by which Mr. Flood, Richard Cory, and Miniver Cheevy are immortalized are the bases for Lowell's characterizations—such as Anne Kavanaugh and Mother Marie Therese. Since Robinson was rather heavy-handed with meter and rarely strayed from end-line rhymes, detractors of Lowell's early poetry (e.g., Bewley; see below) said it resembled Robinson's style. By the time Lowell had created his mature portraits, from *Life Studies* on, the Robinson influence was no longer a point of interest; nonetheless, Robinson played an oblique role in Lowell's writing, early and late.

Frost was a more valuable model for Lowell than Robinson, for in addition to bringing realistic portraits to his verse (as in "Home Burial") he gave his poetic line the natural intonations of speech. In a *Paris Review* interview, Lowell spoke at some length about Frost, using epithets bordering on veneration. For Lowell, the people in Frost's poems had a wonderful quality of life and the authenticity of a "photograph," yet the poems retained artistic polish. (The visual element, here expressed by the metaphor of photography, was a quality Lowell both sought and avoided. On the one hand, he tried to produce the effect of a family album in his poetry, while at the same time he was fearful of the one-dimensionality and flatness of camera reproductions. He told Ian Hamilton in the 1971 *Review* interview that *Notebook* was his attempt to circumvent this: "What I wanted to get away from was the photograph of reality.")

Edgar Lee Masters combined those qualities of Robinson and Frost which made their way into Lowell's style. Masters' impact on Lowell was less pervasive than Robinson's and Frost's, but his portrayal of Puritan, provincial America, in loosely cadenced verse, served as a model for the narrative and dramatic-monologue compositions in *Mills* and *Life Studies*. Though Masters' work has fallen into relative obscurity, his *Spoon River Anthology* was popular in the years Lowell was learning his craft.

Robinson and Masters cannot be mentioned here without also mentioning a poet who was born in the same year (1869) as both: William Vaughn Moody. Moody, a man of New England stock (though born in Indiana), graduated from Harvard, taught there, then taught at the new University of Chicago. His concern with Puritan views of man's essential depravity and a willingness to question official government morality certainly find echoes in Lowell—though Moody's poetry is quite regular in stanza and rhyme. Interestingly, Moody used the St. Gaudens statue of Colonel Shaw prominently in an antiwar poem, "An Ode in Time of Hesitation" (*Atlantic Monthly*, May 1900). As we note below, when Harold Bloom sought a disparaging comparison for Lowell with a poet who had been thought strikingly original and important in his day but had since been largely forgotten, he picked William Vaughn Moody.

Lowell knew that he could not confine himself to the Frostian mode, however, since it was too ingenuous for his purposes. He needed to draw from others—writers with a sense of the elaborate and of the baroque. With witty, erudite poets like Tate, Ransom, and (to some degree) Stevens, he could share his penchant for the metaphysical conceit, the brilliant pun, the inescapable irony. He never abandoned these elements of artifice, even in the late diary-like poems.

Another corner of the quarry to be mined by Lowell was the poetry of William Carlos Williams. While we cannot fix a ratio between Williams' influences and a specific work by Lowell, we know that Lowell was reading Williams "very carefully" while writing *Life Studies* (Lowell's "William Carlos Williams" in *Hudson Review*, Winter 1961/62). Without this information, we might not immediately connect that work with *Paterson* or *The Desert Music*, two volumes Lowell mentioned in the *Hudson Review* piece. Knowing this, we can recognize Williams' prosodic daring and his fidelity to time and place in *Life Studies*. In a sense, Williams' and Lowell's writing careers, if not their social or professional lives, ran parallel. Both began writing in intricate, convoluted meters; both used arcane symbols and motifs; both were determined to dramatize and then eschew, with the fervor of exorcists, elements of Puritanism in their sensibilities.

Also, there was a tragic strain in Williams' poetry to which Lowell was especially sensitive. To a degree, it derived from their similar childhoods: dominant mothers; weak, ineffectual fathers. From a Freudian perspective, this created conflicts in Williams and Lowell, conflicts which they consciously incorporated into their family poems and unconsciously appropriated to all their work. Indeed, in 1936 Williams published a poem entitled "Adam," a biographical sketch of his father which so resembles Lowell's piece on *his* father, "Terminal Days at Beverly Farms," that the early piece must have been Lowell's model (Procopiow, "William Carlos Williams and the Origins of the Confessional Poem," *Ariel*, 1976).

In addition to the influence of Robinson, Frost, and Masters in Lowell's early years, and of Williams during his middle period, Eliot and Pound were the most authoritative models for Lowell throughout his career. Lowell learned from Eliot how to adapt classical myth to contemporary context (e.g., "Ulysses and Circe," *Day by Day*) and from Pound how to convert history into mythos. *History* is in some ways a miniature replica of *The Cantos*, but there are less obvious examples, such as *Life Studies*, which also attest to Pound's presence. The exegetical study of Pound's influence is still in its infancy, but Axelrod has made some valuable inroads:

> *Life Studies* rings with Poundian notes, especially in its vivid portraits of writers and of inmates in mental and penal institutions. For example, the "Fordie" of Cantos 74, 80 and 82 prefigures the "Fordie" of Lowell's "Ford Madox Ford"; and Pound's all-too-human fellow prisoners, Mr. Edwards, Mr. G. Scott and the rest, prefigure the Negro boy, Abramowitz, and the other "jailbirds" of "Memories of West Street and Lepke" [*Robert Lowell*, p. 123].

This shared subject matter—even a shared attitude toward their "all-too-human" fellow prisoners—is surely significant, but —for this chapter at least—is a less telling factor than the style which, despite Lowell's fondness for the rhythms of some of the *Cantos*, is closer here to Eliot than to Pound. (In *Naked Poetry: Recent American Poetry in Open Forms*, an anthology of poems with accompanying statements by the poets represented in the volume, Lowell mentions the *Cantos* as one of

those free-verse masterpieces which would be "thoroughly
marred and would indeed be inconceivable in meter.") Lowell
shared with Pound the need to adapt, rather than translate,
foreign and classical poets to a contemporary idiom (see "The
Poetics of Imitation"). The Eliot legacy, however, is more obvious than Pound's. We have already noted Lowell's debt to
Eliot in thematic matters ("The Puritan Burden"), but when it
comes to style, as we shall see, critics were perhaps too content
with ready-made comparisons of these poets as Symbolists.

There are several other poets who deserve mention for having contributed, in a marginal way, to Lowell's stylistic development. Marianne Moore and Elizabeth Bishop were the two
contemporary women poets Lowell most admired. Moore was
his model of absolute dedication to the craft of writing, but he
had reservations about her "terrible, private, and strange vision."
What is more, her cameo vistas were too precious for his restless, overreaching nature. Chronogically, Moore's work preceded Lowell's by a little more than a decade and seemed to
him "naive" for his day (*Paris Review* interview). Bishop, on
the other hand, had a continuing impact on Lowell throughout
his career. Her poems, with their minute, precise, yet under-
stated details, achieved in words what the Flemish "genre"
painters achieved on canvas. Lowell strove to capture the realism of Vermeer and Rembrandt, and noted early in his career
(*Sewanee Review*, Summer 1947) that Bishop had done just that
in her poetry. Her imagery, prosody, and, more importantly,
the stoic wisdom which informed her poetic themes remained
a source of wonder to Lowell.

The most effective, concrete, and acknowledged example of
Bishop's influence is in "Skunk Hour," which Lowell tells us
was modeled on her "The Armadillo." Since our concern here
is with prosody, not subject matter or theme, the parallels between Bishop's armadillo and Lowell's skunk are not as important as Lowell's announcement that "re-reading Bishop suggested a way of breaking through the shell of my own manner."
Lowell cites as influential her "rhythms, idiom, images, and
stanza structure," and adds that both "Skunk Hour" and "The
Armadillo" "use short line stanzas, start with drifting description and end with a single animal" (Lowell in *The Contemporary Poet as Artist and Critic*; see below).

During the fifties, Lowell declared his independence from
the Fugitives, a group of poets living in Nashville, Tennessee

who numbered in their company John Crowe Ransom, Allen Tate, and Donald Davidson. Essentially conservative in their political views, they published manifestos urging the South not to abandon its character as an agrarian society. When it came to poetry, their stylistic strategies were equally old fashioned. Lowell's strongest link with the Fugitives was Tate, with whom he lived in the spring and summer of 1937. When he disaffiliated himself from this group, he did not stray far. His poet-friends during the fifties, while more politically liberal than the Fugitives, shared with the former group a traditional demand for the well-wrought lyric. John Berryman, Karl Shapiro, Richard Wilbur, and Delmore Schwartz experienced, with Lowell, a post–World War II *Weltschmerz*—a disillusionment which surfaced in their poetry with satiric force. Mutual respect ran high, but there was a feeling among them that Lowell was the most accomplished of the tribe—a feeling now endorsed by literary historians. In the sixties and seventies, Lowell forged ahead with new modes and left those poets (those who survived) behind. Indeed, to draw an analogy from another art, Lowell's career was akin to Picasso's: like this restless painter, who associated himself with movements (Fauvism, Cubism), only to move on when the movements began to enjoy public approval, Lowell always sought new challenges. For a while, in the sixties, he was deeply involved with the group of writers who contributed to the *New York Review of Books* and, like them (Adrienne Rich, Norman Mailer, Tom Wolfe—to name the famous), punctuated his writing with political statement (*Old Glory*, *Near the Ocean*). But this phase, too, was short-lived. Lowell felt a need to escape the oppressively public aspect of his New York life, and typically got as far from the scene as he could, to England, where he lived from 1970 to 1976. There he wrote *Day by Day*.

In many ways, Lowell's career is an account in miniature of modern American poetry. Lowell both influenced and was influenced by some of its stellar figures. There are a few poets who did *not* enter his sphere, and one can easily pick them out: Robinson Jeffers, E. E. Cummings, Carl Sandburg, Conrad Aiken, Archibald MacLeish, failed to capture his interest or imagination. Perhaps it is more accurate to say that they had little to teach him. Their sensibilities were alien to his: too romantic (Cummings, Aiken, Jeffers) or too proletarian (Sandburg, MacLeish). There is more ambiguity about his relationships with Roethke or Hart Crane. Lowell corresponded with

Roethke intermittently for two decades, during which time they exchanged manuscripts. Both believed that visionary poetry constituted some of the best verse in the language, but Roethke consciously aspired toward the mystical in poetry while Lowell moved slowly, but steadily, in the opposite direction. Lowell did not know Crane, who died in 1932, but he was enamored of his poetry during his Kenyon years, and *Land of Unlikeness* shows a distinctly Cranean influence. Lowell copied down several of Crane's lyrics ("Repose of Rivers," "Voyages II," and "For the Marriage of Faustus and Helen") in notebooks he kept between 1939 and 1943. While Lowell continued to respect Roethke and Crane, his mature poetry had no resemblance to theirs.

## *Theoretical Approaches to Style*

Lowell's rank as a stylist has been subject to the mutation of standards. The New Critics, expectedly, treated him well; the postmodern critics found him less than charismatic. A sampling from the assessments of Harold Bloom and Charles Altieri suggests that the more recent the verdict, the less glowing. Bloom's review of the *Selected Poems* (1976) was devastating: the early poems were "hollow" and the late poems were "drafts." Bloom then delivered the unkindest cut of all:

> Either the age is very wrong about this poet, or I am, and so I am willing to record myself against the age, in order to await later verdicts. I prophesy that Lowell will be another William Vaughn Moody, and not an Edward Arlington Robinson [*New Republic*, November 20, 1976].

In Altieri's "From Experience to Discourse: American Poetry and Poetics in the Seventies," Lowell's canon is compared with the work of the young poet Stephen Dunn. Praising Dunn for his unpretentious use of tone, Altieri delivers an "ironic reminder of how melodramatic, how prone to treat basic pleasures in pompously heroic terms, Lowell was, even at his best" (*Contemporary Literature*, Spring 1980). Interestingly, Bloom and Altieri arrive at the same conclusion for opposite reasons: Bloom dislikes Lowell's formlessness, Altieri his excessive formality.

While there seems to be a present dip in enthusiasm over Lowell's poetic style, the sixties and seventies brought a rash of scholarship which, if not consistently favorable, suggested that this style deserved examination. The major stylistic analysis of the volumes up to and including *Notebook* is found in Marjorie Perloff's *The Poetic Art of Robert Lowell* (1973). Rooted in the formalist methodology, this text is a careful and comprehensive exposition of the prosodic, syntactical, and imagistic patterns in the verse. Proceeding inductively and chronologically, Perloff classifies the technical devices common to the volumes. She then demonstrates how Lowell's stylistic habits are affected by his changing reactions to life—public and private. She claims that whatever his changing reactions, all of his seasons are "spent in hell."

Perloff begins her stylistic analysis with a consideration of dominant images. Spring, for example, is not in *Notebook*: "Despite his insistence on the seasonal cycle as organizing principle, Lowell cannot bring himself to include spring in the sequence." Similarly, *Lord Weary's Castle* has an archetypal garden which is either "barren waste land or oppressive jungle." Throughout the volumes, the landscape remains a reflection of the poet's anguish. In Lowell's animal kingdom, the same kind of sensibility applies: serpents give way to lesser reptiles, such as the turtle. Ferocity is tamed, says Perloff, but the ironic context remains nihilistic; tigers are replaced by insects. The healthy, ebullient animal kingdom is nonexistent:

> Lowell's poems have been full of references to mice, cats, moles, chipmunks, otters, worms, caterpillars, gnats, flies, spiders, bats, locusts, parrots, and geese, as images of pettiness, blindness, ugliness, disease, and death.

Such a bestiary, when translated to the social and psychological milieu, becomes a universe of "underworld garages," "industry's dogged, clogged pollution," "graveyards," and "the jerking noose of time."

When she deals with Lowell's syntax, Perloff is equally penetrating. She demonstrates how syntactic structures (adjective strings, participial phrase-piles) qualify and emphasize the emotionally tormented vision. In all, violent action or motion reflects Lowell's psyche in the grammar. Perloff finds a growing slackness in the volumes, so that by the time one arrives at the later work, there is a diminution of stylistic vitality. The poetic self is passive rather than active.

The merit of this study derives from Perloff's ability to translate the mechanics of Lowell's style to an index of his vision. Thus when she argues that *Notebook* is a "falling off," Perloff illustrates how the syntax and meaning are insufficiently related: earlier devices, such as noun-phrase series, which provided so much immediacy in *Life Studies*, have now become "mere mannerism." The poetic cosmos remains intact, but when "the syntactic structures fail to measure its dimensions, its outlines become blurred."

A less ambitious, but similar, appraisal of Lowell's stylistics was attempted by Harvey Gross in his *Sound and Form in Modern Poetry* (1964). Gross takes the standard approaches to Lowell's technique (that the early style is "willed," the later "natural") and shows how prosodic structure supports the claims. Thus the strained awkwardness of the early volumes derives from an obsessive rather than organic prosody. In *Mills*, a transitional book, "we hear the clear rhythms of Lowell's speaking voice unhampered by the exigencies of precise line length and exactly patterned stresses." The greatest achievement, says Gross, is *Life Studies*, where the texture and syntax show "no stitching," where the technique cannot be separated from the feeling. Gross's study is limited by its early date of composition, since the prosodic framework of the later sonnet sequences seems to contraindicate the directions Gross foresaw with the volumes at hand.

Both Perloff and Gross refer to the sources of Lowell's style, taking no exception to the idea that the Romantic poets hover in the background. While Lowell's immersion in literary tradition may be identified with various periods (e.g., British Metaphysical, American Puritan), the idiosyncratic self-accounting found in all of his poetry is primarily Romantic. In chapter III of *Poetic Art*, Perloff explores the properties of the greater Romantic lyric in Lowell's mode. Although the setting is altered (the speaker in the Romantic poem is usually in a localized outdoor setting whereas Lowell's scenes are more often interiors), the Lowellian poem retains the "determinate speaker," who experiences through the setting some integral process of memory, thought, anticipation. The poem closes on an altered mood or deepened understanding, as does the Romantic lyric. The device by which Lowell modernized the Romantic technique was the narrative, used in nineteenth-century Continental

Realist fiction. Perloff explains the dual source for his mode: "In *Life Studies* Lowell is trying to fuse the romantic mode, projects the poet's 'I' in the act of self-discovery, and the Tolstoyan or Chekhovian mode, usually called realism." She posits that it is his manipulation of the realistic convention, rather than the titillating confessional content, that distinguishes the so-called breakthrough of *Life Studies* and elevates it to a status beyond the work of Lowell's less accomplished disciples. Perloff says that the basis for Lowell's realism is the metonymic process: "Following the path of contiguous relations, the realistic author metonymically digresses from the plot to the atmosphere and from the characters to the setting in space and time." When Lowell appropriated this fictional device, his imagery converted documentary details into a mythology of his life. The product: a confessional mode both strikingly personal and objectively formal.

Perloff concludes her chapter on Romanticism and Realism as the bases for confessionalism with an admonition. Whether or not *Life Studies* tells the truth is irrelevant, as long as the reader believes that he or she is "getting the *real* Robert Lowell." Credibility is all. Indeed, Lowell said in his *Paris Review* interview that when he wrote *Life Studies* there was a "great deal of tinkering" with facts.

One critic who considers literal confession the crux of Lowell's style, and the *Paris Review* disclaimer just another of Lowell's truth-fictions, is M. L. Rosenthal. Lowell never stops playing the artist, but neither does he stop exposing his self:

> Lowell removes the mask. His speaker is unequivocally himself, and it is hard not to think of *Life Studies* as a series of personal confidences, rather shameful, that one is honor-bound not to reveal [*Nation*, September 19, 1959].

The "therapeutic confession," as Rosenthal coins Lowell's poetry, is the trademark of poetry of the sixties and its residual may be found in poetry of the seventies. In *The Modern Poets* (1960), Rosenthal continues his discussion of Lowell's style and claims that an entire generation—not just a decade—has been affected by it. The modern emphasis on the "I," which began with Eliot's "Prufrock" and reached its climax in *Life Studies*, was the foundation on which Lowell built his poetics. According to Rosenthal, the startling revelations in the poems actuate a rhetoric—or what in other critical discourses is referred to as "style." Rosenthal is sometimes disaffected by the revelations, especially in Lowell's poems about his father: "Lowell's contempt for him is at last mitigated by adult compassion, though I wonder if a man can allow himself this kind of ghoulish operation on his father without doing his own spirit incalculable damage." But he acknowledges that the shocking admissions are crucial to the poems' stylistic force.

Rosenthal makes some preliminary observations about *Life Studies* as sequence poetry, a topic which should command more attention in the scholarship. He says that the implicit purpose of the sequence is to imitate autobiography, yet create the aura of fiction. Thus " 'To Speak of Woe That Is in Marriage' is a monologue by the wife of a lecherous, 'hopped-up' drunkard. It is placed strategically before the last poem, 'Skunk Hour,' and after 'Man and Wife,' because Lowell wants us to know he is discussing his own marriage."

Not everyone was of the opinion that a rhetoric mobilized by shocking fact is the proper vehicle for poetry. For each of the accolades I have cited there was a detraction. For example, in "Sylvia Plath: A Partial Disagreement" (*Harper's*, January 1972) Irving Howe quibbled with claims that Lowell's style was beneficial to American poetry. Plath, said Howe, was handicapped by it; she felt compelled to tell her personal story, which, though deeply poignant, resulted in severe misuse of her talent. In this mode, the private details slip into self-indulgence —first in *Life Studies*, then in Plath's *Ariel*. The poems fall apart in the middle, says Howe, because once the subject is declared, the poet does nothing universal with it. In "Man and Wife," Lowell declines into a fuzzy recollection about the time he outdrank the Rahvs in Greenwich Village. If readers do not know who the Rahvs are (Philip Rahv was an editor of *Partisan Review*), this passage of the poem loses its force. Thus it was the personal reference—an extension of the cryptic symbol of Lowell's early style—that annoyed critics like Howe. What Howe did not consider was that "Man and Wife," as a commentary on the chic, intellectual New York scene, is full of sad undercurrents in which the Rahv episode is just one example of this group's existential despair. It doesn't matter whether readers know who the Rahvs are.

Any consideration of Lowell's style must take account of the commentary in Anthony Ostroff's *The Contemporary Poet as Artist and Critic: Eight Symposia* (1964)—from which we have drawn Lowell's remarks on Elizabeth Bishop. By Ostroff's scheme, three poets comment on a recent work of one of their contemporaries, who then makes his or her comments. In the Lowell section (or "symposium," as Ostroff calls it), the poem is "Skunk Hour" and the critiques are by Richard Wilbur, John Frederick Nims, and John Berryman. Berryman comments largely on the associations evoked by the poem—so tellingly, in fact, that Lowell says he "comes too close for comfort." (Such matters have been dealt with in our chapter on Puritanism.) Nims offers a close reading which pays careful attention to the nature of "Skunk Hour's" six-line stanza and its normative A–BCBC–A rhyme scheme, often incomplete and with rhymes and off-rhymes running from stanza to stanza. This painstaking demonstration of the craft in the poem is important because it testifies to Lowell's skill in setting up and varying a formal scheme.

Wilbur's comments are perhaps more interesting here, because less limited to the poem at issue and because their author shared many similarities (and differences) with Lowell. Summing up his sense of Lowell's stylistic progress, Wilbur recollects the "crammed, hopped-up lines [which] make continual dazzling transitions" in *Lord Weary*. He finds that

> the dramatic verse of *The Mills of the Kavanaughs* retains, generally speaking, the crammed and racing character of the first book; but not the quick jumps, the surprising collocations, the wrenched rhythms, the sixteen-line sentences full of avalanching particulars, are justified not by prophetic fervor but by the states of mind which Lowell allots to his characters [p. 84].

In "Skunk Hour" Wilbur sees another kind of dramatic verse, with the poet as speaker, in which the lines "are short, the rhymes off-hand, the language specific and conversational, the tone level."

The most interesting comments in the Ostoff "symposium" are by Lowell himself, for they set out the situation and the sources of the change in his style in this period (1957). In March of that year Lowell was, as he tells us, giving readings in San Francisco, "the era and setting of Allen Ginsberg." Although we can accept Lowell's claim that he was not influenced by the "beats," we can see how giving readings in that context of free forms and largely oral structures could convince Lowell that his own poems seemed like "prehistoric monsters dragged down into the bog and death by their ponderous armor." The breakthrough Lowell tells of came not from oral poetry, with which he was disenchanted, but from two other directions. He had at the time been writing prose and felt that the prose styles of Chekhov and Flaubert held promise for a new poetry. In the other direction was his rereading of Elizabeth Bishop, whose influence we have mentioned. In August of 1957 Miss Bishop's verse, presumably because of its literalness and its short-line stanzas, seemed the new idiom. By the end of September "Skunk Hour" was finished, and Lowell had broken away from the tight, armor-clad style of his earlier books. The stylistic accomplishment of "Skunk Hour" is not inconsiderable. Lowell had certainly found great freedom with complexly patterned syntactic and aural units, yet this was not Whitmanesque verse, and those to whom the long line, the catalogue, and the dominantly oral quality were the *sine qua non* of a "new" poetry would never find Lowell convincing.

The British were more inclined to take umbrage at personal references than Americans. While Britons granted that Lowell was the most formal practitioner of the confessional style, they found him too "naked" for their tastes. In a collection of essays entitled *The Modern Poet* (ed. Ian Hamilton, 1968), Colin Falck and other critics presented their case about the prosodic and thematic character of contemporary American poetry. Falck's target was Lowell, whose *Life Studies* "mirrors the chaos of experience without overcoming it." Falck's displeasure had its origin in a preponderant British complaint about American poetry: it is heedless of decorum, technical as well as thematic. Lowell is rambling, contingent, lacking in objectivity, says Falck, who was unimpressed with arguments like Perloff's, that the poems are only meant to "sound like" Lowell. Whether they are fiction or fact is irrelevant: "the end product remains the same."

In another essay in *The Modern Poet* Ian Hamilton attacked the prosodic structure of *Life Studies*, which he believed is prose: "There is no reason why these passages should be syntactically line-broken into verse." Since Lowell had acknowledged in the Ostroff symposium that one part of his inspiration for this *Life Studies* style was the prose of Chekhov and Flaubert, Hamilton's observation is not entirely unexpected, yet the unique syntactical play Lowell manages with many of his line breaks suggests that this critic was not reading very closely. Surveying the dramatic monologue as used in *Mills* and *Life Studies*, Hamilton argues that Lowell cannot fully achieve the synthesis between rhetoric and the "narrative motive," which combine to produce successful dramatic monologues. Lowell is too monotonously single pitched to score brilliant representations of human behavior.

Not so, said Gabriel Pearson, an admirer of Lowell's style for precisely the opposite characteristic: the presentation of life in a process of "depersonalization" (*Review*, March 1969). Despite Lowell's "unbuttoned," informal handling of family figures, his poems insist on structure and are designed to "keep the past past and the dead dead." The poems remain products, Pearson argues, albeit "artfully designed ruins," which transcend the crude stages of nature. As a Briton, Pearson was going against the critical grain, or so it seemed; but he was merely championing the traditional critical standards by a different maneuver.

Thus we encounter the first in a series of problematic topics that engrossed those critics who addressed Lowell's style. Was the style personal or depersonalized? One of the means of clarifying the distinction between the personal and the depersonalized was to investigate Lowell's use of "voice." However, critics had diverse conceptions of what, precisely, "voice" is. In the interest of standardization, I shall use M. H. Abrams' definition when I select examples of the criticisms which apply the term. For Abrams, when one speaks of "voice,"

> We have the sense of all-pervasive presence, a determinate intelligence and moral sensibility, which has selected, ordered, rendered, and expressed these literary materials in just this way [*A Glossary of Literary Terms*].

There is, then, a voice beyond the fictitious voices in a work, and a person behind the *dramatis persona*, even the first-person persona. The Lowell scholarship on his manipulation of voice shows a growing appreciation over the years of Lowell's use of personae. We have, for once, a compatibility between Lowell's stylistic maturation and the critics' reactions. When Marius Bewley wrote about Lowell in 1952 (in *The Complex Fate*, which we have referred to in other contexts), Lowell's portraits were "much nearer Edwin Arlington Robinson than Eliot" (Bewley's observation). Both Robinson and Lowell had a "disastrously 'literary' taste for the more romantic and ancient themes" and their exotic "set pieces" served up wooden personae. Bewley was not deceived by the apparent modernity of

Lowell's verse, but he did detect a growth in *Mills*, which, as an overall experiment, was a qualified success but proved that Lowell could create convincing personae other than his lyric "I." Bewley expressed confidence that Lowell would perfect his dramatic monologues.

After *Mills*, Lowell continued to write dramatic monologues which functioned differently in each volume. By the time he wrote *Notebook*, he had incorporated them into sonnet sequences, and the cast of characters had not only broadened but had ceased to sound like projections of the poet. As Randall Jarrell had remarked of the heroine in *Mills*, "You feel, 'yes, Robert Lowell would act like this if he were a girl'; but whoever saw a girl like Robert Lowell?" (*Poetry and the Age*, 1953).

I must insert a qualification about the praise rendered Lowell's dramatic monologues. When critics were pleased with them, it was often the archetypal echoes which they were really enjoying—that is, the mythopoesis of "Mills of the Kavanaughs" or of "Ulysses and Circe" gave the poems more dramatic power than the characterizations themselves. Few critics separated the effect of mythical overlay from the question of dramatic characterization. Hugh Staples *did* separate the two in his discussion of the symbolic identification of the "Mills" heroine and the central myth of Pluto and Persephone (*Robert Lowell*). The monologue of Anne Kavanaugh, delivered in a state of waking reverie, exists somewhere between exterior and interior reality, says Staples. The heroine's series of conflicts is given emphasis by the resonance of the myth, which juxtaposes spring and fall, fertility and sterility, sanity and madness. Voice here is heightened by myth, according to Staples.

Jerome Mazzaro takes the discussion of mythopoesis one step further ("Robert Lowell and the Kavanaugh Collapse," *University of Windsor Review*, Fall 1969). He says that the mythopsychological level of "Mills" functions as unconscious autobiographical motif, a preliminary use of voice and precursor to the "authentic monologues" of *Life Studies* and later volumes. Mazzaro says that the poem may well have served to rid Lowell's conscience of the sense of his marriage's dissolution and the "significance of this dissolution to his Roman Catholicism by converting both, under the guise of myths, into objective problems."

There exists here a real and unresolved problem which catches Lowell—and Lowell criticism—between his early mentors and the neo-Romantic poets and critics of the turbulent sixties. Following in the steps of T. E. Hulme and the *fin de siècle* revolt against Romanticism, Eliot proclaimed an objective, strictly dramatic poetry in which the persona (e.g., the aging Prufrock) is not the poet, the twenty-three-year old Eliot. Yet, with the subjectivism of the late sixties, poets and critics were discovering (rather late!) that Eliot was a reactionary and were calling for an "unmediated vision" in which the poet, like Keats or Shelley, would come out from behind the mask and the institutional formalities and speak from the soul. The whole issue of voice in Lowell's poetry is confused over the question of whether or not Lowell ever did this *and*, depending on the critic's values, whether this was good or bad. For Marjorie Perloff, Lowell maintains a persona and this was a mark of his excellence. For Altieri, Lowell's persona was a measure of his indirection and essential falseness. For Wilbur, Lowell dropped the persona in "Skunk Hour" (and presumably in the confessional mode generally), and this was a measure of his new success. For critics like Falck, Lowell's failure to depersonalize his poetry was his failure as a poet.

Some critics' uses of the word "tone" coincided with what other critics preferred to call "voice." Although they recognized the nuances between the two, their focus on tone was more concerned with the persona's attitude toward his or her listener. Lowell's poetry scored less well by this criterion, for critics (especially of the early poetry) found Lowell somewhat private and even narcissistic. The function of imagery in the tone of poetic speech was a topic critics were inclined to select when they wrote about voice. Lowell's imagery was not only markedly sensual but imbued with the power to evoke strong emotional reactions (in the reader) to subdued narrative details:

> He was dying of the incurable Hodgkin's disease. . . .
> My hands were warm, then cool, on the piles
> of earth and lime,
> a black pile and white pile. . . .
> Come winter,
> Uncle Devereux would blend to the one color.
>
> ["My Last Afternoon
> with Uncle Devereux Winslow," *Life Studies*]

A. K. Weatherhead attributes Lowell's command of tone to a creative faculty based on the Coleridgean notion of the "organic." Using Coleridge's distinction between Imagination (the "supreme faculty in the making of poetry") and Fancy (a "lower-order faculty"), Weatherhead said that the key to Lowell's forceful imagery is Imagination (*The Edge of the Image*, 1967). The substantial nature of Lowell's image is subordinated to the ideas and feelings it can be made to evoke, an effect best realized in *Lord Weary* but present in all of his poetry. Lowell does not dwell on imagery for its literal sensuous detail, says Weatherhead; in "Quaker Graveyard," for example, "the images of the Atlantic, though they are descriptive, are not a series of independent pictorial entities, associated by sensible features," but a re-creation of "the feeling of God, the omnipotent, terrible God of the Old Testament." The Coleridgean scheme resembles another formula for classifying great poetry: the synthesis of phanopeia (image making) and logopoeia (idea involving). The nomenclature bandied about was as varied as the critiques of style, but it essentially conferred the same meaning. Thus although a late critic, Alan Williamson, concentrates on Lowell's politics in *Pity the Monsters*, he sees the stylistic success of the political message as dependent on a fusion of images: "The irony with which he develops a double ambivalence toward the Edenic vision and the issues of ordinary experience is achieved primarily through imagery." And since imagery's essence comes forth in wordplay, repetition, and other linguistic arrangements, tone was necessarily discovered in their enactment. Early on, John Berryman had found in Lowell's "simultaneous repetition-with-variation, or the serious pun" that fusion of feeling and thought which later impressed Weatherhead (*Partisan Review*, January 1947). Berryman was not completely convinced of its success, however. These lines from "The Exile's Return" (*Lord Weary*) crowd meaning, said Berryman:

> The search-guns click and spit and split up timber
> And nick the slate roofs on the Holstenwall
> Where torn-up tilestones crown the victor

Here "*crown* is effective, if it is, against the implausibility of one meaning (invest, reward) and the infrequency of the other (fall on, finish off): one leg ought to be firmer." It was, of course, lines like these, instanced by Berryman, that later critics would label turgid or confusing.

Berryman was not willing to scrap a poem like "Exile's Return" or *Lord Weary*, which represented a considerable advance in tone:

> By a shift toward the dramatic which is one of the large features
> of his development, he is now peopling it [Lord Weary]. (It is
> to be noted that Lowell is an *objective* poet; except as a Christian
> or a descendant he scarcely appears in his poems.)

The statement in parenthesis was a minority view in the forties
and has remained so to the present. Berryman was confident
that Lowell's overreaching efforts at compression would moderate with time, and they did. *Union Dead* was the volume
which, because of the loosening stylistic facility Lowell achieved
with *Life Studies*, carried out Berryman's prediction.

Christopher Ricks offered some line-by-line readings of sam-
ples from *Union Dead* which were to him a marvel of linguistic
texture (*New Statesman*, March 25, 1965). Noting that *For the
Union Dead* was a "grimly punning title," Ricks quoted one of
his favorite couplets in the volume, and his analysis is so superb
that it deserves full repetition:

> You stare down hallways, mile on stoney mile,
> Where statues of the gods return your smile.
> [From "Caligula"]

> The assurance manifest in the unsignalled pun on "stare down"
> (as the couplet unrolls, the suggestion becomes Gorgonian); the
> way the couplet congeals around "stoney"; the chilling force here
> given to the cliche "return your smile" (not the reciprocity of love
> in the circumstances); and the explicit feeling of vista'd repetition
> which is enforced by the near-identity of the rhyme "mile/smile"
> —all these show a technical mastery that is inescapable from imag-
> inative mastery.

But Lowell's capacity for wit, which Berryman earlier and
Williamson later aligned with seventeenth-century poetics, has
not enjoyed the critical appreciation it deserves. Critics were
disinclined to go beyond the seemingly literal tenor of the
images, especially when they worked with the volumes after
*Life Studies*, a work so vividly (and deceptively) mimetic that
it seems to discourage the notion that a linguistic probe will
unearth hidden meanings. The voice or tone which critics af-
fixed in their minds was that established in *Life Studies*; volumes written before this were considered precursory, volumes
written after were judged by it. Therefore it would be useful
to pause here and examine the critics' perceptions of that phenomenon, known as the "confessional" style, so that later references to tone and voice may fall into place.

In *Robert Lowell*, Axelrod listed what were for him the three essentials of the confessional style: an undisguised exposure of painful personal event; a dialectic of private matter with public matter; and an intimate, unornamented style. Critics came to expect one or more of these features in all confessional poetry. Lowell's poetry was generally a combination of all three, and it was the expert handling of the second feature which accounted for his superiority over other confessional poets. In *The Poet in the Imaginary Museum: Essays of Two Decades* (1976), Donald Davie described the confessional style as one phase in the struggle, which began in the Romantic movement, to free poetry of rhetoric: "As soon as the poet looks outside the circle of his intimates, and thinks of his public (of an anonymous third party—to be interested and intrigued, in short, to be *persuaded*), he is no longer operating as poet but as rhetorician." Davie said that *Life Studies* put an end to reticence and pushed intimacy to a new extreme:

> The right to privacy for one's self, and the right not to look when the privacies of others are exposed, are rights that are now derided, if not yet explicitly denied. And for this surely baleful development, Lowell has to take some of the blame.

Some, but not all, the blame; for if we look at the poetic scene in the United States during the fifties, we find an entire band of culprits—the Beats. Poets were polarized into two categories at this time: Eggheads and Beatniks. This categorization was an oversimplification, naturally, but it provided critics with convenient short cuts for stylistic commentary. Eggheads tended to affiliate themselves with universities, making their living by teaching. They displayed their erudition by filling their verse with literary echoes and allusions. Beatniks advocated a return to primitive expressions and sniffed at the "literary" verse so favored by academia. Three years prior to the appearance of *Life Studies*, Allen Ginsberg, the leading figure in the Beatnik group, had rocked the literary scene with "Howl," which one commentator described as "inspired by heroin and lacking in heroism." Reactions to "Howl" recalled the Paleface/Redskin nomenclature for dividing American literature: Salon vs. Frontier, Learning vs. Feeling, East vs. West. The Eggheads were Paleface, Salon, Learning, East; the Beatniks Redskin, Frontier, Feeling, West. This not only sounded like jargon about sports teams, but it was outdated as well. Critics accused the Beatniks of sloppy writing and placed bets for enduring art on the Egg-heads. They failed to notice that the Beat poets, while noncon-formist, were fiercely obsessed with technique. Donald Hall attempted to correct this misconception in "The Battle of the Bards" (*Horizon*, September 1961), arguing that the Paleface/ Redskin dichotomy was no longer applicable in the twentieth century, where there was considerable blurring of standards. Thus a major poet like Pound could combine the cultivated Eliotic mode and the ingenuous Williamsesque mode and achieve artistic poise. Lowell found "Howl" a breakthrough to direct utterance (*Paris Review* interview).

Actually, poets were crossing the lines in greater numbers than the critics counted at the time. For example, James Wright, who by the standards I have outlined would have been con-sidered an Egghead (he was on the faculty at the University of Minnesota), published a number of his poems in *Origin*, a jour-nal critics considered Beatnik. Nor did the contradiction end there: *Origin* was published at Black Mountain College (North Carolina), an academic institution that was contemptuous of Academe! Lowell never took sides in this "battle of the bards"— which was, in truth, a battle of the critics—and while his pre-ferred social ambience was more staid than that of the Beats, he was very receptive to their free use of idiom and meter. In a sense, his *Life Studies* was a cross between Egghead and Beat poetry, and there is an amusing example of this conflict about classification. In a single issue of *Yugen* (no. 7, 1961) were two essays on *Life Studies*, one praising it, the other panning it. The essay praising it was by LeRoi Jones, who was moved by its humanity. The essay panning it was by a Beat poet, Gilbert Sorrentino, who faulted Lowell for the same defects other critics found in Beat poetry: uncertainty of rhythmic structure and thematic disorientation.

When critics spoke of the stylistic novelty of *Life Studies*, they were alluding to parts II and IV, the sections of the vol-ume which contained poems about Lowell's personal life. Part II was the prose fragment "91 Revere Street," and part IV was a lyric sequence on his family life, past and present. The critics found I and III too much like Lowell's earlier style. The per-sonae in I (e.g., the "Banker's Daughter," the "Mad Negro Soldier Confined at Munich") had the same woodenness as Anne Kavanaugh, who, in her role as victim, was a mouthpiece for Lowell. Part III consists of sketches of four literary figures (Ford, Santayana, Schwartz, Crane) who, in their different

ways, bore resemblances to Lowell and functioned in the poems
as personality projections. The critics preferred the privileged
peek at intimate life in the Lowell household, and part IV
satisfied their voyeurism.

At the time, critics felt that "91 Revere Street" and part IV
were prose and poetry versions of the same story. Few noticed
the difference in characterizations, especially in the portrayal
of Lowell's parents. In a later study, Karl Malkoff made the distinction (*Escape from the Self*, 1977). Malkoff said that the
prose fragment depicted the father as Lowell's mother had
wanted her son to perceive him, while part IV presented the
father as Lowell wanted to perceive him. In IV, the father's
youthful, manly traits are emphasized. Malkoff sees this as
Lowell's way to protect his own sense of manhood through
"restoration of a strong masculine figure" as model. The composition of IV served a therapeutic function. Malkoff's interpretation of the difference may be wide of the mark, but he
at least recognized the difference in the characterizations. Joseph
Bennett lumped parts II and IV together as a "lazy," "snobbish"
name-dropping memoir (*Hudson Review*, Autumn 1959), and
DeSales Standerwick found them both simply "embarrassing"
(*Renascence*, Autumn 1960). But none of them brought up the
use of voice in the two modes of presentation.

It wasn't until the seventies that the notion of fictionalization
of an audience as a way to explain tone was comprehensively
explored. It was then, paradoxically, that confessional poetry
(which claimed to strip off all masks) was said to wear the deep-
est disguise of all. And Lowell, the most skilled of the confessional poets, was seen as the most masked. In an essay entitled
"The Writer's Audience Is Always a Fiction" (*PMLA*, January
1975), Walter Ong argues that the confessional mode is an outgrowth of the Hemingway style. Although Ong does not refer
specifically to Lowell, his argument accounts for the sort of
existential reality Lowell created. According to Ong, Hemingway fictionalized his reader, who, by responding to such features as the extensive use of definite articles in descriptive
passages, became a companion-in-arms or confidant to the
narrator. By using grammatical ploys, such as demonstrative
pronouns, which make the reader feel he's *supposed* to know
what the narrator knows, Hemingway involved the reader in a
personal way. Ong uses as his example the opening sentence of
*A Farewell to Arms*: "In the late summer of that year we lived
in a house in a village that looked across the river and the plain

to the mountains." The reader, says Ong, doesn't ask *what* year. Somehow, "both he and the narrator have been there together." This, of course, is the same tactic that Lowell used in *Life Studies*:

> Father and Mother moved to Beverly Farms
> to be a two minute walk from the station,
> half an hour by train from the Boston doctors.
>             ["Terminal Days at Beverly Farms"]

Early reviewers did not fully appreciate the rhetorical tricks embedded in lines like these, which may explain why W. D. Snodgrass' *Heart's Needle*, which came out the same year as *Life Studies*, was the Pulitzer Prize selection. Time has shifted the status of *Heart's Needle*, which was cited for its imaginative transformation of ordinary experience. Today, Lowell's book is considered both the more authentic and more artistically achieved of the two, but in the September 1960 issue of *Harper's*, the annual "New Books" essay put *Heart's Needle* and *Life Studies* on equal footing. Stanley Kunitz, author of the essay, voiced the critical judgment of the day: All confessional poems are more or less alike.

There was no telling how established critics would react to *Life Studies*. Donald Davie, a respected academician, called the work a "noble achievement" (*Twentieth Century*, August 1959). As we have seen, Davie later felt less enchanted with Lowell's confessionalism (*Imaginary Museum*). In *For Lizzie and Harriet*, for example, the "intimate" game had gone too far:

> We are to be with him, we *have* to be with him, as he runs a distracted hand through his hair. . . . If we don't know about this [Lowell's new marriage] we don't know where to go for information; and we feel like people absentmindedly invited to a party where everyone else is in the know and knows everyone else.

In other words, the gimmick Ong had described was no longer working.

But to return to Davie's reactions to *Life Studies* in 1959. The "hair-raising" treatment of domestic intimacies represented (to Davie) Lowell's triumphant release from the dramatic monologues and historical episodes that "screened" his earlier work. Davie raised a subject pertinent to our discourse on style which one wishes he had developed further: the notion of voice in *Life Studies* as "scrupulously toneless." According to Davie, tone can often exist in poems which are "nothing more than pseudo-statements" working upon readers' emotions. Since the contemporary poet's relationship with his audience is uncertain —or so Davie believes—dependence upon tone as the criterion of successful poetry is a fruitless undertaking. Davie divides "Augustan" from "Romantic" poetry by noting that the former is toneless because it does not address the reader directly, as would the Romantic poem. He abruptly halts his argument here, leaving us to conclude that he is aligning Lowell with the Augustans.

Davie's essay doesn't ring right: how can a "hair-raising" treatment of life be "scrupulously toneless"? A possible answer is that Davie, like Pearson (noted earlier), was championing traditional British standards, which would give little value to the creation of a personal voice speaking through these poems.

John Thompson made a preliminary attempt to explain how the voice in *Life Studies* addressed its audience (*Kenyon Review*, Summer 1959). Lowell's technical strategy lay in the avoidance of metaphor and the refusal to present scenes or images which explain each other; the images spring up as if by chance. Through this procedure the truth emerges, not only about Lowell but "about the reader himself." Thompson stresses the importance of the reader in the composition of *Life Studies*, thus pinpointing the quality which for him makes *Life Studies* seem so modern: one gains knowledge about oneself while reading about another life.

Before we adjust to a critical view of *Life Studies* as eminently modern, we must take into consideration an anthology which appeared in 1960, entitled *The New American Poetry 1945–1960*. Edited by Donald Allen for Grove Press, this volume featured what was then considered avant-garde poetry. Numbered among its contributors were members of the Beat, Black Mountain, and New York schools. Lowell was not included—he was not *that* experimental. Lowell himself would have classified the poetry in *New American Poetry* as "raw." He separated the poetry of the day into two classes: "the raw and the cooked"; the "cooked" was laboriously concocted and meant to be studied, while the "raw" was the product of unseasoned experience, meant to be "dished up for midnight listeners." *Life Studies*, as Kunitz wittily remarked in the *Harper's* essay, was "medium rare."

Because part IV seemed so autobiographical to reviewers, they resorted to the "91 Revere Street" section as a kind of confirmation of facts. Alfred Kazin saw the prose fragment as a preface to IV and considered it a guide to the "more impressionistic poems" (*Reporter*, June 24, 1959). Alden Nowlan said that the poems were dependent on the prose and this created an artistic handicap (*Tamarack Review*, Summer 1960). Yet Robert Phelps liked the idea of a dual presentation, finding the prose something of a sounding-board to the poems (*National Review*, August 29, 1959). Lowell never explained his incorporation of the prose section into the volume. He believed that prose has a greater claim to realism or the fullness of experience than poetry (*Paris Review* interview), but part IV achieved more immediacy and realism than the prose. When critics raved about artistry, they singled out part IV. The factual aura in these lyrics qualified them as more than exquisite patterns of sound and imagery. Lowell had said that, despite his admiration for Hart Crane's poetry, it had no meat; a paraphrase of Crane's poems would "not give any impression whatever" (*Paris Review*). The debate about the function of "91 Revere Street" quickly subsided, in any case. Later scholarship used it as a biographical source. In terms of artistic merit, it was considered a parody of the "genteel traditions" of Bostonian reminiscences (see Axelrod's *Robert Lowell*).

One of the better early analyses of *Life Studies* was John Hollander's (*Poetry*, October 1959). Hollander, interested in how the autobiographical elements actuated poetic expression, noted that although the poems were autobiographical (Hollander was one of the believers), they were constructed around "the glimpse," which was usually a familiar object converted to an image. Thus the *image*, rather than the novelistic use of scene or episode, created the tone. He also noticed a less violent attitude in expression about life (compared with *Lord Weary* and *Mills*), a change which brought better prosodic effects. Lowell appeared to be a bit more relaxed. Hollander concluded that *Life Studies* was "unbelievably moving."

I must emphasize that the stylistic novelty of *Life Studies* put poetry and criticism at a new level of confrontation. Critical schisms increased after the sixties; journals were no sooner inundated with essays in one interpretive methodology than a new one took its place. Although New Criticism no longer provided the only standards by which a book like *Life Studies* could be judged, some practitioners of the new theories (e.g., Deconstructionists, Structuralists) kept away from Lowell. In fact, New Critic Cleanth Brooks, sensing that Lowell was at the center of a simultaneous creative and critical revolution, admitted that the formalist approach might not be the most effectual proving ground for *Life Studies* (*Southern Review*, Summer 1965). During the seventies, interest in the reader's and the author's role in interpreting the text further diminished the authority of New Criticism. Although generally the text still had primacy, critics like Walter Ong, David Bleich, and Stanley Fish believed that intention and affect were not as irrevelant to the success of a text as was previously believed. The self, in both poet and audience, deserved the critics' acquaintance. Actually, the new approach recalled the precepts of I. A. Richards, who was not so interested in what a poem means but in what it does (Richards, *Principles of Literary Criticism*, 1925). A sampling of essays on *Life Studies*, spanning the two decades subsequent to its publication, shows that the later the study the greater the interest in what *Life Studies* does.

Early reviewers devoted most of their commentary to the subject matter of *Life Studies*, exclaiming at Lowell's candor. Some were laudatory (*New Yorker*, October 24, 1959; *Sewanee Review*, Winter 1960); others were not certain of their reactions (*Atlantic*, July 1959; *Saturday Review of Literature*, July 25, 1959). One of the more forthright commentators, Thom Gunn, said that *all* the critics were "guarded" because they were bewildered by part IV (*Yale Review*, December 1959). Gunn found part I stale and was not surprised that Lowell had to break away from its stylistic limitations. The early British reviewers, surprisingly, were kind to *Life Studies*—except Frank Kermode, who found it too loosely organized (*Spectator*, May 1, 1959). Journals whose readership was wide and unspecialized were favorable (*London Sunday Times*, March 9, 1959; *London Times*, August 6, 1959; London *Observer*, April 12, 1959). Poet Philip Larkin didn't quite know what to make of *Life Studies*, since the poems seemed "too personal," yet "accurate and original" (Manchester *Guardian Weekly*, May 21, 1959). In retrospect, we may posit that the work had a greater impact on Larkin than he realized, for shortly after he reviewed the volume he began to write confessional poetry himself (*Whitsun Weddings*, 1964). And in his next volume, *High Windows* (1974), he shattered decorum as well:

> Groping back to bed after a piss
> I part thick curtains, and am startled by
> The rigid clouds, the moon's cleanliness.
>                    [From "Sad Steps"]

> They fuck you up, your mum and dad.
> They may not mean to, but they do.
> They fill you with the faults they had
> And add some extra, just for you.
>                    [From "This Be the Verse"]

Lowell's family poems are tame by contrast:

> "I won't go with you. I want to stay with Grandpa!"
> That's how I threw cold water
> on my Mother and Father's
> watery martini pipe dreams at Sunday dinner.
>                    ["My Last Afternoon with . . ."]

By 1965 A. R. Jones had claimed in a respected British journal, *Critical Quarterly* (Spring), that Lowell was the unquestioned leader of the American confessional poets. While he admitted to reservations about Plath's, Sexton's, and Lowell's "intolerable compulsion to confess," Jones was impressed with their willingness to "take chances and run risks."

Later essays attributed the brilliance of *Life Studies* to its unique use of autobiography. Robert Bagg's "Lowell and the Self" is a study of the distinction between the autobiographical poems of Yeats and Eliot and Lowell's *Life Studies* (*Mosaic*, 2, 1969). Not only does Bagg put Lowell in good company, but he argues that the "objects" in Yeats's and Eliot's works draw their meaning from tradition, whereas Lowell's objects "cannot be objectified." This, says Bagg, is Lowell's point of departure and singularly innovative contribution, since no modern poet has made the personal so immediately classical. And, given the standard response to *Life Studies* as a document of anguish, George McFadden takes an original position by classifying part IV's mythical elements as "comic" (*PMLA*, January 1975). Shattering the impression that this work is a "painful exorcism" or a testament of suffering, McFadden says it is a prototypical Freudian dramatization of "maturation and the family romance." The volume is a rite of passage whose redemptive element issues in artistic terms as a new voice or "speech"; and despite the intimate anecdotes about family quarrels and marital disputes, Lowell, like the rest of us, is making the Everyman journey through life. The humor in the poems, often a reaction to a punishing or humiliating situation, is a "Freudian proof of adulthood."

Finally, Jackson Barry's "Robert Lowell's 'Confessional' Image of an Age: Theme and Language in Poetic Form," thoughtfully analyzes the use of imagery and sound structure by which the forties and fifties, recalled both in Lowell's personal experience and in objective historical events, evoke a "memorable *poetic* image of an age" (*Ariel*, January 1981). Although the opening lines of "Memories of West Street and Lepke" sound like documentary detail, Lowell, in the interest of euphony, may have chosen a different weekday than that on which he really taught ("teaching," "Tuesdays"):

> Only teaching on Tuesdays, book-worming
> in pajamas fresh from the washer each morning,
> I hog a whole house on Boston's
> "hardly passionate Marlborough Street"

When Lowell completed *Life Studies*, he didn't know how or what he would write next. While he was fearful that he would not attain the public acclaim this book brought, he did not want to write another *Life Studies*, which he later described as a "decent book" (interview with V. S. Naipaul, *Listener*, September 4, 1969). Perhaps Stephen Spender's hyperbolic description of Lowell as "an outstanding pioneer extending the frontiers of language" intimidated him (*New Republic*, June 8, 1959). For the fact remains that this volume catapulted him to the sort of fame and publicity that threatened his shaky psychic state. And since it fixed him, in the critics' words, as a "poet of autobiography," he tried to perpetuate that aspect of his style. (Lowell, whether he ever admitted it to himself or not, attended to the critics' assessments and suggestions.)

While the critics have altered the earlier, less august "confessional poet" to "poet of autobiography," they are still at odds about Lowell's integrity in the use of his mode. Burton Raffel, for example, tells us that what Lowell "truly feels is hidden" (*Literary Review*, Spring 1980). Even the poignant poem in *Life Studies* about his reunion with his daughter, after confinement in a mental institution ("Home after Three Months Away"), is deceptive: "Weary, facile, this self-denigrating summation does not reveal anything, though it pretends to." But in the same issue of *Literary Review* Richard Fein claims the opposite: "It is all, strangely and pleasurably, of one piece, of one life—the life we read in all of its disparateness yet come to share, the life we study." By this view, Fein becomes that reader, described by Ong, who enters the world of the text (*PMLA* essay). Indeed, Fein speaks of "Skunk Hour," the volume's last selection, as though he had witnessed a longed-for reconciliation between Lowell and his mother: "The helpful mother had finally appeared in Lowell's poetry, though in a strange form. She brings her children to food."

We might now ask whether, taken as a whole, the critical literature on *Life Studies* advances our understanding of confessional stylistics. Yes and no. Negative observations were generally more concrete than positive ones. (I am excluding those essays which simply condemned the subject matter of *Life Studies* and never bothered with stylistics.) When Spender, in his otherwise glowing *New Republic* review, said that sometimes characterization was "a bit too final" or took the "form of a flat statement," we had tangible ideas to work with, even though we might have wished for more detail. Unfortunately, there was no prolixity of this kind of analysis, and in terms of current scholarship, there is little interest in confessionalism—perhaps because it was a trademark of the sixties, a decade most of us would rather forget. At any rate, there were other aspects of Lowell's stylistics which function as addenda to the discourse on confessional stylistics: the sequence, the confessional theme, the imitation of "realistic" painting techniques.

A spell was broken when Lowell published the *Notebook* volumes and *History*, for these works seemed to fly off in new stylistic directions. Between these volumes and *Life Studies* ten years and several books had intervened, though, besides the plays and translations, only two of them were books of original poems (*Union Dead* and *Near the Ocean*). Neither of these poetry volumes marked out new territory for Lowell. Helen Vendler, to her credit, used one of Lowell's more controversial —if not totally maligned—volumes, *History*, to defend his style ("The Difficult Grandeur of Robert Lowell," *Atlantic*, January 1975). She said that the plethora of "indigestible fragments of experience" in *History* produced a modern Marvellian treatise on the "use and abuse of power and kingship." In order that this be appreciated, we must learn how to read Lowell: "His free association, irritating at first, hovering always dangerously toward the point where unpleasure replaces pleasure, nonetheless becomes bearable, and then even deeply satisfying, on repeated reading." Vendler, then, distinguishes between sequences in earlier volumes (e.g., the Edwards poems in *Lord Weary*) and those in *History*. She says the problem in *Weary* rests with Lowell's difficulty in simultaneously describing the chaos of the present and incorporating his sense of the pressure of the poet. In short, it derives from the "cruel brevity of a fourteen-line form used for encyclopedic material, and the attempt to write of immediate personal interchange." But in *History* and its companion volumes, *Lizzie and Harriet* and *Dolphin*, the fusion of the past and present is achieved. In fact, these volumes, "with their tenderness toward the earth and its offerings, contain the first legitimate continuance of Shakespeare's sonnets since Keats." It is the forging of "maxims in fine-drawn descriptions," the narration of episodes with "pure and detached observation, as an immortal eye, indifferent to its own decay," which bring about the poetic accomplishment.

Vendler's opinion about *History* and the sequence structure is at present a minority view. As far as Davie was concerned, "all the poet has done is sort his poems into loose categories merely by subject matter" (*Imaginary Museum*). Rosenthal, Cooper, Cosgrave, Oberg, and others talk about Lowell's sequence poems, but they stress the thematic rather than prosodic elements. One book-length study, organized around the concept of Lowell's thematic "continuum," moves in the direction of sequence analysis: Stephen Yenser's *Circle to Circle: The Poetry of Robert Lowell* (1975). Yenser, however, does not go far enough with the subject. As his title implies, he sees Lowell's work as a "circularizing" of linear movement, representing a constant return to an organizing core of images and motifs which, even in occasional displacement, espouses an immutable vision. Although Yenser stresses the preponderance of sequences —in prosody, imagery, personae, seasonal patterns—he restricts their larger meaning to the metaphor of the circle. Lowell never moved beyond this circumscribed world, claims Yenser, but moved as in a shuttle from public to personal voice, "from the irrevocable enmity between the world's condition and man's sensibility to the need . . . to endure vicissitude and anguish."

In effect, Yenser's approach is a latter-day variety of New Criticism, which finds in this circularity "a formal unity which is grounded in tension and irony." The chief problem with this thesis is that it does not explain all the stylistic anomalies in Lowell's canon or the differences between the *Lord Weary*, *Life Studies*, and *Notebook* sequences. Moreover, Yenser is so bent on ferreting out every "circle image" that his exegesis is sometimes far fetched. This is especially true of his chapter "The Notebooks," where even Lowell's use of the exclamation "O" is called a circle motif. Yenser unduly emphasizes Lowell's use of the word "round," or any images suggesting this shape: "moon," "funeral wreath," "winding stair," etc. In effect, this becomes a textural reading according to metaphysical design, which may be misleading. What purpose is served by analyzing the "Harriet" sequence (which elucidates the relationship between the poet and his daughter) in this manner?

> Lowell is not specific about the alternative to death, although he alludes to Nietzsche's doctrines of the "eternal return," or rather to Herbert Marcuse's summary of that doctrine; but it is clear that Harriet, one of "earth's fairer children," is as least symbolic of his return.

The paradox is that in the "Harriet" sequence, particularly, Lowell uses the *sequence* with consummate artistry—and with meanings more resonant than is suggested by the circle concept. The variations of monologue, dialogue, recorded thoughts and speech are so exquisitely interwoven that Lowell has here superseded even the most moving moments in *Life Studies*.

One of the topics that sorely needs investigation is the correlation between Lowell's Symbolist mode and the Symbolist *structure* of his sequences. While Lowell abandoned his "clotted" early Symbolist style, he let go mainly of certain lexical features, principally in diction and imagery. Since the sonnet as a form contains philosophical—if not prosodic—attributes which are associated with Symbolist poetics, as derived from Baudelaire, and since Lowell's late volumes are sonnet sequences, the sequence design itself is a Symbolist analogue. The sonnet form recalls, if it does not actually incorporate, the force of rhetoric (often doctrinaire) in which its lineation restriction encourages the poet to summarize a human truth. For those critics who admire *History*, its sonnet structure succeeds in delivering such a summation. The question, so far unanswered, is how does Lowell reconcile his dissatisfaction with the symbolist mode with his return to the sonnet form?

As I stated earlier, critics seldom organized their essays around the analysis of tone as such, yet it entered the discourse in ancillary topics, one of which was the separation of Lowell's self from a more universal persona, and suggested at least a tentative answer to the Symbolist dilemma. Lowell's tonal modifications advanced to a growing recognition of the conflict between change and stasis. Therefore, Lowell could not have written *Life Studies* until he had lived long enough to comprehend man's futile attempt to "escape the flux of the temporal." Staples relegates to "memory" the basis for Lowell's changing tone: "Experience becomes valid only as it is ordered and enriched by the operation of the memory." Thus something as personal as memory is ultimately expressed by a universal persona. In Lowell's earlier style, irony and even invective expressed his solipsistic "wished-for permanence," whereas a gentler diction and rhyme bespoke his new-found awareness of mutability and his "acceptance of man's fate." Richard Poirier, in an essay which was actually a review of *Union Dead* but was also a resumé of all of Lowell's poetry to 1964, did not feel a sharp line between the tone in the early volumes and *Life Studies* (*Book Week*, October 11, 1964). In Poirier's view, *all* the work is happily marked by "an absence of metaphoric nervousness," and because of this "absence" the poems

> seldom invite anyone to expand inside them; they almost yield to generalizations about life or about the present situation. They stifle their own eloquence just at the point where they might publicize rather than serve as a close scrutiny of the poet's feelings.

This is surely a departure, for most critics, even when praising Lowell, do so by referring to his "generalizations about life" and his "eloquence." Poirier ascribes Lowell's "integrity of imagery" to the poet's tenderness for things, people, and the human body, a tenderness which derives from "the discovery he keeps making that persons and things are not something else, something larger." This is a fascinating notion (whether it is true or not is another matter) and in some contiguous way explains how Lowell, by constantly experimenting with diction, freed himself from the Symbolist trap.

To Denis Donoghue, those qualities in Lowell which captivated Poirier were precisely the cause of the poet's stylistic downfall ("Lowell at the End," *Hudson Review*, Spring 1978).

Donoghue asks "why is the relation between personal experience and the produced poem, somehow less fruitful in *Day by Day* than in, say, *Life Studies?*" Referring to the last poem in *Day by Day*, "Epilogue," he finds the poet's lines "I want to make/something imagined, not recalled" the crux of the problem. It is disingenuous, Donoghue argues, to speak of the writing act as recording "what happened." The gap between "what happened" and the "saying," or the question of memory and imagination, is where Lowell failed. Lowell had placed himself in the Wordsworthian camp, using his memory as a form of imagination; but since Lowell was not a Wordsworth, says Donoghue, his poems became (especially in *Day by Day*) machines for transcribing facts that had undergone little artistic transformation: "He writes with the low spirits of a poet who knows that he cannot transform [experience] anymore. In one poem he complains that his words no longer 'sound': and it is true." To Donoghue, the problem is solipsism: "Lowell never had anything to write about but himself," and in the last years he had "used himself up." He was Blakean rather than Wordsworthian, concludes Donoghue, a visionary Romantic who believed in transfiguring his experience; and when he abandoned this aesthetic principle in *Day by Day*, the "joy of words had leaked away." What Donoghue misses is the *basis* for a new poetics in *Day by Day*. Lowell isn't really regretting this disappearance of the "joy of words," but moving on to a more self-referential, antimimetic style which (in Postmodern terms) collapses illusion.

David Kalstone is much more sympathetic to Lowell's objectives (*Five Temperaments*, 1977). He too believes that memory is Lowell's poetic "method" but that he uses it as an impulse, not as an answer: "Memory of and by itself does not animate the present for him. . . . On the contrary, it threatens to overwhelm him." Kalstone, like Donoghue, believes that autobiography is a problematic form for Lowell, but *his* form nonetheless, and that the documentary surface of the poems is his singular contribution to contemporary poetics. Kalstone extends this notion a bit further by arguing that the act of presence achieved through the documentary surface resides in the image of language itself.

This brings us to a sticky area of Lowell's stylistics: his practice of writing about writing. Lowell's later volumes (especially *Notebook* and *Day by Day*) contain poems which metaphorize the poet in the act of writing. What is interesting to us is that writing about writing, a self-reflective stylistic activity, has ordinarily been associated with "postmodern" poetics. Insofar as the statement "the text is about the text" is one criterion for differentiating the Postmodern from the Modern poem, does this suggest that Lowell (at least in late career) was a Postmodern poet? Critics have stayed away from this problem, the solution of which will likely fall to the literary historians. (How, for example, will they classify Wallace Stevens, whose poetry is consistently on the subject of writing poetry but whose Symbolist mode puts him in the Modernist camp?)

We must say a few words about certain personal themes which absorbed Lowell throughout his career (apart from the major and more public ones, like Puritanism, history, religion, which have been treated elsewhere) since their psychological force influenced his stylistic habits. Jerome Mazzaro frequently (and I think correctly) suggested that Lowell's use of voice was dependent on his largely unconscious effort to conceal his conflicts with his mother. Scattered references to Lowell's mother images are made throughout *The Poetic Themes of Robert Lowell* (especially pp. 108–14), but in a *Salmagundi* essay (Winter 1966/67) Mazzaro showed how this familial problem became a thematic motif: Lowell's "heroes, himself and others, even in a post-Christian world, must encounter and subdue their imaginations' Terrible Mothers." The hint of the "evil mother" surfaces in *Life Studies*, he says, but it appears more frequently in the later work. Mazzaro was discreet and perfunctory, perhaps because Lowell was living then. After his death, however, Burton Raffel, in *Literary Review* (mentioned earlier), remarked on these lines from "Sailing Home from Rapallo" in *Life Studies*:

> In the grandiloquent lettering on Mother's coffin,
> *Lowell* had been misspelled LOVEL.
> The corpse
> was wrapped like *panetone* in Italian tinfoil.

To describe one's mother as a Milanese cake wrapped in foil is inexcusably vicious, argues Raffel. And as we shall see in our chronological survey of stylistic approaches to the volumes, critics were more condemnatory of the mother portraits in *Day by Day*. In this volume, Lowell made some effort toward forgiveness—of himself as well as her—in lines such as these:

"It has taken me the time since you died/to discover you are as human as I am" ("To Mother"). But the larger archetypal motif of the "evil mother," as characterized earlier by Mazzaro, continued to make its appearance in poems about *other* men's mothers. In "William Carlos Williams" (*Notebook 1967–68*), for example, Lowell describes Williams' aged mother, whom he had met during a visit to the Williamses:

> the Mother, stonedeaf, her face a wrinkled talon,
> burnt-out ash of her long-haired Puerto Rican grasses;
> the black, blind, bituminous eye is inquisitorial.

The theme of erotic love makes few appearances in Lowell's early volumes, but when it does, the consequence of lovemaking is more often than not tragic (e.g., "The Death of the Sheriff," *Lord Weary*), or occurs in a dream (e.g., "Mills"). In the later volumes—in *Dolphin* especially—the theme is not only rendered in its beauty and joyousness but it also represents Lowell's own experience, rather than that of a fictional persona. Even in the late poems, nonetheless, feelings of guilt threaten the poet's happiness; Lowell seems not only grateful for his new-found love but saddened by it as well.

One of the best essays to explore the manifestations of Lowell's guilt insofar as it affected his writing is G. D. Willis' "Afloat on Lowell's *Dolphin*" (*Critical Quarterly*, Winter 1975). Willis argues that although Lowell's guilt was a burden, its function was not entirely negative: guilt tended to depress Lowell, thereby releasing him from his real mental problem, mania. If mania threatened his creative powers, depression at least restored him to reality and left him free to write. Willis says that Lowell's guilt at leaving Lizzie, his second wife, to marry Caroline, generated the stylistic configurations of *Dolphin* and *Lizzie and Harriet*. Thus the technique of presenting Lizzie through her own words (primarily in letters) releases her from the castrating bitch image he presented in the earlier "Man and Wife." In effect, Willis is defending Lowell against those critics who lacerated him for using bits of conversations, letters, and newspaper clippings to fill his poems. Lowell's newly discovered love, expressed in collage-like poetic structure, imbued his work with a tone of gentle humanity: loving Caroline awakened his capacity to love all people, "so that he can feel more love even for the wife he is deserting than he has for some time."

*Day by Day*, while not entirely devoted—as is *Dolphin*—to poems about Caroline, contains a number of poems about her. "Ulysses and Circe" transforms the myth to a mythification of the relationship between Lowell and Caroline. Robert Fitzgerald's "Notes" on the poem (which is hardly that) correlates the hero of *The Odyssey* with the poet as depicted in the narrative ("Aiaia and Ithaca: Notes on a New Lowell Poem," *Salmagundi*, Spring 1977). Ulysses is a classical figure for a culture at that point of exhaustion which saw Christ come to take his place. To Fitzgerald, the identification Lowell makes with Ulysses enlarges his own image to epic proportions, but also reduces Lowell to a tragic figure whose wanderings have come to an end. Thus the parody of the epic mode, albeit in plain style, produces an inimitable atmosphere and a tone which is "timeless."

One of the subjects related to Lowell's stylistics which has been glancingly addressed and will, hopefully, be more fully attended to in future scholarship is his interest in the Flemish "genre" school of painting, especially the painters Rembrandt, Vermeer, and Van Eyck. One of the discoveries, made by Jack Branscomb, was that Lowell actually paraphrased comments by art historians and incorporated them into the poems (*English Language Notes*, December 1977). The sonnet "Rembrandt," in *History*, relies heavily on Sir Kenneth Clark's language in *The Nude: A Study in Ideal Form*. Branscomb shows how Lowell adds several new elements to his source, transforming the painter's technique to words: "Lowell seems to suggest the similarities of his and Rembrandt's methods while remaining pessimistic about his own success." Like Rembrandt, Lowell deals with the "stubbornly unlovely" things in life and fills his poems with the concrete, specific, everyday details one encounters in Dutch painting. By the time he wrote *Day by Day*, Lowell had gone further with his experiments in realism. Now the "photographic" quality of *Life Studies* and *Union Dead* seemed lifeless to him and he longed to capture the fluid, transfigured quality of the Flemish school. It was this effort that gave *Day by Day* a quality different from his other work. Further investigation into painting as a new source of inspiration for Lowell will likely uncover technical strategies in this volume.

Meanwhile, those critics who believed that *Lord Weary* was Lowell's triumph, and that his downfall began with *Notebook*, were scathing about *Day by Day*. Donald Hall was "depressed by its trashiness" (*Georgia Review*, Spring 1978). Noting that Lowell had been "canonized" and could do no wrong for the critics, he concluded that the trite language and unfixed connections were inexcusable: "Its overall tone proclaims the lassitude and despondency of self-imitation." Hall ignored Lowell's clues within the poems themselves that paintings now informed his compositional procedure:

> Pray for the grace of accuracy
> Vermeer gave to the sun's illumination
> stealing like the tide across a map
> to his girl solid with yearning.

One critic who understood what Lowell was attempting in *Day by Day* was Helen Vendler (*New York Review of Books*, February 8, 1979). Although she did not elaborate on his altered conventions, she made some penetrating comments on his final aesthetic:

> This backward glance to the power of the painter's vision, as it "trembles to caress the light," is paired with a backward glance to "those blessed structures, plot and rhyme," the compositional resources comparable, in the poet's art, to balance of masses and hues in the art of the painter.

Thus the uncomposed aesthetic of the poems aims at a Vermeer-like "writing with light," a reproduction of reality without the mechanical deadness of snapshots. To Vendler, this technique is "only another convention," but she is correct in insisting that it contradicts the convention of *Life Studies*.

*Life Studies* was a liberation through memory, *Day by Day* an effort to understand the present. The images in the earlier volume, although domestic and ordinary, were fixed in such controlled sound and rhythm patterns that they emitted a certain formality; the last volume is more dishevelled in its use of images and rhythms. Vendler's essay reminds us of the critical battles about Lowell's earlier books, which we must turn to now and follow, chronologically, for a fuller picture of the changing critical standards which led to interpretations such as Vendler's.

## Stylistic Commentary on Individual Volumes

The term "symbolism" found its way into most of the critical and theoretical literature of the forties; indeed, excellence in American poets was gauged by their facility with the symbolic mode. Eliot's studies on the French poets and Edmund Wilson's essay on Symbolism in *Axel's Castle* (1936) had provided the terminology and philosophical context needed to evaluate the poetry currently being published. But even such lucid essayists as Eliot and Wilson could not prevent the proliferation of fuzzy commentary on the subject. This is evident when we read essays on Lowell's early style, which was mistakenly wedged into the Symbolist classification. It may be argued that such a misapprehension could easily develop. Symbolism, as practiced by Baudelaire, Valéry, and Mallarmé, stressed the values and social conflicts of isolated man in the modern city. From an aesthetic standpoint, these poets insisted on the autonomy of poetry as a complex interiorization of experience, as depiction not of the thing itself but of the effect it produces. The Symbolist poetic was clearly elitist, its vagueness and suggestiveness formulating a mystery to which only enlightened readers found the key. Lowell's early ideas had something in common with the French poets', but his poetry, as we have seen, had other derivations as well.

Allen Tate was usually named as the link between Lowell and the French school, but the writer who most resembled the French poets was Eliot. In 1970 Haskell Block wrote a retrospective essay which clarified the French connection in the works of poets like Tate and Lowell ("Impact of French Symbolism on Modern American Poetry" in *The Shaken Realist*). Block claimed that what they really learned from the French (via Eliot) was how to widen the range of potential innovation, but that they could not be called Symbolists. This position had been maintained a few years earlier by F. J. Hoffman in "Symbolisme and Modern Poetry in the United States" (*Comparative Literature Studies*, 1967). According to Hoffman, the American poet has always wanted to "hold on to the thing," and has been reluctant to move freely toward the symbol. In fact, it is because the "particulars of our world" are so important to us that Imagism, which brought the poet halfway between thing and symbol, had a certain appeal for native poets. Both Block and Hoffman traced Lowell's and Tate's styles to seventeenth-century Metaphysical poetry, which was not symbolist yet resembled the abstruse diction and witty intellectuality of the French poets. But their essays entered the critical literature long after Lowell's early volumes were reviewed. In a 1963 interview with A. Alvarez (London *Observer*, July 21), Lowell recalled that when he wrote *Unlikeness* and *Lord Weary* he attempted to give his poetry much more formal complexity than Eliot and Pound had used and to write meters which "look hard." There is no mention of an effort to imitate the French poets.

*Land of Unlikeness* (1944) was so immersed in religious myth and intellectualized Catholic symbolism that it was barely comprehensible. Lowell later said that when he was writing this volume he was "much more interested in being a Catholic than in being a writer" (*Paris Review*). His style was really a botched compilation of what he had learned from the Renaissance and Metaphysical poets, and what he had culled from the Fugitives' experiments. Tate, in his Introduction to the volume, stressed the ethical character of the poems but he also made a few comments about stylistics. The text as a whole was a return to formal meters, said Tate, heightened by brilliant puns and shifts of tone. The main flaw was its "willed" symbolic language, which appeared in the explicitly religious poems. When Lowell wrote on personal subjects (e.g., "Death from Cancer"), the symbolism was more "explicit." Through indirection, Tate advised Lowell to write less obscurely, and Lowell listened—perhaps too well, as far as the critics of the later volumes were concerned. Lowell persisted with his metrical experiments, however, evidently not heeding Tate about formal rhythms, and in *Lord Weary* (1947) he tried to vary the poetic line while retaining the iambic measure.

His experiments troubled Howard Moss (*Kenyon Review*, Spring 1947) and Marius Bewley (*Scrutiny*, March 1951), both of whom detected a flaw in Lowell's line: a caesura at line end, just before the first word of a new sentence. Although Lowell tried to domesticate his symbolic patterns, certain critics thought they were still too wild. At least one influential critic, Austin Warren, couldn't understand the poems' order of placement in the text (*Poetry*, August 1947). For the sake of coherence, Lowell should have observed the historical sequence of the themes treated in the poems: he should have opened with the Jonathan Edwards poems, then followed with the poems referring to Emerson and Thoreau, and so forth. Warren wanted a cultural-historical framework to provide the formal pattern. Lowell's organization, however, stemmed from a private rather than chronological pattern of meaning—at times so private that the poems were unintelligible! Critics like Warren and Bewley (in the *Scrutiny* piece) acknowledged, nonetheless, that Lowell's obscurity was one of the troubling results of his originality. For example, in "Quaker Graveyard" Lowell yoked Catholic imagery ("Our Lady") with mythical Indian allusions ("scorched thunder-breasts"). The two references were considered too remote to coalesce successfully. Lowell's symbols were erudite, but did they work? *Lord Weary* showed more artistry than *Unlikeness*, but it had imperfections.

The decade spanning 1950 to 1960 was a transitional period for American poetry, for the formalist style had begun to vanish and poets were moving in the direction of the more open, confessional mode. Lowell's stylistic evolution did not come about promptly or easily—it took eight years for it to mature from the tentative *Mills* (1951) to the triumphant *Life Studies* (1959)—but the psychic and aesthetic problems Lowell grappled with were common to his fellow poets. A postwar sensibility had emerged and a new voice was needed to express it. Poets aimed at a sense of identity between the workings of the unconscious and those of the outer, natural world. For various reasons, neither the old Symbolism (never native, as argued earlier) nor the new Surrealism (also a foreign import) seemed the proper vehicle. The American poet needed a contemporary doctrine of correspondence between a sense of the self (the spiritual residue of Emersonian Transcendentalism) and a sense of the existential angst of modern life. In this search Lowell worked alone, away from programmatic groups or schools of writing. How was he to write in a manner which had access to dream and illusion while, at the same time, retaining access to the world of objective thought and experience?

Others, like Roethke, experimented with the "deep image" poem, or, like John Berryman, with the "dream song." Lowell's device became the "confessional" poem, as we know, but he had to resolve his obsession with the distinctions between public and private experience before he could write confessional poetry. His intermediate solution was the persona in dramatic monologue, a speaker who could incorporate much of his private consciousness and yet expand the boundaries of the self. In "Mills," the title poem, a projected dramatis persona served as his model of the self, and the narrative structure conjoined realistic description with reverie. The poem was a distinct departure from his usual style and the critical response to it was confusion or disappointment. It took some time before the Joycean and Browningesque elements in "Mills" were identified and their thematic functions explained. It was also necessary to relate the mythical echoes in the poem to their contemporary meanings.

Staples' analysis (in *Robert Lowell*) advanced the understanding of the poem. Anne Kavanaugh, the principal persona in the poem, is a modern-day Persephone whose tragic marriage is a metamorphic complex of dualism about life and death, faith and faithfulness, says Staples. She enacts the poet's own marital, spiritual, and artistic struggles; and Lowell's effort to cover these struggles is undoubtedly the reason for the poem's obscurity. According to Staples, Lowell tried to fuse two techniques in "Mills": to use myth, as Joyce did in *Ulysses*, embodying archetypes in a modern environment, and to actualize characters in the form of a Browning monologue. The experiment was ambitious, concluded Staples, but the poem lacked dramatic immediacy.

A few of the early essays on *Mills* have become classic statements on the work, partly because they were written by distinguished men of letters (William Carlos Williams, Randall Jarrell, William Arrowsmith) and partly because the later critics showed little interest in it. Williams' review (*New York Times Book Review*, April 22, 1951) was a little quirky and tended to harp on poetic problems that he himself was encountering at the time—primarily, the difficulty of overcoming the "monotony of the line." He sensed Lowell's need to break through the rhyme-and-meter barrier but felt that he succeeded only partially. Williams claimed that "Mills" was at its best when the "tragic inevitability" inherent in the narrative content forced Lowell to use "violent and sensual" forms, and it was in those tragic passages that Lowell had broken through the barrier. Williams was also pleased with the *range* of themes in the volume: dreams, incest, sainthood. In retrospect, we observe that Lowell did not retain these themes for his later poetry, which suggests that Lowell was still groping for themes that naturally accommodated his sensibility.

Williams did not comment on the length of "Mills" (600 lines). Arrowsmith did, and found it the reason for the poem's failure (*Hudson Review*, Winter 1952). He said that Lowell was a forceful lyric poet who could produce "explosions" on a page, but that his devices did not work in a long poem. When expanded, its power, passion, and violence became "monotonous." Arrowsmith also objected to Lowell's use of the Persephone and Hades myth—and to the use of myth at all. His reason: since such eschatologies are so richly embedded in cultural memory, they tend to keep their own force and to obscure, rather than enhance, the new narrative. Jarrell, one of Lowell's most consistent champions, was nice to *Mills* (*Poetry and the Age*, 1953), but he also sensed that the book had been written by a compulsive act of will rather than by the force of imagination. Jarrell, in his customary practice as critic, was more penetrating in his aperçus than in his systematic analyses.

In effect, these three commentaries, rounded out by Staples' elaborate analysis of "Mills," are the definitive stylistic approaches to the volume. When Ehrenpreis wrote his influential essay "The Age of Lowell" (1965), he reiterated the view of Staples and Jarrell (implied by Williams and Arrowsmith) that the static quality of *Mills* came from its poorly used autobiographical inserts. We must be mindful that "Mills," as narrative verse, was judged against the narrative verse of Frost, who was then considered by the critics the master of this genre. Lowell, expectedly, did not show well, but as Jarrell noted in his essay, everyone who wrote narrative verse in those years was an "amateur" compared with Frost.

Despite these qualifying factors, the reviews of *Mills* were abundant and, generally, favorable. Now considered one of Lowell's weakest volumes, it was uniformly hailed in wide-readership publications, perhaps as a conditioned response to a former Pulitzer Prize winner (*Lord Weary*). Gene Baro saw tremendous growth in *Mills*, for the poet had come to terms with the duality of human nature and his absolutism had deepened to a more tolerant understanding (*New York Herald Tribune Book Review*, April 22, 1951). Paul Engle described the book as transitional, but moving toward a more flexible manner (*Chicago Tribune Magazine of Books*, June 10, 1951); and Charles Poore also detected a spiritual growth in *Mills*, a kind of "shattered fortitude" that ennobled both poet and audience (*New York Times*, May 12, 1951). The one quality that all three reviews emphasized was Lowell's humanism. In the literary journals, Lowell's stylistic growth was praised. Richard Eberhart found Lowell's mixture of classical erudition and rough contemporaneity the "American thing" (*Kenyon Review*, Winter 1952); and Lowell's triumph over his former excesses in imagery and metrics was scored by Byron Vazakas (*New Mexico Quarterly*, Summer 1952), Cudworth Flint (*Virginia Quarterly Review*, Summer 1951), Dudley Fitts (*Furioso*, Fall 1951), and Lloyd Frankenberg (*Harper's*, October 1951). Only David Daiches still had reservations about Lowell's "too venturesome" stylistics (*Yale Review*, Autumn 1951).

After *Life Studies* and *Union Dead*, the two volumes which, through their loose rhythms and personal subject matter, became the trademarks of Lowell's confessional mode, Lowell surprised the critics again and reverted to traditional meters (octosyllabic couplets in the title poem) in his next work, *Near the Ocean* (1967). The prosody in *Ocean* was determined by the thematic imperatives of the poems, which were historical and political. In the period between *Life Studies* and *Ocean*, Lowell was establishing certain principles (which never really amounted to a theory) about the use of free forms. This was verified by Anne Sexton, a fellow confessional poet who audited Lowell's poetry seminar at Boston University in 1959. In a *Paris Review* interview (1971), Sexton, when asked about her own development, said that Lowell had taught her how to transform her daily mental crises into poetry. He told her that his own shaky mental state was the decisive factor in his prosodic options: he could write about madness "more effectively in free verse." And when Lowell himself was asked about his affinities with William Carlos Williams and the Beat poets (interview with A. Alvarez, *Review*, August 1963), he replied that his work was "much more connected with older English poetry than Williams' was, and that the Beat style too easily skirted "the complexities of life."

The fact remains that Lowell always felt that the pentameter was "still very much alive" and that the number of modern poets who haven't written well in this meter was small (*Agenda*, Spring/Summer 1973). In this *Agenda* piece, which was really a response to a questionnaire concerning poets' methods and intentions in the disposition of their poems, Lowell was asked if he was conscious of "a retreat from some norm" when he wrote free verse. He replied that each line should be a "rhythmic whole," even when unprovable by punctuation or even sense. He also endorsed the use of the pentameter line in modern verse, but not in long poems, since it would impose a heavy burden of continuity and monotony on works such as *The Waste Land* or the *Cantos*.

The reviews of *Ocean* were mainly concerned with the thematic content of the book, and the critics devoted little space to stylistic commentary. It is needless, therefore, to enumerate the positive and negative responses, but we should mention Alan Williamson's analysis of the volume in *Pity the Monsters*, since it fittingly summarizes the bases for the history of *Ocean*'s critical reception. Williamson noted that "younger readers" were more excited by *Ocean* than by *Life Studies*, which remained the favorite of critics close to Lowell's age. The younger generation, with its awakened political sensibility, was impatient with the personal whine of *Life Studies* but not with the public whine of *Ocean*. It mattered not that the latter volume had old-fashioned meters. Williamson also speculated on the possible bases for critics' discontent with the volume's title poem. He said that it was in the tradition of the long poem, as descended from Eliot's *Waste Land*, Crane's *The Bridge*, and Berryman's *Homage to Mistress Bradstreet*; this genre, as opposed to the open, almost novelistic personal epic, like *Paterson*, *The Cantos*, or *The Dream Songs*, is more fixed in form. It generally starts from intense personal experience but moves out to a larger realm "by epiphany rather than direct experience." According to Williamson, it is subtler and more interesting than the loose, open form, but is less rapidly acknowledged—largely because of its difficulty.

The greatest stylistic accomplishment one may attribute to the entire volume is its voice, says Williamson. Its "suave and songlike tenderness" and calmer "moral grandeur" derive from Marvell and Blake: from Marvell the subtle and ironic ambivalence toward political realities, from Blake the fiercely bardic vehicle of political attack. The sexual sadism that runs through *Ocean* is transformed into "paranoid murderousness," a condition which has grown from personal to national dimension. The knowledge of this leads Lowell to despair, says Williamson, who locates the despair in the harsh vocabulary as well as in the dissonant sound structure of the title poem. Lowell intermittently combats this and withers into exclamations of impossible longing ("Sing softer!" "O to break loose!" "Anywhere, but somewhere else!"). This brilliant gathering of tonal effects is what most distinguishes *Ocean*, says Williamson.

There appears to be a hiatus in the criticism here, for no one has satisfactorily explained the significance of Lowell's brief return to rhyme. Why would this poet, who had discarded the rhyme schemes of *Lord Weary* (even here rhyme was irregular) and found in *Life Studies* sound schemes of amazing subtlety *and* flexibility, return in *Near the Ocean* to regular rhymed iambic tetrameter in eight-line stanzas, the form of "The Drunken Fisherman"? What bearing, if any, did this prosodic experiment have on his final form, the combination of fixity and freedom he found in the unrhymed sonnets of the later books?

The last decade of Lowell's life was frenzied and chaotic; he did not "go gentle" into the "good night." Both his life and his writing continued to surprise the public. He seemed to be moving in many directions at once: campaigning for presidential candidates, starting a third marriage and a new family, publishing verse which was often a revision of verse published just a year earlier, and translating Greek tragedies. Although this took place over a ten-year period, it was difficult to make an orderly or consistent evaluation of Lowell's stylistic directions. He was prolific but unpredictable. As a result, the criticism had a distant, at times exasperated tone. Some critics gave up on Lowell and turned their attention to the new crop of poets. The New York school, the newly discovered "Objectivists," the mystical and ecological poets, made Lowell's sonnet sequences seem passé. Lowell did not seem to fit anywhere. After *Notebook 1967–68*, which was written in unrhymed iambic sonnets, critics began to have second thoughts about Lowell, calling into question his legacy to American poetry. Some went so far as to label all the volumes, from *Notebook 1967–68* on, the pathetic vestiges of a formerly great poet. Moreover, poets like Robert Bly, David Antin, and Jerome Rothernberg had brought about a revival of primitivist oral poetry, a literature which could be grasped on first hearing. This further reduced interest in Lowell's verbally intricate compositions. Indeed, his poetry was coming to be classified as esoteric. Critics used the same epithets about Lowell that Lowell had used about Stevens in earlier years.

Since most of the poems in *Notebook 1967–68* were later reprinted (generally revised) in *Notebook* and then reprinted in *History, Lizzie and Harriet*, or *Dolphin*, we should take a close look at the stylistic commentary on this volume. Unlike *Life Studies*, which was *sui generis*, *Notebook 1967–68* sent the critics on a stylistic source hunt. Jerome Mazzaro offered the most detailed exegesis of its stylistic origins (*Nation*, July 7, 1969). (Actually, Mazzaro's analysis applies to both *Notebook* versions.) According to Mazzaro, the *Notebooks* derive from Ovid, not from the verse epistles of Horace and Pope. Each entry in the epistle sequences of Horace and Pope emphasized self-containment, yet each of Lowell's entries carried the double burden of leading toward the next while, at the same time, retaining a certain autonomy. Lowell's debt to Ovid is the "unrealism" he evinces, which is closer to *The Metamorphoses* than to the logical modes of Horace or Pope. The stylistic patterns of recurrence and repetition derive from concepts of regeneration which order the myths of *Metamorphoses*.

Moving beyond Ovid, Mazzaro finds Lowell's interpretation of history strongly fashioned after Toynbee; that is, Toynbee's delineation of the growth and breakdown of Western civilization along economic, political, and cultural lines is the "structural principle" for the *Notebooks*. For example, where Toynbee relates historical thought to social environment, Lowell regards his and his daughter's different perspectives as explained by the forty-year gap in their lives: they are "field study" specimens for Toynbee's theory. Finally, Mazzaro argues that these seemingly remote influences are linked by Lowell's resort to the "classic pattern of autobiography," which begins in "personal anomie and alienation" and terminates in harmony and acceptance. By imitating all these conventions, Lowell concretizes his intention to bring epic dimensions to *Notebook* and to have his persona appear as a voyeur rather than as a "self-reflexive, engaged participant."

Mazzaro's sources may seem too broad to provide a useful application to the poems—a possible drawback to his analysis—but he convinces us of Lowell's skill at turning the tools of a rich tradition to his purposes. He also predicts that Lowell's journal-like style, an escape from "the empty formalism of his day," will influence the direction of poetry to come. Lowell's duality of tone (i.e., public and private) gets more of life into the poetry without sacrificing the "opacity" and toughness of tone which was this poet's trademark.

By the late sixties, critics were a little better informed about Lowell's bouts with mental illness than they had been earlier and attributed the *Notebook* style, in part, to his psychic disturbances. *Time*, for example, said that it was the work of "an honest madman and an eloquent one" (June 6, 1969). This casual reference to Lowell's mental illness derived not so much from critics' need to relate style to documentary fact as from the change in the literary establishment: a growing tolerance toward the Beatnik, the mental patient, the addict, as poet. Thus an author like Lowell, who could march on the Pentagon with Allen Ginsberg but at the same time exhibit an easy erudition, had the perfect combination of traits to ensure public adulation. When William Meredith referred to Lowell's "racked" mind and the dual quality of the voice in the poems as a "shuttle between the reporter's view and the mystic's," the public appreciated what he meant (*New York Times Book Review*, June 15, 1969).

The journal-like texture of both *Notebooks* prompted critics to consider the manipulation of voice in the poems. Louis Martz's delight that the voice "irradiated with love," largely stemming from Lowell's happiness at having "a ten-year-old daughter and a lasting marriage," is an amusing example of the biographical fallacy (*Yale Review*, Winter 1970). We now know that when Lowell was working on the *Notebooks* he was in the throes of marital discord and about to embark on his relationship with his future, third wife. But Martz's misconception proves that Lowell never removed his mask (Ong was right!). Martz also found delight in Lowell's skills with the sonnet form. He found in them the whiplash endings of Sidney's sonnets and the "muted" couplets of Shakespeare's sonnets. The strong openings of Lowell's sonnets gave them a strict separation from preceding poems, yet the turn toward resolution in the eighth or ninth line of each sonnet produced the sequential power of a narrative.

Karl Malkoff also stressed Lowell's masterful execution of the sonnet form, which embodied a tension between form and formlessness, and added that, though as sonnets they were full of run-on lines, "order triumphs but not by denying chaos" (*Commonweal*, October 17, 1969). Malkoff praised Lowell's avoidance of propaganda in the poems, despite their strongly political content. He cited as example the poem "April 8, 1968," which is, in its tonal texture, a reaction to the assassination of Martin Luther King, yet makes no mention of the black leader. Malkoff views this absence of factual reference as Lowell's way to dramatize the tension between the world of private experience and public affairs.

One critic who found voice the chief source of disappointment in *Notebook 1967–68* was Dan Jaffe (*Saturday Review of Literature*, September 6, 1969). Whether the topic is the "Chicago convention, Frost, or onion-skin paper," the voice hardly varies, says Jaffe. It would make no difference if lines were switched from one poem to another, and since this is the case, the total effect of the poems is "tedium." Things worsen when we read Peter Cooley's reactions to the *Notebooks* (*North American Review*, Fall 1969). In Cooley's view, Lowell loses voice entirely: Lowell is so busy making his experience "archetypal by implication" that he loses his actual self. This is symptomatic not just of Lowell, however, but is part of a trend in which poets "melt" into what they perceive. The symbolist poets' obsession with finding the right relationship with the object has passed.

This did not entirely facilitate the critics' task in handling the *Notebooks*, for it still left the question: had Lowell really altered his style—that is, apart from his obvious conversion to the sonnet form? George Lensing thought not (*Southern Review*, Winter 1971). Although Lowell had switched to sonnets at the exclusion of other forms, the same Latinate phrases filled these poems that filled those in *Lord Weary*, said Lensing. The reason was attitudinal: Lowell had never altered his "intense distrust of the nature of man," which he expressed with self-indulgence and ennui. Even Lowell's relatives were depicted in the same fashion: the sonnet "My Grandfather" (*Notebook 1967–68*) continues the struggle he had as far back as "In Memory of Arthur Winslow" (*Lord Weary*) between "feeling admiration and condemnation" for this man.

The *Notebooks* also reactivated the critical dissension about Lowell's voice: Was it private or public? Most of the commentary still separated the two by the poems' subject matter. Thus when Lowell wrote on Robert Kennedy or Attila the Hun, he used a public voice, and when he wrote on his daughter or his years at Kenyon, he used a private voice. William Pritchard's review in *Poetry* (December 1971) established such a dichotomy, thereby overlooking the fact that Lowell always considered a poem to be an artifact, separated from life. Speaking about *Life Studies* in an interview with Ian Hamilton, Lowell confessed to having had bouts with mania and depression while he was writing the book but claimed that the volume was "about neither" (*Review*, no. 26, 1971). He told Hamilton that despite some misgivings on other issues, one of the reasons he liked the Beats was that they had little interest in experience but great interest in expression. "Howl" had little to do with the "stir of life," but it was a "stirring sermon."

The simultaneous release of *History*, *Lizzie and Harriet*, and

*Dolphin* (1973) only calcified critics' notions about Lowell's double voice, however. Now the "private experience" label was confidently assigned to the last two volumes. While *Lizzie and Harriet* brought over some poems from *Notebook*, *Dolphin* was entirely new and traced Lowell's relationship with Caroline Blackwood, the birth of his son by her, and his eventual marriage to her. Although for the most part critics were discreet in dealing with the material, a certain archness in their commentary indicated that they were shocked by Lowell's new marriage. What is more, some of the sonnets in *Lizzie and Harriet* described Lowell's quarrels with his second wife over his new liaison. Because there was little to say about the form of these poems, the critics were faced, except in the case of *History*, with the delicate task of discussing their subject matter. Most reviewers had to treat all three books at once and, given space limitations, they were permitted little in-depth analysis for the individual volumes. All these contingencies made it even more difficult to assess "voice" as manifested in the formal features of these volumes.

Lowell's persistence in retaining the sonnet form for *History*, *Lizzie and Harriet*, and *Dolphin* drew mixed critical reactions. Douglas Dunn said that a major poet makes innovation in both "feeling *and* form," but that Lowell had done so only with the former (*Encounter*, October 1973). Unlike Eliot or Pound, who "carried the weight of change," Lowell, by writing sonnets, was of no use to younger writers. Dunn was so strongly convinced that Lowell's poems were "all feeling" that he saw no difference in the voices in the three volumes. *History* was just as personal as the other two, for all of its allusions; Lowell's concept of history had no intellectual purpose. In another essay which concentrates on Lowell's sonnet mode, Christopher Ricks compared *History* with Shakespeare's sonnets and found both "lightly grouped and unpretentious" (*Listener*, June 21, 1973). This rather flattering distinction was amplified by Ricks's admiration for Lowell's manner of dealing with the marriage themes in *Lizzie* and *Dolphin*. Readers may feel pain, outrage, or fervor about these poems, but Lowell makes them *think* about the indignation they feel. Lowell is above "routine responses," says Ricks, and refuses to apologize, confess, or exorcise. Ricks admits to finding something "monstrous" in Lowell's behavior as a poet (not as a man), but concludes that he gives himself pain in writing these poems because he needs the pleasure which comes with that pain. Back to the Puritan Burden!

Marjorie Perloff is less kind to Lowell (*New Republic*, July 7 and 14, 1973), finding all three volumes an embarrassment of subject matter *and* form. She is hardest on *Dolphin*, which contains material tantamount to soap opera. Lowell's sonnet form is "an amorphous container" into which the poet indiscriminately placed whatever came to mind. Modern divorce or erotic love is not a congenial theme for our "great contemporary American Puritan poet," she concludes. And on the subject of love, Arthur Oberg detected a lack of discrimination in Lowell's use of voice: the same expressions of affection were applied to his daughter, to a student, to a political leader (*Modern American Lyric*). Oberg was not the only critic to notice this frequency of love declarations (both sexual and platonic), which appeared to generate from a psychological condition. To Paul Ramsey, the declarations were "poetically boring" (*Sewanee Review*, Spring 1974), but to Axelrod they were redemptive to both the poet and the poems (*Robert Lowell*).

According to Axelrod, *Dolphin* is a modern love poem which reinstates divinity in a world which has lost its gods. The dolphin image is the commingling of physical and spiritual love, and Caroline is the dolphin who brings Lowell to earth and rescues his life. Axelrod does not dwell on the stylistic elements in *Dolphin*, except to identify the dolphin as the poet's muse and to argue that *Dolphin* is *the* poem toward which his poetics had "long been pointing." He acknowledges that this new-found love has pitfalls, both artistic and psychological, and finds evidence of this in ironic anti-dolphin images (e.g., "gaping jaws"); but he believes that Lowell's acceptance of himself and his world for the first time outweighs the sentimental softness (what would be called "bathos" by a harsher critic) of the text.

As a form of tribute to Lowell, Axelrod does a careful analysis of the symbolic patterns in *Dolphin*. To this reader, at least, there is something too pat about the scheme by which "nets," "fishlines," and "mermaids" are joined together. Stephen Yenser's brief treatment of *Dolphin* in *Circle to Circle* is much more censorious about the symbolism, which he finds "platitudinous" and full of "gaffes." The nautical motif is often reduced to absurdity, Yenser feels, as in the following lines which suggest the poet's fear of impotence: "I lack manhood to finish the fishing trip/Glad to escape beguilement and the storm." This critic is quick to note the "monstrous female" elements in the imagery, a thematic constant Mazzaro noticed earlier, but, like

Mazzaro, who remained discreet about Lowell's attitudes on this subject, Yenser is reluctant to amplify.

Lowell-watchers were very curious about his new book, *Day by Day*, which appeared in late summer of 1977. Four years had elapsed since he had published any new work. In between, publishers kept him visible with *Robert Lowell's Poems: A Selection* and *Selected Poems* (1974, 1976). Critics wondered where he was, what he was writing. *Day by Day* told it all: the dissolution of his third marriage, the recurrence of his mental illness, the shuttling between England and the United States. The facts were literally recorded in the poems. Lowell had flung aside his sonnet mania and obsessive dolphin symbolism and gone back to the realism and free verse of *Life Studies*. To most critics it was a welcome change; indeed, a scan of reviews shows that the responses were predominantly favorable: *Los Angeles Times*, September 8, 1977; *Chicago Tribune*, August 28, 1977; *New York Times Book Review*, August 14, 1977; *Time*, August 29, 1977; *Newsweek*, September 5, 1977; *Harper's*, December 1977.

Lowell's death followed so quickly that memorial tributes crowded out—or minimized—attention to *Day by Day*. In fact, full assessment, positive or negative, has yet to be made of this volume. However, I want to mention a few noteworthy essays on the stylistic construct of *Day by Day* insofar as they represented, and suggested for future scholarship, substantial perspectives. W. S. DiPiero (*Southern Review*, Spring 1978) made the most provocative observation about this volume's stylistic problem:

> after years of writing in the serviceable fourteen-liners, Lowell is here writing free verse, casting about for a new measure to serve the large theme of old age. His free verse, however, lacks the driving obsessiveness of the fourteen-liners. He seems genuinely ill at ease in these more open forms.

Helen Vendler made the most innovative observation, that this volume does not look back to *Life Studies* but breaks the hold of his former mode (*New York Times Book Review*, August 14, 1977). We are no longer dealing with the literary reality of *Life Studies*, says Vendler, but with "a landscapist's art, remote, descriptive, unimpassioned." The last example is

John Bayley's essay "Lowell and Hölderlin: A Note and Suggestion" (*Agenda*, Autumn 1980), which, in its comparison of
Lowell's poetics with Hölderlin's, suggests that Lowell had
learned much from the German Romantic poet. Lowell was
still locked in his own dilemma in *Life Studies*, says Bayley, but
in *Day by Day* he was able to express the predicament of his
aloneness without reserve and, consequently, to join it wholly
to a new communion of consciousness. The voice in *Day by
Day*, then, is one of abandon and lack of self-consciousness.

The reception of Lowell's style in these last volumes was far
from auspicious. Even when critics welcomed his return to
more formal structures, they seemed to be doing so in a gesture
of respect for a poet whose time of genius had passed. They
found themselves sighing for the vintage Lowell of *Life Studies*,
*Near the Ocean*, and in some cases *Lord Weary*. The passion
and fierce rhetoric of these earlier works had subsided, and the
formerly eloquent elegiac mode now seemed dulled by exhaustion. Lowell's enervation carried over to the scholarship, for
with the exception of a few memorable essays (whether vitriolic,
as Donald Hall's piece in *Georgia Review*, or complimentary,
as Vendler's review in the *New York Times*) there was no
longer a mood of excitement about Lowell's work. Critics
greeted the volumes, written in the seventies, with curiosity
rather than positive expectation. They were not doing their job
as thoroughly as they should have, however. Perhaps because
Lowell's adoption of the traditional sonnet form may have put
them off, critics glancingly remarked on stylistics and offered
little of the exacting analysis of prosody, imagery, and diction
which might match Perloff's *Poetic Art*. While they concentrated on the subject matter of *Lizzie* and *Dolphin*, they did not
consider that there might be a stylistic evolution in Lowell's
domestic themes.

I, for one, believe that there is a transformation deserving
careful stylistic study in what could be called the "marriage"
poems in the volumes from *Life Studies* to *Day by Day* (e.g.,
"Man and Wife," "The Old Flame," "Near the Ocean," "Marriage," to name the better known). One might even put the
"children" poems (e.g., "Home after Three Months Away,"
"Sheridan") into a special category for study. Did Lowell's
changing view of marriage affect the tonal variations in those
poems about his three wives? For example, "The Old Flame"
(*Union Dead*), which is about Lowell's former marriage to Jean
Stafford, is riddled with irony, as this stanza demonstrates:

> Everything's changed for the best—
> how quivering and fierce we were,
> there snowbound together,
> simmering like wasps
> in our tent of books!

*Is* it "changed for the best"? Or do we detect in these energetic
rhythms a regret that such intensity and passion are gone? And
what are we to make of the tone in "Marriage" (*Day by Day*),
the opening lines of which describe his wedding photograph of
his third marriage:

> We were middle-class and verismo
> enough to suit Van Eyck,
> when we crowded together in Maidstone,
> patriarch and young wife
> with our three small girls
> to pose in Sunday-best.

In these lines Lowell attempts to appropriate the realism of
Dutch painting to the poetic line, which presents in serial (para-
tactic) syntax and simple diction a portrait fashioned after Van
Eyck's *Arnolfini Marriage*. How does such a stripped-down
style affect the tonal structure of this piece? Questions such as
these will, I hope, engage future scholars.

Before turning to the last section of this chapter, I would like
to acknowledge an essay by Terry Miller, "The Prosodies of
Robert Lowell" (*Speech Monographs*, 1968), for its fine treatment of the prosodic transformations which took place in Lowell's style as a result of Elizabeth Bishop's influence. Miller traces
Lowell's prosody in "Quaker Graveyard" to the formalist styles
of Ransom and Tate, and then shows how *Life Studies* reflects
the "muted" but "personal and specific" style of Bishop. Re-
phrasing an acknowledgment by Lowell in Ostroff's *The Contemporary Poet as Artist and Critic* (see above), Miller states
that "Skunk Hour" is a direct offspring of Bishop's "The Armadillo," not only in its rhythmic structure but in the overall
movement of the poem:

> There is a marriage here between Lowell's prophetic corruption-
> involvement-prayer structure and Bishop's general description-
> focus on the speaker-animal, closeup sequence. The first half of

"Skunk Hour," four stanzas, gives us a casual, wide-angle description of the sea-side town. But the description finally adds up to a picture of a decaying society; the Bishop camera has given us the Lowell vision of corruption.

Miller's overhyphenated style is strained, but he suggests some interesting structural habits in the Lowell oeuvre.

## Lowell's Practice of Revision

Lowell believed that poetry is neither transport nor technique but a combination of the two, with emphasis on the latter. Ransom and Tate, the two poets to whom he was apprenticed in his early years, were known for constantly revising their compositions. As Ransom said, "The first version that comes out just drives us wild. . . . We must revise the poem" (*Conversations on the Craft of Poetry*, 1961). Lowell followed in his mentors' steps, and even went beyond them by rewriting a poem as many as thirty times. In the *Salmagundi* essay cited at the beginning of this chapter, Lowell gave a brief description of his writing habits:

> I have spent hundreds and hundreds of hours shaping, extending and changing hopeless or defective work. I lie on a bed staring, crossing out, writing in, crossing out what was written in, again and again, through days and weeks.

Critics knew as early as the publication of *Lord Weary* that Lowell liked to rewrite, because this volume contained some poems that had appeared in *Unlikeness*, all of which had been altered in some small detail. In 1962 Hugh Staples gave further evidence of the extent of Lowell's passion for revision by printing a primary bibliography of Lowell's poetry up to *Life Studies* (appendix 2, *Robert Lowell*). Here is a sample entry:

> "The Capitalist's Meditation by the Civil War Monument, Christmas, 1942." (a) *Partisan Review*, (July–August 1943). (b) *Land of Unlikeness* (revised); (revised title: "Christmas Eve in the Time of War"). (c) *Commonweal*, (11 October 1946), (further revision); (revised title: "Christmas Eve under Hooker's Statue"). (d) *Lord Weary's Castle*. (e) *Poems (1938–1949)*.

Staples' thorough appendix has become one of the most valuable repositories for Lowell scholarship, but few critics have used it to full advantage and schematized Lowell's stylistic evolution. In recent years, however, the notion of Lowell's poetics of revision has begun to interest critics, and there is an indication that "revision research" will increase in the future. While, at present, only a slender corpus of scholarship on Lowell's revisions exists, it is nonetheless of high quality.

Not surprisingly, one especially sensitive analysis of revision comes from a fellow poet, Richard Eberhart, who offered a fine explication of the changes in the *Unlikeness* poems which were incorporated into *Lord Weary* (*Sewanee Review*, Spring 1947). In essence, the changes were mostly in phraseology: away from the vaguely symbolic toward the more concrete. Eberhart is not convinced that the changes bring improvement, however, for in the interest of clarity Lowell sacrifices the direct passion of the earlier poem. According to Eberhart, the later version of these lines from "The Drunken Fisherman" destroys the tone quality:

> are these fit terms
> To mete the worm whose gilded rage
> Havocs the in'ards of old age?
>
> [*Unlikeness*]

> are these fit terms
> To mete the worm whose molten rage
> Boils in the belly of old age?
>
> [*Lord Weary*]

A freshness is lost in the literality of "molten" and "boils," says Eberhart.

I daresay that a present-day critic, comparing these sets of lines, would argue that neither version is fresh and that the diction remains stilted ("To mete the worm"). However, Eberhart correctly concludes that the stylistic harshness in the ten poems taken from *Unlikeness* is by and large replaced by gracefulness and better structural balance. Mazzaro carried the matter of the revision process a bit further by finding evidence of ideological change when passages of original poems have been either altered or omitted (*Poetic Themes of Robert Lowell*). He uses as one of his examples an early magazine version of "Beyond the Alps"

(*Kenyon Review*, Summer 1953) which contained long sections on the death of George Santayana in Rome and reflected on Santayana's disenchantment with fascism, religion, and the world in general. The later version of "Alps" (*Life Studies*) dropped the passages on Santayana and, though it still expressed disenchantment, this feeling was assigned to Lowell himself. In Mazzaro's view, this revision signifies that Lowell has accepted his *own* disenchantment. Santayana's loss of faith becomes the subject of another poem in *Life Studies*, "For George Santayana." I would like to supplement Mazzaro's commentary by arguing that the omitted passage in "Alps," with its abstruse explanation of Santayana's apostasy, lacks the immediacy with which these lines from "For George Santayana" capture the feelings of the dying poet-philosopher:

> There at the monastery hospital,
> you wished those geese-girl sisters wouldn't bother
> their heads and yours by praying for your soul:
> "There is no God and Mary is His Mother."

In the next stage of the study of Lowell's revisions, critics sought to explicate the function of literary allusions. Rudolph Nelson traced the history of "The Public Garden," which was eighteen years in the making before acquiring its final form in *Union Dead* (1946). In "A Note on the Evolution of Robert Lowell's 'The Public Garden'" (*American Literature*, March 1969), Nelson argued that Lowell kept recasting the poem until he could successfully retain the biblical echoes of the David and Bathsheba story in a personal poem about a lost love.

Originally, the poem had two parts, which were published separately in *Nation* ("David to Bathsheba," December 7, 1946; "Bathsheba's Lament in the Garden," May 17, 1947). "David to Bathsheba," printed in dialogue form in Roman italic type, represented Lowell's effort to merge dramatic monologue with intricate symbolic structure. Evidently dissatisfied with the effects achieved in the two *Nation* poems, Lowell fused them into a single composition, "David and Bathsheba in the Public Garden," which was printed in *Mills of the Kavanaughs* (1951). This time he omitted those sections which most directly referred to the incident as recorded in the Bible, but in so doing he rendered the poem almost completely unintelligible. It was not until the *Union Dead* version that the poem (compressed to a thirty-line poem from the original two-poem total of eighty-three lines) took shape as a personal lyric about contemporary experience. The final version is far superior to the earlier ones, argues Nelson, who is convinced that Lowell's process of revision was his pathway to excellence.

The core of the controversy, then, was whether Lowell's compulsive rewriting ultimately yielded superior compositions. It was easier to agree with Nelson's position when the revisions under scrutiny were in draft form in the thirties and forties—as was the case with some poems in *Life Studies* and *Union Dead*. With and after *Notebook*, however, the critics felt that there was no substantial improvement. They exhibited, too, a tendency to consider the final versions of Lowell's most acclaimed poems as unquestionably more accomplished. In *Robert Lowell* (appendix B), Axelrod printed an early draft of "Skunk Hour," originally entitled "Inspiration," noting that the diction and imagery in the draft were melodramatic and hackneyed and arguing that the following changes produced a more vivid, dramatic tone:

> I hear a hollow, sucking moan
> Inside my wild heart's prison cell
> ["Inspiration"]

> I hear
> my ill-spirit sob in each blood cell,
> as if my hand were at its throat
> ["Skunk Hour"]

There are, undoubtedly, critics who would quibble with Axelrod about the actual difference between the two versions and disagree with him that the final version succeeds in "narrowing the distance between the poem and the experience that triggered it." Axelrod is more convincing when he claims that the cultural context, added to the poem (the "fairy decorator" and "hermit heiress" are not in "Inspiration"), makes the speaker (Lowell) more believably a part of the society he represents. And although Axelrod did not compare the titles of the versions, I think most would agree that "Skunk Hour" is far more beguiling than "Inspiration."

When critics turned their attention to Lowell's political views, they found the revisions of "Waking Early Sunday Morning" (*Near the Ocean*) fascinating to investigate. There are numerous drafts of this work, some bearing the title "Waking Up (Too) Early on Sunday." The most exacting analysis of its reshaping is by Alan Williamson (*Agenda*, Autumn 1980), who says that the drafts document Lowell's slowly evolving realization that he does not want to become a public figure. His decision to dismiss megalomaniac "dreams of power" is somehow connected with his decision about using meter in the poem. Thus the earliest draft makes a return to the iambic line, but even as Lowell writes it he distrusts its association as a tool for power: "I cannot take it, I am sick/of stretching for the rhetoric." In the margins of succeeding drafts are lists of rhymed phrases which refer to religion ("dark places crave their stiff control,/and leave a loophole for the soul"). Lowell is still vacillating about religious belief, argues Williamson. But by the time the poem received its first printed version (*New York Review of Books*, August 5, 1965), Lowell had excised the first three stanzas of the early drafts, which were decidedly personal, and incorporated a stanza about President Lyndon Johnson. In the transition, the passage referring to Lowell's distrust of meter and highly formal poetry was eliminated. There was also a change in the persona, who was vaguely identified with the president. In the ultimate draft, however, even this was eliminated, and Lowell's tone was one of "neutral distance." Lowell had bade farewell to his sense of political commitment. Williamson's thesis about Lowell's disenchantment with the public scene is supported by biographical fact: Lowell fled to England shortly after the publication of *Near the Ocean*.

The nadir of Lowell's reputation came in 1970 with the publication of *Notebook*, an expanded version of *Notebook 1967–68*. Lowell added about ninety poems to the earlier edition, but he also extensively revised about one hundred of the earlier selections. The project was considered a failure. Louis Martz attributed the poor performance to Lowell's process of rewriting, which did little more than "drain vitality out of the language" (*Yale Review*, Spring 1971). Martz had been heartened by *Notebook 1967–68*, but now he felt that Lowell's "grim tone" had crept back into his work. There was another hazard in merging new with old poems, said Martz: it wrecked the structure of the volume. The insertion of new poems, which have a different feel from the original ones, prevents a "unified and gradual conclusion." Moreover, in revision, Lowell tends to objectify his feelings and to move farther outside the intimacy of the "family constellation," which is necessary to the poet's tone. Martz offers an example of the depersonalization that damages the version of a line in *Notebook*: "black-bordered letters like stamps from Turkestan." In the 1967-68 version the line had a demonstrative pronoun and a simple predicate, which personalized the meaning: "those black-bordered letters were like attempts from Turkestan!"

Other essays were far more vituperative than Martz's but they offered little comment on the actual revision process. David Bromwich's review of *Notebook* took the standard position: Lowell's style was nothing more than the "flow of an unremitting turbid consciousness" (*Commentary*, August 1971). The poems did not work individually, being too privately allusive, and what was missing was the marvelous persona of *Life Studies*. Bromwich got to the heart of the problem, for Lowell *did* seem to have distanced himself from the poem.

Lowell fared better with *History* (1973), which was mostly comprised of poems taken from *Notebook*, again often heavily revised. Stephen Yenser argued that the reason for *History*'s success was a structural necessity which was never established in *Notebook* (*Circle to Circle*). The speakers in *History*, formerly "mysterious personalities with bizarrre tastes" in the *Notebook* version, were now plausible dramatic characters. Yenser attributes the credibility of the personae to Lowell's adoption of the dramatic monologue and decreased use of the personal lyric. For example, the first line of "The Book of Wisdom" (*Notebook*), "Can I go on loving anyone at fifty?" is converted to "Can I go on keeping a hundred wives at fifty?" in the *History* version of the poem, a dramatic monologue entitled "Solomon's Wisdom." Yenser also argues that *History* relates to *all* of Lowell's earlier poetry and is informed by many poems from previous volumes, which, in their new context, we can now better understand:

> The use of Coleridge in *Life Studies* helps us to realize the use of Stalin in *History*, which in turn enables us to see that he was used in a similar fashion in *Life Studies*, which insight seems to be confirmed by the information provided in this volume ("Mother, 1972") that Lowell's mother died of a cerebral hemorrhage, for in the earlier book Lowell continually regards himself as heir to the family frailties and reminds us that Stalin died of a cerebral hemorrhage.

Thus *History* is a "synecdoche for the career," says Yenser—a repetition of Lowell repeating himself with variations. In this volume, Lowell's poetics of revision is inseparable from structure.

Stylistic studies of Lowell's oeuvre seem perhaps more muddled than those of any other aspect of the poems; yet one could dare to say that Lowell's most lasting contribution may be precisely in his style. He moved from a symbol-laden academic verse to what might seem a free-style transcript of the diurnal scene. He found, in the fifties, the "confessional" mode, which livened personal details into poetic images of a life we all then sought to question. The torment of Arnoldian responsibility or the psychic and familial disorders haunting his homes in Boston, Maine, London, and New York tore at his poetry. He sought a voice—of Anne Kavanaugh, of the preacher, of Lowell the poet himself. All this has been received and integrated into the work of his fellow poets and his critics. Yet, aside from a few brilliant though often impressionistic treatments, especially of the earlier volumes, detailed treatments of his stylistic accomplishment are remarkably sparse. The specific and unique *voice* of Lowell that supports his typically apologetic nostalgia, his disdain of L. L. Bean outfits ("Skunk Hour") or antique-store pewter ("The Old Flame"), seems still to escape us. More directly, it seems disappointing that the amazing gift Lowell possessed for sound (this man had an ear!) has never been systematically studied throughout the work. Consider, for example, the short lines typical of the first poems in *Union Dead*, as in this closing quatrain from "Water":

> We wished our two souls
> might return like gulls
> to the rock. In the end,
> the water was too cold for us.

What patterns of placement exist for the distribution of the aural and thematic repetitions and contrasts? We sense them there—we sense them as typically Lowell; but how has he managed this? Is the climax of the Lowellian line, at its end, stung into sentience by his enjambments? Is one of the problems with the late poems that the long sonnet lines, lacking these breaks, seem flaccid?

# References

Abrams, M. H.
1971. *A Glossary of Literary Terms.* New York: Holt, Rinehart and Winston.

Allen, Donald M.
1960. (editor) *The New American Poetry 1945–1960.* New York: Grove Pr.

Altieri, Charles
1980. "From Experience to Discourse: American Poetry and Poetics in the Seventies." *Contemporary Literature* Spring, pp. 191–224.

Alvarez, A.
1959. "Something New in Verse." London *Observer* Apr. 12, p. 22; revised and reprinted in *Times Literary Supplement* Mar. 23, 1967, pp. 229–32; in his *Beyond All This Fiddle.* New York: Random House, 1968.
1963. "Robert Lowell in Conversation." London *Observer* July 21, p. 19.

Andrews, Lyman
1959. "Voices of America." *London Sunday Times* Mar. 9, p. 56.

Antin, David
1972. "Modernism and Post Modernism: Approaching the Present in American Poetry." *Boundary 2* Fall, pp. 98–133 [109–116].

Arrowsmith, William
1952. "Five Poets." *Hudson Review* Winter, pp. 619–27 [627]; reprinted in *Robert Lowell: A Collection of Critical Essays,* ed. Thomas Parkinson. Englewood Cliffs, N.J.: Prentice-Hall, 1968.

Axelrod, Steven Gould
1978. *Robert Lowell: Life and Art.* Princeton: Princeton Univ. Pr.

Bagg, Robert
1969. "The Rise of Lady Lazaras." *Mosaic* Summer, pp. 9–36 [10].

Baro, Gene
1951. "New Richness from an American Poet." *New York Herald Tribune Weekly Book Review* Apr. 22, p. 4.

Barry, Jackson
1981. "Robert Lowell's 'Confessional' Image of an Age: Theme and Language in Poetic Form." *Ariel* Jan., pp. 51–58.

Bayley, John
1980. "Lowell and Hölderlin: A Note and Suggestion." *Agenda* Autumn, pp. 30–33.

Bennett, Joseph
1959. "Two Americans, a Brahmin and the Bourgeoisie." *Hudson Review* Autumn, pp. 431–39 [435]; reprinted in *Robert Lowell: A Portrait of the Artist in His Time,* ed. Michael London and Robert Boyers. New York: David Lewis, 1970.

Berryman, John

1947. "Lowell, Thomas & Co." *Partisan Review* Jan.–Feb., pp. 73–85 [73–80]; reprinted in his *Freedom of the Poet.* New York: Farrar, Straus & Giroux, 1976.

1964. "On Robert Lowell's 'Skunk Hour.' " In *The Contemporary Poet as Artist and Critic,* pp. 99–106. Boston: Little, Brown.

Bewley, Marius

1950. "Aspects of Modern Poetry." *Scrutiny* Apr., pp. 334–52 [339, 342–48]; reprinted in his *The Complex Fate.* London: Chatto & Windus, 1952; in *Robert Lowell: A Portrait of the Artist in His Time,* ed. Michael London and Robert Boyers. New York: David Lewis, 1970.

Block, Haskell

1970. "The Impact of French Symbolism on Modern American Poetry." In *The Shaken Realist—Essays in Modern Literature in Honor of Frederick J. Hoffman,* ed. Melvin J. Friedman and John B. Vickery, pp. 165–217 [188–89]. Baton Rouge: Louisiana State Univ. Pr.

Bloom, Harold

1976. Review of *Selected Poems. New Republic* Nov. 21, p. 22.

Bogan, Louise

1959. "Verse." *New Yorker* Oct. 24, pp. 186–88 [187].

Branscomb, Jack

1977. "Robert Lowell's Painters: Two Sources." *English Language Notes* Dec., pp. 119–22.

Bromwich, David

1971. "Reading Robert Lowell." *Commentary* Aug., pp. 78–83.

Brooks, Cleanth

1965. "Poetry Since 'The Waste Land.' " *Southern Review* Summer, 487–500 [497].

Carruth, Hayden

1977. "An Appreciation of Robert Lowell." *Harper's* Dec., pp. 110–12.

Cooley, Peter

1969. "Reaching Out, Keeping Position: New Poems by James Wright and Robert Lowell." *North American Review* Fall, pp. [68–70].

Daiches, David

1951. "Some Recent Poetry." *Yale Review* Autumn, pp. 153–57 [157].

Davidson, Peter

1959. "New Poetry." *Atlantic* July, pp. 73–76 [76].

Davie, Donald

1959. Review of *Life Studies. Twentieth Century* Aug., pp. 116–18.

1973. "Robert Lowell." *Parnassus* Fall–Winter, pp. 49–57; reprinted in his *The Poet in the Imaginary Museum: Essays of Two Decades*. New York: Percea, 1976.

Di Piero, W. S.
1978. "Lowell and Ashbery." *Southern Review* Spring, pp. 359–67.

Donoghue, Denis
1978. "Lowell at the End." *Hudson Review* Spring, pp. 196–201.

Dunn, Douglas
1973. "The Big Race." *Encounter* Oct., pp. 107–13.

Easthope, Antony
1981. "Problematizing the Pentameter." *New Literary History* Spring, pp. 475–92.

Eberhart, Richard
1947. "Four Poets." *Sewanee Review* Spring, pp. 324–36 [328]; reprinted in *Robert Lowell: A Collection of Critical Essays*, ed. Thomas Parkinson. Englewood Cliffs, N.J.: Prentice-Hall, 1968.
1952. "Five Poets." *Kenyon Review* Winter, pp. 168–76 [172–74]; reprinted in *Robert Lowell: A Portrait of the Artist in His Time*, ed. Michael London and Robert Boyers. New York: David Lewis, 1970.

Ehrenpreis, Irvin
1965. "The Age of Lowell." In his *American Poetry*, Stratford-upon-Avon-Studies no. 7, pp. 65–95. New York: St. Martin's; reprinted in *Robert Lowell: A Portrait of the Artist in His Time*, ed. Michael London and Robert Boyers. New York: David Lewis, 1970; in *Robert Lowell: A Collection of Critical Essays*, ed. Thomas Parkinson. Englewood Cliffs, N.J.: Prentice-Hall, 1968; in *Critics on Robert Lowell*, ed. Jonathan Price. Coral Gables, Fla.: Univ. of Miami Pr., 1972.

Eliot, T. S.
1942. *The Music of Poetry*. Glasgow: Jackson, Son & Company; reprinted in *Partisan Review* Nov./Dec. 1942, pp. 450–65; in *Modern Writing*, ed. Willard Thorp and Margaret Farrand Thorp. New York: American Book Co., 1944; in his *On Poetry and Poets*. London: Faber and Faber, 1957.

Engle, Paul
1951. "Poems in Which You Hear Human Voices." *Chicago Tribune Magazine of Books* June 10, p. 4.

Falck, Colin
1962. "Dreams and Responsibilities." *Review* June/July, pp. 3–18; reprinted in *The Modern Poet*, ed. Ian Hamilton. New York: Horizon, 1969.

Fein, Richard
1980. "The Life of *Life Studies*." *Literary Review* Spring, pp. 326–38.

Fitts, Dudley
1951. Review of *The Mills of the Kavanaughs*. *Furioso* Fall, pp.

76–78; reprinted in *Profile of Robert Lowell*, ed. Jerome Mazzaro. Columbus: Merrill, 1971.

1959. "New Verse for Midsummer Night Dreamers." *Saturday Review of Literature* July 25, pp. 14–16 [16].

Fitzgerald, Robert

1977. "Aiaia and Ithaca: Notes on a New Lowell Poem." *Salmagundi* Spring, pp. 25–31.

Flint, F. Cudworth

1951. "Let the Snake Wait." *Virginia Quarterly Review* Summer, pp. 471–80 [480].

Frankenberg, Lloyd

1951. "The Year in Poetry." *Harper's* Oct., pp. 108–12 [112].

Gray, Paul

1977. "Trying to Say What Happened." *Time* Aug. 29, pp. 70–71.

Gross, Harvey

1964. *Sound and Form in Modern Poetry*. Ann Arbor: Univ. of Michigan Pr.

1978. "Action and Incantation." *Antaeus* Spring, pp. 283–95.

Gunn, Thom

1959. "Excellence and Variety." *Yale Review* Dec., pp. 295–305 [303–5].

Hall, Donald

1961. "The Battle of the Bards." *Horizon* Sept., pp. 116–21.

1978. "Robert Lowell and the Literature Industry." *Georgia Review* Spring, pp. 7–12.

Hamilton, Ian

1971. "A Conversation with Robert Lowell." *Review* Summer, pp. 10–29.

Hoffman, Daniel G.

1960. "Arrivals and Rebirths." *Sewanee Review* Winter, pp. 118–37 [133].

Hoffman, Frederick J.

1967. "*Symbolisme* and Modern Poetry in the United States." *Comparative Literature Studies* nos. 1 and 2, pp. 193–99.

Hollander, John

1959. "Robert Lowell's New Book." *Poetry* Oct., pp. 41–46; reprinted in *On Contemporary Literature*, ed. Richard Kostelanetz. New York: Avon, 1964; in *Critics on Robert Lowell*, ed. Jonathan Price. Coral Gables, Fla.: Univ. of Miami Pr., 1972.

Howe, Irving

1972. "Sylvia Plath: A Partial Disagreement." *Harper's* Jan., pp. 88–91.

Jaffe, Dan

1969. "Voice of the Poet: Oracular, Eerie, Daring." *Saturday Review of Literature* Sept. 6, pp. 28–29, 62 [28–29].

Jarrell, Randall

1953. *Poetry and the Age*. New York: Knopf.

Jones, A. R.
1965. "Necessity and Freedom: The Poetry of Robert Lowell, Sylvia Plath and Anne Sexton." *Critical Quarterly* Spring, pp. 11–30.

Jones, LeRoi
1961. "Putdown of the Whore of Babylon." *Yugen* no. 7, pp. 4–5.

Kalstone, David
1977. *Five Temperaments: Elizabeth Bishop, Robert Lowell, James Merrill, Adrienne Rich, John Ashbery.* New York: Oxford Univ. Pr.

Kazin, Alfred
1959. "In Praise of Robert Lowell." *Reporter* June 25, pp. 41–42; reprinted in his *Contemporaries.* New York: Little, Brown, 1962.

Kermode, Frank
1959. "Talent and More." *Spectator* May 1, p. 628.

Kevles, Barbara
1971. "The Art of Poetry XV—Anne Sexton." *Paris Review* Summer, pp. 158–91.

Kirsch, Robert
1977. "Lowell in England and in Love." *Los Angeles Times* Sept. 8, sec. 4, p. 9.

Kroll, Jack
1977. "A Poet's Odyssey." *Newsweek* Sept. 5, p. 77.

Kunitz, Stanley
1960. "Process and Thing: A Year of Poetry." *Harper's* Sept., pp. 96–104 [100].

Larkin, Philip
1959. "Collected Poems." Manchester *Guardian Weekly* May 21, p. 10.

Lensing, George
1971. "The Consistency of Robert Lowell." *Southern Review* Winter, pp. 338–44.

Lowell, Robert
1947. "Thomas, Bishop and Williams." *Sewanee Review* Summer, pp. 493–503.
1961/62. "William Carlos Williams." *Hudson Review* Winter, pp. 530–36; reprinted in *William Carlos Williams: A Collection of Critical Essays,* ed. J. Hillis Miller. Englewood Cliffs, N.J.: Prentice-Hall, 1966.
1964. "On 'Skunk Hour.'" In *The Contemporary Poet as Artist and Critic,* pp. 107–10. Boston: Little, Brown.
1969. "On Freedom in Poetry." In *Naked Poetry: Recent American Poetry in Open Forms,* ed. Stephen Berg and Robert Mezey. Indianapolis and New York: Bobbs-Merrill.
1973. "Supplement: On Rhythm from America." *Agenda* Spring/Summer, pp. 51–52.

1977. "After Enjoying Six or Seven Essays on Me." *Salmagundi* Spring, pp. 113–15.

Malkoff, Karl

1969. Review of *Notebook 1967–68. Commonweal* Oct. 17, pp. 85–87.

1977. *Escape from the Self: A Study in Contemporary American Poetry and Poetics.* New York: Columbia Univ. Pr.

Martz, Louis

1970. "Recent Poetry: The End of an Era." *Yale Review* Winter, pp. 252–67 [252–56].

1971. "Recent Poetry: Visions and Revisions." *Yale Review* Spring, pp. 403–17 [403–09].

Mazzaro, Jerome

1965. *The Poetic Themes of Robert Lowell.* Ann Arbor: Univ. of Michigan Pr.

1966–1967. "Lowell after For the Union Dead." *Salmagundi* Winter, pp. 57–68; reprinted in *Robert Lowell: A Portrait of the Artist in His Time*, ed. Michael London and Robert Boyers. New York: David Lewis, 1970.

1969. "Robert Lowell and the Kavanaugh Collapse." *University of Windsor Review* Fall, pp. 1–24.

1969. "Sojourner of the Self." *Nation* July 7, pp. 22, 24.

McFadden, George

1975. "*Life Studies:* Robert Lowell's Comic Breakthrough." *PMLA* Jan. pp. 96–106.

Meredith, William

1969. Review of *Notebook 1967–68. New York Times Book Review* June 15, pp. 1, 27; reprinted in *Critics on Robert Lowell*, ed. Jonathan Price. Coral Gables, Fla.: Univ. of Miami Pr., 1972.

Miller, Terry

1968. "The Prosodies of Robert Lowell." *Speech Monographs* Nov., pp. 425–34.

Moss, Howard

1947. "Ten Poets." *Kenyon Review* Spring, pp. 290–98 [293–94].

Naipaul, V. S.

1969. "Et in America Ego." *Listener* Sept. 4, pp. 302–4; reprinted in *Profile of Robert Lowell*, ed. Jerome Mazzaro. Columbus: Merrill, 1971.

Nelson, Rudolph

1969. "A Note on the Evolution of Robert Lowell's 'The Public Garden.'" *American Literature* Mar., pp. 106–10.

Nims, John Frederick

1964. "On Robert Lowell's 'Skunk Hour.'" In *The Contemporary Poet as Artist and Critic*, pp. 88–98. Boston: Little, Brown.

Nowlan, Alden A.

1960. "Ten Books of Poetry." *Tamarack Review* Summer, pp. 71–79 [74–75].

Oberg, Arthur
1977. *Modern American Lyric: Lowell, Berryman, Creeley and Plath.* New Brunswick: Rutgers Univ. Pr.

Ong, Walter
1975. "The Writer's Audience Is Always a Fiction." *PMLA* Jan., pp. 9–21.

Ostroff, Anthony
1964. *The Contemporary Poet as Artist and Critic.* Boston: Little, Brown.

Parisi, Joseph
1977. "Three Poets Put Life into Words." *Chicago Tribune* Aug. 28, sec., p. 2.

Pearson, Gabriel
1969. "Robert Lowell." *Review* Mar., pp. 3–36; reprinted in *Contemporary Poetry in America: Essays and Interviews,* ed. Robert Boyers. New York: Stockton, 1974.

Perkins, David
1976. *A History of Modern Poetry: From the 1890s to the High Modernist Mode.* Cambridge, Mass.: Harvard Univ. Pr.

Perloff, Marjorie
1973. "The Blank Now." *New Republic* July 7 & 14, pp. 24–26.
1973. *The Poetic Art of Robert Lowell.* Ithaca, N.Y.: Cornell Univ. Pr.

Phelps, Robert
1959. "A Book of Revelations." *National Review* Aug. 29, pp. 307–8.

Poirier, Richard
1964. "Our Truest Historian." *Book Week* Oct. 11, pp. 1, 16; reprinted in *Critics on Robert Lowell,* ed. Jonathan Price. Coral Gables, Fla.: Univ. of Miami Pr.

Poore, Charles
1951. "Books of the Times." *New York Times* May 12, p. 19.

Pritchard, William
1971. "Positives." *Poetry* Dec., pp. 159–69.

Procopiow, Norma
1976. "William Carlos Williams and the Origins of the Confessional Poem." *Ariel* Apr., pp. 63–75.

Raffel, Burton
1980. "Robert Lowell's Life Studies." *Literary Review* Spring, pp. 293–325.

Ramsey, Paul
1974. "American Poetry in 1973." *Sewanee Review* Spring, pp. 393–406 [400].

Ransom, John Crowe
1961. In *Conversations on the Craft of Poetry,* ed. Robert Penn Warren et al., pp. 22, 24. New York: Holt, Rinehart and Winston.

Richards, I. A.

1925. *Principles of Literary Criticism*. London: K. Paul, Trench, Trubner; New York: Harcourt Brace.

Ricks, Christopher

1965. "The Three Lives of Robert Lowell." *New Statesman* Mar. 26, pp. 496–97; reprinted in *Critics on Robert Lowell*, ed. Jonathan Price. Coral Gables, Fla.: Univ. of Miami Pr., 1972.

1973. "The Poet Robert Lowell." *Listener* June 21, pp. 817, 830–32.

Rosenthal, M. L.

1959. "Poetry as Confession." *Nation* Sept. 19, pp. 154–55; reprinted in *Critics on Robert Lowell*, ed. Jonathan Price. Coral Gables, Fla.: Univ. of Miami Pr., 1972.

1960. *Modern Poets: A Critical Introduction*. New York: Oxford Univ. Pr.

Seidel, Frederick

1961. "Interview with Robert Lowell." *Paris Review* Winter–Spring, pp. 56–95; reprinted in *Robert Lowell: A Portrait of the Artist in His Time*, ed. Michael London and Robert Boyers. New York: David Lewis, 1970; in *Robert Lowell: A Collection of Critical Essays*, ed. Thomas Parkinson. Englewood Cliffs, N. J.: Prentice-Hall, 1968; in *Writers at Work, Second Series*, ed. Malcolm Cowley. New York: Viking, 1963; in *Modern Poets on Modern Poetry*, ed. James Scully. London: Collins, 1966.

Sorrentino, Gilbert

1961. Review of *Life Studies*. *Yugen* no. 7, pp. 5–7.

Spender, Stephen

1959. "Robert Lowell's Family Album." *New Republic* June 8, p. 17; reprinted in *Robert Lowell: A Collection of Critical Essays*, ed. Thomas Parkinson. Englewood Cliffs, N.J.: Prentice-Hall, 1968.

Standerwick, De Sales

1960. "Pieces Too Personal." *Renascence* Autumn, pp. 53–56; reprinted in *Profile of Robert Lowell*, ed. Jerome Mazzaro. Columbus: Merrill, 1971; in *Critics on Robert Lowell*, ed. Jonathan Price. Coral Gables, Fla.: Univ. of Miami Pr., 1972.

Staples, Hugh

1962. *Robert Lowell: The First Twenty Years*. New York: Farrar, Straus & Cudahy.

Tate, Allen

1944. "Introduction." In *Land of Unlikeness*, pp. v–vi. Cummington, Mass.: Cummington Pr.

1968. *Essays of Four Decades*. Chicago: Swallow.

Thompson, John

1959. "Two Poets." *Kenyon Review* Summer, pp. 482–90 [482–88].

Time

1969. "The Chameleon Poet." *Time* June 6, pp. 112, 114.

*Times* (London)

1959. "Modern Poets Look Outside Themselves for a Theme." London *Times* Aug. 6, p. 11.

Vazakas, Byron

1952. "Eleven Contemporary Poets." *New Mexico Quarterly* Summer, pp. 213–30 [221–23].

Vendler, Helen

1975. "The Difficult Grandeur of Robert Lowell." *Atlantic* Jan., pp. 68–73.

1977. "The Poetry of Autobiography." *New York Times Book Review* Aug. 14, pp. 1, 24–25.

1979. "Pudding Stone." *New York Review of Books* Feb. 8, pp. 3–4, 6.

Warren, Austin

1947. "Double Discipline." *Poetry* Aug., pp. 262–65.

Weatherhead, A. Kingsley

1967. *The Edge of the Image.* Seattle and London: Univ. of Washington Pr.

Wilbur, Richard

1964. "On Robert Lowell's 'Skunk Hour.'" In *The Contemporary Poet as Artist and Critic,* pp. 84–87. Boston: Little, Brown.

Williams, William Carlos

1951. "In a Mood of Tragedy." *New York Times Book Review* Apr. 22, p. 6; reprinted in *Robert Lowell: A Portrait of the Artist in His Time,* ed. Michael London and Robert Boyers. New York: David Lewis, 1970; in *Robert Lowell: A Collection of Critical Essays,* ed. Thomas Parkinson. Englewood Cliffs, N.J.: Prentice-Hall, 1968; in *The Selected Essays of William Carlos Williams,* ed. John Thirwall. New York: Random House, 1954.

Williamson, Alan

1974. *Pity the Monsters: The Political Vision of Robert Lowell.* New Haven and London: Yale Univ. Pr.

1980. "The Reshaping of 'Waking Early Sunday Morning.'" *Agenda* Autumn, pp. 47–62.

Willis, G. D.

1975. "Afloat on Lowell's *Dolphin.*" *Critical Quarterly* Winter, pp. 363–76.

Yenser, Stephen

1975. *Circle to Circle: The Poetry of Robert Lowell.* Berkeley: Univ. of California Pr.

# CHAPTER 6

# Lowell the Critic

Examination of Lowell's criticism of other poets reveals a unique dimension of his creativity. There are two blocks of time during which Lowell was in and out of step with the state of contemporary literary criticism. In the first block, the forties and fifties, there was little basic difference between the dominant critical trends in the United States and Lowell's own. In the second block, the sixties and seventies, he grew less predictable, more self-indulgent, and evidently less interested in peers' reactions to his judgments. But in both of these time units he was generally shrewd and cautious in his public pronouncements on the work of his contemporaries—self-servingly so, for he feared these poets' retaliation when they reviewed *his* poetry. In his early years the critic he most admired and imitated was Randall Jarrell, whose high standards demanded that one practice candor before benevolence. Lowell always looked for synthesis in a text (synthesis of thought and aesthetic vision) and he often came away disappointed. He also seemed acutely conscious of the tension between the sacred and profane elements in everyday life, and when the sacred elements were absent in a text he felt their absence as a void. The emergent moral insight in a poem was somehow more important than its beauty, order, symmetry.

Lowell's critical writing took the form, largely, of book reviews contributed to journals whose spheres of literary and cultural interest matched his own (e.g., *Kenyon Review, Sewanee Review, Hudson Review*). His output was modest and thinly spread over a forty-year period, which perhaps accounts for the critics' paucity of interest in this area of his productivity. A survey of his criticism indicates that Lowell was extrinsically conditioned by a historical process and, at the same time, intrinsically conditioned by a self-reflexive activity. Lowell always formulated judgments relative to his own compositional problems at the moment, but he seldom atomized his view or relinquished the high seriousness he attached to the critical process. There was, however, some ambivalence between his poetic practice and his theoretical speculations on poetry; the greatest discrepancy was between his insistence on clarity in other poets' work and the obscurity that marred many of his own compositions. This was later verified in an interview statement by Frank Bidart, a poet friend of Lowell's. Bidart, whom Lowell had enlisted as his editorial assistant for the revision of *Notebook 1967–68*, noted that Lowell seemed oblivious to the cryptic character of this volume. Fearful of offending Lowell, Bidart would make delicate inquiries about personal references in the poems, most of which he could not decipher. He discovered that Lowell "did not know when something was unclear" (Hamilton biography, p. 392). Bidart worked with Lowell in the late fall of 1969, a period when Lowell was regularly taking lithium. This medication stabilized his extreme moods of elation and depression, but it also left him slightly removed from reality. Consequently, both his creative *and* critical writing show an increased opacity.

The question of whether the creative writer is capable of first-rate criticism did not arise in this country in the forties, the decade of Lowell's first critical offerings. Indeed, the creative writer was considered by many the only competent judge of literary value. Poet-critic Randall Jarrell scorned the notion of absolutism among critics, which he took to be a form of dehumanized scientism. This horror of scientism left room for poets like Lowell to allow biases, passions, and self-interest to spice their commentary. Moreover, it was not in Lowell's character to feel obliged to deliver "definitive" reading of texts. He was always conscious of the social relevance of a text and was more sensitive to human issues than to metrical matters. And from the start, he neither cowered before giants nor pandered to models of elitism. In his early career, for example, he dealt with Eliot as an equal, as his 1943 review of *Four Quartets* demonstrates (*Sewanee*, Summer). This piece also exemplifies the method he used for critical writing: to familiarize himself with, and often refer to, other critics' views of the work; to compare the work with equivalents or precedents in the literature. This procedure apparently made Lowell feel free to draw honest conclusions, especially when he wanted to admonish. Thus he prefaced the Eliot review with a note that both John Crowe

Ransom and Yvor Winters had censured Eliot's "loose logic and loose meters." Reminding readers that Pound had edited *The Waste Land* down to two-thirds its original length, Lowell argued that *Quartets* suffered from repetitiveness—as well as obscurity. That the work dealt with mystical experience, and that a "contemplative's life," as distinguished from his separate acts, created a structural problem for Eliot, indeed explained why *Quartets'* external unity was a pawn to its unity of intention. Obscurity and fragmentation were part and parcel of its structural necessity.

Today, the established merit of *Quartets* makes Lowell's apologia seem almost naive, but in fact Lowell was repeating the didactical correctives of the New Criticism. Having asserted his reservations, however, Lowell proceeded to defend the work. In *Quartets*, Eliot had at last dispensed with his "sometimes over-stating" satire (i.e., in the pub passages of *Waste Land*) and allowed his deeper reflections to emerge. Like the Christian mystics, reaching toward "union with God," Eliot demonstrated the difficulty of merging visionary experience with craftsmanship. Lowell finds Eliot's use of quotations and parodistic insertions intriguing—presumably because he himself borrows from other poets. A certain anonymity, coupled with a sense of continuity in poetic tradition, results from this process and universalizes the work, says Lowell.

He is also interested in the appropriation of voice in the poem, both to personalize it (Lowell employs the term "confessional" this early on) and to qualify it as a "community product." In addition to his absorption in the possibilities of a confessional voice, we find Lowell cogitating the function of voice in drama: he feels that Eliot's mystical obsessions explain the "relative failure" of his plays. Eliot has just "one theme" (the mystical experience) and it is less congenial to drama than to the long poem, which can accommodate the nonsequentiality of ecstasy.

When we take this essay as a whole, we find that Lowell is more exploratory than critical. He fastens on aspects of the work which interest him rather than viewing the entire poem. What can Eliot, poet-as-mystic, teach Lowell? Not much, we surmise from this essay. Actually, Lowell learned more than he consciously acknowledged at the time, namely, of the poet's need for religious faith. This was not made explicit in the review, but it forms the underlying ethos of *Land of Unlikeness*, which was scheduled for publication in the fall of the same year (1943).

Lowell consistently used literary criticism as a springboard for ideological debates. During the forties, his obsession with Catholicism was noticeable in all of his commentary. Thus, when he was invited to contribute to a "Hopkins Centennial" issue of *Kenyon Review* (Autumn 1944), Hopkins' "sanctity" was the subject of his essay. Here was the offspring of a distinguished "Puritan" family singing the praises of a Jesuit poet. To read Lowell's essay today is to be struck by its almost adolescent fervor. In this instance, Lowell curiously ignores the exacting formalist standards of the period and offers the same kind of doctrinal reading his *own* poetry was receiving in religiously oriented journals like *Commonweal* and *Renascence*. But Lowell redeems himself with his inevitable aperçus, and next to his remarks on Hopkins' "complete Christian life," which involved the "mysterious co-working of grace and free-will," stands commentary evincing solid aesthetic awareness. Lowell enumerated Hopkins' faults as a poet: he knew about nature but little about people; some of his rhythms have the effect of a "hyperthyroid injection"; his diction is too far from human speech. In fact, Hopkins' sanctity is so overreaching that it produces stylistic problems.

In another section of the essay, Lowell insists that certain "highly religious" writers of the past (Wordsworth, Coleridge, Arnold, Browning) stopped living after a point and began to reflect, moralize, preach, fable, because the "whole man had stopped." Yet he believes this never happened to Hopkins, and that if we take the total oeuvre we find Hopkins continuing to progress—in life and art—toward perfection.

Expectedly, there are sections of the essay where Lowell seems to be justifying his own poetry: his statement that Hopkins' obscurity and syntactical violence were probably "unavoidable" sounds like an apologia for *his* style. Such remarks may well have been motivated by Lowell's fearful anticipation of critics' complaints about obscurity in *Unlikeness*, which appeared in the wake of the Hopkins essay. Despite its brilliance, the Hopkins piece remains fragmentary; it never clarifies Lowell's underlying perception of the Jesuit's poetics. Lowell's later pieces contained broader perspectives of texts, but they never lost the quality of fragmentariness. Indeed, they never boasted logical, orderly analysis.

While we are attending to the weaknesses in Lowell's criticism, another might be mentioned: for all his erudition and urbanity, there is little wit in his critical essays. Morality and

earnestness tend to weigh down the lucubrations. Neither Lowell's maturity nor his secularization of values succeed in reliev-
ing his grave tone. In fact, his later work evinces a sadness
caused by more immediate concerns than the abstract (philosophical, religious) problems of his youth. Given this bent, he
was inclined to prefer the serious poets or the more somber
compositions of poets he admired. For example, Auden's sharp
humor and saucy wordplay interested him less than Hardy's
heavy melancholy. This is apparent in his compendium review
of eighteen new volumes of verse (*Sewanee*, Winter 1946).
When we look at an early piece such as this one, in which
Lowell separates the few gold coins from the dross, we discover that with the passage of time historians endorsed his verdict. In just a few pages Lowell showed remarkable discrimina-
tory powers when gauging the talents variously represented.
Apart from dismissing poets whose names are long since forgotten (Carl Carmer, Jeremy Ingalls, Katherine Hosking), Lowell delivers qualified judgments on the modestly capable poets
who enjoyed brief visibility (Winfield Townley Scott, Herbert
Read, George Zabriskie). And among the group of more tal-
ented poets—C. Day Lewis, Richard Eberhart, Louis MacNeice
—he singles out MacNeice as the best, primarily because of his
"observant eye" and "harsh line." There is no little irony in the
fact that he renders a stinging evaluation of Edmund Blunden,
the poet to whom he would lose the Oxford chair twenty years
later. Lowell finds Blunden's *Shells by a Stream* disappointing:

> At his best he is a small Hardy—a Hardy diminished in talent,
> technique and humanity but very solid and original. In this vol-
> ume Mr. Blunden writes formally in the manner of Bridges with
> scraps of tame Hardy and ineffectual Vaughan, Traherne, and
> Herbert. The result is heavy, clumsy, careless, academic, and
> sentimental.

Blunden's resemblance to Hardy, however minimal, was no
doubt the basis for his endearment to British critics. Lowell,
also an admirer of Hardy (especially his concrete and dramatic
regional poems), had the courage to indict a Hardy imitator—
no mean task in those years.

Among other high points of this *Sewanee* essay is an incisive
estimate of Frost's *A Masque of Reason*. Frost was always numbered among Lowell's favorite poets. Perhaps it was Frost's
dark, nearly nihilistic view that attracted the younger New
Englander. But Lowell preferred those Frost poems, with re-

gional dialogues, where the action was "grim, located, and tensely plotted," and he felt that *Masque* was too allegorical, too biblical in its imaginary conversations between Job and God. Here again, Lowell's critique anticipated the historian's appraisals; *Masque* is now considered one of Frost's minor works. But what seems to trouble Lowell most about *Masque* is his *own* temptation toward allegory. Frost, with his anachronistic verbal constructs, failed to construct a contemporary literary reality in this particular composition. Lowell believes that the modern poet must project an image of our technological society, but at no debasement of the mythical imagination. The quibble with *Masque* is ultimately self-reflexive, and reminds Lowell of the pitfalls inherent in allegorizing modern motifs.

Scattered among his notations on Frost, as well as on the other poets reviewed, are Lowell's comments on metrics. Lowell seems to prefer the "rough" or "strong" line which has not strayed far from its iambic base. At this point in his career, he still shows allegiance to traditional prosody, and while he is intolerant of diction which sounds mannered or uncolloquial, he is happy to see it locked into regular rhythms. At the conclusion of the *Sewanee* review, Lowell comments on an anthology edited by Oscar Williams, *The War Poets*, but he seems less austere when he discusses these war poems. Lowell now defends "documentary gravity" in poetry, especially when it affords an honest version of war. This volume shows us the "real war," not the "propaganda war" in newspapers or official announcements. Lowell mentions, in passing, that "men in the armed services"—amateurs, in other words—are heavily represented in this anthology. In effect, we find Lowell playing patriot rather than unwavering aesthete. This switch in priorities comes as a surprise to the reader, but in a sense it replicates the kind of abandon we find in Lowell's poetry when his passions overpower a concern with craft. We find his ardor so moving that we forget how scathing he was toward the poets reviewed earlier in this *Sewanee* essay, who are at least as skilled as these anthology contributors.

Thus Lowell was a capricious critic and his unpredictable approaches gave his essays a certain verve. Just as each of his succeeding verse volumes sought to resolve a new stylistic problem, so did each of his critical essays address a new point of interest. And in his next review in *Sewanee* (Summer 1947) he went far toward proving that the most sensitive judge of poetry is a poet. The essay, entitled "Thomas, Bishop, and Williams," is, in my estimation, Lowell's finest piece of criticism. It pits three major poets each against the other and draws several fascinating conclusions. This trio represents a wide spectrum of stylistic modes, from symbolic (Thomas) to realistic (Bishop) to primitive (Williams). Lowell is harshest on Thomas, a "dazzling writer who can be enjoyed without understanding." But we must not forget that his obscurity is largely responsible for the dazzlement, says Lowell. Thomas is like Hart Crane: mystical, complex, and perhaps too Elizabethan for his time. The only living poet who can compare with Thomas as a formal metrician is Wallace Stevens, says Lowell, but metrics are not enough and sound does not a great poet make. In Thomas' case, sound is a mere lyrical facade, lacking organic function. Moreover, Thomas overloads his poems with symbols, says Lowell, symbols which are not always supported by their context.

At a time in Thomas' career when he was giving flamboyant readings from his work to clamoring fans in packed halls, Lowell was insisting that the Welshman's sonorous effects lacked purpose, that his unremitting chants and pagan use of Christian mythology would work better if he kept his eye on the object. Nonetheless, we grasp from this review that Lowell was intrigued by Thomas, whose repetition of elemental words and motifs seemed to touch some deep recess. Perhaps the staid New Englander envied Thomas' abandon and exuberance.

Lowell felt more comfortable with Elizabeth Bishop's "unrhetorical, cool, and beautifully thought poems." As he put it, Thomas had "greater moments" than Bishop, but fewer successful poems. But he also observed that a "motion-process" seemed to dominate the Bishop poems and that this process was dreary and exhausting, to the point of disintegration. Everything is at a terminus, but at the same time stoically maintained. This odd synthesis of motion and death is so oversimplified that it borders on the trivial; and the trivial is anathema to Lowell. As in his assessment of Thomas, Lowell inflates Bishop's attributes only to conclude by isolating a shortcoming: Thomas is sometimes "swamped in rhetoric"; Bishop is sometimes "pert, banal, and over-pointed." The more Lowell admires the poet, the harder he searches for a radical flaw. This penchant seems to derive more from psychological than aesthetic reactions to the verse. Because Lowell is not confident that he has a worthy center of poetic value, he feels compelled to reject other poets. Such identity reaction gives a slightly perverse tone to this otherwise balanced essay.

We no sooner become adjusted to this pattern of criticism in
the essay, however, than we find Lowell reviewing Williams'
*Paterson* in terms this side of idolatry:

> I can think of no book published in 1946 that is as important, or
> of any living English or American poet who has written anything
> better or more ambitious.

He aligns this text with several majestic precedents (Crane's
*The Bridge*; Wordsworth's *The Prelude*), but not before he
makes clear that there is an inferior precedent:

> This may appear crude and vague, but Williams has nothing in
> common with the coarse, oratorical sentimentalists, most favor-
> ably represented by Carl Sandburg, who have written about cities
> and the people.

Lowell, once again, matched the historians; the wax and wane
of Sandburg's reputation is now familiar to all.

What is more remarkable about Lowell's delight in *Paterson*
is that he expressed it at the time his own *Lord Weary's Castle*,
a volume antithetical to *Paterson*, was drawing praise for its
complex, heavily ornamented style. Lowell reveled in Williams'
Whitmanesque, liberal, anti-orthodox language. *Paterson* proved
that the educated in our land lacked the language to deal with
the particulars and mystery of reality, while the ignorant failed
equally with their "speechless passion." Williams had found
the language to bridge these worlds, said Lowell, but the reader
comes away from this essay feeling that Lowell was more
moved by "the tragedy of Paterson" than by Williams' language. The grimness and strength of the Paterson citizens
whom Williams so dramatically described (walking in the parks
and by the falls, going to the factories) captivated Lowell. This
mill town, indeed, may have found entry into Lowell's imaginative world and provided him with the idea for "Mills of
the Kavanaughs." Williams' "Man-City and Woman-Mountain"
carried enough symbolic force, despite their primal character,
to suit Lowell's metaphoric appetite. Although he stressed Williams' unshadowed vision, his own diction for describing *Paterson* showed that he apprehended the poem as a symbolic essence: "It is the elemental thought that lacks a language, the
source of life and motion."

What we must conclude from Lowell's appraisal of Williams, which in the climate of the essay reduces (if not deni-

grates) Bishop's and Thomas' offerings, is that Lowell is voicing an incipient awareness of the transformation of his own poetics; he will not address poetry in the "old" way again. Of course, he is not yet completely cognizant that he cannot, like Williams, yield openly to the world and reject the intellect, with its quarry of erudition and formal imperatives. For the moment, he has found a compelling touchstone and will labor to achieve Williams' "contact." He seems, primarily, to have grasped from Williams the ways to express a sense of abundance in life, and one device is to soften the jagged breaks in his metrical and imagistic patterns.

Wallace Stevens is the first poet to suffer the slings of Lowell's new standards. In his review of Stevens' *Transport to Summer* (*Nation*, April 5, 1947), Lowell perceives as dandyism what he had formerly considered appropriate rhetoric. He still finds the need to cite other negative assessments, as if to bolster his own, and in this case it is Yvor Winters' dismissal of Stevens in *The Anatomy of Nonsense*. But then his own voice takes command: personae with names like "Canon Aspirin," "Nanzia Nunzio," seem to be created for Stevens' private amusement. "Notes toward a Supreme Fiction," the longest poem in the book, "rambles and rambles without gathering volume, and many of the sections are padded to fill out their twenty-one lines." Lowell notes that Stevens' early *Harmonium* was exciting and magical, but now the magic has been lost. One suspects, however, that it is Lowell who has changed and not Stevens. He no longer finds magic in the whimsy of these lines, which he disparagingly quotes in the essay:

> Angry men and furious machines
> Swarm from the little blue of the horizon
> To the great blue of the middle height.
> Men scatter through the clouds.

Lowell's immersion in Williams' "Falls" caused a conversion; in contrast to Williams, Stevens is "seldom human." Lowell continues to summon forth his formalist criteria to make his case, as though phrases like "loose structures" and "imagistic mannerisms" will verify his objectivity. The lexical surface of the essay, therefore, exhibits his old terminology, but it is turned to new purposes.

During these years when Lowell was discovering Williams and modifying his taste, he failed to grapple with some of the deeper theoretical problems which that shift brought up. Lowell was always skillful at describing how well wrought the urn was, but the theoretical basis on which the New Critics founded their taste for certain urns—namely, that their favored kind of metaphysical wit and irony imaged the complexities and contradictions of mature experience—never seemed to concern him. His move to a taste for the poetry of Williams, which by and large lacked metaphysical wit and was never very popular with the New Critics, would have been impossible for a true believer in the school of which Tate and Ransom were masters. In effect, Lowell was not a card-carrying New Critic; and when he no longer relied on affiliation with the masters of this school, his departure from them was not clearly manifest in his criticism. His device for announcing his changing taste in poetry was to force himself to be original through self-reflexivity and, as he moved away from his mentors, to declare his independence by writing elaborate tributes (farewells, really) to several of these mentors. In "John Crowe Ransom's Conversation" (*Sewanee*, July–September 1948) his strategy was to claim that Ransom's best characteristic as a teacher was to instill selfhood in his pupils: "One took what one could, and went on, God willing, as one's self." It was not possible to become a replica of Ransom, Lowell insisted, but when he described Ransom's poetry he used his mentor's language:

> There is the unusual structural clarity, the rightness of tone and rhythm, the brisk and effective ingenuity, the rhetorical fireworks of exposition, description and dialogue.

Even more surprising, Lowell spoke of Ransom's poems as having the "distinction of good conversation," but the lines by Ransom which Lowell used as an epigraph for his essay hardly sound so:

> Virgin, whose image bent to the small grass
> I keep against this tide of wayfaring,
> O hear the maiden pageant ever sing
> Of that far away time of gentleness.

This was not so much inconsistency on Lowell's part, or even an accolade written for political reasons. (Lowell did not resort to political strategies; even his longstanding friendship with Elizabeth Bishop did not prevent him from labeling her poetry "pert, banal, and over-pointed".) What is more plausible is that

Lowell genuinely preferred the formality of poetry such as Ransom's, but that his characteristic need to rebel brought him over to Williams' camp. There is something absolute, too fiercely laudatory, about his review of *Paterson*. Actually, *Paterson* had sharpened Lowell's interest in the interaction between poem and reader as a permanent motif. Lowell sensed this but was evidently unable to articulate it; he never excelled at intellectual definition. His split with Ransom, whose poetry was so different from Williams', was expressed emotionally.

When we read Lowell's essay on another of his New Critical mentors, Allen Tate, this sense of fading admiration is again evident (*Sewanee*, Autumn 1959). Lowell recounts his stay with the Tates during the summer of 1937, when he "offered" himself as a guest and was told he could sleep on the lawn, which he did—in an "olive Sears-Roebuck-Nashville umbrella tent." Tate delivered pronouncements on poetry all summer long, but the one Lowell repeated was that "a good poem had nothing to do with exalted feelings of being moved by the spirit. It was simply a piece of craftsmanship, an intelligible or *cognitive* object." Here again we sense that Lowell has been, perhaps unconsciously, Mephistophelean in his choice of quotations. Tate's dictum sounds not only contradictory but philistine as well. Lowell seems to be consigning to Tate the role of doctrinaire critic who must instruct young geniuses (Lowell!) how to harness their effusive talent. Thus for all his compliments to Tate, Lowell is sketching a flattering portrait of himself. Tate, like Ransom, figures in the molding of a great poet. None of this is explicit in Lowell's essays, nor is there ever a suggestion of arrogance. It is closer to the mark to argue that Lowell wrote about these men as critics who happened to write poetry, and in each case a handful of permanent lyrics. Again, the historians concur. But the genesis of Lowell's disenchantment with Ransom and Tate, apart from his discovery of Williams, was his discovery that he need not lean on rational faculty to write great poetry. His separation from the Catholic church in the late forties curiously coincided with his separation from the New Critics, who sought to impose order on a universe Lowell increasingly found deranged.

Lowell's bouts of mental illness also had some bearing on his changing critical standards. He became attracted to writers who shunned discipline or system (e.g., the Beats). Yet among the writers he admired for their anti-academicism, *he* had the reputation of scholar-critic. This unique attitude about roles continued to influence Lowell's critical activity. He felt torn between enjoying the Olympian authority of a critic and the delirious surrender of an artist. When I. A. Richards published his first book of verse (*Goodbye Earth*) at age sixty, Lowell said it was the product of a critic who had too long misdirected his creative powers (*Encounter*, February 1960). He did not state this directly, but quoted Coleridge on the hazards of writing verse after the years of youthful spontaneity have passed:

"How difficult and delicate a task even the mere mechanism of verse is, may be conjectured from the failure of those who have attempted to write verse late in life."

Crouching behind Coleridge's anguished observation, Lowell freely expounded on the shortcomings of Richards' volume. Richards was too self-conscious to write great poetry; his mind, brimming with abstractions, semantics, philosophy, too often crowded out his feelings. Clearly, Tate's pronouncement that a "good poem had nothing to do with exalted feelings" but "was simply a piece of craftsmanship" no longer ranked as doctrine with Lowell. The *Encounter* essay, which tested Tate's criteria although it never mentioned his name, not only discounted Richards as a poet but indirectly bade farewell to Tate.

We might backtrack briefly and consider Lowell's review of Robert Penn Warren's *Brother to Dragons* (*Kenyon Review*, Autumn 1953), which tells us more about Lowell's problems with creativity than about Warren's work. *Dragons*, a long narrative poem, is based on the account of two nephews of Thomas Jefferson who in 1811 brutally murdered one of their slaves because he had broken a pitcher prized by their dead mother. Warren hinged his verse melodrama on the paradox that the homicide was committed by relatives of the first truly democratic president in American history, and that the murderers indirectly attributed the act to Jeffersonian idealism. The tale contained all the ingredients for anti-Romantic Southern fiction, but Warren presented it in a blank verse which recalled the Elizabethan tragedies. Lowell was intrigued by the work, which, in scope and mode, resembled his "Mills of the Kavanaughs," published two years earlier. *Dragons* was a better-sustained work than "Mills" and Lowell, bearing no grudge, was generous in his praise. On this count alone, the review was an informative sample of Lowell's nature as a critic.

It also showed that Lowell was searching for a model which successfully applied a documentary approach to a violent event in American history (an approach later utilized in *The Old Glory*).

Beyond this, Lowell used the review to expose his dilemma about the proper limits of literary form, both thematic and linguistic. He said that poetry at that time had become "all that was not prose," meaning that factual items could be incorporated into a poem through quotations, statistics, conversations, and newspaper clippings. But plot and character, in other than fragmentary moments, were still the province of fiction. How did one incorporate these elements without sounding hollow and unreal? Moreover, how did the self-conscious modern poet effect the readability of fiction and yet retain the poetic voice? Warren's solution in *Dragons* is to intrude on the narrative himself, serve as commentator, and then retreat into the background. This is a novelist's device, however, and one which came naturally to Warren but not to Lowell. Lowell concludes his essay with the assertion that "prose genius in verse" must become the new expression for American poets.

We have here, in the guise of a book review, the prolegomena for the poetics of *Life Studies*, a fascinating glimpse of the poet's (as yet unconscious) struggle with his own technical problem. Along the way, Lowell reveals the problems he has with his own writing: how to mix dialogue with narrative voice; how to sustain a long poem without growing "puffy, paralyzed and pretentious"; how to achieve the historical sense with documentary detail. Rather than imitate Warren's intrusive narrator, Lowell uses a strategy of deceptive surfaces in *Life Studies*; bland dialogue and uneventful episodes understate emotionally explosive experiences. As a persona, Lowell does not dominate the text.

I might add that even in the review of a work like *Dragons*, which has little religious content, Lowell tries to locate its underlying religious stance: "I'm not sure of Warren's position but it is often close to neo-Humanism and neo-Thomism." He has a bit of difficulty reconciling this notion with the Southern literary rendition of evil in *Dragons*, but this incongruity does not detract from the force of the essay.

While Lowell never fully internalized the precepts of the New Criticism, as I have noted, he used its phraseology throughout his career. Other theoretical schools came and went, but

Lowell did not seem interested in them. Nowhere in his criticism do we find the terminology of the structuralists, deconstructionists, or phenomenological critics. He seldom engaged in archetypal analysis, although he was highly conscious of biblical motifs (e.g., the Abel-Cain analogue in *Brother to Dragons*). The biblical commentary, at any rate, always remained on an ethical level and was not fused with a larger consideration of mythos. Lowell *did* inject some psychological analysis into his criticism—more Freudian than Jungian. On occasion he mentioned philosophers, but in an elementary way. For example, in his *Nation* review of Stevens' *Transport to Summer* he attempted to define Stevens' philosophical ideas:

> His world is an impartial, hedonistic, speculative world—he is closer to Plato than to Socrates, and closer to the philosophy and temperament of George Santayana than to Plato. Directly or indirectly much of his thought is derived from the dialectical idealism of Hegel.

We might find such a statement maddening, were we not charmed by its confident rhetoric. And this is true of most of his other theoretical claims—literary, philosophical, and otherwise. His commentary is happily free of jargon, and for the most part he makes practical observations, especially in matters metrical and linguistic. He also subscribed to Coleridge's principle that great ideas can only emanate from great feelings, and his essay on the style of the Gettysburg Address (in *Lincoln & The Gettysburg Address*, 1964) demonstrates this. Lincoln could not have written this speech if he had not "symbolically died, just as the Union soldiers really died—and he himself was soon really to die." The Address became part of the battle and added significance to the maneuvers of the soldiers. Lowell, addressing the idea of literature as process, enumerated the birth images in the Address: "brought forth," "conceived," "created," "a new birth of freedom." But even in this essay he found an excuse to incorporate some religious sentiments: "He [Lincoln] left Jefferson's ideals of freedom and equality joined to the Christian sacrificial act of death and rebirth." In his criticism as in his poetry, the Arnoldian strain was never completely absent.

When Lowell was not limited to writing a book review but was asked to do a "profile" on a poet, he showed great skill as a raconteur. In "William Carlos Williams" (*Hudson Review*,

Winter 1961/62), Lowell's portrait is more compelling than his appraisal of Williams as a poet:

> When I think of his last longish autobiographical poems, I remember his last reading I heard. It was at Wellesley. I think about three thousand students attended. It couldn't have been more crowded in the wide-galleried hall and I had to sit in the aisle. The poet appeared, one whole side partly paralyzed, his voice just audible, and here and there a word misread. No one stirred.

When he spoke of Williams' poetry, he delivered fair warning that this "common style" could not be imitated. Without the genius of Williams, the results would be dull. Lowell recalled how, in the late thirties at Kenyon, he and his fellow poets found Williams' poetry "the best that free verse could do." Williams was part of the literary revolution but he remained "fresh, secondary and minor." Lowell later reversed that view, of course, and equated *Paterson* with *Leaves of Grass*. He could not complete this *Hudson Review* piece, however, without discussing his confrontation with Williams' style, which he had tried to imitate: "The difficulties I found in Williams twenty-five years ago are still difficulties for me. Williams enters me, but I cannot enter him." Williams loves America so excessively that Lowell finds his poetry "Dantesque." Indeed, Williams looks on the American scene with "exasperation, terror and a kind of love."

Lowell is surely tranferring some of his own impressions to Williams, for those familiar with *Spring and All* and other Williams poems know that the dazzling natural world is as frequently present as the grim industrial world of "By the Road to the Contagious Hospital." It is clear from this review, however, that Lowell has internalized Williams' belief that the only legitimate formal rules for prosody are those determined by the pulse rate and breath of the individual poet. The principle had not been so much disputed as bypassed by the New Critics. Thus Lowell's separation from his old metrical theory was established.

We noted elsewhere that Lowell's "Skunk Hour" was the subject-poem for the symposia volume *The Contemporary Poet as Artist and Critic*. In one of these symposia, Stanley Kunitz' "Father and Son" was the subject-poem and Lowell was one of the critics. Lowell's essay is especially interesting because it is his first public statement about the confessional mode, of which Kunitz' poem is an example (albeit a rather conservative one). In considering what Lowell has to say, it should be noted that "Father and Son" (1958) has a strong tonal resemblance to some of Lowell's family poems, but it withers in soft sentimentality—a weakness we cannot attribute to the author of *Life Studies*. Here, for example, is a stanza from "Father and Son":

> At the water's edge, where the smothering ferns lifted
> Their arms, "Father!" I cried, "Return! You know
> The way. I'll wipe the mudstains from your clothes;
> No trace, I promise, will remain. Instruct
> Your son, whirling between two wars,
> In the Gemara of your gentleness,
> For I would be a child to those who mourn
> And brother to the foundlings of the field
> And friend of innocence and all bright eyes.
> O teach me how to work and keep me kind."

Prior to embarking on his analysis, Lowell expresses skepticism about the current critical process. Analysis doesn't make for interesting reading, he says, and "One knows ahead of time how the machine will grind." Exegesis has taken over the industry and the poets are pandering to the trend: "There is even a kind of modern poem, now produced in bulk, that seems written to be explained. Training and labor are required for such efforts, but this can't be the way good poems are written." There is a weariness in Lowell's tone and a sense of nostalgia for earlier days, when Marianne Moore and Stevens and Eliot "came as a revelation." The academies had turned literary criticism into a dull, conventional practice: "A glow seems to be gone." Nonetheless, once past his admission of indifference toward the "industry," he launched into his exacting analysis of Kunitz' poem.

It has an "embarrassing" lack of difficulty, says Lowell—and we, as readers, recall his own dense and reverberating compositions. Without directly denigrating the piece, Lowell reminds us how "open and apparent" the expression is. Indeed, this is one essay where Lowell tries to conceal his reservations about a composition, but dissatisfaction leaks out ("The meter is a tolerably regular blank verse"; "What's the point of the pond? Did the father drown himself, or was his favorite sport fishing or wading for water bugs?"). What is more important, Lowell, by not addressing the poem as a confessional work, implies that it offers nothing new or momentous. It was difficult for Lowell to be unkind to a fellow poet, but it was even more difficult to show enthusiasm when he was bored or apathetic about a work.

His next essay, the Foreword to Sylvia Plath's *Ariel*, which was posthumously published in 1966, was the sort of commentary he preferred to write. He was familiar with Plath's brand of existential dread. She validated his belief that there was a curse on the poets of his generation, that they were traveling in dangerous psychological territory. Paying his respects to a poet whose promising career was abruptly terminated, Lowell admitted that he had earlier sensed her distinction but "never guessed her later appalling and triumphant fulfillment." He calls *Ariel* "the autobiography of a fever," then plunges in—exhibiting intensity equal to the work he describes —with words of praise. It is apparent that Lowell is identifying with Plath and her hallucinatory manner; but he is reminded of the risk in writing such death-bent poems: "These poems are playing Russian roulette with six cartridges in the cylinder, a game of 'chicken,' the wheels of both cars locked and unable to swerve." Turning to technical matters, he finds her metrical structure formidably expert and her voice representative of "Massachusetts' low-tide dolor" (here he is self-reflexive). The dark strains in poetry by New Englanders prompt Lowell to critical praise. He is intrigued by Plath's courage to apostrophize death in sensual language:

> He tells me how sweet
> The babies look in their hospital
> Icebox, a simple
> Frill at the neck,
> Then the flutings of their Ionian
> Death-gowns,
> Then two little feet.

Surely, here Lowell exposes his Puritanical fascination with morbidity; but he is also reflecting a pathological aspect of the criticism in this period, whereby the death of the poet elevates his or her art, in some sacrificial way, to the status of a cultural statement. The confessional poets, especially, had an obsession with the survivor syndrome and viewed their predicaments as paradigms of civilization's destructive power. As M. L. Rosenthal said of the confessional poets: "It was the old romantic fallacy, if you will, of confusing motive and art, or the real and ideal—private obsession and disorientation become normalized as they are organized into a structure outside themselves" (*The New Poets*, 1967).

The cultist aura surrounding Plath in the sixties no doubt came into play when Lowell wrote his Foreword. He was at the same time cognizant that *Ariel* left readers feeling "empty, evasive and inarticulate," and a certain objectivity—or perhaps sanity—kept him from sinking into total commitment. After the *Ariel* Foreword there was no instance (either in interviews or essays on other poets) in which he singled out Plath—or any other confessional poets, for that matter—in a preferential way. In fact, his later commentaries almost reverted to sighs of longing for poets of the earlier generation.

When the Oxford edition of *Twentieth Century English Poetry* (1973), edited by Philip Larkin, was the subject of his review (*Encounter*, May 1973), Lowell championed the "golden oldies," poets like A. E. Housman, who would blush at the thought of unleashing private urges, preferring to sublimate them in mournful, yearning lyrics. Indeed, to those who turned to Lowell for commentary on contemporary verse, it must have been disappointing to read these words: "The one who most moves me to tears—when poetry can—is Housman. His iron quatrains are sometimes like tomb-inscriptions for the Athenian youths who died at Marathon."

His other reflections in this review were even more mystifying, for he averred that one must like Hardy, who was "the greatest poet of the century." When we carefully attend to what it is in Hardy that so attracted Lowell, we discover that Lowell the man, rather than Lowell the critic, had taken command:

> He [Hardy] had to be old to find natural inspiration in nostalgia, things changing, the days of his courtship, eternal then quickly gone, when love turned terrible and the marriage endured.

The *Encounter* review is a milestone in Lowell's critical repertory. Here, still, is the critic whose humanism and rhetoric will sway us no matter what he says. But here, too, is a creative mind that has forgotten its old exacting criteria. To give him his due, Lowell recognizes the transitory value of the Movement school (the 1950s British poets whose leader was Philip Larkin) and singles out their "low-voiced insularity." Actually, an anthology of twentieth-century British verse was not the best vehicle to test Lowell's critical observations. It was too broad in scope and included too many poets for individual analysis.

Lowell's review of Larkin's anthology was the last of his strictly critical publications. During these years he wrote several wayward, affectionate reminiscences ("For John Berryman," *New York Review of Books*; "Tribute to John Crowe Ransom," *New Review*) but brought little of his critical acumen to the occasion. Lowell was now designated an elder statesman in letters and his role was perceived as largely ceremonial. These were the seventies and the Modernist poets' popularity had declined. The *Sewanee* and *Kenyon* reviews no longer claimed the authority they had in the past. Journals based in academia, such as *Boundary 2* (at the State University of New York), were singing the praises of the Black Mountain and Oral poets, and Lowell was not numbered among them. Indeed, as the most gifted poet of the modes these journals were now electing to excoriate, Lowell became their whipping boy. Classified as a Modernist, he was, consequently, not invited to review the new poets. His later critical statements came from requests to comment on his own work.

It is hard to know how he reacted to this neglect, after his reign of "influence" during the sixties. His last official essay on his own work, in the special Lowell issue of *Salmagundi* (Spring 1977), evinced no bitterness or sense of rejection. His melancholy tone ("I hope there has been increase of beauty, wisdom, tragedy, and all the blessings of this consuming chance") was consistent with his tone throughout his career, but in this essay he managed to synthesize all the ideas that had been fragmentarily suggested in his earlier critiques. He reiterated his concern about America, capitalism, totalitarianism, and predicted the world would not survive if we continued on the same course. All the sentiments poetically expressed in such famous poems as "Quaker Graveyard" were here repeated in prose. He added that all of his poems had been written "for catharsis"— something he had never admitted before but which came as no surprise to readers now familiar with the psychological torments from which he had sought relief.

Lowell sprinkled into his discourse on his poetry some critical notes on other writers. The only modern poets whom he bothered to acknowledge were Pound, Williams, and Bishop; for the rest, it was back to the Romantics, the Victorians. Browning, whom he had expressed doubts about in his 1961

*Paris Review* interview, was now "the large poet of the nineteenth century." There was such a variety of rich characterization in Browning, said Lowell, that his poems would outlast much major fiction.

At this point in his career, Lowell was still obsessed with the problem of "ventriloquism," of projecting voices other than his own. How many modern poets could people their verses with Napoleon III, St. John, Cardinal Manning, even another fictional character, Caliban? Prose fiction seemed to have become the ideal mode for Lowell, who now dwelt on George Eliot, Samuel Butler, Flaubert. One wonders if, had he lived longer, he would have attempted to write a novel himself.

The challenge of producing meters had obviously passed; he had used nearly every variety in the tradition of English literature and now seemed ready for something new. In a brief but instructive earlier comment on the writing of free verse ("On Freedom in Poetry," *Naked Poetry*, 1969), Lowell had said that when he dropped one style of writing it was usually "a surprise" to him. He never worked his intuitions into a theory, far less a program for his writing objectives. But even in this essay, which is a defense of license in meter, Lowell says that "the joy and strength of unscanned verse is that it can be as natural as conversation or prose, or can follow the rhythm of the ear that knows no measure." When we recall the diction, values, and religious interest that colored his review of *Four Quartets* in 1943, we can see that Lowell had substantially broadened his horizons.

In chapter 1 we noted that Lowell's interviews became, for the critics, seminal guides to the interpretation of his poetry. In conclusion, we must turn again to the interviews, which, while they do not qualify as formal criticism, served as the platforms from which Lowell launched some of his most trenchant comments. These remarks often took up themes that flowed through the journal articles but were revivified in the informality of the interview situation. Thus it was in conversation with Alvarez (London *Observer*, July 21, 1963) that we learned that Lowell found Ted Hughes "just a sort of thunderbolt," but also a poet who had written some of the best animal poems in English. This casual comment should remind us of Lowell's very professional interest in such works and send us back to his formal piece in *The Contemporary Poet as Artist and Critic*. It was in this article (which we have commented on elsewhere) that Lowell stressed how important Elizabeth Bishop's animal poem "The Armadillo" had been to him at a crucial point in his career and how her words had inspired his best-known poem in that genre, "Skunk Hour." And it was in a conversation with Stanley Kunitz (*New York Times Book Review*, October 4, 1964), in which that poet had said that the strain of modern living produced the tragic, violent, and disintegrated poetic structures we encounter in current poetry, that Lowell supplied the opinion that he found Eliot "no sadder at the heart or more vulnerable" than Keats or Coleridge.

Lowell's sense of history took him beyond such facile generalizing. One came to Marianne Moore's "The Frigate Pelican" with a sense of "relief and liberation," he said, implying that not all modern poetry is sad at the heart. Taken as a whole, Lowell's interview pieces are filled with innumerable insights that suggest a catholicity of taste. There was no single literary epoch that commanded his interest, and no single poet elected for his pedestal. Lowell seemed reluctant to speak of specific poets, and did so only in reply to pointed inquiries. He often sidetracked the conversation by referring to prose, as in this *Paris Review* statement:

> The ideal modern form seems to me to be the novel and certain short stories. Maybe Tolstoi would be the perfect example—his work is imagistic, it deals with all experience, and there seems to be no conflict of the form and content.

Why would a poet, so dedicated to his craft, speak with such admiration of other genres? Possibly because it relieved him of the task of evaluating his peers in an informal context. More importantly, it suited his temperament to deliver "off track" opinions. When asked (also in *Paris Review* interview) why he had written so little criticism, Lowell replied: "Sometimes I wish I did more, but I'm very anxious in criticism not to do the standard analytical essay. I'd like my essay to be much sloppier and more intuitive."

Just as he instructed us on how to apprehend his poetry, he aptly described his criticism.

## References

Lowell, Robert.
    1943. "A Review of *Four Quartets*." *Sewanee Review* Summer, pp. 432–35.

1944. "A Note." *Kenyon Review* Autumn, pp. 583–86.

1946. "Current Poetry." *Sewanee Review* Winter, pp. 145–53.

1947. "Imagination and Reality." *The Nation* April 5, pp. 400–02.

1948. "Homage to John Crowe Ransom." *Sewanee Review* July–September, pp. 374–77.

1953. "Prose Genius in Verse." *Kenyon Review* Autumn, pp. 619–25.

1959. "Visiting the Tates." *Sewanee Review* Autumn, pp. 557–59.

1960. "I. A. Richards as Poet." *Encounter* February, pp. 77–78.

1961–62. "William Carlos Williams." *Hudson Review* Winter, pp. 530–36. Reprinted in *William Carlos Williams: A Collection of Critical Essays*, ed. J. Hillis Miller. Englewood Cliffs, N.J.: Prentice-Hall, 1966.

1964. "On the Gettysburg Address." In *Lincoln and the Gettysburg Address*, ed. Allan Nevins. Urbana: University of Illinois Press, 1964, pp. 88–89.

1964. "On Stanley Kunitz' 'Father and Son.' " In *The Contemporary Poet as Artist and Critic*, ed. Anthony Ostroff. Boston: Little, Brown, pp. 71–75.

1966. Foreword to *Ariel*, by Sylvia Plath. New York: Harper & Row.

1969. "On Freedom in Poetry." *Naked Poetry*, ed. Stephen Berg and Robert Mezey. Indianapolis: Bobbs-Merrill, p. 124.

1972. "For John Berryman." *New York Review of Books* April 6, pp. 3–4.

1974. "Tribute to John Crowe Ransom." *The New Review* August, pp. 3–6.

1977. "Digressions from Larkin's 20th Century Verse." *American Poetry Review* January–February, pp. 33–34.

1977. "After Enjoying Six or Seven Essays on Me." *Salmagundi* Spring, pp. 113–15.

Interviews

1961. "Interview with Robert Lowell." *Paris Review* Winter–Spring, pp. 56–95. Reprinted in *Writers at Work, Second Series*, ed. Malcolm Cowley. New York: Viking, 1963.

1963. "Robert Lowell in Conversation." London *Observer* July 21, p. 19.

1964. "Talk with Robert Lowell." *New York Times Book Review* October 4, pp. 34–38.

Hamilton, Ian.

1982. *Robert Lowell: A Biography*. New York: Random House.

Rosenthal, M. L.

1967. *The New Poets*. New York: Oxford University Press.

# CHAPTER 7

# Conclusion

Poetry today is no longer the definitive medium we ordinarily associate with the Modernist poetry of the early twentieth century. The first and founding members of Modernism—Pound, Eliot, Williams—institutionalized their undertaking by campaigning in numerous journalistic essays and in critical essays of great originality and force. Journals promoting the cause, the "little magazines," multiplied in this country and in England in the twenties. Important writers became their editors or founded their own magazines as outlets for their work: *The Fugitive* (1922–25) in Memphis, Tennessee; *The Dial* (1880–1925) in New York City; and *The Criterion* (1922–29) in London, the most influential critical journal, which was founded and edited by Eliot. Eliot became a senior editor at Faber & Faber in London and Allen Tate became poetry editor at Henry Holt in New York.

Beginning with John Crowe Ransom at the end of World War I and with increasing frequency after 1930, prominent writers, like Tate, Warren, and Ransom, secured posts in colleges and universities, which facilitated acceptance of the new literature in academia and among younger generations of students. After 1940, established poets like Frost and Eliot recorded their works for commercial companies, finding new and widening audiences. By the time Lowell came along, in what is now considered the second and final phase of the Modernist movement, the principles and practices of the founders dominated the literary scene. The principles and practices need no recital here; they have been referred to in chapter 5 of this study in conjunction with source-study examination of Lowell's stylistics. What is most pertinent here is Lowell's reaction to the movement and how (or whether) he placed his imprimatur on it.

There is no denying that, at least in the sixties decade and several years prior to and after it, Lowell enjoyed a magisterial role as arbiter of literary taste. He was considered uncompromising and impervious to the limitations of readers; the poet was there to edify. Although his reputation never reached the heights that Eliot's did, critics often used the same terminology to describe Lowell that they had used for Eliot ("classicist," "prophetic," "spokesman for the age"). Even after the appearance of Hamilton's revealing, occasionally unflattering biography, critics, reviewing the biography, felt that Lowell was larger than life, or was never as "shockingly personal as he thought he was." These are Alfred Kazin's words, to whom Lowell was "too well bred and by nature even more elusive than he knew. His style in its expert fluidity was not only catch-as-catch-can but really said 'catch me if you can'" (*Times Literary Supplement*, May 6, 1983). Stephen Spender (also in a review of the Hamilton biography) concluded that Lowell "wrote the greatest poems of the generation with which he identified himself" (*Washington Post Book World*, November 14, 1982). Spender forgave Lowell's obliviousness of others, his childish, sometimes brutal behavior toward those who loved him. For Spender, it sufficed that he had "an inescapable quality of greatness about him." Finally, Richard Ellmann, in *his* review of Hamilton, said that

> though there were rival claimants, Robert Lowell throned it over American poetry for 20 years. . . . His aim was to make himself a representative man, whose reactions to war, politics, love, family and friends would add up to archetypal completeness. For a man so unlike other men, it was a singular ambition. That he largely achieved it was a triumph [*New York Times Book Review*, November 28, 1982].

Kazin, Spender, and Ellmann are roughly in the same age bracket as Lowell, and being contemporaries may have some bearing on their sympathetic appraisals. Whatever the reason, the three reviews confirm the fact that Lowell's mystique is still acknowledged by influential men of letters.

Disparate as they seem and indeed are, writers like Frost, Eliot, Pound, and Stevens nonetheless formed the crest of a rebellion which ironically carried poetry toward a classic direction. Although they would presumably agree that a modern poet cannot profitably assume the roles of philosopher or theologian, all of these writers played the traditional philosopher or "priest" at some point in their writing careers. Eliot, for example, considered Modernism a gesture or method of doing away with Romantic (ego-bound) notions of "originality" in poetry. He wished to subvert those Wordsworthian criteria of poetic discourse which deliberately foregrounded a poet's feelings. Yet other Modernist poets, in obeisance to that other Romantic, Coleridge, advocated a poetry which was organic, open, derived from nature. A split developed between the poets, for while they were consolidated on certain issues (new rhythms, compression of statement), they also formed splinter groups with factional strategies. Thus we find that we must stretch, rather than reinforce, the boundaries which define Modernism in literature; and so, in this closing chapter, I should like to suggest some of the difficulties critics have encountered in their assessment of Lowell's role in the Modernist movement, as well as his legacy to the ensuing generation of poets.

Lowell was every bit as ambitious as the poets of both phases of the Modernist movement. He wanted to be "major," and watched with vigilance the fluctuations of rank among his poetic peers. His affected humility, and reticence concealed the fact that he was perpetually wary of contenders. Thus he "kept up" with trends and critical upheavals. At the same time he had two trenchant fears about his profession: the unsteadiness of his world of literary friends and mentors, and the absolute critical authority certain luminaries wielded in his day. As an example of the first fear, Lowell followed reports of Berryman's bad health, drinking, and breakdowns with muted dread. He identified with Berryman as a kind of victim-hero, whose *Dream Songs* had been something of a model for his own later volumes. With Berryman's example in *Dream Songs*, Lowell realized that domestic trivia, random conversations, private anecdotes, could be contained in a text which give the illusion of structure. But was suicide the price one had to pay in order to reproduce life's haphazard flow in writing? As an example of the second fear, Lowell worried that a stylistic "breaking loose" would bring the wrath of stringent critics upon his head. The death of Randall Jarrell (1965), whom Lowell considered a genuine friend, actually relieved him: it removed a potential verdict of *Notebook* as slack, self-indulgent jotting. The tension between wanting to break loose and satisfying the standards of certain critics was at times more than Lowell could bear. In a sense, however, this tension was not the privileged psychic property of Lowell; it was an "accent" which characterized the Modernist movement.

Lowell's relationship to the Modernist movement functions largely as a dialectic of generations, a debate about continuing values, about closed and repetitive verse forms, about the nature of pure speech. In 1960, when Charles Olson asserted that poetry could only move forward by "getting rid of the lyrical interference of the individual ego, of the subject and his soul," he was advocating a sociopolitical as well as literary ideology. The single voice (Lowell's centrality of the personal) must become a thing of the past (*Poetics of the New American Poetry*). Other critics, however, would disagree. A. Poulin (editor of *Contemporary American Poetry*, 1980) feels that one of the major differences between Modernist and contemporary poetry is that the *latter* is more personal, that poets like Eliot, Frost, even Lowell, always assured a certain distance between themselves and their poems. The objectification of subject, emotion, and medium is not present in a text by an Adrienne Rich, a Gary Snyder, a Robert Bly, he insists. These poets' objectivity becomes evident in their moral stance toward sociopolitical events, but in the process of debunking egoism in verse, they merely succeed in reinstating it.

The issue has been complicated by another theory: that iambic pentameter is a historically constituted form, coterminous with bourgeois culture, and that bourgeois culture has had its day. In his groundbreaking study *Poetry as Discourse* (1983), Antony Easthope ascribes the death of Modernism and, parenthetically, the death of iambic pentameter to political conditions. By "pentameter" he means not only a metric system but all the other patterns inherent in the "traditional" forms practiced by Modernist poets (Lowell numbered among them). Because pentameter provides space for "certain polysyllabic words," Easthope postulates that "it encourages a certain vocabulary and register in poetry." This vocabulary has been associated with certain ideological meanings, meanings which are elitist and invite the reader into "a position of imaginary *identification* with this single voice, this represented presence." Here, indeed, is where Lowell's reputation, if it falters in the near future, may be subject to harsh examination. It is not so much the loose, quasi-chaotic volumes of the late sixties and early seventies which will undermine Lowell's credibility; it is the traditional meters of his early volumes, which, while moving toward impersonal meditation, too emphatically return one to the self (both Lowell's *and* the reader's). There is a certain self-aggrandizement in this process which goes contrary to the ideologies of current literary scholars.

Laszlo Géfin is a recent exponent of this view. In *Ideogram: History of a Poetic Method* (1982), Géfin ascribes the fall of Modernism to "metaphoric construction." He argues that Pound was the first to espouse the idea that the ideogram was the only alternative to metaphor, and that those poets who followed in his trail (e.g., Williams, the Beats, the Objectivists) became the true "post-modernists." Lowell is not numbered among those poets who made the crucial transition; he never abandoned Modernism, even in its demise. Thus when we examine studies which emphasize the strong difference between Modernism and Postmodernism—or whatever nomenclature one applies to poetry being written today—Lowell is consigned to a dark corner. Géfin, using the term "analytical" in a nearly derogatory sense, believes that "synthetical" texts (e.g., Zukofsky's "A," Williams' *Paterson*, Olson's *Maximus Poems*, Ginsberg's *The Fall of America*, Snyder's *Myths and Texts*) are "ideogrammic" and "enact natural processes." As such, they embody "an aesthetic form extending from a postlogical and even posthumanist consciousness, according to which the human being is not the apex but a creature of the universe." On the other hand, "analytical" poets, like Eliot, and by extension Lowell, never abandoned the logic and ratiocination that subscribes to a human-centered world.

The history of Lowell criticism, then, is a complex one. One finds, since Lowell's death, that when a critic has evaluated the Lowell canon in chronological order (Yenser and Williamson come to mind), he (or she) has envisaged a curve in which the peak is *Life Studies*; subsequent to this volume there is a gradual downward line, which is again reversed when works like *Day by Day* restore Lowell's confessional voice. The rationale for this kind of reading is that *Life Studies* was a liberation from the restricting modes of the earlier volumes. But recent critics, such as Géfin and Easthope, would presumably disagree. It is precisely the anguished personal voice in *Life Studies* that represents a throwback to the Romantic tradition. The tendency at present is to strengthen that view of Lowellian poetics which regards the personal as so crucial to his vision that discussion of his changing modes is really irrelevant.

Religious intolerance is another topic frequently raised when Modernist poets are discussed. Considering Lowell's beliefs, critics offer revisionist bases of assessment, partly because of recently available personal commentary about him. For example, in a recent article in *Atlantic Monthly* (June 1983), James Atlas recounts a conversation he had with Jean Stafford, Lowell's first wife. Atlas does not give the date of this conversation, but merely notes that Stafford was "nearly sixty" when he had visited her and that it was while Lowell was a visiting professor at Harvard. Stafford talked about Lowell's friendship with Delmore Schwartz and the conversation turned on Jews in general. She said:

> "Cal was a terrible anti-Semite. He once told me he could never have a close friend who was a Jew." She waited for that revelation to sink in, studying its effect with a clinical eye. "We all had dinner at the Lowells' one night—Cal's parents—and Cal kept going on about this ancient relative of his who was Jewish, and how this made Cal himself one-eighth Jewish until Delmore was just livid."

One might, of course, take Stafford's interpretation of events as personal venom, the bitter words of a woman whose divorce from Lowell colored her comments. Hamilton's biography omits any consideration of Stafford's reliability in documenting the past. Hamilton merely remarks that Lowell had avoided Schwartz toward the end of his life because of "his [Schwartz's] suspiciousness, his paranoia," but Hamilton takes this to be a character trait in Lowell rather than a sign of prejudice. These personal accounts must be factored into appraisals, however; and at present they place Lowell squarely in the reactionary group of Modernists.

When it came to political belief, Lowell was a product of that system to which he subscribed. His aestheticism changed as political trends changed in this country. For example, in the United States the New Criticism of the forties was a reaction, primarily by Southern "Agrarian" conservatives (like Ransom and Tate), to the radical progressivism of the Roosevelt era. Lowell, though not a Southerner, found the mechanism of New Criticism congenial to his longing for *noblesse oblige*, idyllic nature, traditional continuity. New Criticism represented an ideal which, if it could not be realized in historical events, could at least be expressed in art. Similarly, when the ecological pacificism of the 1960s emerged in the United States, it was as a reaction to the conservative politics of the Eisenhower years; this time Lowell moved *against* conservatism and in favor of a progressive atmosphere.

His conversions were not so contradictory as they seem. Roughly speaking, they were utopian, as was much of American literature in both periods insofar as it sought solutions to historical crisis. When we look now at "The Quaker Graveyard in Nantucket" (written in 1945), its condemnations of wartime devotees and the military establishment are arrestingly clear. And "Waking Early Sunday Morning" (composed during the summer of 1965) expresses the same sentiments. Each of these poems derives from a different stage of political belief for Lowell; each is a polemic against the national policy at the time. Nevertheless, Lowell's views on war cannot be epitomized by these examples; it is difficult to square their message with an essay Lowell published at age eighteen in the St. Mark's school magazine *Vindex* (1935). In this essay, entitled "War: A Justification," he *advocates* war as a test of man's moral, physical, and mental resources. He concedes that there are serious objections to war, but is convinced that "not only the good that [wars] bring far outweighs the evil, but also they are essential for the preservation of life in its highest forms." In peacetime, the world is in a "pitiful condition" and people are not united by a common goal. War gives "cowards and thieves . . . a chance to gain self-respect and honour."

If we wish further to shatter the image of Lowell as a pacifist liberal, we can refer to Jonathan Miller's conversation with Lowell in January of 1965. Miller (the director of *Old Glory*), who tells this anecdote about Lowell, who spent some time with him while preparing for a Broadway run of *Benito Cereno*, describes his meeting with Lowell at the Kennedy airport:

> As he greeted me there were three or four Hasidic rabbis coming off the plane and a sort of mischievous look came into his eyes, and he said, "Oh Jonathan, the Germans were not responsible for World War II" [Hamilton, p. 315].

This seems to convince us of Jean Stafford's anti-Semitism story; but Hamilton, taking the cue from Miller, who told him about the airport incident during an interview, attributes Lowell's behavior to the onset of one of his manic attacks. Lowell's medical history supports the generalization that his fascination with Hitler (and other tyrants) signaled an impending manic episode. Thus we have no consistent theoretical formula for Lowell as a political thinker, but the passage of time and new release of information increasingly undermine his reputation as a progressive liberal.

To be sure, Lowell's political ideology has little bearing on his merit as a poet. When one considers how many important writers of the twentieth century held reactionary (or what some would consider anti-humanist) views, the question seems irrelevant. Pound, Yeats, Lawrence, Eliot—to name a few examples—have not suffered disfavor as artists because of their political philosophies. At the same time, since critics are not only aestheticians but also men of ethical consciousness, and since present-day views about fascism and war are more censorious than in the period these other writers lived, Lowell may be subject to more discriminating evaluation. It is difficult to predict the extent of damage Stafford's or Miller's disclosures may bring. It is also possible that critics, now apprised of the severity of Lowell's mental illness and his persistent effort to overcome it, will hold him in higher esteem than they had in the past. The mythos of the poet as suffering victim is still very much with us.

Perceptions of Modernism in American poetry are as numerous as the scholars who have written on it. Apart from its stylistic identification with a pattern loosely described as moving "from what is closed to what is open" (Jarrell's words), the spirit of existentialism, with its chronic and sometimes systematic pessimism, has been the most consistently accepted philosophical context for the movement. Spanning two world wars, Modernism bespoke an ontological nostalgia for earlier, more peaceful times, even while its daring prosodic experiments looked forward to a better future. Change the structure of verse, adherents believed, and the world will somehow change. Some of the nostalgia was conditioned and simply vestigial—an expected component in poetry of any period. But some of the nostalgia moved into a Nietzschean "nihilism of affirmation" in the face of the void. Lowell's work qualifies in both categories, depending on which of his texts is examined. He moved, as many poets do, toward a state of acceptance or reconciliation in his later years, but he never truly broke into a celebration of life. Critics' impression of him as an existential figure has been largely intuitive and dealt with impressionistically. There has not really been a systematic study of the impact of existential thought on Lowell's writing.

At the moment, Lowell's legacy to the younger generation of American poets is apprehended by critics as essentially parallel to the entire Modernist legacy. The new modes of writing in the twenties and thirties have won acceptance, but not without opposition. The poetry of Eliot's and Pound's generation *did* surrender to alienation, political conservatism, and the pathos of individual isolation. Younger poets' repudiation of such a sensibility forced them to make renewed efforts with both form and content. Yet, as different as their programs may be, they have in principle revamped the Modernist tradition, obeyed Pound's prescription to "make it new," and extended the literary revolution which began in the twenties. Poets like Galway Kinnell, Allen Ginsberg, W. S. Merwin, Adrienne Rich, and LeRoi Jones are stylistic pluralists who have absorbed a variety of the Modernist influences. They took from Pound, Eliot, and Williams a number of poetic resources. What did they take from Lowell?

I would posit that, because of works like *Notebook*, the single perfect and self-contained lyric has ceased to define the parameters of poetic expression. In *Notebook*, Lowell once again fulfilled the Romantic poets' ambition to record "the growth of a poet's mind"; he moved away from the single lyric and toward shorter poetic efforts which could be incorporated into a large construction. The journal became the basis for a modern epic of consciousness. As an illustration of Lowell's influence, one could compare the diary poems of Frank O'Hara —which O'Hara preferred to associate with contemporary music and art rather than with what was going on in American poetry—with Lowell's sonnets, filled with jottings, distractions, random jumps. O'Hara's mock-heroic persona, his masks, his richly varied exposures of the self (especially in *Lunch Poems*, 1964) owe more to the Lowellian poetic than O'Hara may have realized. The cultivation of a private vision by poets writing in the seventies and eighties has a new autobiographical intensity that comes directly from—indeed, is a bequest from—Lowell.

## References

Atlas, James
    1983. "Unsentimental Education." *Atlantic Monthly* June, pp. 78–90.

Easthope, Antony
  1983. *Poetry as Discourse*. London and New York: Methuen.
Ellmann, Richard
  1982. "The Poet at the Center." *New York Times Book Review*
  Nov. 28, pp. 1, 14.
Géfin, Laszlo
  1982. *Ideogram: History of a Poetic Method*. Austin: Univ. of
  Texas Press.
Hamilton, Ian
  1982. *Robert Lowell: A Biography*. New York: Random House.
Kazin, Alfred
  1983. "The Case History of Cal." *Times Literary Supplement*
  May 6, pp. 447–48.
Lowell, Robert
  1935. "War: A Justification." *Vindex* no. 59, pp. 156–58.
Olson, Charles
  1973. "Projective Verse." In *Poetics of the New American Poetry*,
  ed. Donald Allen & Warren Tallman. New York: Grove Pr.
Poulin, A., Jr.
  1980. (editor) *Contemporary American Poetry*, 3d ed. Boston:
  Houghton Mifflin.
Spender, Stephen
  1982. "Life Studies in Poetry, History and Madness." *Washington
  Post Book World* Nov. 14, pp. 1, 9.

# Index

WORKS

Norma Procopiow is a visiting instructor at Catholic University of America, Washington, D.C. She previously was on the faculty of the University of Maryland. She is active in the Modern Language Association and has published in *College Literature*, *Illinois Quarterly*, *Ariel*, *Modernist Studies*, and *Centennial Review*. She is the editor of *The New American Prosody*.